Illuminate Publishing

AQA
GCSE Drama
Designing Drama

Lighting, Sound, Set, Costume & Puppet Design

Sue Shewring

Published in 2020 by Illuminate Publishing Ltd,
PO Box 1160, Cheltenham, Gloucestershire GL50 9RW

Orders: Please visit www.illuminatepublishing.com
or email sales@illuminatepublishing.com

© Sue Shewring 2020

The moral rights of the author have been asserted.

All rights reserved. No part of this book may be reprinted, reproduced, or utilised in any form or by any electronic, mechanical, or other means, now known or hereafter invented, including photocopying and recording, or in any information storage and retrieval system, without permission in writing from the publishers.

British Library Cataloguing-in-Publication Data

A catalogue record of this book is available from the British Library.

ISBN 978-1-912820-24-5

Printed in Gloucester by Severn.

03.21

The publisher's policy is to use papers that are natural, renewable and recyclable products made from wood grown in sustainable forests. The logging and manufacturing processes are expected to conform to the environmental regulations in the country of origin.

Every effort has been made to contact copyright holders of material reproduced in this book. Great care has been taken by the author and publisher to ensure that either formal permission has been granted for the use of copyright material reproduced, or that copyright material has been used under the provision of fair-dealing guidelines in the UK – specifically that it has been used sparingly, solely for the purpose of criticism and review, and has been properly acknowledged. If notified, the publisher will be pleased to rectify any errors or omissions at the earliest opportunity.

We have made every effort to ensure that website addresses are correct at the time of printing, and links are provided for information only. Illuminate Publishing cannot be held responsible for the content of any website listed or detailed in this book.

Editor: Roanne Charles, abc Editorial
Design and layout and Cover design: EMC Design Ltd
Cover photograph: Ivan Yohan / Alamy Stock Photo

Text acknowledgements

Extracts from *Collected Grimm Tales* by Carol Ann Duffy. Published by Faber & Faber. Copyright © Carol Ann Duffy. Reproduced by permission of the author c/o Rogers, Coleridge & White Ltd., 20 Powis Mews, London W11 1JN.

Extract from *A Christmas Carol* by Charles Dickens adapted by Conor McReynolds and Richard Kidd. Published by Oxford University Press (UK). Copyright © Conor McReynolds and Richard Kidd. Reproduced with permission of the Licensor through PLSclear.

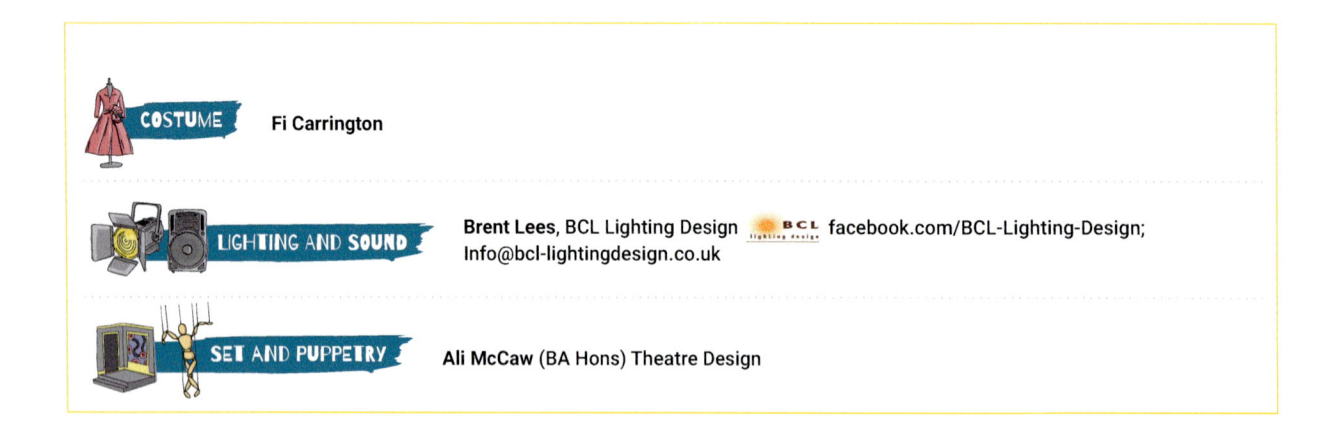

COSTUME — Fi Carrington

LIGHTING AND SOUND — Brent Lees, BCL Lighting Design, facebook.com/BCL-Lighting-Design; Info@bcl-lightingdesign.co.uk

SET AND PUPPETRY — Ali McCaw (BA Hons) Theatre Design

CONTENTS

Everything But the Acting — 5
Design in drama and theatre — 5
How to get the most from this book — 5

How You will be Assessed — 7
Components and assessment objectives — 7
The written exam — 8
Practical components — 9

Understanding Design in Drama and Theatre — 11
Theatre design — 11

Chapter 1 Practical Guide to Lighting Design — 13
Introduction to lighting design — 14
Types of stage lantern — 16
Understanding your lighting resources — 18
Angles, colour and intensity — 20
Special effects in lighting — 24
Lighting transitions — 26
Research for lighting — 27
How to document your lighting design — 28
Plotting the lighting design — 30
Rigging and focusing — 32
Health and safety in lighting design — 34
Operating the lighting — 35
Technical and dress rehearsals for lighting designers — 36
Evaluating your lighting design — 37
Lighting design vocabulary — 38

Chapter 2 Practical Guide to Sound Design — 39
Introduction to sound design — 40
How to produce sound for the stage — 42
Research for sound design — 44
Sourcing, creating and mixing sounds — 46
Health and safety in sound design — 49
Special sound effects — 50
How to document your sound design — 52
Directional sound — 54
Plotting the sound design — 56
Operating sound equipment — 58
Technical and dress rehearsals for sound designers — 60
Evaluating your sound design — 61
Sound design vocabulary — 62

Chapter 3 Practical Guide to Set Design — 63
Introduction to set design — 64
Two styles of set design — 66
Research for set design — 67
Using levels in set design — 68
How to document your set design — 69

Understanding your resources — 73
Sourcing materials for the set — 74
Health and safety in set design — 75
Creating your set design for the stage — 76
Technical and dress rehearsals for set designers — 77
Evaluating your set design — 78
Set design vocabulary — 80

Chapter 4 Practical Guide to Costume Design — 81
Introduction to costume design — 82
Placing costume in history — 84
Style: what we wear, and why — 85
Colour and fabric for the stage — 86
Developing and using your costume resources — 90
Key process – sewing — 92
Adapting costume items — 94
Health and safety in costume design — 95
Hair, make-up and masks — 96
How to document your costume design — 98
Fitting the costume — 100
Technical and dress rehearsals for costume designers — 104
Evaluating your costume design — 105
Costume design vocabulary — 106

Chapter 5 Practical Guide to Puppet Design — 107
Introduction to puppet design — 108
Why choose puppets? — 109
The cultural and historical importance of puppets — 110
Types of puppet — 112
Which type of puppet should I design? — 116
Research for puppet design — 118
How to document your puppet design — 119
Health and safety in puppet design — 119
Creating your puppet for the stage — 120
Animating puppets — 122
Technical and dress rehearsals for puppet designers — 124
Evaluating your puppet design — 125
Puppet design vocabulary — 126

Chapter 6: Component 1: Understanding drama — 127
Introduction to design in the written exam — 128
Section A: Theatre roles and terminology — 132
Section B: Study of the set play — 137
Section C: Live theatre evaluation — 137

Lighting design in the set play (Section B) — 138
Lighting design in live theatre (Section C) — 144

Sound design in the set play (Section B) — 148
Sound design in live theatre (Section C) — 154

Set design in the set play (Section B)	157
Set design in live theatre (Section C)	161
Costume design in the set play (Section B)	164
Costume design in live theatre (Section C)	168
Puppet design in the set play (Section B)	172
Puppet design in live theatre (Section C)	175

Chapter 7 Component 2: Devising Drama – a Practical Guide — 179

Your design challenge	180
How your design for the devised piece will be assessed	182
Responding to stimuli	183
Agreeing on your artistic intentions	184
Genre, style, structure, form, character and language	186
Working positively as a group	190
Production meetings	191
Using rehearsals to develop and refine your designs	192
Final rehearsals	194

Lighting Design for the Devised Piece — 195

Section 1: Response to a stimulus	196
Section 2: Development and collaboration	198
Reviewing sections 1 and 2	200
Producing and documenting your lighting design	201
Section 3: Analysis and evaluation	202

Sound Design for the Devised Piece — 203

Section 1: Response to a stimulus	204
Section 2: Development and collaboration	206
Reviewing sections 1 and 2	208
Producing and documenting your sound design	209
Section 3: Analysis and evaluation	210

Set Design for the Devised Piece — 212

Section 1: Response to a stimulus	213
Section 2: Development and collaboration	215
Reviewing sections 1 and 2	217
Producing and documenting your set design	218
Section 3: Analysis and evaluation	219

Costume Design for the Devised Piece — 221

Section 1: Response to a stimulus	222
Section 2: Development and collaboration	224
Reviewing sections 1 and 2	226
Producing and documenting your costume design	227
Section 3: Analysis and evaluation	228

Puppet Design for the Devised Piece — 230

Section 1: Response to a stimulus	231
Section 2: Development and collaboration	233
Reviewing sections 1 and 2	235
Producing and documenting your puppet design	236
Section 3: Analysis and evaluation	237

Chapter 8 Component 3: Designing for Texts in Practice — 239

How your design skills will be assessed	240

Six Steps to Lighting Design for Texts in Practice — 242

1 Working on your own with the script	242
2 The design brief meeting and rehearsals	244
3 Revisiting the script	245
4 Confirming your lighting designs	246
5 The final design meeting	247
6 The completed lighting design	248
The Statement of Dramatic Intentions for lighting design	249

Six Steps to Sound Design for Texts in Practice — 250

1 Working on your own with the script	250
2 The design brief meeting and rehearsals	252
3 Revisiting the script	253
4 Confirming your sound designs	254
5 The final design meeting	255
6 The completed sound design	256
The Statement of Dramatic Intentions for sound design	257

Six Steps to Set Design for Texts in Practice — 258

1 Working on your own with the script	258
2 The design brief meeting and rehearsals	260
3 Revisiting the script	261
4 Confirming your set designs	262
5 The final design meeting	263
6 The completed set design	264
The Statement of Dramatic Intentions for set design	265

Six Steps to Costume Design for Texts in Practice — 266

1 Working on your own with the script	266
2 The design brief meeting and rehearsals	268
3 Revisiting the script	269
4 Confirming your costume designs	270
5 The final design meeting	271
6 The completed costume design	272
The Statement of Dramatic Intentions for costume design	273

Six Steps to Puppet Design for Texts in Practice — 274

1 Working on your own with the script	274
2 The design brief meeting and rehearsals	276
3 Revisiting the script	277
4 Confirming your puppet designs	278
5 The final design meeting	279
6 The completed puppet design	279
The Statement of Dramatic Intentions for puppet design	280

Glossary — 281

Index — 285

Acknowledgements — 288

EVERYTHING BUT THE ACTING

DESIGN IN DRAMA AND THEATRE

This book is about everything that happens on the stage except for the acting!

Designing Drama will help you to costume actors and give them a set to perform on. It will guide you through the process that fills their world with sound and floods the stage with light.

More than that, you will come to understand how the work of the theatre designer brings the world of the stage to life for the most important people in the theatre – the audience.

Whether you are designing sound for a devised piece of drama, or costume for a scripted one, this book offers practical advice and activities to help you develop your knowledge, understanding and creativity.

If you are a performer at heart, this book will help you to master the knowledge and skills needed to write about design in the exam. You will need a good level of knowledge for all the design elements that exam questions could be about. Performance and design work hand in hand to create the harmonious world of the stage. *Designing Drama* will help you to understand how to be part of this creative process from every angle.

HOW TO GET THE MOST FROM THIS BOOK

Practical guides to design roles

Chapters 1 to 5 are the practical guides to each of the Drama design elements:

- LIGHTING
- SOUND
- SET
- COSTUME
- PUPPETRY

These chapters introduce you to each design role and provide practical guidance, advice and activities to help you through the design process. They will give you a good grounding in your chosen design specialism, enabling you to develop your skills, boost your confidence and explore your creativity.

Drama course content

Refer back to the practical chapters as you move on to the chapters that cover design for each assessed component of the course:

- Component 1: Understanding drama (Chapter 6)
- Component 2: Devising drama (Chapter 7)
- Component 3: Texts in practice (Chapter 8).

Features of the book

In order to highlight important information, activities and assessment objectives, we have included some special features:

FOCUS
A note to summarise the main content of the section.

ASSESSMENT CHECK
Details from the AQA specification documents to show you which elements of the assessment criteria the guidance and activities will help you to achieve.

SIGNPOST
These direct you to supporting content from other sections that you are likely to need before you attempt the activities.

TASKS
Activities and exercises to help you learn, practise and develop your design skills.

DESIGN TIPS
Quick ideas, things to remember and helpful tips from professional theatre design.

LOOK HERE
A guide to the most suitable sections of support from other chapters.

This symbol indicates that there is a free download available at www.illuminatepublishing.com. Simply navigate to the product page for this book.

Important technical drama terms are highlighted and collected in a Glossary at the back of the book.

We have also included some sample exam questions and example student-style answers. These will give you an idea of the type of questions that will come up in the exam and how some students might have responded.

In addition, the notes are illustrated by diagrams, sketches, plans and photographs to help you visualise the practical elements of theatre that you can achieve as a Drama designer.

Everything But the Acting

HOW YOU WILL BE ASSESSED

COMPONENTS AND ASSESSMENT OBJECTIVES

The three components of the AQA GCSE Drama course are:
1 **Understanding drama** (written exam)
2 **Devising drama** (assessed by your teacher)
3 **Texts in practice** (assessed by a visiting examiner).

For these components, the assessment objectives, total marks and percentages of the overall GCSE are:

Component	Assessment objectives and percentages					Overall percentage in GCSE	Total marks
	AO1: Create and develop ideas to communicate meaning for theatrical performance.	**AO2:** Apply theatrical skills to realise artistic intentions in live performance.	**AO3:** Demonstrate knowledge and understanding of how drama and theatre is developed and performed.	**AO4:** Analyse and evaluate their own work and the work of others.		
Component 1: Understanding drama	0	0	30%	10%	40	80
Component 2: Devising drama	20%	10%	0	10%	40	80
Component 3: Texts in practice	0	20%	0	0	20	40

THE WRITTEN EXAM

Component 1: Understanding drama

There is a written exam at the end of the course that is 1 hour 45 minutes.

Section A: Theatre roles and terminologies

You are tested on your knowledge of the roles of professional theatre makers and other terminology, such as stage configurations and positioning. Each of the four multiple-choice questions in this section is worth 1 mark.

Section B: Study of a set play

The questions here relate to an extract from the play you have studied in lessons. You will take a clean copy of the play into the exam.

You will answer a 4-mark question about how you would design a given element of the play, such as costume or lighting. There will be no choice of design element. At the end of the section, you will have a choice of question to answer as a performer or as any type of designer. There are 20 marks available for this question. Other questions in this section are performance based.

Section C: Live theatre production

This section has a choice of three questions worth 32 marks. One will be about performance, the other two about design. You will use your experience as an audience member and are expected to describe and evaluate.

Practical components

You can work practically as a designer for Components 2 and/or 3.

Your teacher will assess your work for Component 2, and external examiners will standardise the marking by looking at examples of videos and devising logs.

For Component 3, a visiting examiner will assess your work in performance.

Component 2: Devising drama

As a designer, you will work as part of a group to create, develop and produce an original piece of drama, devised from a **stimulus**. This is assessed in two parts.

A devised design realisation in the performance

This is worth 20 marks and covers AO2. A mark out of 4 is given for each of the following:
- Level of theatrical skill
- Range of theatrical skills demonstrated
- Contribution to the effectiveness of the piece
- Inventiveness of individual's work
- Success in realising individual artistic intention.

Your designs will be assessed in live performance, in which you create a single choice from the following. **Your design must meet the demands of the devised piece being performed.**

> **One lighting design** that shows a range of lighting effects/states and cues/transitions.
>
> **One sound design** that shows a range of sound effects and cues/transitions.
>
> **One set design** for one setting, showing dressings and props.
>
> **One costume design** to be worn by one performer, showing clothing and accessories (and hair and make-up if applicable).
>
> **One puppet design** realised as a complete puppet used in the performance.

A devising log

This log consists of three sections, each marked out of 20.
- Section 1: Response to a stimulus (AO1)
- Section 2: Development and collaboration (AO1)
- Section 3: Analysis and evaluation (AO4).

Evidence for the devising log	Suggested length per section	The devising log must not exceed in total (evidence beyond this will not count towards the mark)
Entirely written	400–600 words	2500 words
Written accompanied by: • annotated photographs • annotated sketches/drawings • annotated cue sheets	2–4 A4 pages	15 pages
Written accompanied by audio/visual/audiovisual recording(s)	200–400 words and 2–3 minutes	1500 words and 12 minutes
Entirely audio/visual/audiovisual recording(s)	3–4 minutes	15 minutes

Component 3: Texts in practice

In your group, you will interpret a playscript. You will design for **two extracts** from the text (unless you opt for performance, of course). Your teacher can direct and support you; a visiting examiner will assess you.

This component covers AO2. Twenty marks are available for each extract.

Practical design requirements

For your choice from the five design roles, you need to produce **one design for each extract**. The realised designs must then be seen/heard in the live performance. So, if you choose puppet design, for example, you should design one puppet for each extract, which is then made and used in the performance of that extract.

You must also produce an individual **Statement of Dramatic Intentions** to justify your theatrical choices.

UNDERSTANDING DESIGN IN DRAMA AND THEATRE

THEATRE DESIGN

The focus of this book is design: the theatrical elements of set, costume, lighting, sound and puppetry. Often known as stagecraft, design covers all the creative, non-performing aspects of staging a theatrical production for an audience.

As a student of Drama, you might have experienced the thrill that comes from putting on a costume or feeling the lights come up on you at the beginning of a scene. While actors wearing simple black outfits can create powerful drama on their own, the integration of performance and theatrical design generally lifts the experience to another, higher, level.

Working in design

Theatre design has evolved over the centuries, and the roles of the designers are as necessary in today's professional theatre as those of director and actor. If theatre design and the technical elements of puppetry, lighting, sound, costume or set excite you – and you don't mind the travelling that is often involved – careers in the backstage elements of theatre are certainly to be found.

Many colleges, universities and drama schools have courses for designers and technicians that you could investigate to follow on from your Drama courses in school. In addition, the skills required for theatre lighting, costume, make-up and sound apply equally well to the music, television, film and festival industries. These are interesting careers with potentially more employment opportunities compared with acting for example.

> **Fi Carrington, a freelance wardrobe supervisor and costume designer, says:**
>
> *I trained on a theatre costume design course and now do some teaching on a degree course. Most of the students don't have too much difficulty getting freelance work in theatre, film and television.*

The role of design in drama

The role of a theatre designer involves working with a director and other designers to produce workable design ideas for a drama production. There is usually an element of research to be done in relation to the script and historical **periods** and contexts, for example. The designer and director will eventually agree final, budgeted designs and then begin the creation of these in terms of:

- making costumes, puppets and sets
- setting plans for rigging, operating and cueing lighting and sounds.

Adaptations to these final designs might be needed as the performance grows closer and issues crop up during rehearsals.

> Theatre designers, directors and performers work together to create an artistic vision. Most often, this theatrical vision creates a harmonious world on the stage.

FOCUS
- How design elements enhance theatre.
- A brief guide to the design process.

Understanding Design in Drama and Theatre 11

The design process: rehearsal and performance

The technical rehearsal

An important moment in the design process is the technical rehearsal. Here, the performers 'walk' through a complete performance during which they will need to stop, re-perform and skip sections of the play as design details are finalised. This is known as working cue to cue, meaning that each sound and lighting cue is covered and repeated as necessary. This happens until the designers and technicians are confident that the production can run smoothly and maintain the desired artistic intentions. Set and costume changes and puppet animation will also be run through.

Technical rehearsals are notoriously long and taxing for all those involved, but no professional or amateur production can be satisfactorily achieved without one – or sometimes two!

Dress rehearsals

The dress rehearsal is a designer's opportunity to test their design in real time. Lighting and sound designers can practise operating their designs following the script. This means that they can prepare for and then activate their plotted cues. Meanwhile, costume, puppet and set designers will often sit in the auditorium with the director, taking notes on what has and hasn't worked well, so that problems can be addressed before the first performance.

Work during the performance

Once a show or run, if there are multiple performances, is underway, there is still work to be done. Costumes have to be cleaned and maintained (although this is done by wardrobe maintenance or dressers in professional theatre). Similarly, sets (including props and set dressings), puppets and technical equipment need to be checked and maintained.

Stage management

In charge of this whole process is the **stage manager**, who co-ordinates all the backstage and technical elements during rehearsals and performances. The stage manager works closely with designers and technicians as well as performers, controlling the production. If you continue your involvement in theatre after your course, stage management is a very important role that could interest you.

Practical design and the exam

Practical components and the written exam are closely related!

- Try to see all your practical work in Components 2 and 3 as preparation for the written exam, where you will have opportunities to use your developing knowledge and skills.
- Even if you are working as a performer for one or both of the practical components, be aware of the design work and opportunities for all the design elements: lighting, sound, set, costume and puppetry.

TASK I.1

In your next practical drama lesson, where an improvisation or piece of scripted performance is shown, decide on the following in your group:

- What costumes would enhance your performance?
- How could a puppet help with characterisation?
- How could set be used to add meaning and interest to the performance?
- How might you use coloured stage lighting or spotlights to help focus the audience?
- Can you plan one sound cue to emphasise a significant moment in the performance?

---

12   Understanding Design in Drama and Theatre

PRACTICAL GUIDE TO LIGHTING DESIGN

Chapter 1

Introduction to lighting design	14
Types of stage lantern	16
Understanding your lighting resources	18
Angles, colour and intensity	20
Special effects in lighting	24
Lighting transitions	26
Research for lighting	27
How to document your lighting design	28
Plotting the lighting design	30
Rigging and focusing	32
Health and safety in lighting design	34
Operating the lighting	35
Technical and dress rehearsals for lighting designers	36
Evaluating your lighting design	37
Lighting design vocabulary	38

FOCUS

- The purpose and power of stage lighting.
- The technical and creative skills in lighting design.

ASSESSMENT CHECK

This section will help you to understand how to:

- design and realise a range of lighting effects that contribute to the performance
- gain knowledge and understanding of how drama and theatre is developed and performed (AO3).

INTRODUCTION TO LIGHTING DESIGN

The purpose of stage lighting

At the moment when the house lights go down in the theatre, the lighting designer introduces the audience to the world of the performance. It is as though the audience holds its collective breath ready to enter that world. The first lights that illuminate the stage can create a magical moment. If the lighting design is not right, however, the cast might struggle to grab and keep the audience's attention, and other design elements might not combine well.

Stage lighting can be described as having four main functions:

VISIBILITY
Audience members need to be able to see the actors and the set.

FOCUS
Lighting draws attention to specific areas of the stage.

MOOD
The uses of colour and **intensity** (brightness) have a powerful **atmospheric** affect. These choices can also link to a play's themes and meanings.

LOCATION/SETTING
Similarly, colour choices, intensity and effects (such as a wash or a spotlight) can create a sense of time and place for the audience.

This lighting design is by Nic Farman (with a set by Lily Arnold) for Hornchurch Queens Theatre. It is suitably mysterious and sinister, arousing the audience's curiosity and setting an atmospheric scene for *The Invisible Man*.

TASK 1.1

In a darkened room, experiment with the effects of torchlight. Choose an object in the room and investigate:

- how visible you can make it using a different number of beams
- what size and shape of shadow you can produce
- the different effects produced by front, back and side lighting
- how you can change the atmosphere by using fewer or more torches
- how the **intensity** changes when you move closer or further away.

The power of lighting

A significant difference between lighting a room in your house and lighting the stage is that you should have a blank 'canvas'. Another is that you have considerably more choice of varied and exciting effects. The thinking that determines where you put your desk light and which lightshade you choose is intensified in the role of stage lighting designer as you can use different heights, colours, shapes, shadows and **fades**. You could move suddenly or gradually from one **lighting state** to another and build or reduce intensity of light as the scene demands.

Chapter 1   Practical Guide to Lighting Design

The importance of lighting design

You will find that, as lighting designer, you have a unique power to influence the focus and mood of the audience. You can 'create' sunlight or moonlight, fires and lightning. You can be really creative and your work is an extremely important contribution to a harmonious world for the audience.

Lighting styles

Different genres, styles and forms of performance call for different types of lighting. Bertolt Brecht, for example, often **flooded** the stage with harsh white light. He wanted the audience to be constantly aware that they were watching a play rather than real life. For the same reason, he would keep **lanterns** in full view and sometimes leave the house lights on too.

On the other hand, Konstantin Stanislavski developed a style of theatre that sought realism in every aspect. He used lighting to focus the audience on, for example, an item of set. In today's theatre, **backlighting**, and projections of, for example, clouds would add atmosphere and realism.

DESIGN TIP
The best designers and operators are so skilful that the audience is not consciously aware of the stage lights at all. Unless the designers specifically want them to be...!

TASK 1.2

Watch some different styles and genres of film and/or television. (Here are a couple of example scenes where lighting makes a powerful impact.) Pay particular attention to the lighting effects.

Use the following chart to record what you notice about the effects created. Include, for example, the use of colours and intensity and the mood of the scene.

Title	Genre	Special effects	Time of day / season of the year / weather	How atmosphere is produced and impact it has
Chicago	Musical comedy/ drama	Overhead **spotlight** picks out the character and creates a halo effect on her blonde hair. She is the star!	Stage conditions – general coverage of blue light on the stage creates a cool effect; the character stands out.	Blue lights in the background with possible use of fog machine help the main character to 'shine'.
Star Wars: The Empire Strikes Back				

How can I design lighting as part of this course?

Component 1 is the written exam. Working practically with lighting will give you the knowledge and understanding to write confidently about lighting in your set text or a performance you have seen.

You can opt for lighting design in either or both of the practical sections of the course. If you choose to work as lighting designer in Component 2, you will work in a small group and help to develop the piece, but your specific responsibility will be to create a lighting design for the performance.

Component 3 is similar, but you will work with a script.

TYPES OF STAGE LANTERN

Your school or college might have these types of lighting fixture. Each has its own particular purpose.

FOCUS
The different types of lantern and their variety of uses.

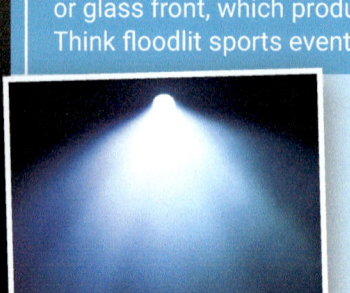

ASSESSMENT CHECK
Learning some of the technicalities of stage lanterns works towards AO3. You will also show that you can select appropriate equipment and determine its position in order to realise the intended design.

NOTE
Stage lights are called **lanterns** or **lighting fixtures** because **bulbs** are known as **lights** (or **lamps**).

BIRDIES
Birdies are very small lanterns (as small as 12cm). Tiny par cans are the most frequently used type of birdie.

Benefit: Surprisingly bright, they are ideal for hiding on stage or using on the stage edge as footlights.

FLOOD
These are basic lanterns, generally with an open or glass front, which produce a wide flood of light. Think floodlit sports events.

Useful for: Lighting large areas of the stage or back cloths: generating a 'flood' of light.

Limitation: The beams' size or shape cannot be controlled.

NB: Where you place and direct these lights is very important as the light will 'spill' everywhere it points.

FRESNEL
Pronounced 'freh-nell', these lanterns have a lens at the front with a 'stepped ring' finish to it.

Useful for: Lighting large or small areas of the stage.

Benefits: The steps on the lens make the light even, making it easy to blend the **focus** of one light to the next.

Several fresnels focused onto several areas can light the whole stage evenly (giving general cover).

By moving the lamp closer to or further away from the lens, you can control the size of the beam.

Barn doors (shutters that fit onto the front of the lantern) can control the spread of the beam.

PAR CANS
These beam lights (lens-less lanterns) get their name from the lamp inside. The lantern itself is simply a '**can**' in which the **par** lamp is contained. The PAR (Parabolic Aluminised Reflector) is a sealed beam unit consisting of a lamp, reflector and lens in one.

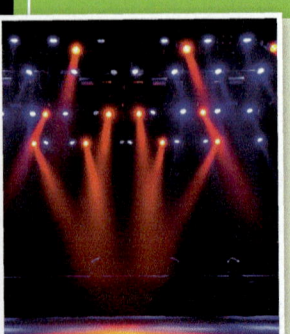

Useful for: Producing a very bright beam, something like a cross between a floodlight and a Fresnel.

Benefits: These lights are excellent for highlighting an area or using with colour filters or gels to produce the bright colourful beams often seen at pop and rock concerts.

Limitation: The only way to change the beam size is either to move the whole fixture, or to physically change the lamp to narrow, medium or wide.

Chapter 1 Practical Guide to Lighting Design

PROFILE SPOT

These versatile lanterns are longer and thinner than floods and spotlights. They also have levers half way down, which are the shutters that control the size and shape of the beam.

Useful for: A soft- or hard-edged beam, produced by moving the lens (not the lamp as in fresnels) forwards or backwards. **Profile** lights with hard edges can create a typical 'spotlight' beam. Alternatively, several profiles focused with a soft edge can overlap for general cover. Profile spots are the type of lantern used to project images with **gobos**.

Benefits: The beam control is generally narrower and more controllable than a fresnel, so a profile spotlight can be further away, while still remaining bright, without 'spilling' light into unwanted areas. The built-in shutters of a profile spotlight mean that barn doors are not needed. They are used to shield areas of the stage that you don't want to light. They can also shape the beam to create a square of light or to focus a tight beam on a particular object or performer.

Follow spot

Follow spots are modified profiles mounted on a tripod and operated manually to track an individual as they move around the stage. You will have seen them used in events such as ice skating.

Gobo

A gobo is a very thin steel plate with a cut-out pattern that fixes over a lens. It is used to project a **silhouette** of images such as trees or windows. The images produced are mainly two-dimensional. The colour is dictated by the colour **filter** or **gel** put in front of the lens. They can produce stunning effects.

LED LANTERN

Many schools are now using theatre lanterns with an **LED** source. The most common is probably an LED par can, but there are now LED floods, profiles and fresnels.

Useful for: The light inside is most commonly made up of red, green and blue LEDs which can be selected or combined to create a variety of colours.

Benefits: LED lights use less power, generate less heat and save on the cost of replacing bulbs and buying colour filters or gels.

Limitations: They can be expensive, and controlling their **colour palette** requires computer software.

AUTOMATED MOVING LANTERNS

Often seen at concerts and large-scale events, moving lanterns are very versatile. They are generally manufactured as profile spots or fresnels.

Benefit: The focus, beam size, gobo and colour are controlled by the software on a **lighting desk** or **console**. The desks usually have libraries of different light fixtures, which enables relatively easy programming and operation, and adds versatility and complexity to a design.

Limitations: They are expensive and require a computerised lighting desk.

UNDERSTANDING YOUR LIGHTING RESOURCES

What lighting equipment is available?

It is essential to know what resources are available, so you can create a practical design. Typical lighting equipment includes:

- lanterns (as we saw on the previous pages)
- colour gels and gobos
- a lighting desk (a manual **board**, or computer software)
- a lighting **rig** or lighting stands
- a **dimmer** (unless your school uses only LED lights).

Don't be put off if your school or college does not have lots of lighting equipment. As long as you have at least two different types of lantern and a way of controlling them, you can light an acting area.

Ask your teacher if you can run an audit of the available lanterns. This could mean looking up into the rigging and identifying the numbers of different types of lantern, or checking in the storeroom. The following tasks will also help you to document and rig your production.

Identifying what lighting fixtures you have and what works best where will avoid having to move lanterns to a completely different area of the rig.

FOCUS
Organising your equipment and resources.

ASSESSMENT CHECK
Knowing the equipment you have and how to use it helps you to realise a range of lighting effects. This works towards AO2: 'Apply theatrical skills to realise artistic intentions in live performance.'

DESIGN TIP
If you are not familiar with some of the equipment, learn about it before you start any major design work. Don't be frustrated if this takes time. And don't be afraid to ask for help.

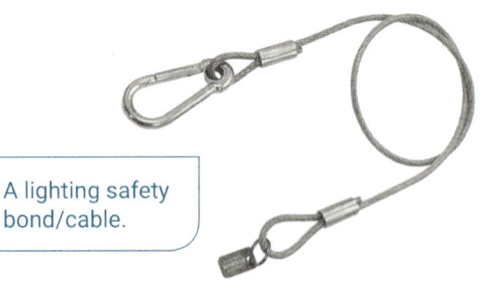

A lighting safety bond/cable.

TASK 1.3

1. Make notes on the operating equipment you have and any queries about it. (Some examples have been given to start you off.)

Lighting desk	Lighting rig/stands	Dimmer	Lantern accessories
Manual or **digital**?	• Number of sockets on the rig? • Number and types of stand or boom?	Position and type of **dimmer rack**?	• Gobos • Barn doors • Gels • **Safety bonds** (There must be one for each lantern you rig!)

2. Identify the lanterns available in school (including quantities). Note down ideas on how you might use them in your design, for example:

Type	How many?	Key features and uses
Fresnels		• Soft-edged beam. • Best used close to the stage. • Barn doors can alter shape and size of beam. • Gobos and colour gels can be added.
Profile spots		• Powerful enough to use further from the stage.
LEDs		
Par cans		
Automated moving lanterns		

TASK 1.4

Sketch a simple diagram to show the position, type and angle of rigged lights relative to the stage. Identify gels, gobos and barn doors that are in place. (An example lighting plot is given on page 29.)

Taking care of your lanterns

Lanterns need to be kept clean. Dusty lanterns give off a burning smell and dirty lenses are less effective at transmitting light. If you can clean your lanterns (de-rigged and unplugged, of course) it is important to:

- use a window cleaning product and soft cloths for lenses, avoiding smears
- wipe the metal body with a damp cloth
- avoid touching halogen lamps because fingerprints cause hot spots that quickly degrade the lamp. If a lamp is accidentally touched it should be cleaned with methylated spirit or isopropyl alcohol.

Controlling your lighting

Every lighting system is controlled by a desk, which can be manual (with or without a computer facility) or a software programme. It does not matter what type of desk you have as long as you can use it confidently.

Online manuals are available for many modern desks and software programmes along with tutorials. This is very useful research, particularly when your teacher and performers are busy.

> **TASK 1.5**
>
> 1 Find time to develop your knowledge and skill with the lighting desk. See if you can achieve:
>   - a **snap** between two lighting states (for example DSL and USR)
>   - a **cross-fade** between two lighting states
>   - fading up a lighting state at a **pace** that feels right for the start of a performance and fading out for the ending
>   - a sequence that brings a sense of excitement (This might involve moving between a number of states at a high pace. Would you end the sequence with a snap to **blackout** or a fade?)
>   - an effect that adds tension. (Could you end with a snap to blackout?)
> 2 Switch everything off carefully.

Human resources

You must understand how to apply rigging, positioning, angling and focusing. You need to be centrally involved in these aspects of the design, but, for health and safety reasons, you almost certainly will not be rigging and focusing lanterns yourself. So, you will need help!

> **TASK 1.6**
>
> As soon as possible, meet the person with the knowledge, clearance and time to be involved. Find out:
> - what they are prepared to do
> - what their availability is
> - how much notice they need to rig and focus the lanterns.

NOTE

Your site supervisor or a technician is likely to be responsible for the electrical maintenance of school equipment and you should never be involved in that aspect of upkeep. If you have any concerns about the safety of a piece of electrical equipment, such as exposed or loose wiring, report this immediately to your teacher.

DESIGN TIP

You must never distract the actors during rehearsal. Ideally, arrange a time slot during rehearsal times in which you can experiment without disturbing the cast.

DESIGN TIP

Be appreciative and flexible with your human resources. They will already be busy!

Chapter 1 Practical Guide to Lighting Design 19

FOCUS
Three key components of lighting design.

ASSESSMENT CHECK
For AO1 and AO2, you will develop skills in:
- designing and realising a range of lighting effects
- selecting appropriate equipment and determining its position
- rigging, positioning, angling and focusing.

DESIGN TIP
Be aware that light bounces off surfaces – particularly light-coloured and shiny ones.

ANGLES, COLOUR AND INTENSITY

Light in the real world

Daylight
Theatre lighting frequently seeks to re-create natural lighting, so begin your design thinking in the real world.

During daylight hours our light source is the Sun. The time of day affects the angle at which the Sun's light hits the Earth. The season and the weather (amount of cloud cover) affect the intensity (brightness) of the sunlight.

TASK 1.7
1. Assuming you are in a room with at least one window, and it is daytime, turn off any artificial lights. Look around you for a minute and note the following:
   - How many sides of the room have portals (windows/doors)?
   - Where can you see bright light? Where does it come from?
   - Where are the shadows? What shape and length are they? Why?
   - How deep (dark) are the shadows?
   - Does the atmosphere vary in the room because of the light? How?
2. Draw a sketch of the room, representing areas of light and shade.

Night-time
When the Sun sets, the Moon and stars create significantly less natural light, so we use artificial light.

TASK 1.8
Thinking about inside and outside:
1. Write down three sources of artificial light.
2. Use them to write two or three sentences about how artificial light has different affects from natural light. An angle-poise lamp, for example, creates a small area of intense white light, whereas a candle creates a dim, flickering warm light.

Think about angle, colour, intensity and atmosphere when comparing natural and artificial light.

Chapter 1 Practical Guide to Lighting Design

Naturalistic (real-world) lighting on stage

Light in the real world is usually the starting point for stage lighting. (You might explore **non-naturalistic** effects later.) As the lighting designer, you have a number of tools with which to control light on the stage:

- the number of stage lanterns
- the types of lantern (see pages 16–17)
- where lanterns are positioned (angle and distance)
- the shape of beam produced
- the intensity of the beam projected
- The colour of the beam.

Key lights

There is always a **key light** in the real world. It might be natural sunlight coming through a window, or moonlight, or the artificial light of a desk lamp, for example. A lighting designer will always be aware of the key light and will generally reproduce it on stage with a lantern or group that is more intense than the others. If the light is supposed to be coming from inside the room through artificial lighting, you could show the source of this light, such as a bedside lamp.

Angles

The angle of lighting to suggest sunlight, for example, is also very important. If it was early morning sunlight, would you want your 'sunlight' to come from a steep angle or a shallow one? (How high is the Sun in the early morning?) Side lights at different heights can create the same effect.

Natural light

The key to natural lighting is to re-create the quality that comes with different times of day and weather conditions. There are several shades of warm, straw-coloured gels available that suggest sunlight. You could use cooler blue colours for an overcast day, and paler blues for moonlight.

Lighting in *The Wider Earth* creates ripples, waves and sparkles as well as the naturalistic blue of under the sea.

TASK 1.9

Create a mini world and light it artificially to create the senses of sunlight and moonlight.
1. Use cardboard to create a small scene which includes a cut-out window.
2. Use torches (perhaps on a mini tripod) to experiment with lighting the scene.
3. Try coloured gels to create different times of day and night. You could also consider different weather conditions.

DESIGN TIP

Stage lanterns are very bright. It is crucial that they do not shine onto the audience and dazzle them.

Chapter 1 Practical Guide to Lighting Design

Front-lit, from straight ahead.

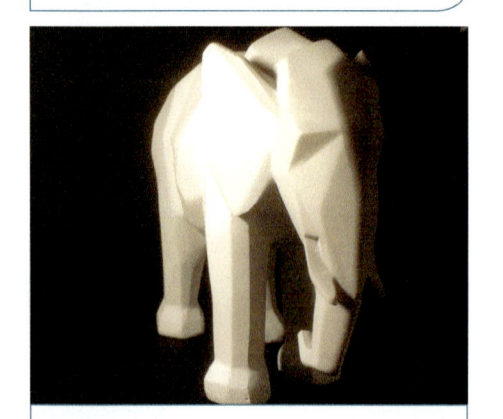

Lit by one light from the front at one side.

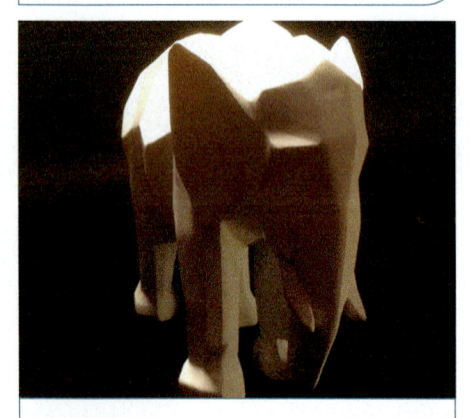

Back-lit.

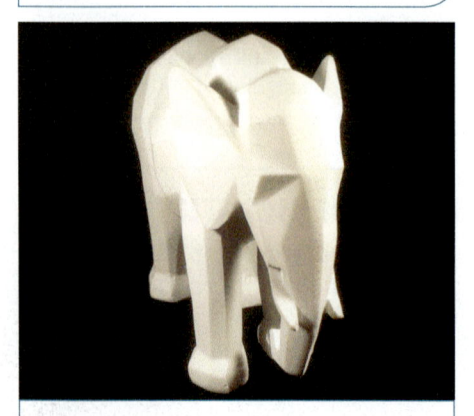

All three lights used equally.

Three-point lighting

Three-point lighting is widely accepted as an ideal starting point for naturalistic lighting. Light coming form only one angle would produce unwanted shadows. So, a second lantern is placed at a 45-degree angle to balance this. In addition, if you only light from the front, the effect is rather flat. To solve this, back light would give a naturalistic, 3D effect.

One of your three lights is the key light. This is likely to be a light that comes from the front, as is the **fill light**, which reduces shadow.

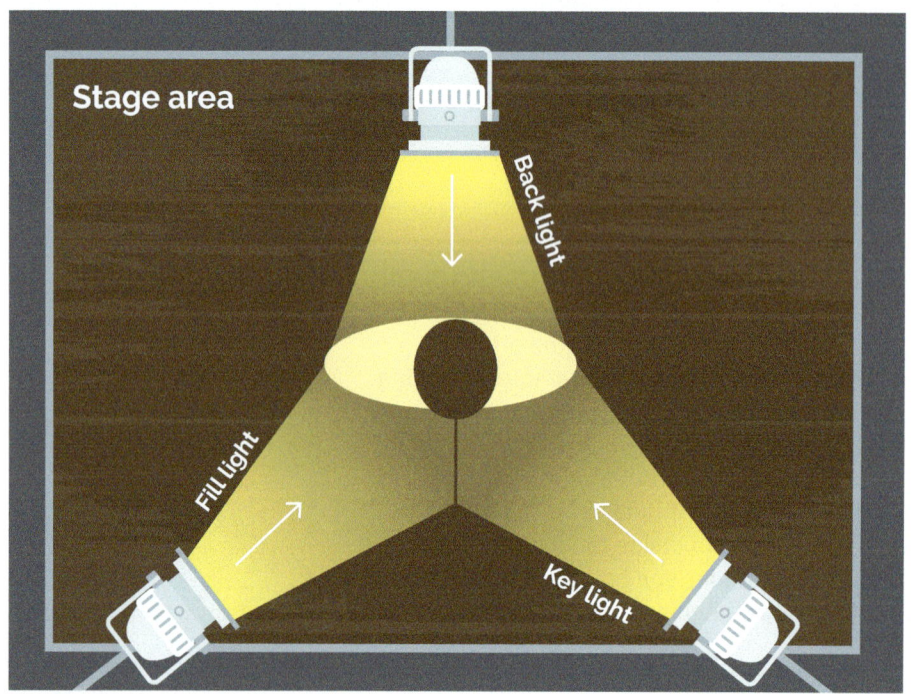

Colour

Colour is one of the most important keys to adding mood and atmosphere to stage lighting. You can see this above, in the explanation of how different colours are used to imitate sunlight and moonlight.

Technical points

White light is produced when a lantern does not have a coloured gel (filter) in front of the lens. In LED lights, white light is produced when all four colours are equally balanced. White light is the brightest light.

Introducing colour is a crucial part of any lighting design. With LED lanterns, you can programme each lighting cue to a specific colour by altering the balance between primary colours (red, green and blue). This versatility means each lantern can project a different colour for every cue if necessary.

Traditional (often older) lanterns use filters or gels to add colour to the beam. Unlike LEDs, each lantern can only be used to project one colour within a single performance. Gels are specially made sheets of thin, transparent, heat-resistant plastic. They are available in a wide range of colours, and can often be bought as a set. Sheets can be cut to fit gel holders that slide into or onto the front of the lantern.

Creative notes

White light is very bright and quite harsh and hard. Simply changing the intensity of the beam is very limiting. To produce more natural or atmospheric effects, you need to add colour.

The following suggestions are starting points for naturalistic lighting.
- Straw gels give a natural sunlight effect.
- Yellows and oranges create a warm, happy atmosphere.
- Pale blue adds a moonlit quality.
- Blues generally create colder and sadder moods.
- Lavenders and lilacs are neutral colours and work well in balancing other colours for a subtle effect.

As a general rule, it is best to use paler colours out front and darker colours from the sides or back of the stage.

Intensity (brightness)

Along with colour, changing the intensity of light is a powerful creator of atmosphere.

The lighting desk gives you as designer control over how bright the beam is (think of household dimmer switches).

Individual lanterns can be made brighter or dimmer using the controls on the lighting desk or board. It is usual to start at 70 per cent and then move up or down to create the effect you want. Be aware that taking the brightness below 20 per cent is likely to give too dim a beam. Coloured filters will also affect the power of a lantern's beam, with darker colours creating a significantly dimmer light.

DESIGN TIP
Always remember to consider coloured lighting alongside set and costume to avoid disrupting the desired overall effect.

LOOK HERE
You will find more information about colour in 'Special effects in lighting' on the following pages.

TASK 1.10

Watch a short interior scene from a TV drama or film in which lighting is important. Concentrate on the effect of lighting in the scene and note the following.
- How intense does the light seem to be, in percentage terms?
- Do the light sources seem natural, artificial or a mixture?
- What angle is the dominant light coming from?
- What colour(s) does the lighting designer appear to be using?

A typically shadowy scene as Eleven takes a call in *Stranger Things*.

FOCUS

Different lighting effects and how they might be created.

ASSESSMENT CHECK

Here, you will develop your ability to design and realise lighting that:

- contributes to the effect of a performance
- establishes location and time and/or enhances mood or atmosphere.

These will help you towards AO1: 'Create and develop ideas to communicate meaning for theatrical performance.'

DESIGN TIP

Modern LED lights are a good option for lighting designers. They are very useful for practical effects. You could, for example, adapt a bicycle headlight, adhesive cupboard lights or the flashing lights designed for pet collars!

SPECIAL EFFECTS IN LIGHTING

What are special effects?

All theatre lighting has a powerful effect. It can be difficult to separate special effects (or specials) from other lighting states and there are no strict rules. Generally speaking, special effects (FX or SFX) are those that have a very specific, short-term purpose in a theatre performance.

The Rocky Horror Picture Show at the Winnipesaukee Playhouse combines performer spotlights and LED lanterns with the naturalistic lighting (such as the chandeliers) from the room created by the set. (Lighting design by Matthew Guminski.)

In the scene above, for example, overhead spotlights create four distinct areas. They have the effect of isolating each performer. If this lighting effect was only used once or twice during a production, it would probably be 'special'. If it was used frequently, however, it would be the production's typical spot lighting state.

TASK 1.11

1. In the script or devised piece you are currently involved in, identify a moment that might be enhanced by a special effect. (This could be a **practical effect**, or one involving a spotlight that uses a particular angle, colour or gobo.)
2. What effect do you want the special effect to have on the audience? How could you create the effect?
3. If possible, test your ideas. How does the special effect influence meaning, mood, style or characterisation?
4. Take a photograph and make notes to remind yourself of what you have achieved.

Practical special effects

These effects are closely linked to the performers, who generally operate or wear them. Examples include:
- a camp-fire flame made of a battery-operated red light, switched on by an actor
- an 'oil' lamp with a flickering LED candle in it, again operated by the actor
- a light on a costume or at the end of a fairy wand.

Using key lights with special effects lighting

In the illustration below, a key light is used alongside the practical special effect of a camp fire to complete the illusion. The key light illuminates the face of the performer because the practical effect is not bright enough. A key light like this could be positioned at the front of the stage or at a low level in the wings to shine up onto the actor's face.

In this production of Harry Potter and the Cursed Child, the actors have practical battery lights on their wands, which they can turn on and off themselves.

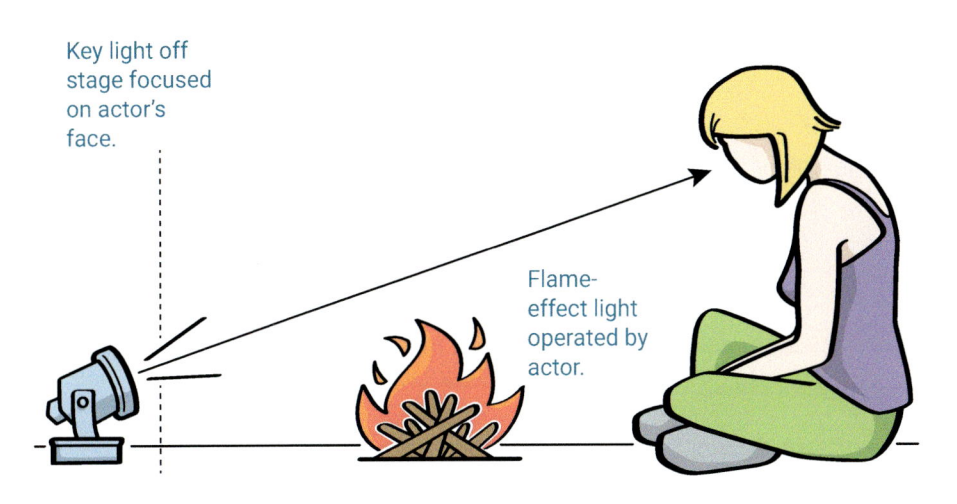

Key light off stage focused on actor's face.

Flame-effect light operated by actor.

This small fire-effect bulb can be used to simulate orange flames and embers with a flicker-effect control.

The opposite of key lighting is fill light, which is often softer. It could be another, less bright, light source, or it could come from general light reflected off surrounding walls, for example.

Naturalistic special effects

Naturalistic effects reproduce particular lighting that you might find in real life, and that the characters in their world would be able to see. Examples include:
- a lightning strike, which can be produced by quickly flashing a white floodlight. (This would be enhanced by an accompanying sound effect!)
- a disco effect, which could be created with LED lanterns or by manually flashing red, blue and green filtered spotlights. (Of course, it is also possible to use an automated moving lantern or a mirror/disco ball.)

Non-naturalistic special effects

These are the weird and wonderful, supernatural types of effect and could include, for example:
- the use of red and green filters combined with a fog machine to suggest an alien planet
- a slowly pulsing red spotlight focused on a character who is being aggressively questioned.

This production of The Tempest uses red, green and blue lighting together with an eerie set design and translucent costume to present the other-worldly nature of the island.

Chapter 1   Practical Guide to Lighting Design   25

FOCUS
The critical skill of how to move from one lighting cue to the next.

ASSESSMENT CHECK
This design skill is included in AO2: 'Apply theatrical skills to realise artistic intentions in live performance.'

DESIGN TIP
A seven-second cross-fade would be a good place to start your experiments.

LIGHTING TRANSITIONS

What is a lighting transition?

In your own home, you simply switch a light on or off: you move from darkness to light and vice versa at the flick of a switch. You might have some rooms with dimmer switches, allowing you to gradually increase or decrease the light's brightness.

In the theatre, in a more sophisticated way, a lighting designer can use the lighting desk to control the speed at which each lantern is made dimmer or brighter. This is known as a **transition**.

Types of transition

Snap
As the name suggests, a snap transition is a sudden movement of lights from on to off or vice versa.

Cross-snap
The sudden movement from one lighting state to another.

Fade
In lighting terms, this means making the lights gradually brighter and dimmer with a high degree of control.

Cross-fade
The gradual movement from one lighting state to another. This is achieved by simultaneously dimming one lighting state and brightening another until one is fully down and the other is fully up.

Choosing which type of transition to use

The more gradually you fade or cross-fade, the less aware the audience will be of the transition. This creates a calmer atmosphere. At the end of a performance, you might fade the lights to **blackout** over about five seconds to give the audience time to recognise that the performance is over. A slow fade to black also gives the audience time to reflect on what they have just seen.

On the other hand, a snap or cross-snap transition has a startling effect. It might jolt the audience and make a sharp contrast to the previous scene.

TASK 1.12

Harold Pinter's play *The Caretaker* includes a long speech in which a man reveals his life story. It is not a happy one. This is the stage direction:

> During Aston's speech the room grows darker. By the close of the speech only Aston can be seen clearly. Davies and all the others objects are in the shadow. The fade down of the light must be as gradual, as protracted [drawn out] and as unobtrusive as possible.

Work with a partner to discuss:
- Why was this detailed stage direction about lighting given?
- What effect might it have on the audience?

The stage darkens around Daniel Mays as Aston in *The Caretaker* at The Old Vic.

Chapter 1 Practical Guide to Lighting Design

RESEARCH FOR LIGHTING

Assessing additional lighting needs

As you progress with your lighting design, you will identify what additional resources you need, if any. In addition to basic equipment such as lanterns and safety bonds, you might find that you need, for example:

- gel sheets in specific colours
- gobos
- filter and/or gobo holders for lanterns
- small LED lights to use as part of a special effect.

Budget

Once you have an idea of the costs of these items, present this to your teacher. If your teacher agrees that these things should be bought, you will be given a small budget. Once this has also been agreed in your group's design meetings, you need to stick to it.

Finding the best deal

It is well worth shopping around for the best-value products. The internet will be the place for much of what you are looking for. Local pound shops and charity shops, however, might be a cheaper source of some practical effect components, such as bicycle lights.

Alternatively, you might be able to borrow or hire items like gobos and their holders from a local theatre. If so, make sure that their accessories fit your equipment.

Battery-operated bicycle safety lights can be useful in special effects.

FOCUS
Finding and costing additional items to complete your lighting designs.

ASSESSMENT CHECK
This research and decision-making helps to show that you can assess the merit of different approaches and judge the overall impact you are having. You should also begin to analyse and evaluate your research findings.

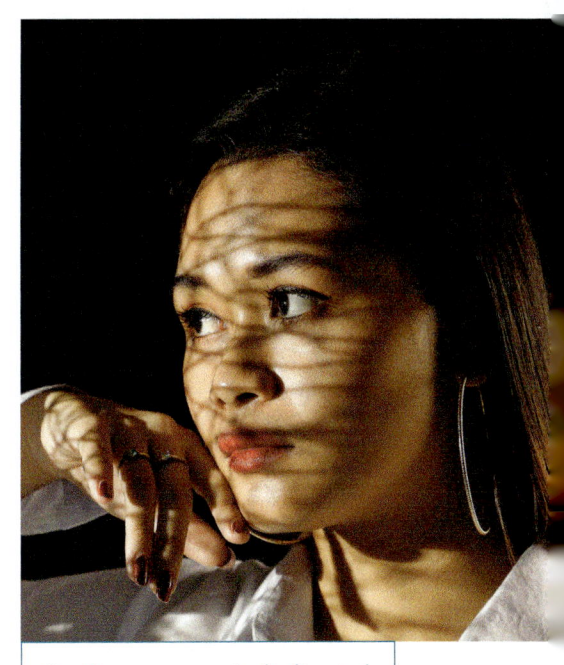

A gobo over a precisely directed light can have a striking effect.

DESIGN TIP
Make sure you know exactly what you need before you begin shopping.

TASK 1.13

Find good sources – in terms of choice, availability and stock – of:
- a colour filter (gel) sheet
- a B-sized gobo of a window
- a replacement lamp (bulb) for a 1kw fresnel.

Chapter 1   Practical Guide to Lighting Design

FOCUS
Examples and guidance to help you prepare the diagrams and charts you need.

ASSESSMENT CHECK
Your diagrams and documents will help you to:
- create and develop ideas to communicate meaning (AO1)
- apply theatrical skills to realise your artistic intentions (AO2).

SIGNPOST
Complete Task 1.3 on page 18 first to check what resources you have. There is no point creating a lighting design for 28 lanterns if you only have access to 18!

LOOK HERE
There is guidance on compiling and using a cue sheet on pages 30–31.

If you are devising, go through the stages in 'Lighting Design for the Devised Piece', beginning on page 195.

LOOK HERE
A detailed example of a lighting cue sheet for *Hansel and Gretel* is available on the *Designing Drama* product page at illuminatepublishing.com.

HOW TO DOCUMENT YOUR LIGHTING DESIGN

What documents should I produce?
You need to create a detailed **cue sheet**, **lighting plot** (rigging diagram) and schedule (list of all the equipment you have used).

These diagrams and charts can look complicated, but the advice on these pages will help you to complete excellent documents.

Why should I create these documents?
Plans and cue sheets provide lighting technicians with plans to follow. Even if a designer were to do all the technical work themselves, they could not carry in their heads all the information needed to rig and operate. Lighting charts and plans serve the same purpose as ground plans and model boxes do for set designers.

The documents you draw up will help you practically as well as going in your devising log and being shown to the visiting examiner.

The lighting plot and schedule provide details of the lanterns and their accessories, along with a plan of where they are rigged. The plan should include a key that explains any symbols used in it.

The cue sheet contains details of every lighting change. It contains all the information needed to operate the lighting in performance.

The equipment and its location
You can only group and rig your lanterns once you know what lighting states and effects are required and where. So, you will already have marked your lighting ideas on the script. You might even have an early cue sheet.

If you are working on a devised piece, you will be becoming clear about all the lighting states and special effects that you are setting out to achieve.

As you get closer to rigging, you will need to produce finished versions of the following documents.

TASK 1.14
Practise drawing up each document as you go along with your design, so that you are confident by the time you are working on the production.

The lighting schedule
You can organise details of all the lanterns, gobos, barn doors and so on in any way you want.

Types and quantities of lanterns
A simple list like the one below is fine.

Lighting schedule: *Hansel and Gretel*	
Type of lantern	**Quantity**
Fresnel	11
Par can	2
Profile spotlight	11

28 Chapter 1 Practical Guide to Lighting Design

Accessories

Here is an example of a **colour count** (using Lee brand filters). It records the different gels used, the size of the colour frames they fit into and how many gels of each you will need. In other words, how many lanterns each colour is going to be used in.

Show	Hansel and Gretel		
Venue	Main Hall		
Colour code	Name	Type (of frame)	Count (number of gels required)
L020	Medium Amber	7.5" colour frame	1
L117	Steel Blue	10" colour frame	2
L132	Medium Blue	7.5" colour frame	2
L201	Full CT Blue	7.5" colour frame	2
L203	¼ CT Blue	7.5" colour frame	8
L770	Burnt Yellow	7.5" colour frame	3

The lighting plot

This document (a detailed example is given below) can contain a great deal of information. The most important is the type of lantern and where it is to be positioned on the rig.

The key to the plot

This tells the reader what the symbols and numbers on the lighting plot mean. Yours could be simpler than this one, on the left, which also shows some different lantern types.

DESIGN TIP

You could create a similar document to a colour count to give details of gobos used.

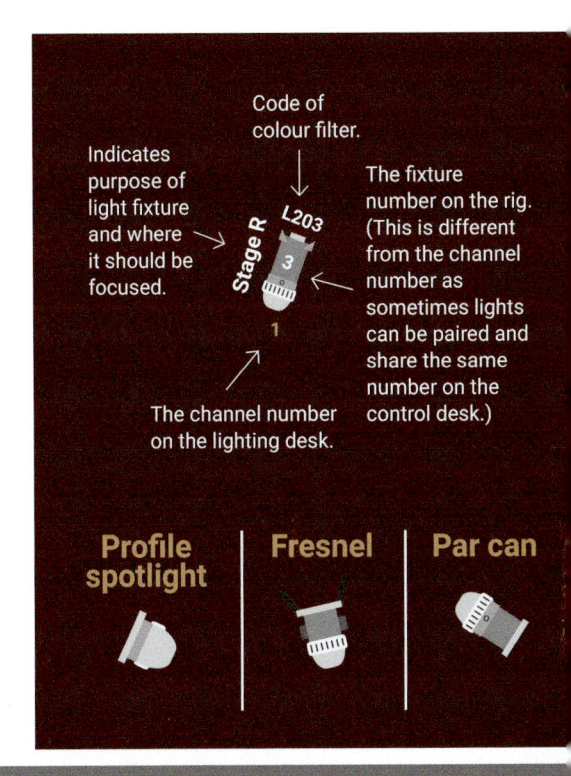

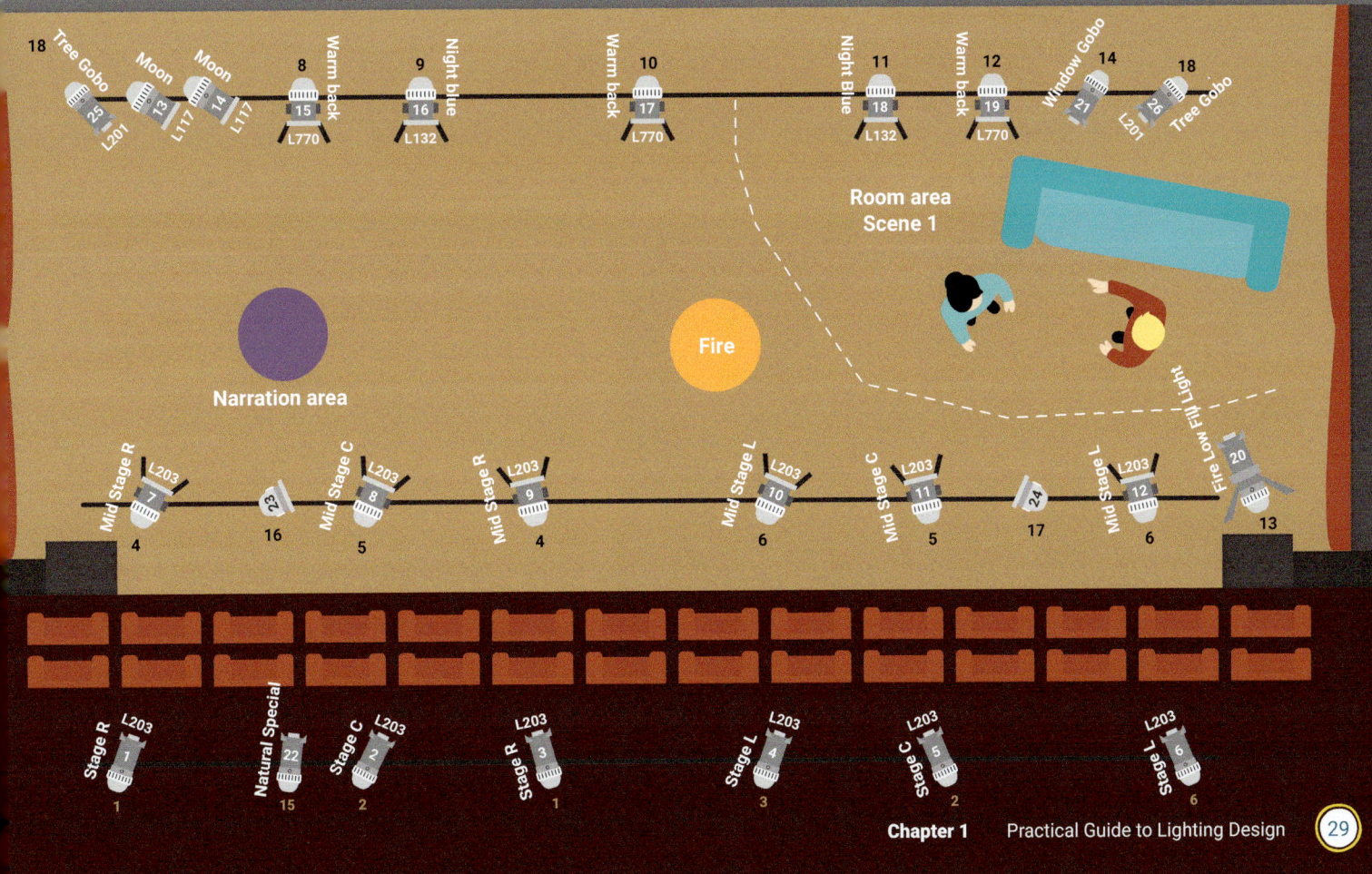

- **Indicates purpose of light fixture and where it should be focused.**
- **Code of colour filter.**
- **The fixture number on the rig.** (This is different from the channel number as sometimes lights can be paired and share the same number on the control desk.)
- **The channel number on the lighting desk.**

Profile spotlight | Fresnel | Par can

Chapter 1   Practical Guide to Lighting Design   29

FOCUS

- The stage at which your lighting design really comes together.
- Creating a lighting cue sheet, which is essential for running a show's lighting and required for assessment.

ASSESSMENT CHECK

Achieving the important goal of the cue sheet means that you can design and realise a range of lighting effects.

You can also use your cue sheet to analyse and evaluate your ideas and the reasons for key decisions.

LOOK HERE

Check how you might use transitions by revisiting page 26.

PLOTTING THE LIGHTING DESIGN

Fixing your cues

In this book, we are using the term **plotting** to mean the act of setting the lighting for every part of the production. The cue sheet should record details of every lighting cue decided. If you have lighting software, record each cue digitally, as you go along.

You will need to make several decisions for each cue, including:

- which lanterns are used
- how bright they should be
- what colours (if any) are needed
- whether any special effects are required
- the type and length of transitions.

Conditions for successful plotting

- Enlist a helper! If you can, invite a younger student who is already involved or interested in lighting to be your assistant – they will be learning too. Your assistant can walk around the acting area so that you can see the effect of your work clearly.
- Choose a quiet time. There is no point trying to plot during a rehearsal or when people need the main (house) lights on.
- Collect everything you need, including:
  - the annotated script or scene list
  - your lighting-rig plan
  - a task light (such as an angle-poise lamp)
  - a template for your cue sheet.

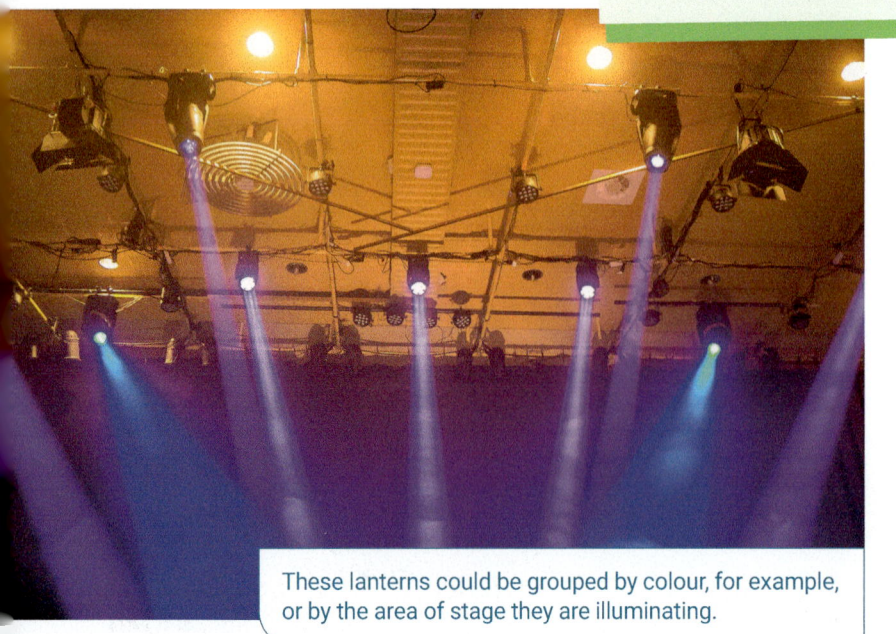

Grouping individual lanterns

The first stage in plotting is likely to be putting lanterns into groups. Creating groups means that you can quickly bring up and mix your lighting states.

A group of lanterns is several lights working together to give a particular look, such as **general cover** or warm colours; to light a specific area of the stage (DSL for example), create a special effect (sfx) and so on.

You could also group lanterns by their position on the rig, such as those at the front lighting bar, **sidelights** and so on.

A lantern could be in more than one group, and you will often use more than one group at a time.

These lanterns could be grouped by colour, for example, or by the area of stage they are illuminating.

Chapter 1   Practical Guide to Lighting Design

Identifying and documenting lantern groups

You will need your lighting plot and script (or detailed performance notes).

TASK 1.15

1. Go through your script and identify the **distinct** groups in your design. Aim for the building blocks. You might find it useful to group by area on the stage or colour, tone, special effects, for example.
2. Give each group a number. You are likely to have between four and ten groupings. Limit the number to the amount of master **channels** on your lighting desk.
3. Select a group to start on. Use your lighting desk to bring up individual lanterns in that group. Keep experimenting until you are happy. You could also make some lights brighter or dimmer to achieve the balance you like.
4. Write down the channel numbers of all the lanterns in the group. Add intensity levels as a percentage as necessary. (F means 'full': 100%.) For example:

Lantern groupings		
Group 1: General cover	**Group 2: DSL (house interior)**	**Group 3: sfx (camp fire)**
3 (F)	3 (70%)	Key light – 6 (variable %)
5 (70%)	8 (F)	
11 (F)	21 (40%)	

> **DESIGN TIP**
> Make separate notes on **why** you are making decisions. These will help you to **analyse** and **evaluate** your design.

Creating your lighting cue sheet

This document is your ultimate guide to operating the lighting for your production. It plots precisely which groups are in use for each cue along with their intensity and the timings involved.

TASK 1.16

1. Lay your script, groupings chart and a cue sheet template around your lighting desk. If you have software for storing your cues, bring it into action.
2. Starting at the beginning of the show, work through the production cue by cue and scene by scene to build and chart each lighting state.
3. Check that cue numbers are clearly and correctly marked in your script so that the operator can track approaching cues. You could add '6a' and '6b' and so on later, if needed.
4. Continue to fill in your cue sheet until you have plotted the entire production.

> **DESIGN TIP**
> Note that blackouts are a cue in themselves. So are all transitions.

> **LOOK HERE**
> Go to www.illuminatepublishing.com for a detailed cue sheet example.

RIGGING AND FOCUSING

FOCUS
The method by which lanterns are positioned and focused.

ASSESSMENT CHECK
You are expected to understand how to apply rigging, positioning, angling and focusing for your lighting design. This will help you towards AO2: 'Apply theatrical skills to realise artistic intentions in live performance.'

This process takes its name from the rig, which, in this case, is the construction of bars from which the lanterns are suspended.

PREPARATION

Complete the checklist on page 248.
⇩
Gather all your resources.
⇩
Check your rigging diagram.
⇩
Set up your lighting desk.
⇩
Switch on the dimmer rack.

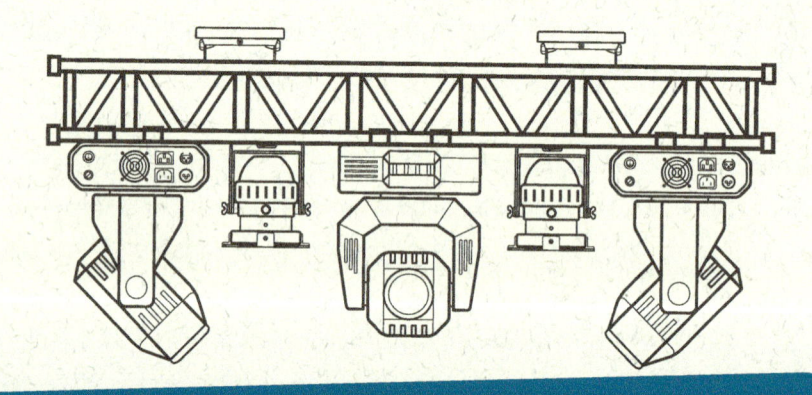

Steps for safe and successful rigging

NB: Lanterns should be checked before rigging by a qualified person.
NB: Nobody should be underneath the rig when lanterns are being mounted.
Check that all climbing equipment can be secured and 'guarded'.
Check that all the lantern attachments, such as barn doors, gels, gobos and the safety bond work properly and are secure.

DESIGN TIP
These rigging notes are for your information as you supervise the process. (You will not be rigging the lights yourself.)

The sequence for rigging lanterns is:
1. Hook over bar and tighten wing nut.
2. Attach safety bond.
3. Point the lantern towards the area you want to light.
4. Adjust shutters and barn doors.
5. Plug in the lantern, wrapping any extra cable loosely around the bar.

Focusing

Focusing involves fine-tuning a lantern's beam size, shape and spread.

Each lantern needs to be adjusted so that it lights the required area precisely. You might want a tight, round spotlight to pick out an individual actor. Alternatively, you might focus a group of lanterns for a subtle wash of light. For this effect, look to make the edges of the beams very soft.

You need a minimum of two people, but three are better. Ideally, one will rig and focus; one brings up the working light on the desk and the third moves around the performance area as the subject for the lighting so that the focusing effect can be seen.

A technician needs the following equipment, so provide them if you can:

- **an adjustable wrench** (to tighten and loosen nuts)
- **heat-resistant gloves** 
- **a small torch or headlamp** 
- **a tool belt or pouch** 

To focus a lantern, the following actions might be required:
- Moving shutters or barn doors
- Inserting or removing coloured filters and gobos (Gobos get very hot!)
- Moving lenses backwards or forwards.

House lights need to be off and one lantern needs to be focused at a time. Some lights can be brought up together to test their combined effect.

DESIGN TIP
You will nearly always want to light the performer, not the floor!

LOOK HERE
Use the information on pages 20–23 to guide your positioning and focusing.

DESIGN TIP
Try to get rigging and focusing correct first time to avoid having to get the people and equipment together again and doing tasks more than once.

Chapter 1   Practical Guide to Lighting Design   33

FOCUS

This section offers potentially life-saving information!

ASSESSMENT CHECK

Throughout Components 2 and 3, you must adopt the latest safe working practices.

This is also covered in AO3: 'Demonstrate knowledge and understanding of how drama and theatre is developed and performed.'

HEALTH AND SAFETY IN LIGHTING DESIGN

Any activity that involves electricity and hanging heavy objects above people's heads needs to be treated with a great deal of care. Stop and think about the risks for a moment!

If I'm not allowed to rig lights, why do I need to know about health and safety?

The exam board does not want you to take on much responsibility for your own and other people's safety when it comes to lighting. Your school must not allow students to put themselves or others at risk either.

However, there are good reasons why you still need to know about it:

- Everyone bears some responsibility for the safety of their environment. If people look out for potential dangers, the better it is for everyone.
- Assessing risks and avoiding hazards is part of being a responsible member of the group.
- You are expected to show your knowledge and understanding of health and safety issues.
- If you progress to make your living in this field, you need to consider health and safety issues and how to tackle them.

Take notes on any risks and hazards you encounter in your practical work. As well as making sure that they are attended to by an adult, you could mention them in your devising log if you design lighting for Component 2.

Using your common sense

Many dangerous situations can be avoided when people are sensible. Here are some basic issues to be aware of before your lights are set up.

! Hazards	Safety measures ✓
⚠ Loose electrical cables	✅ Tape them down or cordon off the area.
⚠ Damaged cables or electrical items ⚠ Lack of or out-of-date PAT (electrical safety) test label	✅ Report the problem immediately to someone in authority.
⚠ Having the wrong tool for a job, such as a knife instead of a screwdriver	✅ Find out what the right tool is and make sure it is available and used.
⚠ Working at height	✅ See 'Rigging and focusing', pages 32–33.
⚠ Unsecured lanterns or fixtures on the lighting bars	✅ Make sure no one is underneath. Ask a suitable person (not yourself!) to attach a safety bond (cable).
⚠ Hot lanterns and gobos	✅ Wear safety gloves.

Chapter 1   Practical Guide to Lighting Design

OPERATING THE LIGHTING

I don't need to operate the lights, do I?

You are not required to operate the lighting desk, but there is no reason why you shouldn't. If you design the lighting for Component 2, learning how to operate the lighting and evaluating your success would be very useful. Similarly, operating skills will be impressive if you design lighting for Component 3. Most importantly, perhaps, it is a thrilling, satisfying experience.

Operating lighting equipment

The following items need to be in place:

- a working lighting desk that you have been able to practise using
- rigged and focused lanterns
- a task light (angle-poise)
- script (if applicable), marked up with the cues (two scripts are ideal – one for your assistant)
- your completed cue sheet.

If there is a sound operator, you will need to co-ordinate certain effects with them. You might need to fade sound and lights precisely at the same time, for example. Unless you are wearing cans (linked headphones), it is wise to operate sound and lights next to each other.

Practising lighting operation

- Take time to check that you are comfortable using your lighting desk. Your preparation could include labelling master channels with group numbers – on a manual board. (You can write on masking tape and it is easily removed.)
- It is useful to have at least one person 'walking' the acting area with a marked-up script. They can work **cue to cue** with you. The script will keep you in time with the action and enable you to see where cues need to happen, such as on a particular word in the performance.
- Make sure you practise transitions, as well as changes within cues, such as dimming and intensifying lighting states.
- If there are long fades and you are using a manual board, make sure that you can operate them smoothly. This is a benefit of a manual desk, as you can 'feel' the action.

FOCUS
Advice for the lighting operator.

ASSESSMENT CHECK
Your lighting knowledge and skills show that you can design and realise lighting that contributes positively to the performance and communicates meaning.

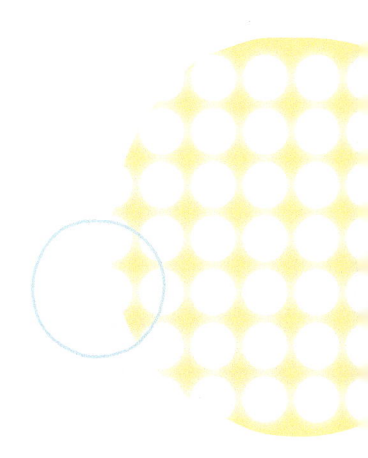

LOOK HERE
See 'Plotting the lighting design', page 30, for details on cues.

Some additional health and safety points

Beware of blackouts! In rehearsals, always call out that you are about to do them, so people are not unexpectedly plunged into darkness.

Be very aware that flashing lights can trigger epilepsy.

Chapter 1   Practical Guide to Lighting Design

FOCUS
Your design role during final rehearsals.

DESIGN TIP
If you are struggling with a technical aspect, ask your group if you can run a cue again. This is the purpose of the techs.

ASSESSMENT CHECK
Rehearsals give you the chance to:
- select appropriate equipment and determine its position
- understand the performer/audience relationship
- apply theatrical skills to realise your artistic intentions (AO2).

TASK 1.17
1. Update your notebook and script with any issues to be resolved before the dress rehearsal.
2. Arrange some time to work things through with other designers if there are any clashes.

LOOK HERE
Technical equipment doesn't always work properly. Use the troubleshooting guide on page 59 to help you cope.

TECHNICAL AND DRESS REHEARSALS FOR LIGHTING DESIGNERS

These are the final rehearsals before the performance.

The technical rehearsal

Technical rehearsals ('techs') are lengthy rehearsals because they need to let lighting and sound operators test their designs in practice.

At the same time, the director and other designers are checking that all the technical aspects of the production work smoothly and harmoniously. The performers get to experience the piece with the design elements in place.

You will need to decide as a group whether to run the production in its entirety or move from cue to cue, missing out certain sections. All the different design roles will need to work closely to make sure that everyone is confident that the process can be repeated when the piece is performed without interruptions.

During technical rehearsals, make sure performers know which areas of the stage will not be lit during particular lighting states. These areas could be marked with tape so that cast and crew can practise moving around safely.

Making technical and artistic improvements

Unlike set and costume designers, who will have completed the bulk of their job by now, you are likely to be heavily involved in the tech. Even if someone else is operating the lighting, you need to guide them through the cues and make adjustments to levels, timings of fades and so on.

You will also need to watch the acting area and check that:
- lighting states allow all sections of the audience to see the actors
- coloured lighting works harmoniously with set and costume
- practical special effects are managed successfully
- the lighting design overall is working well in practice.

The dress rehearsal

The important thing about the dress rehearsal ('dress') is that is runs through the whole production without interruption, except in an emergency. The performers can experience the whole show with all the technical elements, but without an audience to see the actors. The lighting designer can test that the lighting design can be carried out successfully.

Until the dress, none of you will be sure that the performance can run smoothly. For lighting, these are some issues you might face:

Lighting problem	Possible solution
Lack of time between cues in a specific section.	Simplify your design by removing or changing a cue to make it manageable.
The show is 'running away with you' in general. It is a struggle to keep track of the cues, desk, script and stage at the same time.	Don't panic! Get through the dress rehearsal as best you can. It might be a particularly demanding design or production. Practice as much as possible before the performance. Consider simplifying the cues.

EVALUATING YOUR LIGHTING DESIGN

Examining the detail of your design

Once you are clear about what evaluation is and the best way of approaching it, you can focus on assessing the success of your lighting design.

Whenever you evaluate, you should make at least three different points. These points should be illustrated with specific examples. Each time, you should also explain the reason why you have made a particular value judgement. You should highlight anything that could have gone better.

TASK 1.18

1. Copy and complete a table like this one (some examples have been included). The notes will provide a solid basis for your evaluation writing.

Lighting design evaluation			
Design element	**Example/ moment in the play**	**Evaluation**	**Reason for evaluation**
Pre-set lighting state – down-lit white fresnels over the stage. Enhanced by fog machine.	Before the performance began.	Engaging and created powerful atmosphere.	Audience feedback suggested that the eerie atmosphere was established from the start of the play. This was a key part of our artistic intentions.
Practical special effect – camp fire plus key light.	Hansel lights a fire in the forest.	Convincing in setting scene and contributing to action.	The practical effect of the red lamp in the 'fire' was operated well by the actor. Gradually increasing the intensity of the key light on her face gave a convincing illusion of a fire.
Use of cobalt blue filter from side of stage.	The moonlit forest.	Atmospheric; helped in characterisation.	The blue lighting that side-lit the acting area created an atmosphere of fear. Lighting combined well with the soundscape to emphasise the characters' feelings.

2. Expand your notes into three paragraphs of evaluative writing. Remember that you should compare your finished lighting with your agreed artistic intentions.

FOCUS
Placing a value judgement on design.

ASSESSMENT CHECK
This part of the design process is the essential element of AO4: 'Analyse and evaluate your own work and the work of others.'

SIGNPOST
Use the evaluation guidance on page 78 before you start.

LOOK HERE
More examples of analysis and evaluation can be found in Chapter 6 of this book.

Chapter 1 Practical Guide to Lighting Design

LIGHTING DESIGN VOCABULARY

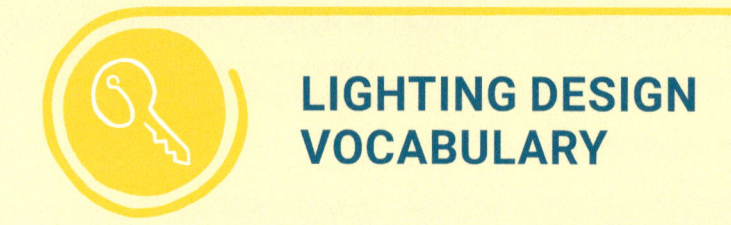

AML (automated moving lantern) Operated digitally, these lanterns can swivel and tilt.

Analyse Examine in detail, thinking about parts in relation to the whole.

Atmospheric A sound, for example, that creates a strong feeling or mood.

Backlight/backlighting Lighting that comes from the back of the acting area.

Barn door A metal attachment that slides into the front of a lantern, with hinged flaps to control the beam.

Birdie A miniature lantern ideal for hiding in small parts of a set or along the front edge of the stage.

Blackout A moment when all the lights are dimmed, often suddenly.

Channel A number given to a **lantern** that corresponds to a number on the **lighting board** or **desk**.

Colour count A record of the number of gels of each colour required.

Colour palette A complementary set of colours that belong to a group, such as pastel or dark.

Cross-fade Fading up one lantern or group while fading down another.

Cue sheet A list of cues along with timings.

Cue to cue Going through a play from one sound or lighting cue to the next, missing out the parts in between.

Digital Using computer technology. Digital lighting desks, for example, are programmed using software.

Dimmer/Fader A way of controlling the intensity (brightness) of the light. These are often manual or digital sliders.

Dimmer rack The control centre for changing the **intensity** of each channel.

Evaluate Give an opinion, a value judgement, backed up with examples and reasons.

Fade A gradual increase or decrease.

Fill light Working with a **key light**, fill light is less intense (bright) and is often used to lessen shadows.

Filter/gel A piece/sheet of coloured plastic/resin that fits at the front of a lantern to change the colour of the beam.

Flood A type of lantern that produces a wide spread of light; a broad cover of light.

Focus Adjust the angle and beam size of a lantern so that it lights the exact area required

Fresnel A type of lantern that is good for lighting large areas and which blends easily with other fresnels or spotlights to create a wash of light.

Gel See **Filter**.

General cover Lanterns that provide overall lighting to the acting area.

Gobo A metal cut-out plate that fits in front of a lantern and casts a shadow shape onto the stage (such as a tree outline, window frames and so on).

Intensity The brightness of lighting. Intensity is generally measured as a percentage (such as 60%).

Key light The main, strongest, most intense light, designed to copy the main light source (natural or artificial) in the real world.

Lamp The technical name for a light bulb.

Lantern The technical term for a **lighting fixture** that contains a light source, such as a lamp.

LED (Light Emitting Diode) Lighting fixtures that use less energy and create less heat than other types of lantern. LEDs are the most popular type of fixture in professional theatres.

Lighting desk/board/console The means of operating the lighting, with channels, dimmers and faders.

Lighting fixture A stage light unit.

Lighting plot The diagram that shows where the lanterns are hung on the rigging.

Lighting state The term used to describe the way a lantern or group of lanterns is used on the stage. For example, a particular lighting state could create a moonlit effect.

Manual Operated by hand as opposed to digitally.

Naturalistic A set or lighting effect, for example, with characteristics of reality; having the appearance of a real place.

Non-naturalistic A set or lighting design, for example, that aims not to look like a real place.

Pace The speed with which lighting effects transition from one to the next.

Par can A type of lantern that produces a very strong beam of light.

Plotting The process of creating a cue sheet to show choices of what light effect happens when and where.

Practical effect A lighting effect that is operated or worn by a performer.

Profile spotlight A versatile lantern that can be used to create tight spots of light or bigger areas as required.

Rig The bars that lanterns are hung on.

Safety bond/cable/chain The metal chain or cable that attaches the lantern to the rigging.

Sidelight Light that shines from the side of the stage, perhaps from the wings.

Silhouette The dark shape of a person or object against a lighter background.

Snap A sudden change such as a **blackout**.

Special effect A lighting effect that has a specific purpose, such as a colour wash to suggest a flashback.

Spotlight A type of lantern that can create a tight circle of light or a larger, softer-edged one.

Three-point lighting A method that shines light from three different directions to give good coverage.

Transition A change between lighting states, such as a snap or a fade.

PRACTICAL GUIDE TO SOUND DESIGN

Chapter 2

Introduction to sound design	40
How to produce sound for the stage	42
Research for sound design	44
Sourcing, creating and mixing sounds	46
Health and safety in sound design	49
Special sound effects	50
How to document your sound design	52
Directional sound	54
Plotting the sound design	56
Operating sound equipment	58
Technical and dress rehearsals for sound designers	60
Evaluating your sound design	61
Sound design vocabulary	62

FOCUS
The power of sound in theatrical performance.

ASSESSMENT CHECK
This section develops your ability to create and develop ideas to communicate meaning (AO1).

You will develop:
- as a creative, effective, independent and reflective student, able to make informed choices in process and performance
- an awareness and understanding of the roles and processes undertaken in contemporary professional theatre practice.

INTRODUCTION TO SOUND DESIGN

How can I design sound as part of this course?

Component 1 is the written exam. Working practically with sound will give you the knowledge and understanding to write confidently about sound in your set text or a performance you have seen.

You can opt for sound design in either or both of the practical sections of the course. If you choose to work as sound designer in Component 2, you will work in a small group and help to develop the piece, but your specific responsibility will be to create a sound design for the performance. Component 3 is similar, but you will work with a script.

Sound in the real world

Sound is one of the five senses that connect human beings with the world. We hear things in the womb before we are born, and it is generally accepted that hearing is the last sense to fail when we die. Sound is possibly the most evocative sensation.

We are not particularly conscious of many of the sounds that most of us hear every day. Traffic noises, people chatting, bird song, the wind and so on often fade into the background. Our brains filter them out so that we can focus on more important sounds.

Other sound choices, such as our ringtones and the volume of our video games, are very conscious. Similarly, we choose our music to suit our situation and the mood we want to create.

Then there are the sounds that are signals in our life, such as a doorbell, text alert, smoke detector or siren of an ambulance. This kind of sound alerts us to actions that we might need to take.

TASK 2.1

1. Take a few moments to listen carefully and identify all of the sounds you can hear right now. Note them in a chart like this one (some examples have been included for guidance.)

Sounds in life		
Closest sound: Computer whirring	**Sound(s) that suggest mood and atmosphere**: Breeze, clock ticking, songbirds, crows…	**Intermittent sound(s)**: Toddler whinging
Most distant sound: Football on playing field (whistle, shouts, ball being kicked)	**Constant sound(s)**: Clock ticking	**Other sounds**: Car door slamming

2. On a scale of 1 to 5, at what level of volume would you place each sound?
3. Finally, try to imagine the blend of sounds you are hearing as a **soundscape** for the stage. What sounds might you take out or add in order to add meaning or atmosphere?

Sound and the stage

In the theatre, the sound designer re-creates many different types of sound to convey meaning and add atmosphere to a production and fit into the harmonious world of the stage. Every sound is included for a reason, including those that help to create location. The sounds feed the imagination of the audience.

Different types of stage sound

There are broadly two types of theatre sound. **Diegetic sounds** are those that seem to come from the world of the stage, such as a scene's background noise, doorbells, music that is put on by an actor, phone ringtones. **Non-diegetic sounds** are those used to add mood and ambience for the audience, such as **atmospheric** sound effects and music. Non-diegetic sounds would not be 'heard' by the characters.

TASK 2.2

Look at this image on the right from *The 39 Steps*. Imagine you are creating a soundscape for it.

1 What sounds would you create? Describe them here.

An atmospheric soundscape	
Diegetic sounds	**Non-diegetic sounds**

2 For each sound, add a volume level from 1 to 5 to create the blend of sounds that you think is suitable. Think about the atmosphere you wish to create.

3 Using CDs, online sound effects and/or (with permission from your teacher) a smartphone, create a version of your soundscape. Even if you are not able yet to mix the sounds, you will be able to blend at least three.

4 Play your soundscape to others. Note their responses regarding the meaning and atmosphere your blend of sounds create for them.

- Was it what you hoped for?
- What could you change to achieve your desired effect?

Chapter 2 Practical Guide to Sound Design 41

FOCUS

The different equipment needed to produce stage sound.

ASSESSMENT CHECK

You need to deploy different types of sounds as appropriate to realise the intended sound design. This is part of of AO2: 'Apply theatrical skills to realise artistic intentions in live performance.'

HOW TO PRODUCE SOUND FOR THE STAGE

Resources for producing sound

Every professional designer needs to understand the mechanics of how sound is produced and most professionals will have significant skills and knowledge. Once you have gained a good understanding of the technical aspects of theatrical sound design, you will be able to unleash your creativity. At GCSE level, it is your design that is assessed, but you need to have sufficient knowledge and understanding to create and transmit sounds for the stage.

As a sound designer, your tools are:

- **sources** of sound (microphones, CDs, **digital** recordings, musical instruments)
- mixing desk (**manual** or digital) and **playback device**
- **amplifier** (produces the signals for the speakers)
- **speaker** (broadcasts the sound).

If we add an 'H' for the person who **h**ears the sound, we can make a mnemonic for the sequence of sound production:

S	Source (CD, microphone, and so on)
M	Mixer (sounds are refined and exported)
A	Amplifier (signal is boosted)
S	Speaker (sound is transmitted)
H	Hearing (sound reaches the listener)

Getting to grips with your resources

Experiment with sound technology until you feel confident. It can be quite easy to produce impressive results.

TASK 2.3

Draw a flow chart to show your understanding of SMASH. Use symbols to help you include details.

DESIGN TIP

If your mixing desk runs from a laptop, check what your operating system provides. Apple has a free version of *QLab*, for example, which enables you to mix and pre-programme sound **cues**.

TASK 2.4

Complete this table to take stock of the sound equipment you have available.

Number of speakers, their positions and if they can be moved	Mixing desk: manual or electronic? Number of channels?	Playback device: type and details	Other resources

Chapter 2 Practical Guide to Sound Design

Sound sources

The source of a sound is simply the place where you 'grab' the sound you want. You can find a piece of music, for example, on a CD, online music service or, with the help of microphones, from live instruments or voices.

Mixing desk

As its name suggests, a sound mixer is the device where a designer or technician refines and blends sounds. Digital mixers are more complex than manual ones, but work on the same principles.

If you don't have a mixing desk, sounds can be mixed and edited in software and played through a computer or amplifier during the performance.

> The input section is where the raw sound enters the system. You can then balance the sound. This might be to equalise it (improve tone) and add effects (such as **reverb**). Several channels mean you can mix several sounds.

> Once the sounds have been adjusted, a **fader** is used to set the volume of each sound. Each input can then be routed to one or all of the outputs.

> The output section also has faders. These are where the final volume for the blend of sounds is adjusted. The mixed sound(s) go from here to the amplifier(s).

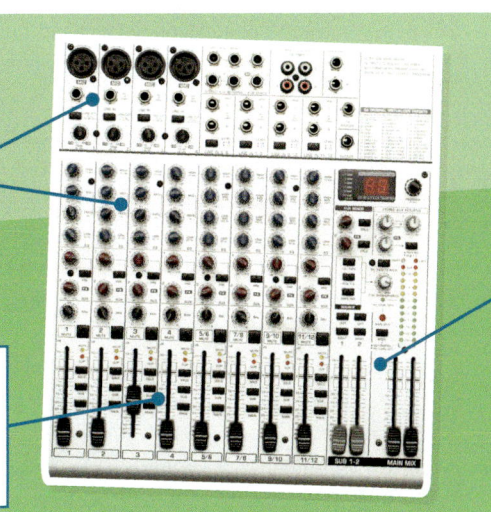

Amplifier

To amplify means 'to make louder or bigger'. In sound design, the amplifier (amp) boosts the signal from the mixing desk to a level where it can be 'read' by the speakers.

Some venues have more than one amplifier. One might connect to the speakers on stage, for example, and another to speakers in the audience.

Speaker

Speakers might be the piece of equipment you are most familiar with. They broadcast sound! Find out early on what speakers you have and whether they are fixed or moveable.

Microphones

In larger spaces, performers sometimes struggle to make themselves heard. This is an issue for sound designers, particularly as you might want to use other sounds under dialogue. In a smaller space, you might not need a microphone, but might want to create specific effects, such as a voice-over.

Radio mics are used in many theatres to amplify actors' voices. Your school or college might have some or can hire them. If so, it is part of your job to make sure they are working and fitted properly.

Floating mics tend to be positioned at the front of the stage. They can be problematic unless used and positioned carefully. They tend to pick up unwanted sounds, such as footsteps on stage.

Hanging mics are suspended above the stage. Again, they will pick up all the sounds on the stage, not just voices.

DESIGN TIP

Store all your sourced sound effects into a computer file in a folder that you can find easily for editing and/or mixing.

LOOK HERE

For more on using sound software, see page 59.
For advice on positioning speakers, see page 54.

FOCUS
Developing ideas and making approximate costings of equipment and materials.

ASSESSMENT CHECK
This research will help you towards AO1: 'Create and develop ideas to communicate meaning for theatrical performance.'

You are also working towards AO2: 'Apply theatrical skills to realise artistic intentions in live performance.'

RESEARCH FOR SOUND DESIGN

Where can I find inspiration for sound design?

If you are new to sound design, an effective and fun way to learn is to study how the professionals work.

TASK 2.5

1. Search the internet for something like 'best sound design'. It should produce a wide choice of videos and articles to inspire you. They might be mainly about film sound, but the basic ideas are the same. Watch, listen and read, and use your notebook!

2. Now turn away from your screen as you play some film trailers. Listen carefully, using headphones if possible. You should be impressed by the clever use of sound to create mood and atmosphere as well as suggesting location, **genre** and style. One trailer for *La Haine*, for example, ends with the slam of a garage door. It is highly effective!

3. Fill out a version of the following table using two or three different film trailers. (This example is based on *Titanic*.)

Analysis of sound design: film trailers	
Title: *Titanic*	
Use of voice (dialogue, monologue, voiceover)	**Montage** of character voices. Short clips from key moments in film. Chilling shouts and screams gradually increase after ship hits iceberg.
Diegetic sound	Waves. Water gushing into the ship. Hull creaking slowly.
Non-diegetic sound	**Echo** on voices suggests the past. Bells (single chimes) are like ship bells and church bells at a funeral. These bells are at the start and end of the trailer.
Music	Orchestral soundtrack suggests romance, drama and tension at different moments. Use of Celine Dion song is moving.
Impact on audience	Strong sense of genre – Action and Romance comes from music and sound effects. Layering of music, dialogue and effects creates different atmospheres. Excitement, panic and sorrow suggested by varied **pace** and volume.
Useful ideas for my stage sound design	Different volumes and pace of music and sound create different moods. Could I use actors' voices off stage to suggest memories? A simple sound could be repeated at different moments to suggest theme or time passing (motif).

TASK 2.6

Repeat Task 2.5, but search specifically for clips from musical theatre. **Analyse** the sounds using the same table.

44 Chapter 2 Practical Guide to Sound Design

Finding the sounds you need

If you need an ambulance siren, you will probably need to look online. There are many websites that provide free sound effects. Others might charge a small fee. There are also sound effects CDs available. Some are general; others specific. Don't buy any until you know just what you need.

There is also the possibility of recording your own effects. For instance, you might not be able to find the exact playground sound effect that you want. You could take out a microphone with a simple recording device (or possibly a smartphone) to record the right sound.

Don't settle for the first effect you find. Select the effect that exactly fits the meaning, mood and style for your drama piece.

TASK 2.7

1. Search 'temple bell sound' on the internet. You should discover many versions that you can listen to without paying for or downloading.
2. Choose one that you think would work well diegetically in a **naturalistic** setting, for example, when a character visits a temple.
3. Now choose another that you might use in a non-diegetic way. For example, to represent a character having an idea.
4. Think about what it was that made you choose each sound. What mood or atmosphere did each effect create?

How do I find technical sound support?

If you are not quite confident yet, or need further help:

Read...
For additional technical information, refer to stage sound books.

Watch...
There are many online videos and guides that should help.

Ask...
Consider your human resources. Are there people in your school who could help? Approach the music department. They are very likely to have staff and students with the skills you need.

Visit...
Local theatres should have a sound specialist. They will probably be keen to share their expertise. Is there a local youth theatre that encourages technicians as well as performers?

Continuous research

Make sure that you visit your group's rehearsals regularly. You are likely to be inspired with new ideas, or note the need for:

- new or different sound effects
- opportunities for performers to be involved with sound effects.

If you discover that your performers do need radio mics, or you want to use floating mics, for example, find out if you can hire them.

ASSESSMENT CHECK

Pinning down the sounds you need shows that you can:

- apply theatrical skills to realise artistic intentions in live performance (AO2)
- show knowledge and understanding of how theatre is developed and performed (AO3).

DESIGN TIP

Always make notes on your research to include in your devising log or supporting documents. Examiners will be impressed by your ability to go into the community as part of your research.

DESIGN TIP

The more you experiment, the more you will discover. Your knowledge and skills will really develop and improve and you will have plenty to write about in Component 2, for example.

FOCUS
Combining sounds and being adventurous as you put your sound design together.

ASSESSMENT CHECK
Choosing, finding and building sounds are important aspects of AO1. You are also beginning to apply the theatrical skills needed for AO2 and developing knowledge and understanding of drama and theatre (AO3).

DESIGN TIP
If permitted, you could download suitable software or an app so that a phone or tablet could be used as a recording device.

DESIGN TIP
Listen out for what you don't want to hear! Recording an outdoor sound on a windy day, for example, is pretty much impossible.

Do we have to pay for the music we use?
Your school or college will have its own policy regarding copyright and royalties, and might already have a licence to play your choices of music to the general public. It can be a complicated issue, so make sure you check with your teachers.

SOURCING, CREATING AND MIXING SOUNDS

Can I make my own recordings?
You might want, for example, the sound effect of a bath filling or emptying. It is possible to create it yourself – with a recording device and patience. How authentic it sounds is something you will need to discover! You might end up with something different but magical. Simply taking a recording device out and about with you and recording in different locations can provide very useful sound material. Similarly, experimenting with musical instruments can produce effects that will be unique to your design.

Styles and places
Trying different locations for your effect recordings can produce interesting variations. Recording in a small space like a bathroom will generate a different effect from that in a big, empty space. Experiment to find styles of sound that suit your group's artistic intentions.

Music
You are familiar with where to find the music you like. You might be knowledgeable about different types and styles of music. But, can you select music that will enhance the performance you are involved in?

TASK 2.8
Imagine you are working on a devised piece about the threat of climate change. The **structure** is episodic, and the style is **non-naturalistic**. You need to find a piece of music to use during each scene change. Research three different types of music that might be suitable; then complete the following chart.

Specific music requirement: Scene changes		
Music type	Suggested piece	Notes on meaning and atmosphere
Classical music (Orchestral? Chamber?)		
Modern instrumental (Atmospheric?)		
Contemporary song with lyrics (Try your own ideas here.)		

Chapter 2 Practical Guide to Sound Design

How do I create a particular mood for a scene?

Your sound design is made up of all the individual sounds you source and mix. They must have a sense of belonging together.

Let's suppose that you want non-diegetic sound or some music that will build tension or romance underneath onstage dialogue. This is **underscoring**.

You might find music tracks that are up to 15 minutes long, so you should be able to find a piece suitable for your scene. If you have the right technical equipment (*Audacity*, for example), you can edit tracks to put together particular sections.

DESIGN TIP
If you are searching online for underscoring pieces, try something like 'ambient soundtrack'. Streaming services like Spotify are a good place to start.

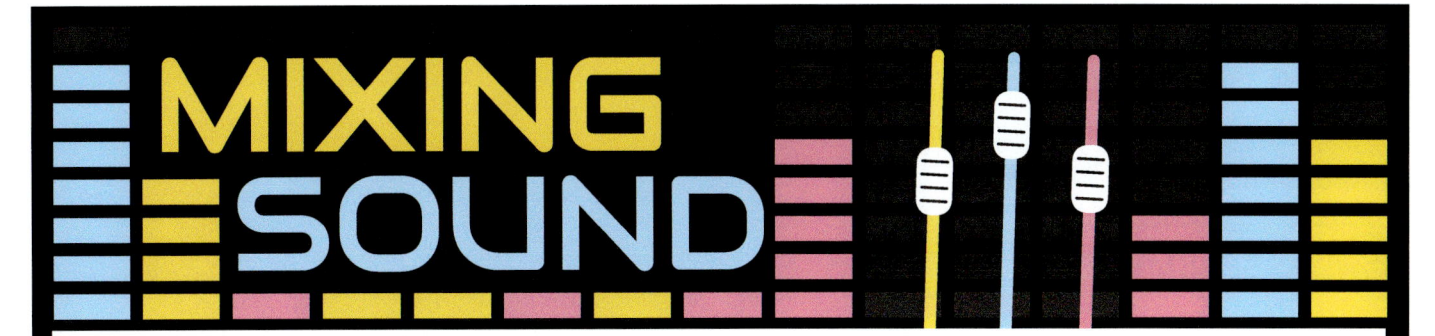

MIXING SOUND

Live mixing

Live mixing of sounds occurs in performance. At some point, you will probably want to combine sounds. This is done by bringing up individual channels on your mixing desk so that sounds come in, are added to and are taken out. This is fine as long as you are not setting yourself too many things to do at once. You can set volume levels during the **plotting** process (see 'Plotting the sound design', on pages 56–57).

Pre-recording soundscapes

You could combine a number of sounds onto a single track to make operating easier. If you have sound-mixing software, you will be able to do this quite easily. You could start with some music as your base sound, for example. Then, using timing controls, set sound effects, such as echoing voices and a siren, to come in and go out automatically. You can set the relative volume levels as you go along. Then, come performance time, it is simply a matter of hitting the space bar on your laptop!

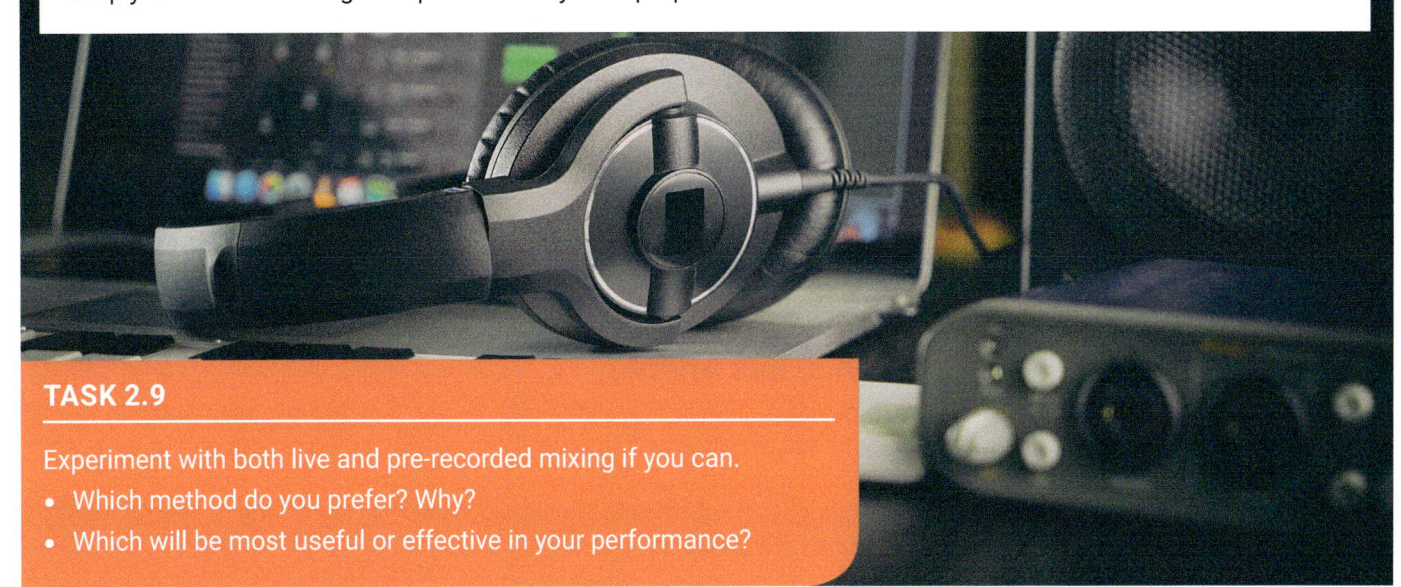

TASK 2.9

Experiment with both live and pre-recorded mixing if you can.
- Which method do you prefer? Why?
- Which will be most useful or effective in your performance?

Chapter 2   Practical Guide to Sound Design

Live sound effects

Does all my sound design have to be recorded?

It is most certainly possible to create **live sound** during the performance. You could play a musical instrument, for example, create thunder with a metal sheet, or ring a real school hand bell.

Depending on the style of your production, the performers could create sound effects as part of your sound design. A **drone**, for example, can be made by the cast, or they could make percussion sounds by tapping different parts of their bodies or costumes. Generally, this kind of sound design suits a non-naturalistic performance style.

In one production of Richard Shannon's play *Sabbat*, performers made whistling noises with their voices and also used an old wind machine to create atmosphere. The audience saw them creating their own sound effects and it had a powerful impact. In this scene, an actor plays hand bells to accompany a song. (Music and sound design by John Biddle.)

ASSESSMENT CHECK

In creating your own sounds, you are applying theatrical skills in order to realise your artistic intentions (AO2).

DESIGN TIP

You, and your performers, will need plenty of practice for live sounds to be successful in the performance.

TASK 2.10

Think about the performance you are working on now or a one you were recently involved in. Find a particular moment in the piece at which a live sound effect could be included.
- Why is that moment suitable?
- What sound effect would you use?
- How would the effect be produced?
- What impact are you trying to achieve?

TASK 2.11

Study the sound design ideas you have so far. Where might a period of silence be effective?

Silence has impact

Silence has a definite place in sound design. In a performance that might be quite full of dialogue, music and sound effects, quietness can make a significant impact. It gives time for the audience to pause and think and, depending where the silence is placed, can be a very effective contribution to mood and atmosphere.

Chapter 2 Practical Guide to Sound Design

HEALTH AND SAFETY IN SOUND DESIGN

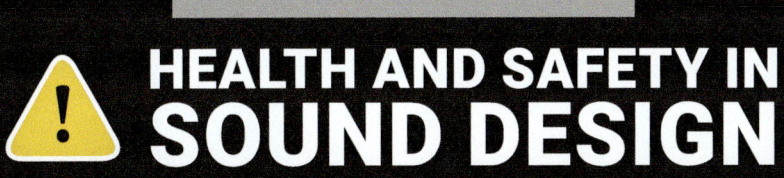

Using your common sense

Many dangerous situations can be avoided when people are sensible. Here are some basic issues to be aware of when using sound equipment:

⚠ Hazards	✓ Safety measures
Loose or unsafe electrical cables.	Tape them down or cordon off the area. Don't use electric cables outdoors.
Damaged cables or electrical items Lack of or out-of-date PAT test label.	Report the problem immediately to someone in authority.
Having the wrong tool for a job, such as a knife instead of a screwdriver.	Find out what the right tool is and make sure it is available and used.
Damaging ear drums. This applies to people wearing headphones as well as in the rehearsal and performances spaces.	Check – beforehand – that volume levels are not too loud.
Startling people with sudden, loud sounds during rehearsals	Fade sounds in during practice sessions. Warn people if you are about to bring up loud sounds.
Negative effects of sudden loud noises or loud continuous sound.	Monitor sound levels carefully. Post a notice in the show programme or in the performance space as a warning.

FOCUS
Some rules and reminders for keeping yourself and others safe.

ASSESSMENT CHECK
Throughout Components 2 and 3, you must adopt the latest safe working practices.

This is also included in AO3: 'Demonstrate knowledge and understanding of how drama and theatre is developed and performed.'

DESIGN TIP
In practice, health and safety needs to be your top priority!

Chapter 2 Practical Guide to Sound Design

FOCUS
Adding extra features to your sounds.

ASSESSMENT CHECK
Complexity in your sound design shows that you can use an extensive range of skills when you apply theatrical skills to realise your artistic intentions (AO2).

SPECIAL SOUND EFFECTS

What are special effects in sound?
As with lighting special effects, it can be tricky to decide what makes a special effect as opposed to a regular sound effect. For now, we will define a special sound effect as one that has additional features such as reverb, echo and **pitch-shift**.

You can add these effects to voices, instruments and other sounds.

Reverb
Reverb is short for 'reverberation'. Sound waves hit surrounding surfaces and we hear the original sound plus its sound reflections. Reverb is always there to some degree, but we don't often notice it. Reverb **is** noticeable when we increase the effect of sound bouncing back to us. This adds depth and fullness to a sound. The sound becomes somehow longer and weightier. It then gradually dies away.

You can record a sound effect in a specific space to affect the reverb acoustically.

TASK 2.12
Take a simple recording device (a phone with a suitable app is fine) to a variety of spaces, such as a cupboard or small bathroom and a large hard-surfaced space such as a sports hall.

In each space, record your voice saying the same thing. You could also take a percussion instrument to experiment with.
- Which space(s) gives you the most reverb?
- Why do you think that is?
- Can you describe what you do and do not like about the special effect created?
- Is there a moment in your devised or scripted piece where it would be useful?

Echo
Echo is another specific quality that can be added to an existing sound effect. Echoes occur when sound bounces off surfaces that are at least 17 metres away from the source of the sound. Echo is different from reverb: the sound has time to repeat rather than blend into the original one.

Chapter 2   Practical Guide to Sound Design

How do I add reverb and echo?

You can add these effects easily and effectively with the help of technology:

- Digital **sound desks** are likely to have reverb and echo settings.
- *QLab* (the Mac sound programme) and Windows-compatible software, such as *Audacity* and *CSC Show Control*, should have reverb built into them.

Your music department might have a reverb unit you can feed into your mixing desk. Most reverb units have a range of settings, which could include echo.

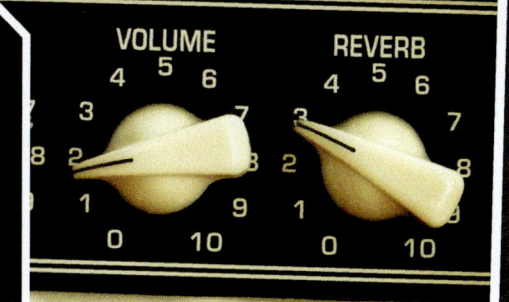

TASK 2.13

Using reverb or echo to add meaning or atmosphere

1. Choose a sound effect from the design you are working on. Alternatively, think of a sound that is rather 'flat', such as a ball thudding onto a rug or long grass.
2. Fill in the following table. (An example has been included to guide you.)

Sound effect	Echo or reverb	Notes on the special effect and meaning or atmosphere
Pre-recorded voice of narrator	Auditorium-style reverb added	• Reverb gave the narrator's voice much more depth. • It sounds more important and more powerful.

This vintage guitar amplifier has a reverb control.

Pitch-shifting

People might think about singers who can't stay in tune when they consider pitch-shifting! There are many uses for this technology, however. You could alter a sound effect, for example, by having three differently pitched versions of the same effect. One would be left at its original pitch. One could be pitch-shifted to 10 per cent below the original, and the third copy could be pitch-shifted to 10 per cent above. The final version – the three mixed together – should have a richer, thicker sound.

High-pitched sound

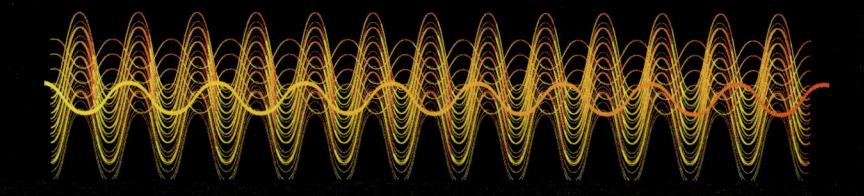

Sound at low pitch

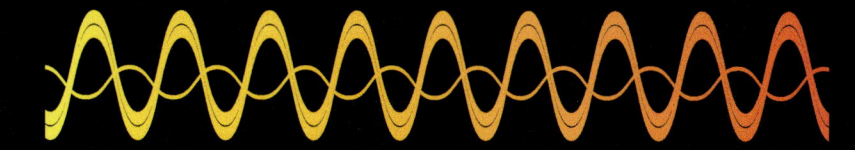

TASK 2.14

1. Pick one of the additional special effects in this section (reverb, echo or pitch-shift).
2. Conduct some research and explore the effect in practice on some potential sounds for your design.
3. Create a short presentation for other students who are interested in sound design, or for other members of your performance group. (Your presentation could be live or recorded.) Explain the impressions the different effects should make on the listener.

DESIGN TIP

By experimenting, you will discover what type of special effect lends the right meaning and atmosphere to your sound design.

Chapter 2   Practical Guide to Sound Design

FOCUS
Examples and guidance to help you prepare the plans and charts you need.

ASSESSMENT CHECK
These documents will help you towards AO1 and AO2: 'Create and develop ideas to communicate meaning' and 'Apply theatrical skills to realise artistic intentions.'

LOOK HERE
If you are devising, go through the stages in 'Sound Design for the Devised Piece', beginning page 203.

Task 2.19 on page 57 provides detail on how to use your cue sheet when plotting your sound design.

TASK 2.15
1. Practise drawing up each type of document as you go along with your design, so that you are confident by the time you are working on an actual production.
2. Work through all of the documents detailed here in the order they appear.

LOOK HERE
A detailed sound cue sheet for *Hansel and Gretel* is available on the *Designing Drama* product page at illuminatepublishing.com.

HOW TO DOCUMENT YOUR SOUND DESIGN

What documents should I produce?
You should create a source sheet, which details whether each sound you use is live or a piece of **recorded sound**. You should also put forward a **cue sheet**, which shows the source, order, length and output level of each cue.

These plans and tables can look complicated, but the advice on these pages will help you to complete excellent documents.

Why should I have these documents?
Source and cue sheets provide the sound operator (whether this is your or a technician) with plans to follow.

The documents will help you practically as well as going in your devising log and being seen by the examiner who watches the scripted performances.

A sound plot is not essential, but does show you (or anyone else) what speakers are used and where they should be positioned. It should include a key that explains any symbols used in it.

The completed cue sheet and source sheet contain all the information needed to complete the design and operate the sound during the production.

Source sheet
A simple list like this is fine:

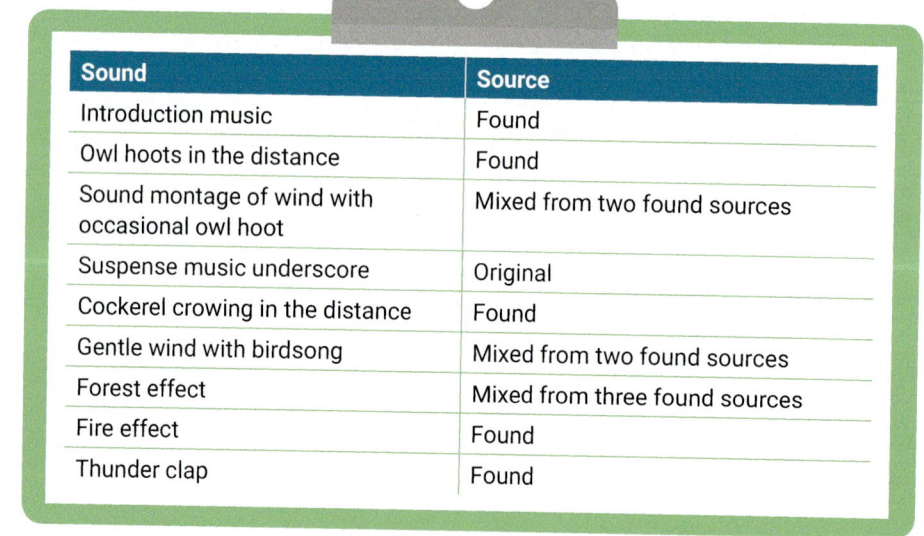

Sound	Source
Introduction music	Found
Owl hoots in the distance	Found
Sound montage of wind with occasional owl hoot	Mixed from two found sources
Suspense music underscore	Original
Cockerel crowing in the distance	Found
Gentle wind with birdsong	Mixed from two found sources
Forest effect	Mixed from three found sources
Fire effect	Found
Thunder clap	Found

Cue sheet
You cannot plot the sound for the production until you know what your music and effects are going to be. So, you will already have marked your sound ideas on your script or notes. You might even have an early version of a cue sheet as well as a source sheet.

The key to the sound plot on the following page explains the different types of speaker that are detailed in a cue sheet.

Sound plot

This diagram is not essential, but will be useful (and should be included in your devising log if you design sound in Component 2, for example). It shows the positioning and type of speakers to be used in the production.

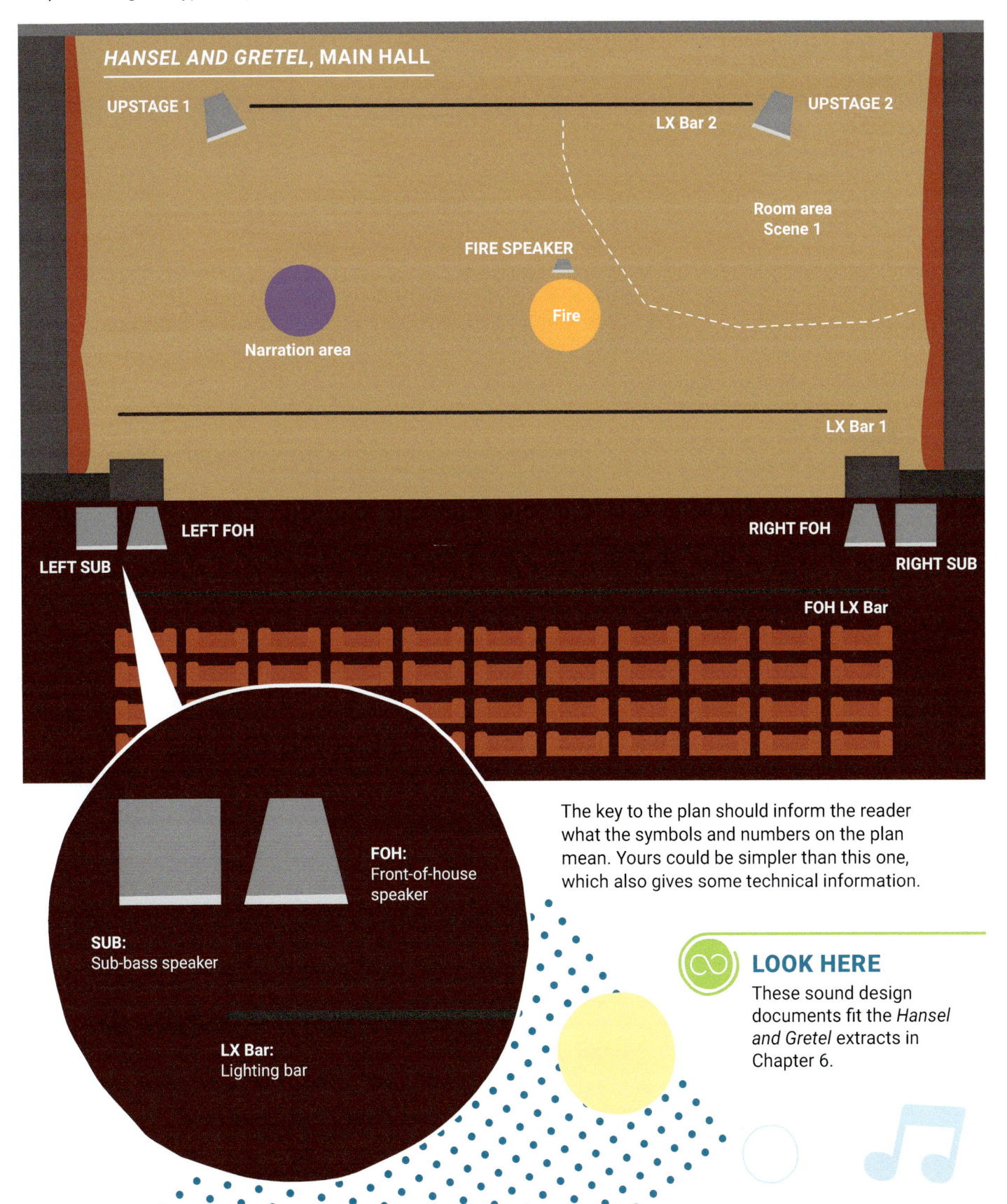

HANSEL AND GRETEL, MAIN HALL

- UPSTAGE 1
- UPSTAGE 2
- LX Bar 2
- Room area Scene 1
- FIRE SPEAKER
- Fire
- Narration area
- LX Bar 1
- LEFT SUB
- LEFT FOH
- RIGHT FOH
- RIGHT SUB
- FOH LX Bar

Key:
- **FOH:** Front-of-house speaker
- **SUB:** Sub-bass speaker
- **LX Bar:** Lighting bar

The key to the plan should inform the reader what the symbols and numbers on the plan mean. Yours could be simpler than this one, which also gives some technical information.

LOOK HERE
These sound design documents fit the *Hansel and Gretel* extracts in Chapter 6.

Chapter 2   Practical Guide to Sound Design   53

FOCUS
How to position sound equipment.

ASSESSMENT CHECK
This section will help you to deploy a range of sound effects to realise your intended sound design as part of AO2.

DESIGN TIP
Add your own notes to the table as you progress with your design.

DIRECTIONAL SOUND

An important aspect of your sound design and practical skills is taking care with the placement of your speakers.

As a general rule, you would have at least one speaker for each section of the audience.

Where do I put moveable speakers?

If the sound speakers in your performance area are fixed, you need to consider that in your design. It is likely, however, that there will be some speakers that you can position yourself. Ask the music department. The table below indicates ideal placements in common configurations.

Once they are in position, you might need to secure speakers with safety bonds or cargo straps.

Minimum number of speakers and their positions

Stage configuration	Position of speakers	Notes
Proscenium arch / **end on**	Front of stage – left and right	If possible, all speakers should be positioned at ear height for the audience.
Traverse	Facing the audience from the acting area (minimum of 2)	See above.
Thrust	Front and sides of stage (3 in total)	See above.
In the round	All four sides, facing the audience	Ideally, these speakers would be hung discreetly above the acting area.

Are mini-speakers useful?

The short answer is that it depends on your sound design. One good example of their use is on stage as part of a diegetic sound device, such as a radio or phone. You could use a powerful bluetooth speaker that the performers would activate themselves. This is a good example of directional sound.

DESIGN TIP
For Component 2, the diagram that you draw in Task 2.16 should be included in your devising log.

TASK 2.16
Draw a plan diagram of your performance space. Pick a simple icon to show the position of your speakers. Be sure to mark the position(s) of the audience too.

Note that 'left' and 'right' in sound usually refers to the audience's right and left, rather than stage left and stage right. (Think about where the sound operator is likely to be.)

Sub-bass speakers produce very low-frequency sounds. They produce the 'thump' in music tracks. They can be useful for sound effects such as thunder.

FOH speakers produce mid- to high-frequency sounds and are the most common type in school halls, for example.

The fire speaker in the plan on page 53 is a small speaker concealed within the fire set on stage and used to make fire crackle sounds. As in lighting, this kind of speaker is called a 'special'.

Is there an ideal place to position the sound desk?

The best place for the sound desk is in the audience area. (Why do you think this is?)

In some venues, there is a 'box' at the back of the auditorium where technical equipment is fixed. Sometimes, these have a sliding window that allows the sound operator to hear what the audience is hearing.

The other element to consider is communication with the lighting operator. There are likely to be times when lighting and sound effects should be **synchronised**. If they can't sit near each other, how could the operators for sound and lighting communicate?

TASK 2.17

1. Walk your performance space with your teacher or other human resource. Identify the ideal location for your sound desk and establish whether it is a practical and safe site.
2. When you have settled on the best place for the sound operating equipment, use a simple icon to add to the diagram that you made in Task 2.16. Add a key to your sketch.

Chapter 2   Practical Guide to Sound Design   55

FOCUS

Creating the cue sheet that will guide you through a performance.

ASSESSMENT CHECK

Achieving your cue sheet means that you can (for AO2 and AO3):

- design and realise a range of sound effects
- realise sound capable of establishing location and time and/or enhancing mood or atmosphere.

You can also use your cue sheet to analyse and evaluate developing ideas and the reasons for decisions (AO4).

DESIGN TIP

Don't try to plot the performance until you have sourced your sounds and know where in the performance you are putting them!

PLOTTING THE SOUND DESIGN

As sound designer, you are contributing to and supporting a performance as a whole. So, the sound operator needs to be able to run the 'sound show' smoothly and accurately. Plotting the sound and creating the cue sheet makes this possible.

What is plotting sound?

In this book, we use the term **plotting** to mean the act of fixing the sound for every part of the production. The **cue sheet** should record details of every sound cue decided. If you have sound design software, record each cue digitally as you go along.

You will need to make several decisions for each cue, including:

- what the sound is and from where it is sourced
- when it happens
- how loud it is
- how long it lasts (Does it snap off or fade?)
- what sounds are combined (if not plotted in software)
- the type and length of transitions.

Conditions for successful sound plotting

Don't underestimate the amount of time plotting will take. You might need more than one session if the performance is lengthy or complex.

- Make sure you plot sound in the performance space that you will be using!
- Choose a time when you can have the space to yourself. There is no point trying to plot during a rehearsal or when people are talking loudly. Setting volume levels, for instance, requires quiet and concentration.
- Collect everything you need, including:
  - your annotated script and notes
  - sound equipment
  - prepared sound effects
  - a task light (such as an angle-poise lamp)
  - a template for your cue sheet.
- You might also find it useful to ask an assistant to read lines of dialogue and check volume in various parts of the audience areas.

Understanding the terminology of sound levels

Unless you have worked with a sound desk before, you would probably expect that 0 on a fader would mean that the sound was off… In fact, sound is measured in decibels, which is a complex unit using a scale. All you really need to know is that 0 decibels is in fact quite loud.

TASK 2.18

Experiment with the faders on your sound desk, keeping your drama piece in mind. Make notes for yourself or use masking tape to label points on the scales that are quiet, average and loud.

Creating your cue sheet

When you have good sound conditions and clear understanding of both your design and the technology, you are ready to plot the production.

TASK 2.19

1. Lay your script and a cue sheet template around your sound desk. If you have a software package for storing your cues, bring it into action.
2. Starting at the beginning of the show, work through the production cue by cue and scene by scene to build and chart each sound cue. (An example is given to show you how it works.)
3. Check that cue numbers are clearly and correctly marked in your script so that the operator can track approaching cues. You could add '6a', '6b' and so on, if needed.
4. Continue to fill in your cue sheet until you have plotted the entire production.

Sound cue sheet

Cue number and script page	Cue signal	Sound	Playback device (if more than one)	Level (dB)	Transition	Notes with timings
1 pre-set	House open	Play music	CD player	−10		Pre-set from time house is open. Visual.
2 p1	Visual – actors walk on	Music off		All out	Fade out	Over 10 seconds (in time with lighting transition).
3 p3	"Come over here!"	Soundscape 1	Laptop	+6	Fade up	Over 5 seconds – gradual fade up.

DESIGN TIP

Take your time with plotting. Continue to check that you are supporting the artistic intentions of the piece. If you miss a cue, add it later, as '3a', for example.

ASSESSMENT CHECK

Here, you are applying your theatrical skills to realise your artistic intentions (AO2).

FOCUS
Advice on putting your sound design into practice.

OPERATING SOUND EQUIPMENT

Creating impact for an audience involves delivering sound cues skilfully in performance. You will need these items in place:

- a working sound desk that you have practised using
- playback device(s), such as a laptop and sound software, CD or mp3 player
- speakers
- a task light
- script (if applicable), marked up with the cues
- the completed cue sheet.

A complex set of sound equipment at Helsinki City Theatre.

ASSESSMENT CHECK

Whether you operate or supervise the sound, your knowledge and skills demonstrate that you can:

- design and realise sound that contributes positively to the performance and communicates meaning
- apply theatrical skills to realise your artistic intentions (AO2).

TASK 2.20

Practise operating sound, even if you will not be responsible for it in the final rehearsals and performance.
1. Set up your equipment and test that it is working.
2. Run through all your cues and check them for volume and effect.
3. Refer to 'Troubleshooting', on the following page, if needed!

Facing the challenges of operating sound

You might not be operating the sound for your production. It is not a requirement for the assessment, but you should know what the challenges are. Remember too that operating sound sensitively will be a significant aspect of the performance.

For now, let's assume that you **are** the sound operator. An early hurdle you might face is equipment not working properly. Your human resources are likely to have more experience than you, so do ask them for support.

DESIGN TIP
Set up a small angle-poise light next to you.

Chapter 2 Practical Guide to Sound Design

Troubleshooting

Here are some common issues and suggestions for overcoming them.

Problem	Checks and possible solutions
No power to desk.	Are other electrical items working, such as the angle-poise lamp? If so, the problem lies with the desk's connection to the electricity supply. Check sockets and cables.
One element of the system, radio mics, for example, is not working.	Is it reaching the desk? Does a light come on for it? If so, the problem is in the output. If not, it is in the input. Is it plugged in to the right socket?
Everything seems to be coming in, but there is still a fault.	There must be a problem with output. Are the masters up? Can you isolate the issue by eliminating things that are working?

Coping with the pressure

If there are a number of cues that are close together, the operator is under pressure to get the timings right. Badly timed sound cues can make a mess of things for the cast and for the audience.

Using software

If you are using software to operate your sound, you are hopefully simply pressing the space bar to trigger the next cue. However, you need to be very familiar with the software so that you know what to do if you fall out of sequence or trigger a cue too early. Practise as much as possible.

Operating a manual desk

You are likely to be busy with both hands and working much harder if you do not have pre-programmed effects. Prepare as much as possible to simplify the process. This could mean labelling master channels, for example. You can write on masking tape, which is easily removed. Always use your pre-set sections to prepare the next cue, and stay focused so that you are always ready for the next cue.

Practising sound operation

You should already be familiar with your sound desk and playback devices, but take time to ensure that you are comfortable using them. Go **cue to cue** through the script, practising the types of fades and effects that you are aiming for. Make sure you can operate them smoothly.

The script will keep you in time with the action and enable you to see where cues need to happen, such as on a word in the performance. You will begin to realise that you can 'feel' the action.

Live music

Many theatrical performances include a band or live performance onstage. This has implications for the sound designer and operator. If you do have instruments onstage, establish how these requirements fold into your sound design and operation. Practise this aspect as early as you can in the design and rehearsal process.

DESIGN TIP

The key to technical troubleshooting is to work through things logically and try to isolate exactly where the problem is. Only then do you stand a chance of fixing it!

DESIGN TIP

QLab (for Mac) is very useful for assembling and mixing sounds. It can also simplify the control of lights, video playback and the settings on a digital mixer.

DESIGN TIP

Be very aware of radio mics and when they need to be live. Keeping their fader down or channel muted at all other times is very important.

Chapter 2 Practical Guide to Sound Design

FOCUS

Making sure everything runs smoothly.

ASSESSMENT CHECK

Rehearsals allow you to:
- select the appropriate equipment and determine its position
- create a design that shows an understanding of the performer/audience relationship
- apply theatrical skills to realise your artistic intentions (AO2).

LOOK HERE

The notes on pages 58–59 will help you to put everything in place before the tech.

DESIGN TIP

If you are using *QLab* or *SCS*, the software can trigger sound cues as well as lighting ones. This can be very useful if you want to precisely co-ordinate a blackout, for example.

DESIGN TIP

Sound levels vary depending on how full the space is. So, you might need to turn up the volume if you have a full house!

TECHNICAL AND DRESS REHEARSALS FOR SOUND DESIGNERS

The final rehearsals are your chance to check that you have a creative sound design that works well in practice. You might have a lot of equipment to set up, so try to complete this before the technical rehearsal ('tech').

The technical rehearsal

Techs are lengthy because they must allow lighting and sound operators to test their designs. At the same time, the director and other designers are checking that other aspects of the production are working smoothly.

Decide as a group whether to run the performance in full or move from cue to cue, missing out some sections. Make sure that everyone is confident that the process can then be repeated without interruptions.

As sound designer, you are likely to be heavily involved in the tech. If someone else is operating the sound, you need to guide them through the cues and make adjustments to levels, timings of fades and so on.

You will also need to watch the acting area to check the following points.

- Are sound effects and music coming in and going out correctly?
- Is sound that involves the performers managed successfully?
- Is the music long enough to cover scene changes, for example?
- Does the music or sound effect fit the piece as intended?
- Do any vocals in music or effects clash with dialogue?
- Is timing with lighting correct?
- Are any long pieces of underscoring at a suitable level? Should this vary in sympathy with the action?

You (or an assistant) should also move around the audience area to hear volume levels. It is likely that levels and timings will need to change for some cues. Set these as you go along, even if it means holding up the tech for a couple of minutes.

If you or the sound operator are struggling with a technical aspect, ask your group if you can run a cue again. This is the purpose of the tech.

TASK 2.21

1. Update your notebook and script with any issues to be resolved before the dress rehearsal.
2. Arrange some time to work things through with other designers.

The dress rehearsal

The dress rehearsal ('dress') runs through the whole production without interruption. The performers can experience the full show with all the technical elements, but without an audience. You can test that the sound design can be operated successfully and works effectively in performance.

EVALUATING YOUR SOUND DESIGN

Once you are clear about what **evaluation** is and the best way of approaching it, you can focus on assessing the success of your sound design.

Examining the detail of your design

You need to provide a careful evaluation of your design skills demonstrated in performance. The only way that you can do this really well is to give detailed examples.

Whenever you evaluate, you should make at least three different points. These points should be illustrated with specific examples. Each time, you should also explain the reason why you have made a particular value judgement. You should highlight things that could have gone better.

It is very important to compare your finished sound design against your artistic intentions. Check your notes and make sure you include the success of this aspect in your evaluation.

Try not to repeat yourself when you evaluate. Discuss different types of sound and use a wide technical vocabulary.

FOCUS
Placing a value judgement on design.

ASSESSMENT CHECK
This part of the design process is the essential element of AO4: 'Analyse and evaluate your own work and the work of others.'

SIGNPOST
Use the evaluation guidance on page 78 before you start.

DESIGN TIP
No process is complete until you reflect upon it. Evaluation is a skill that will be important in all your exam subjects.

TASK 2.22

1. Complete a table like this (some examples have been suggested). The notes will provide a solid basis for your evaluation writing.

Design element	Example / moment in the play	Evaluation	Reason for evaluation
Pre-set music	Before the performance began.	Engaging. Helped to create mood and place piece in time.	The music was chosen to put the audience into the right time period and to create the mood we wanted in our artistic intentions for the start of the piece.
Underscoring	The increasingly tense duologue between the two characters.	Atmospheric and contributed to action.	The underscoring track that I mixed included the use of reverb, which added depth. The pace increased as it went along, but was quiet enough for the actors' voices to be heard clearly.
The live sound from the performers	The end of the piece.	Successfully performed. Suited the ending.	As the performers linked hands and moved around the stage, they used their voices to make a humming sound. As they varied pitch and volume, there was a strong sense of their connection. I do wish that it could have been a little louder.

2. Expand your notes into three paragraphs of evaluative writing.

Chapter 2 Practical Guide to Sound Design 61

SOUND DESIGN VOCABULARY

Amplifier A piece of equipment that produces the sound for the speakers, primarily used to increase volume.

Analyse Examine in detail, thinking about parts in relation to the whole.

Atmospheric A sound, for example, that creates a strong feeling or mood.

Constant sound An uninterrupted sound.

Cue sheet A list of cues with timings.

Cue to cue Going through a play from one sound or lighting cue to the next, missing out the parts in between.

Diegetic sound A sound that the characters would hear within their world, such as a phone ringing.

Digital Using computer technology. Digital lighting desks, for example, are programmed using software.

Directional sound Sound technology that produces a sound in a highly focused way, particularly so that the sound travels a long way. It also refers to the location and angle of a speaker, for example using an offstage speaker to suggest the location of a car.

Drone A constant sound that is often in the background. Drones are often used in non-naturalistic sound effects and are very good for creating atmosphere such as tension.

Echo The effect that occurs when a sound bounces off surfaces.

End on A stage configuration that places the audience on one side of an open stage.

Evaluate Give an opinion, a value judgement, backed up with examples and reasons.

Fade A gradual transition from quiet to loud, or vice versa.

Fader A device to control the volume of a sound.

Floating mic A microphone positioned on the front of the stage.

Hanging mic A microphone suspended above the performance area.

Intermittent sound A sound that is not constant; it comes and goes.

Live sound A sound that is played directly for the audience.

Manual Operated by hand, rather than digitally.

Mixer A device that can change and combine sounds.

Montage A sequence or joining together of sounds to make a new piece of sound.

Naturalistic A set or lighting effect, for example, with characteristics of reality; having the appearance of a real place.

Non-diegetic sound Sound that can be heard by the audience, but would not be heard by the characters (such as atmospheric music to encourage the audience to feel something).

Non-naturalistic A set or lighting design, for example, that aims not to appear like reality.

Pace The speed with which lighting or sound effects transition from one to the next.

Pitch-shifting Altering the pitch of a sound which, when mixed with other differently pitched versions of the same sound, makes it have a richer, thicker sound.

Playback device The means through which recorded sound is played, such as a CD player or smartphone.

Plotting The process of creating a cue sheet to show choices of what sound happens when.

Proscenium (arch) A stage configuration where the audience are where the 'fourth wall' of a room would be – similar to **end on**, but with the addition of a picture-frame effect around the stage.

Radio mic A microphone that is worn by a performer, often taped to the cheek.

Recorded sound Sound that is captured electronically, such as onto a computer file.

Reverb The effect that occurs when sound waves hit surrounding surfaces and we hear the original sound plus its reflections. Adding reverb to a sound makes it longer and weightier.

Snap A quick and sudden transition, such as from loud to silent or a blackout.

Sound desk The means of operating the different sounds.

Soundscape An effect made up of several sounds to give the impression of a city street, for example.

Source Where the sound comes from, such as a computer file. Also used to describe the sound itself, such as a bell ringing.

Speaker The device that transmits the sound. Its volume level can be altered.

Structure The way that something is sequenced, put together or built.

Synchronised Two or more sounds operating at the same time.

Transition Movement between sound cues, such as fade and snap.

Traverse A stage configuration where the audience is in two parts that are seated opposite each other along two sides of the stage.

Underscore Sound (often non-diegetic) that is played quietly while performers are speaking, to add atmosphere.

PRACTICAL GUIDE TO SET DESIGN

Chapter 3

- Introduction to set design — 64
- Two styles of set design — 66
- Research for set design — 67
- Using levels in set design — 68
- How to document your set design — 69
- Understanding your resources — 73
- Sourcing materials for the set — 74
- Health and safety in set design — 75
- Creating your set design for the stage — 76
- Technical and dress rehearsals for set designers — 77
- Evaluating your set design — 78
- Set design vocabulary — 80

FOCUS
Some tasks to get you thinking like a set designer.

ASSESSMENT CHECK
In beginning your journey as a set designer, you will start to:
- design and realise sets that contribute positively to the overall performance and communicate meaning
- understand how drama and theatre is developed and performed (AO3).

DESIGN TIP
Pay attention to your **pre-set**. This can include light and sound too and is seen or heard before the performance begins. It establishes setting and style and lets the audience think, 'I know where we are.'

INTRODUCTION TO SET DESIGN

What is a set designer?
In a sense, you are already a set designer. You probably have opportunities to influence the layout and colour scheme in your bedroom, for example.

Your choices are influenced by practicality, style, comfort and image. An observer might also learn something about you based on the books or games on your shelf or the posters on your wall.

A set designer is very different from an interior designer, however: they think about space from the audience's point of view, not the occupant's. This means that they help to communicate meaning, artistic intentions, style and atmosphere through the **scenery** they design and the stage furniture they select.

What can you tell about the person who occupies this room? What clues give you those ideas?

How can I design sets as part of this course?
You can opt for set design in either or both of the practical sections of the course. Component 1 is the written exam. You will write about design for at least one of the questions.

If you choose to work as set designer in Component 2, you will work in a small group to devise a piece of theatre. You will help to develop the piece as a whole, but your specific responsibility will be to design the set. Component 3 is similar, but you work with a script instead of devising your own drama.

When you **evaluate** a performance you have seen, you might have to write about set design. Practical work will give you the knowledge and understanding to write confidently.

How can set design communicate meaning?
We all 'read' peoples, places and situations, but do not always realise it.

TASK 3.1

Study this set for *Blithe Sprit*, then answer the questions, giving specific examples from the set.

1. What room is shown?
2. The play is set in the 1930s. Are there any clues to this? (Look at styles and shapes of **furnishings**, scenery and fabrics.)
3. What seems to be the economic background of the people who live in this house? (Do they seem wealthy? How does the set suggest this?)
4. What **colour palette** is used?
5. What mood or atmosphere is suggested? (Consider, for example, whether colours are light or dark and whether there is clutter or space. Does the set suggest a calm life or hectic one?)

Chapter 3 Practical Guide to Set Design

Creating a location (place)

Location is a key starting point for most set designs. A set designer must be able to design both **interior** and **exterior** locations. The following tasks will help you to explore these in more detail.

Interior spaces

TASK 3.2

1. Look around the room you are in and notice its shape and features.
2. Now imagine it as a theatre set.
3. In a group, discuss what elements you should keep in order to maintain the room's meaning as, for example, a classroom or drama studio.
4. Then share ideas on how you could re-create the space for staging a drama **in the round**. Think about your audience, furniture, scenery, lighting fixtures and flooring.

Exterior settings

TASK 3.3

This scene from *The Woman in Black* uses back projection to place the character outside a mansion.

1. Imagine that you have been asked to create a set design for the same location, but without the use of projection. This means that you would have to place **constructions**, stage furniture and/or **props** on the stage. You could also consider a painted backdrop. You have a small budget of £100–200.

   Use a chart like this to note down items that you could include.

Location set design: Mansion exterior		
Scenery (flats, backdrops, etc.)	**Furniture**	**Props**
		Plant pots.

2. Next, imagine that a set designer has a budget of several £1000s and is designing the same exterior location, for an **end-on** stage configuration. The designer has provided this sketch ⟶

   Work with a partner to give oral feedback to the designer.
   - What do you like about the set design? Why?
   - How could it be improved?

3. Now **you** are the set designer in a school production of the same scene from *A Woman in Black*. It is an end-on stage configuration. Draw and label your own design.

Painted backdrop of mansion façade

Path (brick-pattern lino)

Free-standing wooden gate

Garden planter with olive tree

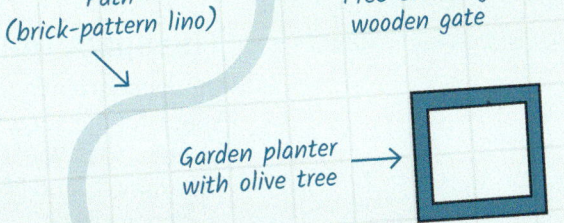

Chapter 3 Practical Guide to Set Design

FOCUS
Naturalistic and non-naturalistic set designs.

ASSESSMENT CHECK
Analysing choices of set design will help you to:
- design and realise sets capable of establishing the location and time and/or enhancing mood or atmosphere
- show an understanding of stage configuration; performer/audience relationship; action, positioning of entrances/exits; effective, smooth and fluent scene changes; use of space, scale and levels.

TASK 3.4
Study the set, right, for *Crocodile Fever*. Write down three details of the design that make it look like a real kitchen. Remember that set design usually includes large props, furniture, **set dressings**, furnishings and accessories, as well as the 'frame' and 'backdrop' of the space.

TASK 3.5
Write down three thoughts or questions that spring to mind when studying the set on the right. These could be linked to the set itself, the performance or the characters within it.

TWO STYLES OF SET DESIGN
Although there are many ways of categorising types of set design, it is helpful to start with these two basic ideas of **realistic**, **naturalistic** sets and **non-naturalistic** sets. They are clear and recognisable styles, and the choice between the two is one of the first decisions a set designer makes.

Naturalistic sets
A naturalist set could also be described as 'realistic'. It aims for immediately recognisable locations and to make the set appear as natural as possible. The audience does not need to use their imagination to understand the setting, as the **illusion** is complete.

A highly detailed set for Crocodile Fever at the Traverse Theatre in Edinburgh.

Non-naturalistic sets
A **representative** or non-naturalistic set might include key items that 'shout' the location within an otherwise **stylised** setting. The set on the right, for example, creates the illusion of a bedroom, but leaves scope for the audience to **interpret** the setting. Lighting and sound can be effective in enhancing meaning with this type of set design.

The use of a non-naturalistic set does not have to be restricted to non-naturalistic texts. They can be used to 'modernise' older plays or 'move' the original location.

The minimalist pre-set for a student production on a thrust stage at the University of Michigan.

The space you are designing for
Other important points in the early stages of set design are the size of the space for the set and what the stage configuration will be. Your teacher will be able to tell you if the performance will be in the drama studio or the hall, for example, and help you with the layout of the acting area and where the audience will sit.

Pay attention to safety issues in your design. It could be very difficult to remove hazards once the set has been constructed.

RESEARCH FOR SET DESIGN

Don't start online! Your first instinct might be to browse the internet, but there is no better place for inspiration and information than the real world.

Ask...

If your set text or devised piece is set in the 20th century, try talking to your family and their friends. You can't beat first-hand experience, and they might have photos.

Visit...

Museums and galleries often have exhibitions linked to particular periods in history. You might get ideas for furnishings and props as well as the set. A visit to a heritage site can be highly inspirational. These places include back-to-back terraces, art deco houses and so on. Take notes and photos, if permitted.

Watch...

There have been some entertaining television documentaries on social history. *Turn Back Time*, for example, placed different families in various historical eras. *A House Through Time* put a modern family in a house that changed to show life from the 19th century to the present day.

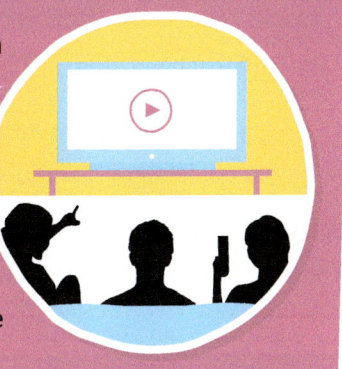

Track down some films that are made or set in the period for your drama. Focus on the settings as you watch.

Online research

Use specific key words in your internet searches. Furniture is a good place to start, and 'Ikea 1970s', for example, should bring up some very useful images. A heritage website will also provide inspiration and information.

Just a couple of props and furnishings or pieces of stage furniture will give your set an authentic feel and help to communicate meaning. It is important to reflect the social and economic contexts of your drama.

TASK 3.6

1. Search for '1930s house interior' and choose an image that interests you. (If you want to, narrow down your search by specifying 'working class' or 'art deco', for example.)
2. From it, pick an item or two that you might be able to use in a set.
3. What colours and patterns from the image might also be suitable for your set?

FOCUS

How to start generating ideas for you set designs.

ASSESSMENT CHECK

This research will help you towards AO1: 'Create and develop ideas to communicate meaning for theatrical performance.'

You are also required to describe your research findings.

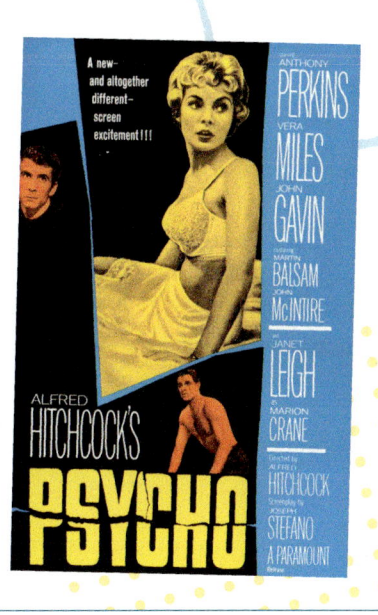

If your design allows it, a print or painting that strongly identifies the period or social context is well worth hanging on a wall. This 1960s film poster adds atmosphere as well as a sense of the period.

FOCUS
Including different heights and positions in your design.

DESIGN TIP
Take care to ensure that seats, steps or platforms are sturdily built and safe to use.

DESIGN TIP
Think carefully about where levels could be used in the acting area. Performance should still be versatile, and sightlines considered.

USING LEVELS IN SET DESIGN

When writing about your own set design or one that you have seen, the use of levels is an important consideration. As well as adding interest, raising areas of the acting area offers potential for:

- creating more than one location
- enhancing a split focus (with the aid of lighting)
- suggesting power relationships.

How to include levels

Professional productions might use expensive methods to create levels, but they can be created without spending much at all. For example:

- Purpose-made staging blocks might be available in your school. Some versions are stackable. Alternatively, you might be able to borrow blocks from another learning setting, your local hall or a theatre nearby. If not, it is possible to hire stage blocks reasonably cheaply.
- If there is a fixed stage (in the hall, for example), you could design a set with some action taking place on the floor and some on the stage.
- A technical department might be able to build some simple levels.
- Actors could sit or stand on low benches, chairs or stools.

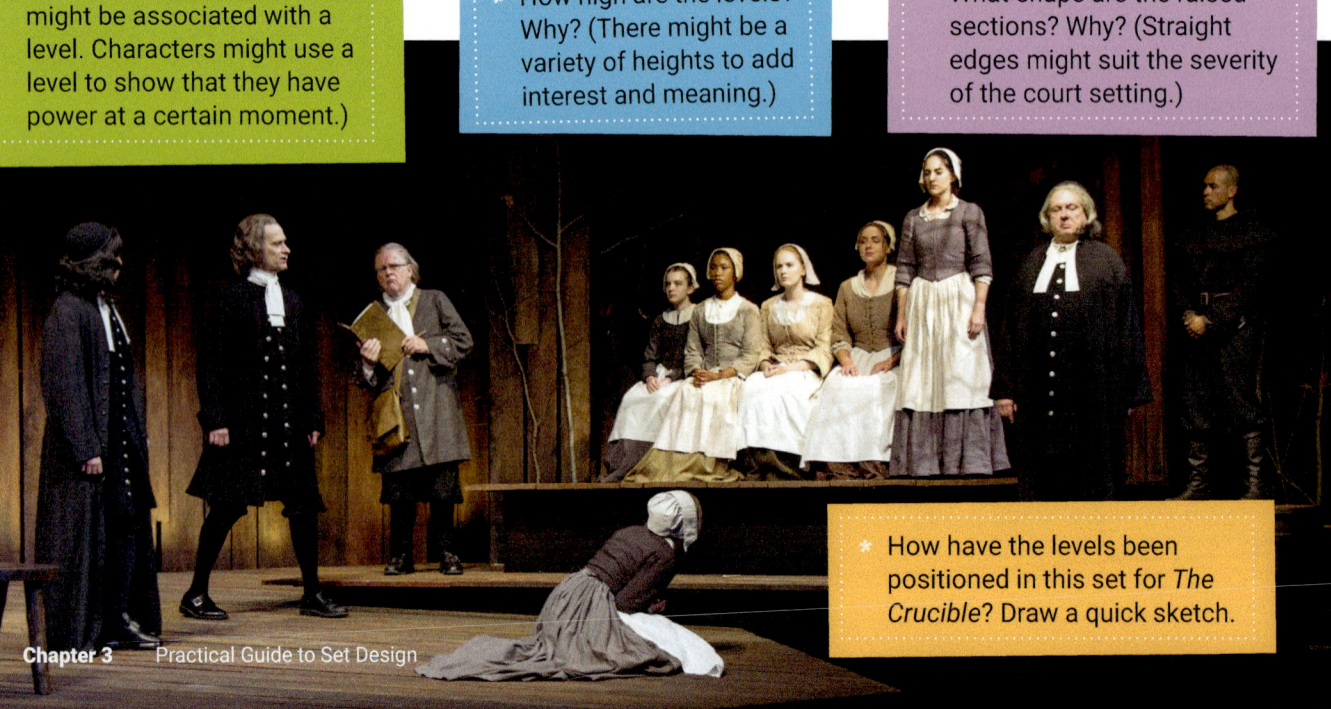

Professional set designers often include more than one level in their designs. This one by Tony Ferrieri for *The Morini Strad* takes place in a stringed-instrument repair shop. The platform is in the shape of a violin. The polished wood tones also match the material of a violin.

Writing about levels in set design

You should explain the significance of levels in the set design you are writing about. Ask yourself questions similar to those below.

* How are levels used by performers? Be specific here. (A character or location might be associated with a level. Characters might use a level to show that they have power at a certain moment.)

* How high are the levels? Why? (There might be a variety of heights to add interest and meaning.)

* What shape are the raised sections? Why? (Straight edges might suit the severity of the court setting.)

* How have the levels been positioned in this set for *The Crucible*? Draw a quick sketch.

Chapter 3 Practical Guide to Set Design

HOW TO DOCUMENT YOUR SET DESIGN

Set designers need to produce their designs very early in the process as lighting, in particular, cannot be designed without knowledge of the set. The director and performers also need to lay out the rehearsal area in a way that represents the set.

What documents should I produce?

All types of theatre designer must be able to show their design ideas long before their designs are actually created. Sketches, ground plans and models are useful ways of doing this.

Clear drawings and ground plans are the best way to begin. These do not need to be drawn to **scale**, but showing scale on the ground plan, in particular, is very useful. When your set is constructed, the builders will use the ground plan to check measurements.

Set designs are created for a specific space. Produce plans that reflect the size of this space as well as the appropriate stage configuration.

Drawings of the final design

This example draft sketch shows a design idea for Oscar Wilde's Victorian social comedy *The Importance of Being Earnest*. It includes enough detail to base a ground plan on.

FOCUS
- Clearly presenting your set design as a ground plan.
- Using 3D models to visualise the design.

ASSESSMENT CHECK
Your plans will show that you understand stage configuration, performer/audience relationship, action, entrances/exits, scene changes and use of space, scale and levels.

- Two portraits are hung at either side of the doors.
- Three **flats** are joined to make a **run** at the back of an end-on stage configuration.
- The centre section is hinged to form outward-opening **French windows**.
- Two more flats are free-standing centre left and centre right.
- Two chairs and a small table stand on the rug.
- A large Victorian-style rug centre stage.

Chapter 3 Practical Guide to Set Design

DESIGN TIP
Keep a tape measure handy!

LOOK HERE
See page 68 for advice on including levels in your design.

DESIGN TIP
Some theatre designers use a scale of 1:25. Choose a scale that is most suitable to you.

Find out the exact size of the area you are designing for. Then you can work out a realistic size for the scenery you are placing in it.

Let's say that your stage area for an end-on configuration is: 5 metres wide by 4 metres deep.

- You have allowed 1m behind the run of flats at the back so that the doors can open outwards. This means the acting area will be 5m wide and 3m deep.
- The two outer flats at the back are going to be 1m wide. The centre one will be 2m wide to include the opening doors.
- Your **free-standing flats** are 1m wide (2m high works well).
- The rug is 2m square, laid at an angle.
- A net/voile curtain does not appear on the sketch, but will be added to the ground plan.

Ground plans

A ground plan is a bird's eye view. If you are looking straight down you would see width and depth, but not height. It should represent the performance space, 'including entrances and exits, audience positioning and stage furniture (as appropriate)'.

The information and sketch on the previous page can be transformed into a ground plan at 1:20 scale, below.

Use an ordinary metal rule to create a 1:20 scale: 5cm on the plan represents 100cm (1 metre) on the stage. Simple annotations and a key help to make details clear.

TASK 3.7

Drawing a ground plan

1. Sketch a **simple** set design for the play you are working on.
2. Measure the performance area in whole or half metres. (Anything else will be complicated to use on a ground plan.)
3. List the dimensions (measurements) of the stage area and the width and depth of all items of scenery to be included.
4. Go on to draw a 1:20-scale ground plan of your design.
5. Add annotations, such as 'rug', main measurements and a key that explains any symbols you use. Note the scale here too.
6. Share your sketch and ground plan with a group member. If they can't understand them, note where the difficulties are, and try again!

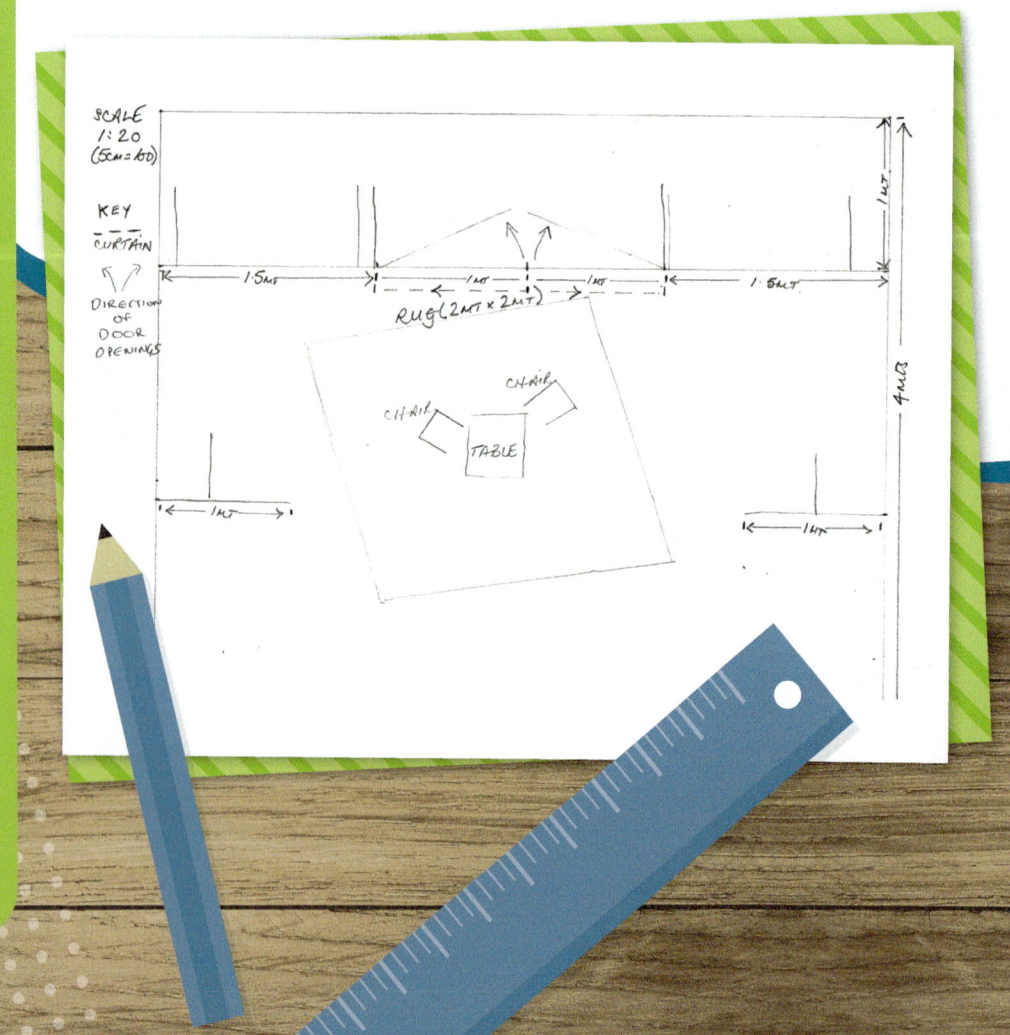

3D models

You are not required to make models, but they are an excellent form in which to show your set designs. Models are widely used because:

- they allow the director and performers to visualise the set clearly
- free-standing parts of the model can be moved around during design meetings, aiding discussion and decision making
- they give valuable information to the set builders.

If you choose to make a 3D model of your set, you might need:

- Paper, pencils, paints and small brushes
- Collage items (magazines and so on)
- Foam board
- Plasticine
- Lolly sticks
- Cardboard
- Plywood offcuts
- Scraps of light weight fabrics
- Glue sticks
- Electrical tape
- Sculpting tools
- Dressmakers' pins
- Cotton reels (about the right scale for tables)

LOOK HERE
Follow the checklist in 'Health and safety notes for set designers', page 75.

DESIGN TIP
Start gathering useful modelling materials as soon as you begin the design process.

White card models

These 3D models are relatively quick and easy to make because they are not detailed. You simply use cardboard. They allow you to experiment with, for example, positioning flats. Moving elements of the model around enables you to see what effects are created in terms of entrances and exits, for instance.

The pictures below show **white-card** elements of a set design for *Hansel and Gretel*. The maker has experimented with **book flats** in different positions.

DESIGN TIP
Include an 'actor' that can be moved around the 'set'. This is very helpful in understanding the space for various scenes. (At 1:20 scale, you could make your figure 7cm tall.)

These book flats have been made from 10cm-square sheets of card, scored and folded to be free-standing. They are at 1:20 scale. The textures are experiments with origami paper, fabric and string for a non-naturalistic forest effect.

Chapter 3 Practical Guide to Set Design

Model boxes

Model boxes are generally made when a designer is fairly certain of their set design. They can be seen as more complete versions of white card models. They can be as simple or as highly detailed as you wish. Some model boxes even include lights!

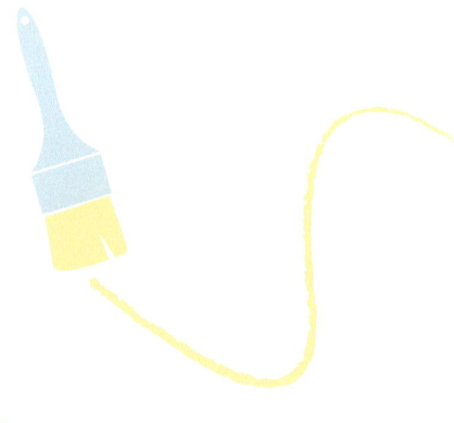

A model of the set for Kindertransport at Coventry Belgrade Theatre by Juliet Shillingford.

A fairly quickly made model box, developed from the ground plan on page 70.

TASK 3.8

Making a 3D model

1. Choose a design from which to create a model box or white card model. You could use the ground plan from Task 3.7.
2. Gather the materials to work with.
3. Make your model at a scale of 1:20.
4. Take feedback on your model and make the necessary changes if you can.

Chapter 3 Practical Guide to Set Design

UNDERSTANDING YOUR RESOURCES

Materials, tools and equipment

At an early stage of the design process, you should make yourself aware of the materials available for creating the set.

> **TASK 3.9**
>
> Select from the following list the items you would like to use for your set. Then highlight which are available in your school or college.
>
> This will give you a good starting point, but if you think you need further items, add them to the list and begin to think where you could source them.

Building MATERIALS and TOOLS

- ○ Cardboard sheets and boxes
- ○ Large pieces of sturdy cloth such as canvas
- ○ Plywood sheets
- ○ Timber strips
- ○ Staple gun
- ○ Glue gun
- ○ Heavy-duty gaffer tape
- ○ Metal brackets and hinges
- ○ Cable ties
- ○ Drill
- ○ Screwdriver
- ○ Flooring offcuts
- ○ Water-based paint, brushes
- ○ Marker pens
- ○ PVA glue

Human resources

The exam board states that 'set designers are not assessed on the set's construction.' This means that you can get help with building your set.

The most likely source of support is your technology department, especially if topics such as construction and working with resistant materials are on the curriculum. Remember that you need to be closely involved in what is made and how it is constructed. Perhaps a technology teacher or student could construct the set or scenery item while you assist, for you to paint afterwards. Discuss this with your Drama teacher.

You might not even need to build a set. You can hire or borrow items, but you need to be involved with the process, and the **design** of the set must be yours.

> **TASK 3.10**
>
> Arrange to visit the construction rooms of the technology department. Discuss with a teacher:
> - How might they set about constructing a scenery item such as a flat?
> - What materials would they suggest using for your design?
> - What tools and equipment would you need?

FOCUS
Practical aspects you need to know about before you create your design.

ASSESSMENT CHECK
Being aware of the possibilities and limits to your design means that you can realise sets with appropriate dressings, furnishings, material, colour, texture and props.

A Drama student mixes and choose paint for her set.

DESIGN TIP
Ask around! There might be a family friend who has a workshop, for example, and a trailer to transport the set to school.

FOCUS

How to find, recycle or buy the materials for your set and meet your artistic intentions.

ASSESSMENT CHECK

By making considered choices, you are demonstrating the ability to select the appropriate materials and equipment to realise your set design.

This works towards AO1: 'Create and develop ideas to communicate meaning for theatrical performance.'

DESIGN TIP

Be resilient. Tackle problems step by step. If an item is difficult to get, think:

- Can you make a saving elsewhere?
- Could you use a similar but cheaper version?
- Do you really need it?

SOURCING MATERIALS FOR THE SET

Once your set design has been agreed with your group, it is time to think about the actual set.

What do I need and what will it cost?

Keep in mind while designing that you will only have a small amount to spend on your set. Don't buy anything until you know:

- what your budget is
- everything you will need to design and make your set
- where you might get it
- how much it will all cost.

TASK 3.11

Copy and complete a chart like this to keep track of what you need.

Item	Source	Approximate cost
Large pot plant	Borrow from family or friends	None
Backcloth	Pre-painted: hire for 5 days	£100? Too much?
	Make own: canvas and paint	£60? Too much?
	Make own: 2 **tarpaulins** and paint	£40?
	Make own: sewn-together sheets, rough wooden frame, paint	£30?
	Make own: cardboard boxes taped together	£10? Will they look poor?
	Watered-down PVA as fire retardant	£2
Stage flat	Ply-board sheet from DIY shop	£20
	Rough-cut lengths from wood yard	£5
	Water-based paints and cheap acrylic	£10?
	Watered-down PVA as fire retardant	£2
3ft round table	Borrow	None
Round white tablecloth	Charity shop or make?	£3?

Recycling and borrowing

It is unlikely that you will be able to buy everything needed for your set. Is everything in your design essential? Can anything be changed to something you can borrow or recycle?

Recycling here simply means making an item into something else. For example, you could fix small wheels to a table to make it a trolley. A large scarf can become a tablecloth. A green tarpaulin over a stepladder could be a mountain.

- Find out what is already available in school. Could you borrow a table? Is there an existing stage flat that you can paint over?
- Try pound shops for craft materials and acrylic paint.
- Go to builders' merchants for offcuts.
- Pallets (often free) are useful for timber or even basic furniture.

Health and safety in set design

Taking care of yourselves

You are responsible for the set, so you need to be aware of safety issues around construction, such as the examples below. This applies even if you are supervising others building a set on your behalf.

- Follow all instructions and guidance given.
- Make sure electrical equipment has an up-to-date PAT (Portable Appliance Testing) certificate.
- Check cables and machinery for damage. Make them secure.
- Wear safety goggles and gloves whenever necessary.
- Some paints and varnishes need to be applied in an airy space. Open windows and wear masks.
- Glue and staple guns are popular with set designers: they are quick and effective. Handle all such tools and materials with care and respect.
- Use the correct tool for the job.
- Store tools and materials neatly and out of the way.
- Be aware of what other people are doing around you.

Taking care of performers

On stage, actors need to concentrate on staying in role and immersing themselves in the world of the drama. Your set needs to enhance this world. It must also ensure the performers' safety.

Risks to **avoid** include:
- Trip hazards (rugs, for instance, should be secured with double-sided tape)
- Unstable pieces of scenery (brace items with stage weights)
- Glass in windows or doors (use Perspex or leave them empty)
- Slippery floor finishes (avoid gloss)
- Unsuitable access or space for performers with impaired mobility
- Large or uneven steps and levels
- Unmarked edges of steps (try a textured surface if tape will be seen by the audience).

Making your set fire-safe

Fire regulations for public performances are very strict. (If your show is just for staff and students in school, it is not considered a public performance.) If a prop is always held in a performer's hand, it does not need to be flame proofed. However, any scenery or large prop that is free-standing **must** be made of fire-retardant material or treated to be flame proof. You could:

- Buy fire-retardant timber and cloth (effective, but expensive)
- Use fire-retardant spray for the fabric parts of your set
- Cover painted wood surfaces with water-based matt varnish or watered-down PVA glue (about 5 parts water to 1 part PVA).

FOCUS
Keeping yourself and others safe.

ASSESSMENT CHECK
The requirement that your set is designed and made safely comes under AO2: 'Use theatrical skills to realise artistic intentions in live performance.'

For both Components 2 and 3, you are expected to adopt the latest safe working practices.

DESIGN TIP
It is important to consider safety issues before you start construction. It could be difficult to remove hazards afterwards.

Chapter 3 Practical Guide to Set Design

FOCUS
Pointers for constructing the set once the design has been agreed.

ASSESSMENT CHECK
In creating a set from your design, you are realising a set that contributes positively to the overall performance and communicates meaning.

LOOK HERE
See page 75 for health and safety tips for set construction, and page 68 for advice on including different levels.

DESIGN TIP
Make sure that your set is completed in good time. The performers need time to rehearse on it!

CREATING YOUR SET DESIGN FOR THE STAGE

Your responsibility
The exam specification states that you do not have to build the set yourself, as you will not be assessed on its construction. Before you begin, however, there are some points to consider.

Which parts of the set need to function?
The most important thing to remember is that you are creating an illusion when you make a theatre set. Many aspects of your set will not need to 'do' anything. A painted shop front, for example, might not need to have a door that opens, it simply gives the illusion of a shop.

Some parts of your set, however, might need to be bear the weight of an actor, or a window might need to open and close. If this is the case, ask yourself:

- What am I making?
- How will it be used?
- Who is using it?

The answers will guide you towards the materials to use and how sturdy your construction needs to be.

Scenery on flats
You might need to make flats: upright pieces of scenery. Usually made from sheets of plywood about 1.2 metres by 2.4 metres, flats are braced and weighted so that they stand securely. Another way of making a flat is to stretch canvas over a wooden frame. Both types can then be painted.

Painted backcloths and panels
Traditionally, many stage sets had a painted cloth at the back of the acting area. It depicted the location for the play. If you have the time and resources, you could use a canvas or canvas-stretched frames. You would need to have a way of hanging them from the lighting bars or make them free-standing. Or, a run of painted flats could work just as well. Your human resources will help you to establish what is possible.

This painted cloth of a riverbank scene was created for, and can be hired from, the Yvonne Arnaud Theatre.

Be creative!
Some of the best set designs are made with non-standard materials. Try the following crafty shortcuts.

- Reinforce large cardboard boxes with gaffer tape. Use them to build pieces of scenery. Paint different sides to give varied scenes and you have an original way of changing the set.
- Ask to borrow a metal trolley from the school canteen. You could attach two different pieces of flat scenery (made from cardboard perhaps) with cable ties. Just swivel them as needed.

Chapter 3 Practical Guide to Set Design

TECHNICAL AND DRESS REHEARSALS FOR SET DESIGNERS

The rehearsal schedule works towards a technical and then a dress rehearsal. These are the rehearsals that draw everything together.

As set designer, you should sit in the audience area for the technical and dress rehearsals. You need your notebook to hand and should change your seat every now and again to check sightlines.

Technical rehearsal

This rehearsal is for technicians and designers. It will probably be the first chance to put all the elements of the production (performers, lights, sound, costumes and set) together. Everything might look and work as planned, but take the opportunity to change things if not. If you encounter some typical problems, try the suggestions in the table below.

Potential problems	Possible solutions and timings
Parts of the set are not finished. Perhaps the edge of a flat has not been painted or a vase does not have flowers.	List outstanding tasks. Ensure they are done before the dress rehearsal (and allow time for paint and glue to dry).
A set element is not functioning properly. For example, a door isn't opening and closing smoothly.	Make adjustments so that the issue is fixed before the dress rehearsal.
A piece of set does not look or feel right. For example, a bookcase looks too empty, too full or too tidy.	Decide if you can make changes before the dress rehearsal. If not, get it done before the performance.
The actors are struggling with some aspect of the set. Perhaps they have to squeeze between items of furniture or cannot move scenery smoothly.	Make a list or annotate your design. Work with the actors after the 'tech' to rearrange the furniture or practise moving the scenery.
The set does not appear as you had hoped under some of the lighting states.	Note which scenes are causing the problem. Talk to the lighting designer before the dress rehearsal and see if you can come to a compromise in the intensity or colour of the lighting.
Part of the set is obscuring sightlines from some areas of the audience.	Sketch where problems occur. Adjust the positioning of the set if possible. Otherwise, remove the awkward seats from the audience.

Dress rehearsal

The 'dress' is the final, timed, **run** before the performance. Now that technical issues have been addressed, the actors can perform uninterrupted.

Again, watch from the audience area with a notebook. Remember to move around and look out for the following:

- Have changes from the tech been made successfully?
- Are sightlines clear from every position in the audience?
- Are set changes working smoothly and in reasonable time?
- Are the actors happy moving around the set?

If there are still issues, revisit your notes and the table above. Work with your colleagues to tackle problems. Make final tweaks as necessary.

FOCUS

- The role of the set designer during final rehearsals.
- How potential problems might be overcome.

ASSESSMENT CHECK

Rehearsals will help you to reflect, analyse and evaluate (AO4), and develop your skills in:

- assessing the merit of different approaches and formulating judgements about the overall impact
- identifying and investigating how far you have developed theatrical skills and how successfully you contributed to the devising process and the final piece.

You will also demonstrate knowledge and understanding of how drama and theatre is developed and performed (AO3).

DESIGN TIP

Try not to interrupt the rehearsal unless there is a health and safety issue, so that you can see how elements work in real time and support the performers.

FOCUS

Placing a value judgement on drama is key to Components 1 and 2. These pages will help you to develop the habit of reflecting on your work.

ASSESSMENT CHECK

Essential for AO4 is the ability to analyse and evaluate your own work and the work of others in the written exam as well as in your practical work.

LOOK HERE

'Set Design for the Devised Piece' from page 212, has more guidance on the devising process and evaluating as you go through it. See Chapter 6 for more examples of evaluation.

Lord of the Flies by A Theatre Near U.

EVALUATING YOUR SET DESIGN

What is evaluation?

Evaluation is a skill that you will use in many of your GCSE subjects. It is the process of judging something's quality, importance or value. In other words, you give your considered opinion on how 'good' or successful something is when you evaluate it. Evaluation is a valued skill because it requires reflection and reasoning.

When do I evaluate?

You will be reflecting on and assessing the success of your set throughout any designing process.

In Component 2, the most crucial analysis comes after the production, when you evaluate the effectiveness of your contribution to the final performance. A strong ability to evaluate will contribute significant marks to the devising log, which is a key part of the devising component.

Evaluation is also an essential skill in Component 1, when you **analyse** and form **critical judgements** on the work of other theatre makers.

How do I evaluate successfully?

Evaluation becomes convincing when you build an argument to support your opinions. The way to do this involves giving clear examples. You should aim to use a range of vocabulary for the different evaluations you make because if you always say something is 'effective' it starts to lose its impact.

TASK 3.12

Copy the following diagram, adding some adjectives of your own. Use it when writing about your set.

Helpful words for evaluation

Poor	Successful	Excellent	
Rushed	Effective	Engaging	Powerful

You will be expected to choose a few details from your set and give reasons why you think they were effective in performance. This student has begun to do this as well as using some evaluative words like the ones above:

> I believe that one **powerful element** of my set design was how it **allowed the performers** to use different **levels**. The **moment** when Jack looks down from a height onto Piggy lying on the floor is **a good example of this**. The set **helped to emphasise** the amount of control and power Jack has over Piggy. Also, the set **combined with lighting** in an **engaging** way for the audience...

Examining the details of your set design

In your evaluation, you will need to make at least three different points with examples that help to illustrate why you have made a particular value judgement.

TASK 3.13

The geometric shapes used consistently throughout this set design are simple to achieve but give flexibility and create a striking effect. (*Brokers* by Tylar Pendgraft performed by the USC School of Dramatic Arts.)

1. Copy and complete your own version of this table (examples are given based on the set design above). These notes will form a solid basis for your evaluative writing.

Set design evaluation			
Design element	**Example / moment in the play**	**Evaluation**	**Reason for evaluation**
Suspended frames	Pre-set and throughout the play.	Engaging. Encouraged audience to ask questions and become involved.	Encouraged the audience to think about uncertainty and things falling. Linked to the theme of the play.
Movable cubes	Scene changes.	Effective in setting scenes quickly and simply.	The fact that the boxes could be easily moved by the actors made it easy and quick to create different locations.
Use of the colour white	The moment when the character became depressed.	Powerful in creating atmosphere and helping characterisation.	The use of white in the set combined with the blue lighting created an atmosphere of emptiness and despair.

2. Once you have made your evaluation into a table like this, turn it into three paragraphs. Remember that you are evaluating. This means that you add a value judgement to an opinion and support it with examples.

Chapter 3 Practical Guide to Set Design   79

SET DESIGN VOCABULARY

Analyse Examine in detail, thinking about parts in relation to the whole.

Backcloth A large piece of canvas or cloth which is often painted with a setting.

Colour palette A complementary set of colours that belong to a group, such as pastel or dark.

Construction Something that has been built (a set for example); the act of building.

Critical judgement Analysing the merits and faults of something to decide its worth or success.

End on A stage configuration that places the audience on one side of an open stage.

Evaluate Give an opinion, a value judgement, backed up with examples and reasons.

Exterior (setting/location) An outdoor space, such as a garden, street or outside a building.

Flat A tall, main piece of scenery that, as its name suggests, generally carries a 2D image.

- **Book flat** Two flats that are hinged along their 'spine'.
- **Free-standing flat** A braced, single flat that can stand anywhere on the set.
- **Run of flats** Two or more flats joined as a length to achieve a wall, for example.

French doors/windows A pair of outward-opening doors often fully glazed, functioning as both windows and doors.

Furnishings Set furniture (sometimes including curtains, rugs and so on).

Illusion Something that is not as it seems; something that is not real, but often gives an impression of reality.

In the round A stage configuration in which the audience encircles the acting area.

Interior (setting/location) An indoor space, such as a kitchen or a school hall.

Interpret Express your own ideas about intended meaning; your choice where there are a number of correct possibilities.

Location The place or setting where action takes place, such as a forest, a bedroom or a park.

Model box A 3D set design, often presented within a box of some sort.

Naturalistic A set, for example, with characteristics of reality; having the appearance of a real place.

Non-naturalistic A set design, for example, that aims not to look like a real place.

Pre-set Features of the drama onstage that are already in place before the audience enters.

Props Short for 'properties' (suggesting ownership): objects that would be owned by a character such as a torch, phone, set of keys.

Realistic A set, for example, that sets out to be like real life (naturalistic).

Representative Something that represents (stands for) something else: for example, a non-naturalistic set that 'represents' and suggests rather than copies real life.

Run Either a rehearsal of the whole play, or the number of times a play will be performed (*The Crucible* has a three-week run at this theatre).

Scale The size of something relative to something else.

Scenery Parts of the set that represent locations or surroundings – on cloth or flats.

Set dressings Accessories such as tablecloths, cushions and other decorative items.

Stylised Non-realistic, non-naturalistic, where style features are dominant.

Tarpaulin Large, heavy-duty, waterproof cloth/sheet, usually of woven plastic.

White-card model A simple 3D representation of a set design.

PRACTICAL GUIDE TO COSTUME DESIGN

Chapter 4

Introduction to costume design	82
Placing costume in history	84
Style: what we wear, and why	85
Colour and fabric for the stage	86
Developing and using your costume resources	90
Key process – sewing	92
Adapting costume items	94
Health and safety in costume design	95
Hair, make-up and masks	96
How to document your costume design	98
Fitting the costume	100
Technical and dress rehearsals for costume designers	104
Evaluating your costume design	105
Costume design vocabulary	106

FOCUS
The importance of costume design.

ASSESSMENT CHECK
As you gain awareness and understanding of costume choices, you are:
- learning how to design and realise costumes that contribute positively to the overall performance and communicate meaning
- gaining knowledge and understanding of how drama and theatre is developed and performed (AO3).

INTRODUCTION TO COSTUME DESIGN

Everyday costumes
At least once every day we all use costume design skills. When you open your drawer or look in your **wardrobe**, you are choosing clothing to suit your day. Consciously or otherwise, you might be thinking:
- Am I going to be outside much and what will I be doing?
- How do I feel and what image do I want to project?
- Do I just want to be comfortable or do I want to make an impression?

Everyday make-up
Some people wouldn't leave the house without make-up. For others, they wear it for an evening out or not at all. Make-up also has strong cultural and religious meanings for some communities.

There are numerous reasons why make-up can be important, including:
- sharing your culture and identity
- boosting confidence
- helping you to feel older or younger.

How should a character be made-up and costumed?
When you design costumes for the stage, you are making decisions for a character rather than for yourself, but you can start with the same three questions above. Then go on to ask yourself these more specific questions:

TASK 4.1
1. Take a few moments to look at the people around you and what they are wearing. Apply the three bullet-point questions above to each person and put yourself in their shoes.
2. If you can, try this task in a range of locations, such as a park and a café. Build up a picture of each person. What other clothing do you imagine they have in their wardrobe?

How does their occupation (or lack of it) influence their clothing and make-up choices?

What fashions and fabrics would be available given the period of history in which the play is to be staged?

Does the character have any particular personality traits that might influence their choices? (Are they vain? Do they tend to feel anxious?)

How interested is the character in clothes and make-up?

Does the character undergo a journey through the play, or a transformation? How could that be communicated through costume and make-up?

To what extent do they care about how they look? To what extent can they afford to care?

Using costume to enhance meaning

As a costume designer, you have the power to influence how an audience perceives a character before they speak or move. Your design input might immediately inform the audience that a character is a pilot in the Second World War, for example, or an impoverished child in the 1960s.

Stylistic and artistic collaboration

Reflecting the context – such as historical and economic signs – is crucial in design. At the same time, a costume designer needs to work in harmony with other designers and the director to achieve the stylistic and artistic intentions of the drama. This might mean, for example, working within a particular **colour palette**, designing a costume that allows an actor to safely climb part of the set, or working with the lighting designer to ensure that your **fabric choices** will be appropriate under particular stage lights.

Costume and the actor

Costuming and make-up are very important for the actor as they help them to portray the character. Costumes also need to be comfortable enough for the actor to move freely. Costume designers will often provide **rehearsal costumes** that help the actor to behave like the character.

Removing or putting on potentially 'fiddly' garments, such as jackets, scarves and headwear, need to be practised and timed in the rehearsal room.

How can I design costumes as part of this course?

Component 1 is the written exam. When you **evaluate** a performance you have seen, you might write about costume design. Practical work will help you to write confidently about costume and make-up.

You can opt for costume design in either or both of the practical sections of the course. If you choose to work as costume designer in Component 2, you will work in a small group to devise a piece of theatre. Your specific responsibility will be to create two costume designs for the performance.

Component 3 is similar, but you will work with a script, instead of devising your own drama.

Research

Even if you are creating a contemporary (modern) world for the stage, you will still need to complete research so that your design:

- suits the personality of the character
- reflects the right economic and social contexts.

For period costumes, remember that many museums have a fashion and clothing section. Study clothing from different centuries and decades.

Also browse the internet, fashion magazines, history books and crafting and sewing magazines. Look for clothing worn by a particular type of person during the historical period of your drama piece.

TASK 4.2

Watch a few minutes of an unfamiliar television drama or film that happens to be on. Focus on one character's costume:

- What historical period is represented?
- What social and economic conditions are being suggested?
- What can you tell about the character's personality?

DESIGN TIP

Find out early on whether actors have health issues with particular fibres or make-up ingredients, so that you have time to explore options.

TASK 4.3

Ask your teacher if you can bring in some rehearsal costumes for a practical performance lesson. Afterwards, discuss how the use of rehearsal costumes affected the performance.

DESIGN TIP

Keep downloaded and bookmarked resources in a research folder on your computer. Keep magazine pages and so on in your paper folder. If you design for Component 2, these will go in your devising log.

FOCUS
A short history of clothing to give you a starting point for including authenticity in your design work.

ASSESSMENT CHECK
This section provides useful background for your set play study and your understanding of its social, historical and/or cultural contexts.

A re-creation of Elizabethan hair (wig) and make-up by Alanna Sadler.

TASK 4.4
Look at the labels in some of your own clothing. What is the fabric made up of? Can you find out where some of the more unusual materials might have been produced?

PLACING COSTUME IN HISTORY
Professional costume designers understand the relationship between historical period, including today, and clothing. What people wear is largely dictated by the society and time that they live in.

Before the 19th century
Pre-industrialisation, poorer people would typically wear **natural**, cotton, linen and wool, and **styles** were broadly modest, simple and functional. If you were wealthy, you might have silk, taffeta and satin. These fabrics could be dyed with beetroot, berries and onion skins, for example. Fashion played a significant role for those that could afford it. At the highest level of society, there were certain items that only royalty wore, such as purple velvet, gold fabric and some types of fur.

The use of make-up also has an interesting history and is used differently across the world. Very pale skin, for example, was desirable in Europe for several hundred years up until the 20th century.

The mid 19th century onwards
Industrialisation paved the way for a broader range of materials. Textile factories meant that the speed and ease of fabric production increased, allowing a wider section of the population to add variety to their clothing.

The first sewing machines were developed around the 1830s, gradually leading to **mass-produced** clothing. As home sewing machines became popular too, ordinary people could copy fashions that they saw the wealthy enjoying.

In the early 20th century, the chemical industry began to produce man-made dyes, along with fabrics such as polyester and nylon that added stretch to clothing. **Textured** fabrics such as corduroy and polyester also developed.

Some periods, such as the 1920s and 1960s, saw iconic fashion and make-up.

TASK 4.5
These photographs of 1940s film star Ava Gardner show her without and with costume make-up.
1. Write a short paragraph describing her 'look' in each picture.
2. Think of at least three adjectives to describe what her made-up look says about her character (for example, *powerful*).

STYLE: WHAT WE WEAR, AND WHY

Some of the most distinctive aspects of costume design are shape and particular features of style.

Historical period

Certain times can be identified by typical clothing styles. Fashion and the availability of fabric are the major influences when it comes to shape, which might include skirt and trouser length, neckline, and so on. Oversized flared cords or jeans, for example, place a costume in the late 1960s to early 1970s. A cloche hat would be from the 1920s.

> **TASK 4.6**
>
> Look through magazines, shops and your own clothes for distinctive shapes or styles of cut. What features stand out (in terms of outline, sleeves, leg shape and length, fullness, **silhouette**)?

Social economics

A person's ability to update and maintain their wardrobe depends largely on the amount of income they are prepared to spend on clothes. Historically, only wealthier members of society could buy more than just essential garments. Today, many people shop widely and frequently for clothes.

For many decades, brand names have been an important influence on purchasing, and favoured brands command a high price tag. Displaying brand names prominently on clothes can be seen as a **status symbol**.

Identity and image

Clothing and make-up are often expressions of our character and personality. Many periods of history have **subculture** fashions, such as punk or mod, that identify the wearers as belonging to that subculture. These are often linked to other areas of popular culture or art, such as music and film.

Suitability

There are two main factors that affect the suitability of clothing.

- Someone's occupation and way of life will affect what they wear in particular situations. It needs to be practical and functional.
- Body shape and confidence levels can play their part when people think about what suits them.

> **TASK 4.7**
>
> Design a new uniform for **one** of the following (male or female):
> - manual council worker, such as a refuse collector
> - primary school pupil
> - supermarket checkout assistant.
>
> Consider suitability, socio-economic factors and identity.

FOCUS

Some of the factors that affect clothing choices.

ASSESSMENT CHECK

Here, you begin to design and realise costumes capable of establishing the character, period and location.

You should also begin to see how costume can contribute to communicating meaning through genre and style.

Goth fans pose at a music festival.

Chapter 4 Practical Guide to Costume Design 85

FOCUS
What to consider when choosing costume material.

ASSESSMENT CHECK
Exploring costume choices will help you to realise costumes that show an understanding of fabrics, textures, trimmings, accessories and colour and work towards AO3: 'Demonstrate knowledge and understanding of how drama and theatre is developed and performed.'

COLOUR AND FABRIC FOR THE STAGE

Selecting colours, patterns and materials

There are eight main considerations for costume designers when selecting which colour and type of fabric to use.

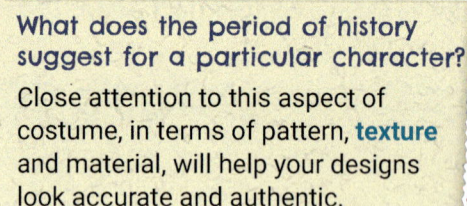

1 What does the period of history suggest for a particular character?
Close attention to this aspect of costume, in terms of pattern, **texture** and material, will help your designs look accurate and authentic.

Paisley patterns were introduced into Britain from India in the 18th century.

2 What **colour palette** is the **set designer** working with?
In the harmonious world of the stage, a unified colour theme is likely to be desired. This does not mean you have to use the same colours as the set, but you might want them to blend or have a complementary use of bold, muted or primary colours.

3 Do the **artistic intentions** of the theatre piece call for any **symbolic use of colour**?
A **stylised** drama might call for all black or all white costumes with the addition of a meaningful colour, such as red to suggest the theme of danger or violence. **Monochrome** (shades of black and white only) can be used for entire sets or costume designs and can be full of impact. Such designs have a clarity and lack of complication that could also be used alongside one or more characters being dressed in colour to emphasise them. White is very effective under coloured lights.

White often has connotations of purity and innocence, while we might associate black fabric with death or evil. Purple has links to royalty and wealth.

A play with opposing groups, such as the Capulets and the Montagues in *Romeo and Juliet*, might use an element of colour coding.

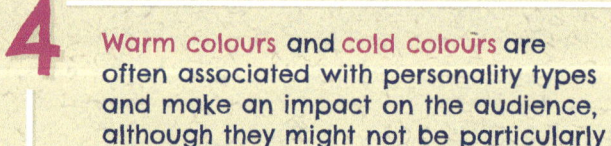

4 **Warm colours** and **cold colours** are often associated with personality types and make an impact on the audience, although they might not be particularly conscious of it.

Warm colours, such as shades of red, orange and yellow, suggest a bold, strong and confident person. Cold colours, such as shades of blue and grey, can suggest a more distant or withdrawn type of person.

This modern production of Hamlet in Berlin uses all-white costumes and an all-white set.

86　Chapter 4　Practical Guide to Costume Design

5 Even in everyday life, the appearance of coloured fabric varies in different lighting conditions, but the intensity of stage lighting takes this to another level.

A new white shirt can be glaring under white stage lights, so costume designers might knock back the brightness by running the garment through a washing machine with other items a couple of times or dye it off-white.

Coloured lights can neutralise or drain the colour from fabric. This is particularly true with subtle tones and you should always work alongside the lighting designer to test the appearance of your fabrics before you finalise your designs.

Aguecheek's bright yellow jumpsuit in Twelfth Night looks its best under 'neutral' lighting.

6 We all have different skin-tones, and costume designers might take account of this when they select colours for their actors. Pale skins, for example, often do not blend particularly well with yellow.

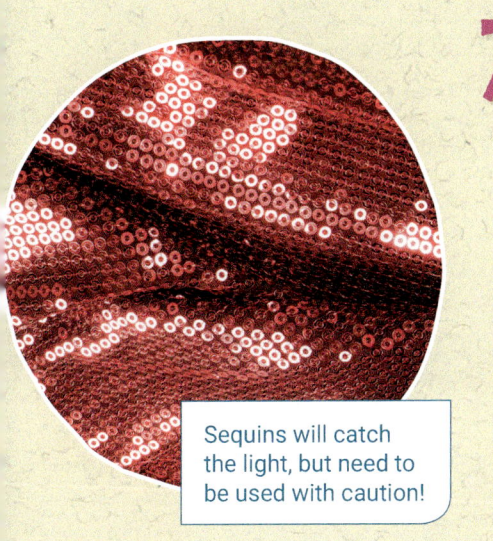

7 Mood, atmosphere and the feel of the play or character affect colour choice for costume designers. A tragic play might call for darker, more muted shades, while bright colours might suit a comedy. Professional directors are notorious for telling designers that something doesn't match the feel of their production. A design might be described as 'too fluffy' or 'not sharp enough', which the costumier has to interpret in terms of changing the shape or colour scheme of costumes.

Sequins will catch the light, but need to be used with caution!

The brightly coloured costumes in Dream Girls reflect the upbeat mood of the production.

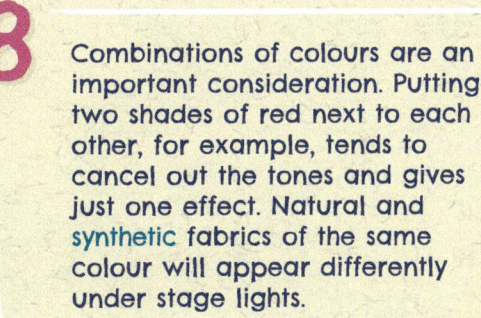

8 Combinations of colours are an important consideration. Putting two shades of red next to each other, for example, tends to cancel out the tones and gives just one effect. Natural and synthetic fabrics of the same colour will appear differently under stage lights.

ASSESSMENT CHECK

You are using the key skill of interpretation here as you develop ideas to communicate meaning to your audience.

> **TASK 4.8**
>
> 1. Choose a character from a play that you have been studying.
>   - Would you costume this character in warm or cool colours? Why?
>   - Does the historical context of the play suggest particular types of fabric, styles and patterns and make-up?
> 2. Sketch a quick costume design. Bear in mind the points above, as well as suitability in terms of characterisation. Add notes on hairstyle and make-up, if appropriate.

Selecting fabrics for stage costumes

In the modern world, there are very many types of material available, and costume designers need to consider a number of factors.

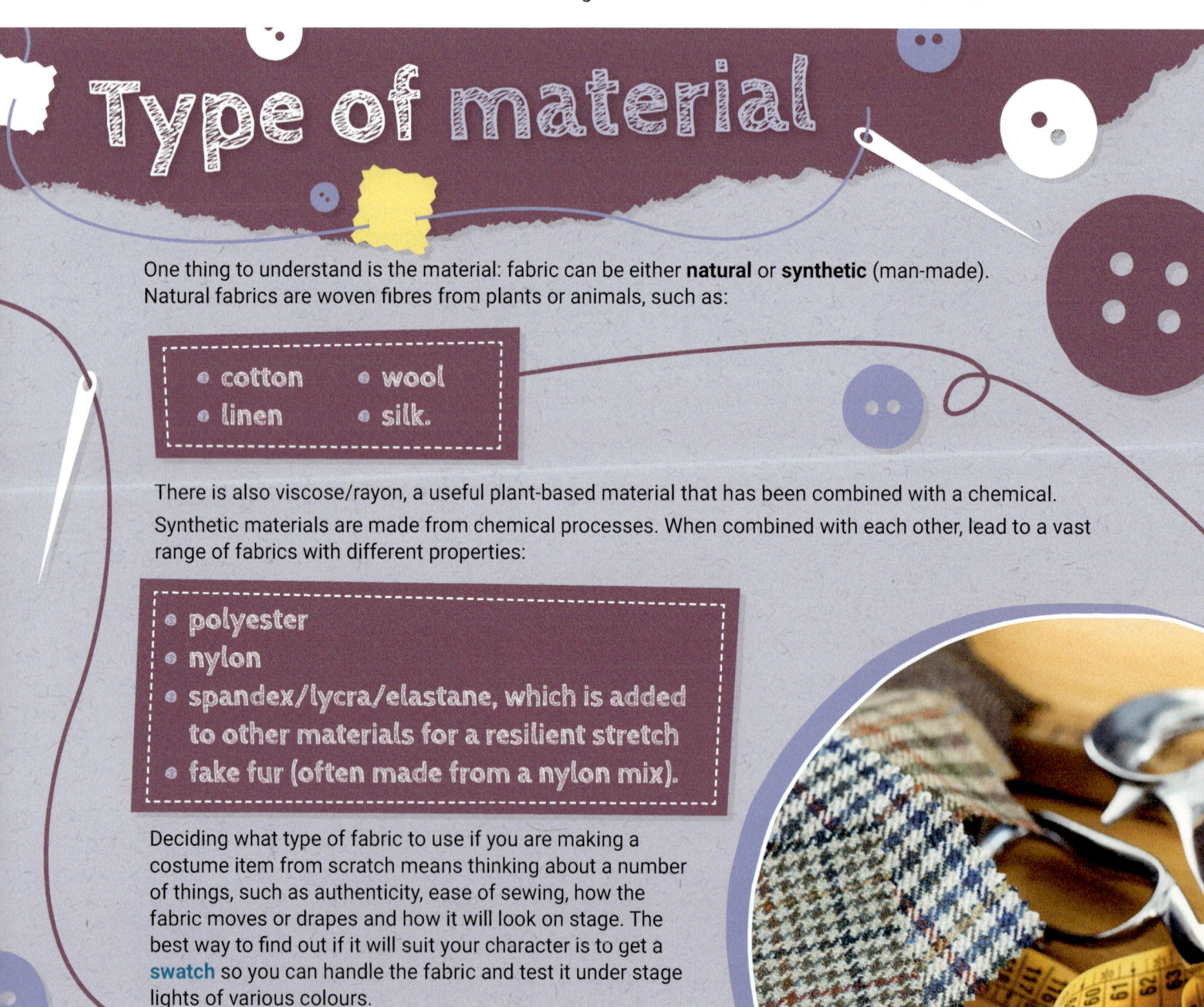

Type of material

One thing to understand is the material: fabric can be either **natural** or **synthetic** (man-made). Natural fabrics are woven fibres from plants or animals, such as:

- cotton
- wool
- linen
- silk.

There is also viscose/rayon, a useful plant-based material that has been combined with a chemical.

Synthetic materials are made from chemical processes. When combined with each other, lead to a vast range of fabrics with different properties:

- polyester
- nylon
- spandex/lycra/elastane, which is added to other materials for a resilient stretch
- fake fur (often made from a nylon mix).

Deciding what type of fabric to use if you are making a costume item from scratch means thinking about a number of things, such as authenticity, ease of sewing, how the fabric moves or drapes and how it will look on stage. The best way to find out if it will suit your character is to get a swatch so you can handle the fabric and test it under stage lights of various colours.

Chapter 4 Practical Guide to Costume Design

Weight and texture

The **weight** of fabric can be read clearly by the audience. Lightweight, flowing fabrics have more movement. If they are used with lots of fullness, they might give impressions of freedom and wealth.

Flimsy fabrics like this are not hard-wearing and therefore could suggest that the people wearing them do not do much work and can afford for their clothes not to last as long as heavier weight fabrics.

In modern clothing, the time of year and weather is a big hint as to what weight of clothing would be worn, unless it's evening-wear, when anything goes!

Corduroy.

Fabric comes in a wide range of textures such as:

- velvet
- cord
- denim
- coarse-woven
- brushed (including tweed)
- brocade/embroidered
- sequinned
- smooth.

Whether the **finish** of the fabric is dull or shiny affects its appearance significantly. Fabrics with a sheen include:

- satin
- silk
- taffeta (usually made from silk).

Tweed.

A fine taffeta dress embroidered with silk flowers.

These fabrics give the wearer an air of wealth and status, and can be expensive to use in a costume. A cheaper option is to use a synthetic version, or add **embellishments** to less expensive fabric, including:

- braid (narrow, plaited trim)
- sequins (which can be bought in strips)
- bright buttons
- jewellery
- trim, such as a fur collar or lace cuffs.

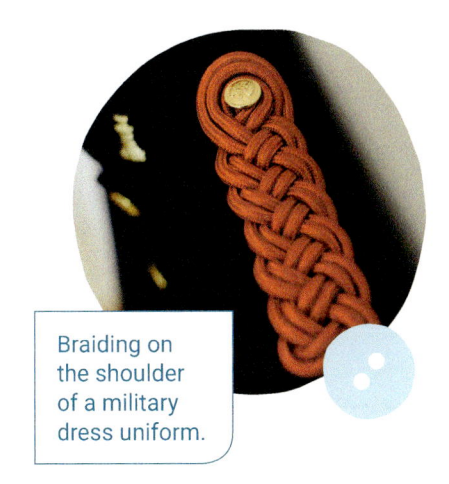

Braiding on the shoulder of a military dress uniform.

TASK 4.9

Find a simple garment from a charity shop (or use one of your own) and **upcycle** it into a more interesting and attractive version with the use of embellishments. Check the effect of the garment before and after under stage lights.

LOOK HERE

For more on altering and adapting clothing and fabric, see 'Adapting costume items' on page 94.

Chapter 4 Practical Guide to Costume Design 89

FOCUS
- Deciding what costume items you need – and where to find them.
- Making use of what you already have.

ASSESSMENT CHECK
This research will help you towards AO1: 'Create and develop ideas to communicate meaning for theatrical performance.' You are also working towards AO2: 'Apply theatrical skills to realise artistic intentions in live performance.'

DESIGN TIP
The skill of collaboration is included in your assessment, so keep notes on your work with performers and other designers.

DESIGN TIP
Selecting and sewing on decorations and trims contribute to the assessed design and creating process.

DEVELOPING AND USING YOUR COSTUME RESOURCES

There is no point designing a costume that you cannot then create, so it is essential to know what resources are available to you, including people.

Human resources

As a costume designer, you must 'be involved in' the making and putting together of costumes, but you can also 'supervise' construction and sourcing. You will not be assessed on the costume's construction.

So, it is acceptable for someone to help you with sewing and sourcing, as long as you stay in charge of the process. It is essential that there is a process. You must not buy an entire costume, put it on an actor and say you designed it: that would just be finding a costume!

Working collaboratively

Work closely with your designing and performing colleagues to stay in touch and share ideas. Your costume will benefit from effective **collaboration**.

Physical resources

Sewing materials and equipment

Your school or college will give you access to at least the basic tools you need to produce your costumes. Sewing machines are ideal, but you might manage with tape measure, tailor's chalk, scissors, iron, pins, needles and thread to hand sew with. These can be bought cheaply if not available in school. Your local market is a good starting point. You might also be given a small budget for fabric and/or clothing.

Items of clothing

Have a good hunt around first in your school's costume room and family's and friends' wardrobes. Even if items are not quite what you have in mind, you might be able to alter and add items to achieve the costume you want. Make sure you get permission first, of course!

Making a costume from scratch

If you plan to make, or supervise, the main part of the costume, list all the materials you need before you begin shopping.

Finding fabric

This flow-chart should help you to decide where to source your fabric.

I need fabric.

Do I already have, or know I can get, some for free?

- **Yes** → Do that!
- **No** →
  - I need less than 1 metre.
    - Fabric needs to be a specific type or have a certain print, colour or texture.
      - **No** → Search charity shops, car boot sales for clothing or household items that can be cut up.
      - **Yes** → Search fabric shops locally or online.
  - I need more than 1 metre.
    - Fabric needs to be a specific type or have a certain print, colour or texture.
      - **Yes** → Search fabric shops locally or online.
      - **No** → Find a sheet, duvet cover or tablecloth from a charity shop or discount store.

Using historical costume patterns

Some excellent **patterns** are available for most historical periods. If you, or one of your human resources, is able and willing to sew a costume from scratch, this could be an excellent way to go. Even if you can't face making the entire costume, patterns are very useful for caps, collars and so on.

Getting the most from your budget

Priorities

It is essential to balance the cost of fabric or a garment and the way it will feel on the actor and appear to the audience. You must not overspend, but you do not want an outfit that feels and looks poor.

Making a costume does not have to be expensive, however. Remember that you can modify found garments to good effect by altering the length, shape or fit and adding accessories, for example. Shop around.

You need to decide on the most important aspects of your design. This will help you to spend your money wisely. There is no point buying an amazing hat, for example, if it leaves you short of money to buy the dress.

Essential extras

Accessories can make a big difference to a costume, often without costing much. Think about your character and their world. They might need a few pairs of shoes and perhaps a bag. A suit might not be finished without a tie. Allow a little of your budget for items such as socks and tights too.

DESIGN TIP

Create and update an expenses spreadsheet in which you itemise every item you buy or hire.

DESIGN TIP

You might be able to hire part of your costume. Make sure that you don't just use a whole costume off the rail, however, as this will not be **your** design.

Chapter 4 Practical Guide to Costume Design

FOCUS
A basic skill for costume design.

ASSESSMENT CHECK
These practical techniques will help you to apply theatrical skills in order to realise your artistic intentions in the performance (AO2).

KEY PROCESS – SEWING

At some point in your work as a costume designer you should sew something! This book won't teach you to become a dressmaker, but these pages show you the key process that securely holds one piece of fabric to another. It really is quite easy.

You can make a bag, for example, or simple garment even if you just have some fabric and basic sewing equipment. Sewing machines are quick, but hand sewing works well too. The following are two simple hand-sewn stitches.

TACKING temporarily holds two pieces of fabric together loosely so that they can be tried on (carefully) or held in place while you sew them together permanently. It is a long up-and-down stitch that you make with the right (outer) sides of the fabric together.

BACK STITCH uses small stitches with no gaps between them. It is strong, permanent stitching which will hold fabric together securely.

MAKING YOUR FIRST PIECE OF COSTUME: A DRAWSTRING BAG

Drawstring bags were popular in Britain from Victorian times until the 1920s, and versions of it are still used today. You could make one for yourself, a friend or as part of a finished costume design.

You can buy the fabric new, but even better for developing your skills as a costume designer, would be to source, from a charity shop or second-hand sale, a garment or home furnishing item with an interesting pattern. Existing buttons or embroidery could be left on for instant embellishment. Of course, choosing and adding your own embellishments would enhance the impact of your bag as well.

Cotton fabric is the easiest to work with as it does not stretch, fray or slip around. Or you could try heavier, textured fabrics, such as velvet, cord or brocade. These bring glamour and interest, but can be more awkward to work with. You could experiment with several fabrics to make a range of bags.

Method

*Back-stitch steps can also be done on a sewing machine.

You will need

- Approximately half a metre of fabric
- Three-quarters of a metre of narrow ribbon, piping or cord
- Pins
- Needles and thread
- Flexible tape measure
- Steel and/or wooden ruler
- Scissors
- Iron
- A safety pin
- Buttons, sequins, beads and so on (optional)

1. Cut two identical oblong pieces of fabric. Your bag will end up about 4cm smaller, so 18cm by 26cm would give you a make-up bag.

2. Using a hard edge to guide you, such as a steel ruler, iron a 1cm fold onto the wrong side (inside) of the fabric over one short side of each piece of fabric. This will be the top of your bag.

3. Pin the two pieces of fabric, wrong sides together. Leave 5cm unpinned at the top on each side.

4. Tack where you have pinned, about 2cm from the edge, on the long sides. Remove the pins.

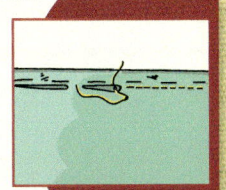

5. Back-stitch next to where you have tacked.

6. Unpick the tacking.

7. Press the **seam** open with the iron. Press up to the top of the bag (the unstitched section).

8. Fold the unstitched sections in half onto the wrong sides.

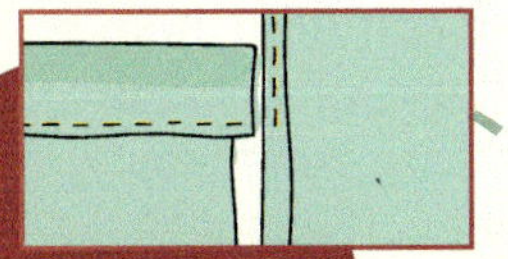

9. Pin, tack and then remove the pins.

10. Back-stitch next to the tacking and remove the tacking. You now have a channel to put your ribbon through.

11. Cut your ribbon in half and attach a safety pin to the end of one piece.

12. Turn your bag the right way out and use the safety pin to thread the ribbon through the channel of one side of the bag.

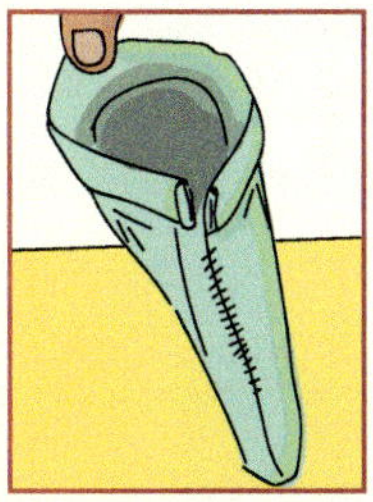

13. Thread the other half of the ribbon through the other channel and press the whole thing.

14. Sew on any embellishments, making sure that you fix them to one side of the bag only.

Chapter 4   Practical Guide to Costume Design   93

FOCUS

Thinking of existing items of clothing and furnishings that you can alter.

ASSESSMENT CHECK

Your imagination and creativity here will help you towards AO1: 'Create and develop ideas to communicate meaning for theatrical performance.'

Charity shops can be a source of inspiration as well as materials and resources.

LOOK HERE

See pages 90–91 for ideas on sourcing items, and pages 92–93 for the sewing techniques.

TASK 4.10

1. Look at the costume design you are currently working on.
2. Could parts of it be made, or all of it adapted, from an existing garment?
3. Could items you need be cut from a large domestic item such as a sheet? Should this be plain or patterned? Light or dark? Does it need certain qualities, such as being strong, lightweight or shiny?

ADAPTING COSTUME ITEMS

Why should I think about upcycling?

Your budget will be small and you need to stay within it. This does not mean, however, that your design cannot be creative, imaginative and effective.

You can be very successful in starting a costume with an item of clothing to upcycle. It minimises waste and is cheap. It can also help with your choices of colours, textures and patterns.

Recycling fabric

Buying a curtain, tablecloth or duvet cover that you can cut up to make an apron or skirt, for example, is a cheap and easy way of finding suitable fabric.

You can then use the offcuts to make accessories such as a headscarf, belt, collars and cuffs. This complementary use of fabric can pull a costume together and create an impression of the character.

Modifying and adapting clothing

Many items of found or cheaply bought clothing can be remodelled by:

- lengthening or shortening
- adding or removing collars
- changing or replacing sleeves
- adding accessories and embellishments
- altering the shape and fit, including padding or panelling.

Here are a few ideas:

- Buy a jacket and remove or shorten the sleeves. You could also change or remove the buttons. Perhaps eyelets and lacing could be added for a different period, such as this 16th-century-style jerkin.
- Find a skirt of suitable fabric and alter the length or silhouette.
- Remove the cuff from the gathered sleeve of a blouse to create a flare. Alternatively, add a longer cuff to suggest a different era.
- Use a cheap prom or bridesmaid's dress as the basis of a period ball gown or evening dress.
- Add sleeves in a contrasting fabric to a top to change its look.
- Customise an item with embellishments such as buttons, feathers, bows, **appliqués**, sequins, lace and beads.

94 Chapter 4 Practical Guide to Costume Design

Health and safety in costume design

You hold some responsibility for the safety of the actors you costume and also for your own health and safety. Your examiners need to know that you have considered the risks and have acted accordingly.

Thinking about yourself as designer and maker, take care that you:

- ! Use scissors, sewing equipment and irons appropriately and extremely carefully.
- ! Work in adequate light.
- ! Tidy away equipment carefully after use to protect everyone using the space.
- ! Take frequent breaks – at least a ten-minute break every hour.

It is very important that you gather information about your actors, as they might have sensitive skin or allergies to things such as:

- ! Certain metals, that might be used in jewellery
- ! Specific fabrics or fibres
- ! Detergents (washing powders and fabric softeners)
- ! Ingredients in make-up products
- ! Adhesives that might be used for masks, wigs or make-up features.

The use of make-up and hair products has potential risks. Some important considerations are:

- ! Use clean hands.
- ! Avoid putting your fingers in make-up in order to prevent contamination.
- ! Wash brushes, sponges and applicators thoroughly at the end of every session.
- ! Have a ready supply of basic cleansers, toners and moisturisers, and cotton wool pads.
- ! Check beforehand with your actors that they are not allergic to any of the chemicals or ingredients in the products.

Heavy or restrictive costumes could prevent actors moving freely and potentially be dangerous. The same could be said for high-heeled footwear, for example, and very long skirts. Collaboration with the actors and the set designer should help to avoid hazards.

FOCUS
Considerations for keeping yourself, your group members and your audience safe.

ASSESSMENT CHECK
The requirement that your costumes are designed and made safely comes under AO2: 'Use theatrical skills to realise artistic intentions in live performance.'

For both Components 2 and 3, you are expected to adopt the latest safe working practices.

Chapter 4 Practical Guide to Costume Design 95

FOCUS

The role of hair and make-up in costume design and how you can make your own interpretations.

ASSESSMENT CHECK

This knowledge should help you to:

- select appropriate materials to realise a make-up design showing an understanding of different types of make-up
- create hairstyles appropriate to character, period, age, ethnicity
- create character through make-up: aging, fantasy characters.

DESIGN TIP

Research the look you need, based on your knowledge of the text and character, to arrive at a workable design.

DESIGN TIP

If you buy a mask, try to add your own embellishments to enhance your role as a designer. This will make the mask unique.

HAIR, MAKE-UP AND MASKS

No costume design is complete without a consideration of hair and make-up.

HAIR AND WIGS

Hairstyles need to suit the characters and match the style of the costumes and period of the play. Assess whether you can work with the actor's own hairstyle to suit the style of the play and the context of the character.

Also think about the character's personality and any changes they undergo. Hair in a bun, for example, could be let down as an effective way to show that a character is relaxing or is distraught, for instance. Putting hair up neatly could indicate an upward change of status.

Wigs are very useful for completely changing a hairstyle. A wig can have instant impact in period plays or for styles that are not easily achievable with the actor's own hair. They can also be cut and coloured as needed. They are fairly cheaply available from specialist stores.

HAIR SPECIAL EFFECTS

Ageing or unconventional looks can be aided with wash-out colour sprays, but don't exaggerate the use of grey unless you are aiming for comedy. Colours might be useful for a fantasy or science-fiction play or as part of an animal costume. Use fake facial hair sparingly to avoid unwanted humour. Always use specialist adhesive!

Careful use of back-combing adds volume to hair, and products such as gel can smooth and flatten, which can significantly change a hairstyle.

If your school or college has a hairdressing department, you might find that teachers and students are keen to be involved. This is extremely helpful for you and can often contribute to those students' coursework.

MASKS

Masks can have a dramatic impact and make a significant contribution to your costume design. However, they should always be an integral part of your design rather than an add on. Ask yourself how your decision to incorporate a mask contributes to the dramatic intentions of the piece as a whole.

Note that covering a performer's face with a neutral mask distances the audience. The actor must rely on physicality to convey mood and character.

Edward Hogg as Romeo at the Globe Theatre.

96 Chapter 4 Practical Guide to Costume Design

Make-up

Stage make-up is important for a number of reasons:

- It helps make facial features more visible, which helps the audience to see expressions clearly. Even when a character would not be wearing make-up, a little carefully applied lipstick in one shade darker than the lips accentuates the mouth, and eyes could be lightly lined. A base layer (foundation or powder) can be helpful in reducing shine under stage lights.
- It can help to establish period, setting and character.
- It can suggest significant aspects of a character, such as age or job.

What products should I use?

Everyday cosmetics are fine for use on stage, but always check with actors for any allergies. For more unusual looks, theatrical make-up can be well worth the expense.

As with shapes and styles of clothing and hair, different cultures and periods of history are associated with certain make-up styles. These are easily researched and should form the basis of your designs.

Useful 'extras' include:

- false eyelashes
- temporary tattoos
- stick-on jewels
- nail polish.

Have a good supply of different brushes to obtain good quality, varied effects. Keep them (and everything else you use) very clean!

Special effects

Ageing make-up should be applied carefully and sparingly or it will look comical. A useful tip is to add shading or highlighting to existing laughter and frown lines.

Bruise wheels are highly effective and easy to use when you follow the instructions. They are useful for creating a range of injuries. Similar effects can be created with inexpensive specialist products, such as scar/modelling wax or liquid latex, and your imagination. You might find that even if a bruise, for instance, is not specified in the script, your interpretation of the character could mean that it reveals something about their broader life.

Be very careful with fake blood. It often contains dye that is difficult to remove from skin and fabric. Avoid very cheap products.

Christopher Ainslie has a completely green costume – including his hair and eyebrows – in his role as Oberon, king of the fairies, from *A Midsummer Night's Dream* (English National Opera).

LOOK HERE

Try Task 4.5 on page 84 to see how make-up can contribute to characterisation and meaning.

Make sure you follow the health and safety guidance on page 95 when trying out make-up and masks.

TASK 4.11

Draw a detailed hair and make-up design for a character you are currently studying. If you have tools and products available, ask your teacher if you can create the look on yourself or another member of your group.

Chapter 4 Practical Guide to Costume Design

FOCUS
Increasing your confidence in drawing clearly presented designs.

ASSESSMENT CHECK
Improving the quality of your presentation will help you to communicate your artistic intentions in your final designs.

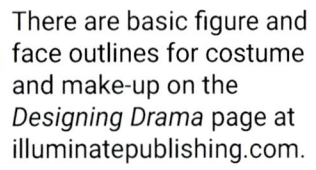

LOOK HERE
There are basic figure and face outlines for costume and make-up on the *Designing Drama* page at illuminatepublishing.com.

TASK 4.12
1. Browse magazines to find a standing, full-length figure of a man or woman. It is ideal if they are in underwear or swimwear.
2. Trace the outline of the figure onto plain paper. You do not need facial features or fingers.
3. On another piece of paper, have a go at sketching the figure freehand. Use short pencil strokes to create lines and curves. Be as basic or detailed as you like.
4. Look at your two versions. Decide which feels most promising and continue with that method. (You can always change your mind later.)
5. If both versions fill you with fear, try a fashion template. There are many online.

HOW TO DOCUMENT YOUR COSTUME DESIGN

All types of theatre designer must be able to show their design ideas long before the costumes, set, lighting and sound are actually created.

Costume design sketches by Alice Smith for Jude and Lynette in *Noughts & Crosses* at Nottingham Playhouse.

You do not need to be good at art to sketch your designs, but you certainly need to include drawn designs when working on your supporting documents for Component 2.

What documents do I need to produce?
In addition to making or supervising the construction of your costumes, you must produce on paper the final costume designs for:
- one character in Component 2
- one character per extract in Component 3.

If appropriate you must incorporate hair, make-up and mask considerations.

How do I create costume designs on paper?
It is entirely up to you whether you work **freehand** or use guides such as templates. Your drawings do not have to be 'pretty': the costume details are the important things.

The first thing to discover is what method of sketching suits you best.

If you choose to draw your designs from scratch, you might find the guidance on the following page helpful.

Chapter 4 Practical Guide to Costume Design

BODY PROPORTIONS

This guide should help you get the proportion of your figures correct if you are not a confident artist, but prefer to work without a ready-made template. Fashion drawings tend to elongate the body, so you should find that the following ratio is more suitable for costume design.

The head of the figure can be drawn as an oval of any size. Two further ovals underneath will take you down to the waistline, and a further three will take you to the ankles.

Developing your design

Below is a suggested sequence for moving from initial sketches to a finished costume design.

You will need to annotate or redraw your first designs after discussion with other designers and performers, and during and after rehearsals.

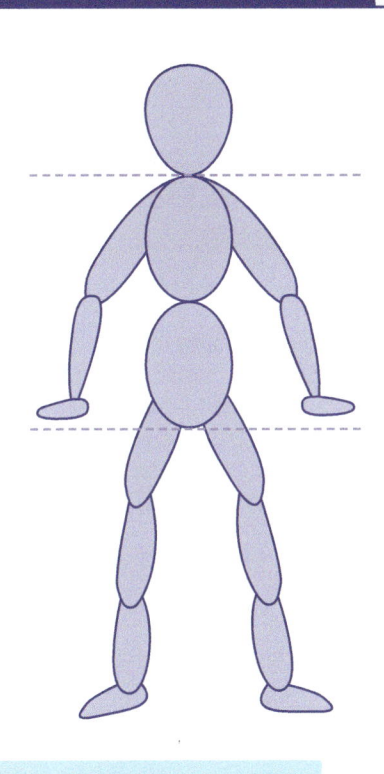

Smaller ovals can be used for hands and feet at the ends of approximated arms and legs.

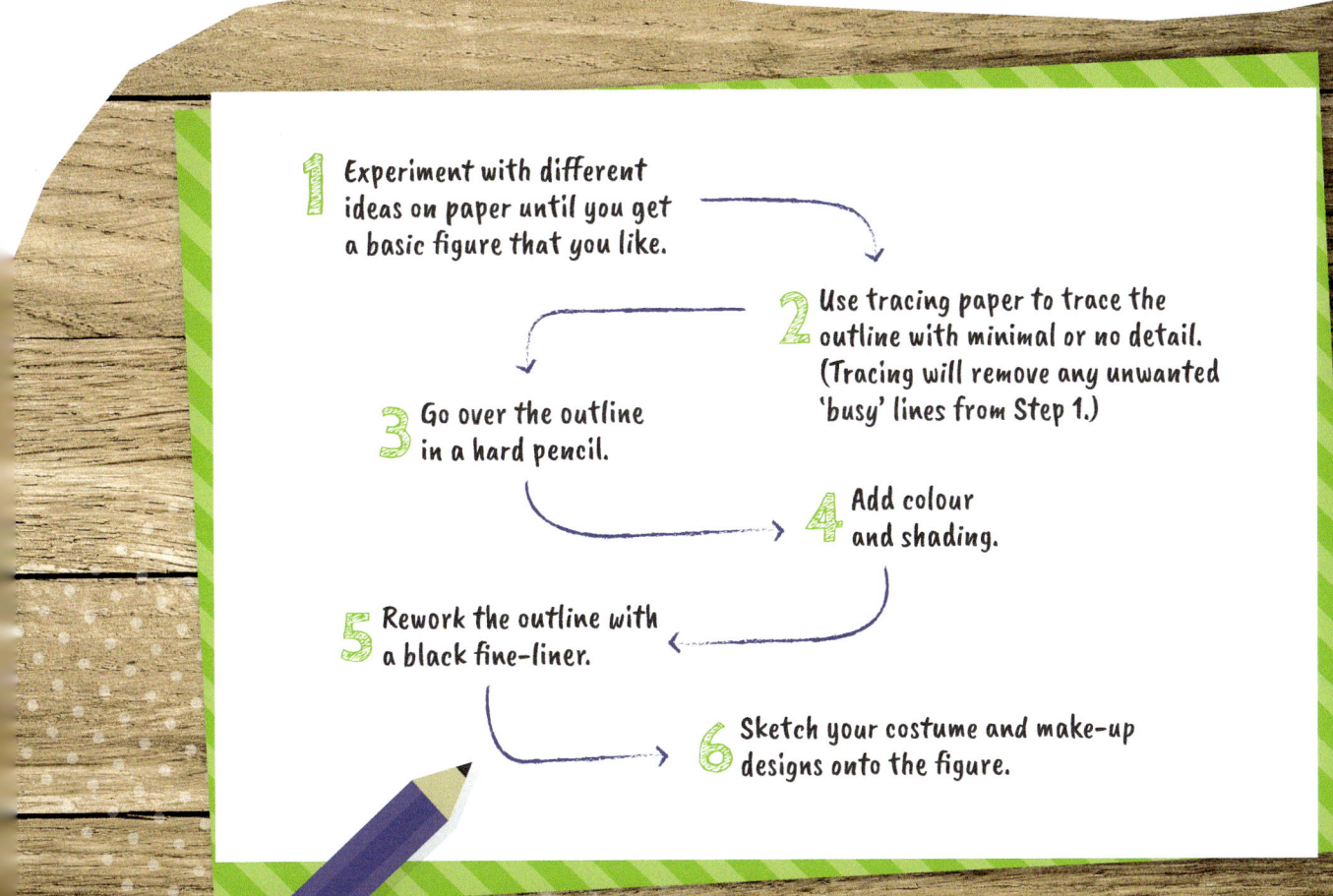

1. Experiment with different ideas on paper until you get a basic figure that you like.
2. Use tracing paper to trace the outline with minimal or no detail. (Tracing will remove any unwanted 'busy' lines from Step 1.)
3. Go over the outline in a hard pencil.
4. Add colour and shading.
5. Rework the outline with a black fine-liner.
6. Sketch your costume and make-up designs onto the figure.

Chapter 4   Practical Guide to Costume Design

FOCUS
Ensuring your costume fits and looks its best.

ASSESSMENT CHECK
Adjusting and fitting costumes shows that you are using refined theatrical skills and ideas and applying theatrical skills to realise your artistic intentions in the performance (AO2).

FITTING THE COSTUME

Your design needs to be 'refined and dynamic'. An ill-fitting costume will be neither of these.

To put together a costume that fits the performer early on, they need to try it on as you source, make and alter it.

Professionals continuously adjust a costume through a series of fitting sessions with the actor. This might even be right up to the performance.

Darts from the waistband of a skirt give a slim, fitted shape.

THE IMPORTANCE OF A WELL-FITTING COSTUME

Appearance
A badly fitting costume will not show your design as it should be. The silhouette will be altered if the costume doesn't hang properly, for example. Make sure that it is neither too big nor too tight.

Comfort
A badly fitting costume will hinder the actor's movements. The actor needs to be able to breathe, walk, stretch and sit in the costume. There are safety implications here too. An actor also needs a costume that will enhance the posture of their character. A casual item such as a sloppy jumper needs to be fitted to the actor, even if a 'bad' fit is a design choice.

How can I make my costume fit?
Everyone has an individual body shape proportioned in a unique way. This is why one pair of size 16 or 32" jeans will fit you very well, but a pair from another shop will not. You are unlikely to start altering the size of jeans, but it can be quite easy to adjust the fit of most garments for the stage.

The **type of fabric** a garment is made of will influence how you fit it.

Stiff fabric
This won't have much stretch, so you might need to use darts, tucks or gathers to alter the shape and make the garment smaller. Alternatively, a belt could be used to pull an item in.

Could you put a panel in the front or the back to make it bigger? For example, a panel of jersey fabric would give more ease as well as more volume. It could also add interest in terms of texture and colour

Stretchy fabric
Fabric with stretch has more ease of wear and movement. It can hug the figure but allow the actor freedom of movement.

You can try similar fitting techniques as for non-elastic fabric, above. In addition, you can alter the side seams on skirts or trousers and add elastic to necklines and waistbands.

Chapter 4 Practical Guide to Costume Design

COMMON FITTING ISSUES AND HOW YOU MIGHT SOLVE THEM

Avoid attempting to make a radical change to a sourced garment. If it is much too big or too small, get something else! Minor adjustments, however, can be very successful.

All of the following ideas can be achieved without taking a garment apart.

Too long

It is not difficult to reduce the length of everything from hems to sleeves. You could carefully cut away excess fabric and re-hem the garment, as long as the style is not complicated. If the bottom of a dress or skirt is very fancy, you might be able to take it up at the waist. You could add elastic to the bottom of long sleeves or simply fold them upwards.

If the top half of a garment looks saggy, try lifting it at the shoulders by shortening its straps or creating a dart. You need to remember, however, that the armholes will also be lifted and that it won't lie properly if the garment has sleeves. Shoulder pads are a possibility, but they are generally best in science-fiction, fantasy or costumes for the 1950s or 1980s.

Too short

Solving this can be a bit trickier than lengthening garments, but there are a couple of tricks you can try. Add borders or frills to sleeves and/or hems, for example. Simply seam them together on the wrong side. You will probably need to use a different material, so, unless you can find something very similar, choose fabric with a strong contrast (difference) in colour and perhaps texture. If you can add a piece of the same material in another place on the costume, this will give a well-finished look.

Darting the shoulders will lift the arm section of a garment. The darted section of fabric should be wider at the shoulder edge than the neck edge.

TASK 4.13

On the dress above, can you see two other places where the same white material could be added to give a considered, balanced look?

LOOK HERE

'Key process – sewing' on pages 92–93 will show you how to make a seam.

Chapter 4   Practical Guide to Costume Design   101

Too big

First, ask the actor to put on the costume to find out where there is too much fabric. Depending on the style of the garment, you might be able to simply sew in some elastic or add a belt. If so, carefully consider shape and size to ensure the whole costume suits the required period and style.

Another possibility would be to remove fabric by taking in the side seams. However, you can only take in side seams all the way from top to bottom if the garment doesn't have sleeves. If most of the extra fabric is around the waistline, you could try adding diamond-shaped darts on each side of the centre-front and centre-back lines.

The costume designer has added a wide elasticated belt to improve the fit and style of this dress.

A good alternative might also be to add wide pieces of elastic to pull a garment in. This could be done at the back or the sides for a natural look or vertically to add a more stylised effect. You could make a feature of the gathering by adding a button or bow, for example. This would make the gather appear to be a deliberate aspect of the design.

Shirred waistband.
Paperbag waistband.
Tiered waistband.
Fold-down waistband.

Necklines

Necklines can be adjusted and embellished to great effect. This is easier if the garment does not have a collar. You could add elastic, a drawstring or laces to a loose neck or one where you have removed the collar. This kind of technique can be useful for creating a period costume for characters in *The Crucible*, for example.

An infill can solve the problem of a neckline that is too low, as well as improving the appearance. Use lace or a contrasting stiff fabric.

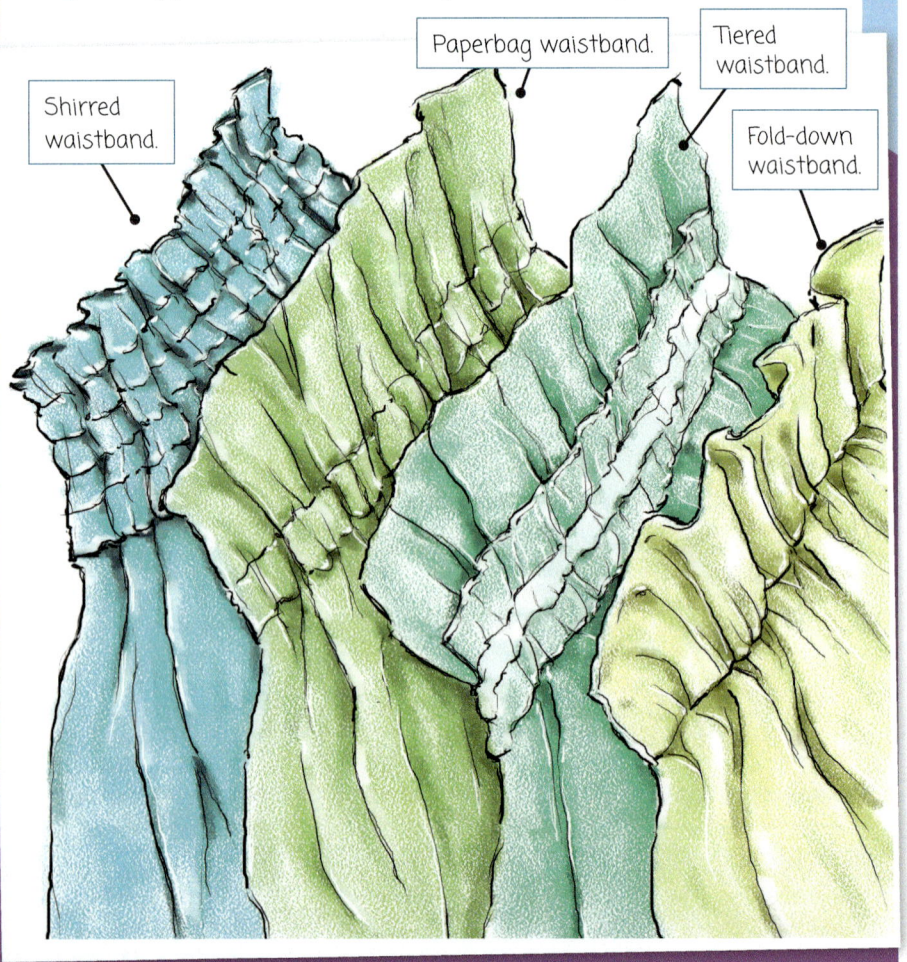

Button extenders can add a little more room and stretch to a waistband.

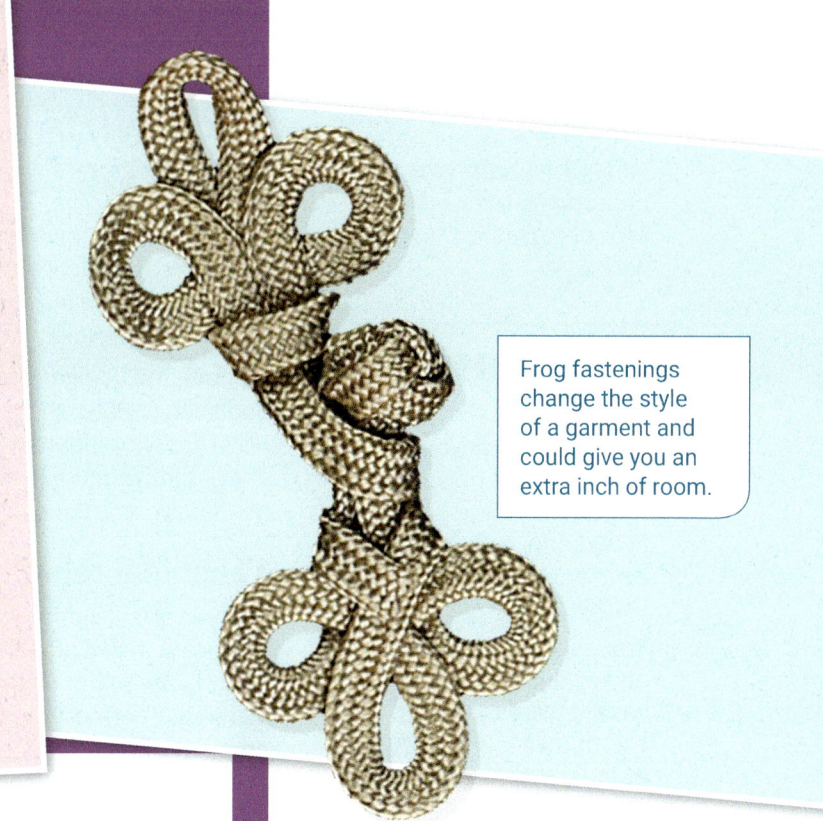

Frog fastenings change the style of a garment and could give you an extra inch of room.

Too small

It is often more difficult to add fabric than to take it away, but there are tricks that can solve the problem. If a garment pulls at the front because it is too tight, for example, you could move the buttons or change the type of fastening. Button extenders are useful too.

If skirts or trousers are too tight at the waist, you could move a button (or use extenders). If there is not a waistband, you could let out a seam. Another option would be to insert a panel of appropriate shape in a similar or contrasting fabric. You would probably need to cut the garment and use seams to insert extra fabric. Stretch fabrics would give extra ease. It is a good idea to balance the contrast fabric elsewhere on the costume if the panel is visible.

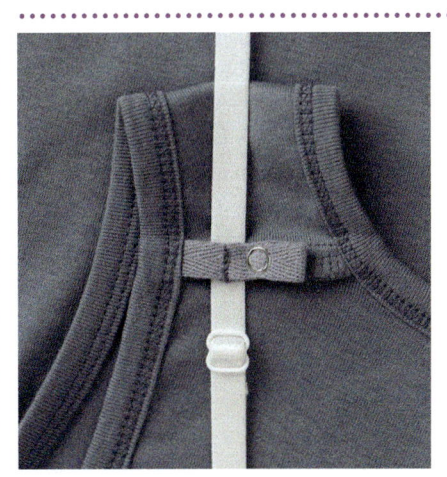

Underwear matters

If the costume has a fitted silhouette, it is very important to consider what will be underneath it. For a good fit, you need to think about the style of underwear your actors should wear. Adding bra-strap loops to a neckline will keep straps hidden.

You might also need to advise your male actors on the question of briefs or boxers if it could affect the costume!

DESIGN TIP
Be adventurous! Costume design is a great opportunity to unleash your creativity.

TASK 4.14
Select a garment that you are thinking of using for your costume. Try it on the actor and experiment with adjusting the fit using some of the techniques above.

Chapter 4 Practical Guide to Costume Design

FOCUS

Final rehearsals: your last opportunity to check that your design is working well.

ASSESSMENT CHECK

Rehearsals help you to develop your knowledge and understanding of how drama and theatre is developed and performed (AO3).

You also reflect, analyse and evaluate (AO4), and work towards a design that shows understanding of the peformer/audience relationship.

DESIGN TIP

Try not to interrupt the rehearsal unless there is a health and safety issue.

TECHNICAL AND DRESS REHEARSALS FOR COSTUME DESIGNERS

The rehearsal schedule works towards a technical and then a dress rehearsal. These are the rehearsals that draw everything together.

As costume designer, sit in the audience area for the rehearsals. Have your notebook to hand and check that your costumes are meeting your artistic intentions.

Technical rehearsal

This rehearsal is for technicians and designers. It will probably be the first opportunity to put all the production elements (performers, lights, sound, costumes and set) together. If you encounter some typical problems, try the suggestions below.

Potential problems	Possible solutions and timings
An element of the costume does not look right. Perhaps the skirt looks too long or the actor is pulling the top down all the time.	Decide if you can make changes before the dress rehearsal. If not, get it done before the performance.
An actor is having difficulties with some aspect of a costume. For example, they struggle to make a costume change onstage or in the wings.	Work with the actor after the tech to see if the costume can be altered with a change of fastenings, for example. Or, another cast member could help with changing.
A costume does not look as good as you had hoped under some of the lighting states.	Note down which scenes are causing the problem. Talk to the lighting designer before the dress rehearsal and see if you can come to a compromise in the intensity or colour of lighting.

Dress rehearsal

The 'dress' is the final, timed, **run** before the performance. Now that technical issues have been addressed, the performers can run through the production uninterrupted.

Again, watch from the audience area with a notebook. Move around and look out for the following:

- Have changes from the tech been made successfully?
- Are the actors happy with their costumes and any changes they need to make during the performance?

If there are still issues, revisit your notes and the table above. Work with your colleagues to tackle problems. Make final tweaks as necessary.

Chapter 4 Practical Guide to Costume Design

EVALUATING YOUR COSTUME DESIGN

Once you are clear about what evaluation is and the best way of approaching it, you can focus on assessing the success of your costume design.

> Using tops that contain lots of stretch was a very effective choice because it meant that the performers could move freely. There was good definition of their arms and legs too, which was important for the physical theatre aspects of the devised piece. One part of my design that was particularly successful in supporting our artistic intentions was the use of colour. Green and earthy colours are associated with nature...

Lord of the Flies at Theatr Clwyd. (S R Taylor Photography.)

Examining the detail of your design

Whenever you evaluate, you should make at least three different points. These points should be illustrated with specific examples. Each time, you should also explain the reason why you have made a particular value judgement. You should highlight anything that could have gone better.

TASK 4.15

1. Use a table like this (some examples have been included) to make notes for your evaluation.

Costume design evaluation			
Design element	**Moment in the play**	**Evaluation**	**Reason for evaluation**
Stretch in T-shirts	Physical theatre sections.	Effective in performance.	Performers were able to move freely and extend clearly defined arms fully.
Colour – greens and browns	Throughout, but particularly full of impact in the poem section.	Successful in supporting artistic intentions.	I avoided making the costumes look like uniforms, but similarity suited context and added mood and atmosphere. Combined well with set and lighting. Addition of costume items for poem added meaning.
Masks	NB: Use image – refer to drawings and photos.	Powerful, darkly comic effect.	Masks enhanced black comedy of the scene. Clear impact on audience.

2. Expand your notes into three paragraphs of evaluative writing. Make sure you relate your finished design to your artistic intentions.

FOCUS
Placing a value judgement on design.

ASSESSMENT CHECK
In Component 2, you need to demonstrate your ability to analyse and evaluate the realisation of creative intentions. In the written exam for Component 1, you might evaluate a professional costume designer's work.

SIGNPOST
Read the evaluation guidance on page 78.

LOOK HERE
More examples of evaluation can be found in Chapter 7.

COSTUME VOCABULARY

Accessories Items such as bags, jewellery and small items that accompany garments.

Allergies Adverse reactions in the body (for example to breathing or the skin) to certain products or ingredients.

Appliqué A small colourful piece of embroidery – often a picture or pattern – sewn onto an item of clothing.

Back stitch A closely worked stitch done by hand.

Bruise wheel Available from theatre make-up sellers, a palette of yellows, reds, browns and cream make-up, excellent for a range of special effects.

Collaboration Working with others towards a common aim.

Colour palette A complementary set of colours that belong to a group, such as pastel or dark.

Darting Sewing small, tapered folds into a garment to provide shape or otherwise alter the fit.

Embellishments Added extras such as lace, buttons, braids and so on; decorative details.

Evaluate Give an opinion, a value judgement, backed up with examples and reasons.

Fabric choice Considerations such as suitability and effect under lights.

Finish The surface of fabric – usually shiny or dull.

Freehand Drawing something without a tracing or template to guide you.

Mass-produced Made in great numbers, usually in a factory.

Monochrome Black, white and grey only.

Natural In terms of fabric – not man-made. Examples of natural fabric are cotton and wool.

Pattern Design printed onto or woven into fabric, including tartan, paisley, stripes. A paper pattern is the template pieces that guide sewers as they cut cloth out to make into garments.

Rehearsal costumes Practice clothes or shoes that bear some similarity to the final costume.

Run Either a rehearsal or read-through of the whole play, or the number of times a play will be performed (for example, *The Crucible* has a three-week run at this theatre).

Seam The joining of two pieces of fabric on the wrong side.

Silhouette The outline shape of a costume.

Status symbol A possession that is seen to show someone's wealth, social position or sense of style.

Style Distinctive appearance, often typical of a particular person, period or place.

Subculture A cultural trend in society that is not the dominant one, such as goth, punk.

Symbolic use of colour The use of colour to communicate a certain meaning or represent a particular theme or mood.

Stylised Non-realistic, non-naturalistic, where style features are dominant.

Swatch A small sample of fabric that gives an idea of how an item made from it would look and feel.

Synthetic Man-made (fabric).

Tacking A fast, long, hand-made, temporary stitch to hold seams together ready for trying on or for permanent stitching.

Texture The surface feel of fabric, for example. Raised fabrics, such as velvet and cord, have a different texture from smooth ones, such as silk, which are flat.

Upcycle Taking an existing garment and changing it in some way to make something different.

Wardrobe The wardrobe department is where the costumes are produced in a theatre. Alternatively, our wardrobe is the collection of clothes we own.

Weight How heavy or light is the fabric? Does it drape or hang heavily?

PRACTICAL GUIDE TO PUPPET DESIGN

Chapter 5

Introduction to puppet design	108
Why choose puppets?	109
The cultural and historical importance of puppets	110
Types of puppet	112
Which type of puppet should I design?	116
Research for puppet design	118
How to document your puppet design	119
Health and safety in puppet design	119
Creating your puppet for the stage	120
Animating puppets	122
Technical and dress rehearsals for puppet designers	124
Evaluating your puppet design	125
Puppet design vocabulary	126

FOCUS

Understanding the potential that puppet design has for creating exciting theatre.

ASSESSMENT CHECK

As you gain awareness and understanding of puppetry as a design element, you are:

- learning how to design and realise puppets that contribute positively to the overall performance and communicate meaning
- gaining knowledge and understanding of how drama and theatre is developed and performed (AO3).

INTRODUCTION TO PUPPET DESIGN

Puppetry might seem rather unfamiliar to you as a student of drama. However, if you have seen *War Horse* or *The Lion King* on stage, your interest might have been kindled. Puppets have a unique role in the world of theatre and, in recent years, have been central to some memorable, groundbreaking productions.

The Lion King uses stunning puppetry to re-create the plains of the savannah.

War Horse is an outstanding example of complex and emotive animal puppetry.

TASK 5.1

1. Think back over your life to identify moments where you have:
   - seen a puppet in everyday life or on stage
   - used or played with a puppet
   - made a puppet
   - seen puppets used on film or television.
2. Share your experiences with a classmate. What similarities and differences do you find?

Puppets take you into another world, and almost anything can be used to make one. They can also be thought of as the earliest form of **animation**.

Puppets can have immense impact. Sometimes, this is because of their size.

Although **shadow puppetry** originated for use on a simple stage, its effects can be found in films, such as this example from *Harry Potter and the Deathly Hallows*. Its presence has a distancing and magical effect.

The Little Girl starts her journey at Liverpool King's Dock as part of the Royal de Luxe *Sea Odyssey* street theatre.

Chapter 5 Practical Guide to Puppet Design

WHY CHOOSE PUPPETS?

FOCUS
Reasons for considering puppetry as for your practical design work.

ASSESSMENT CHECK
Exploring puppetry helps you to create and develop ideas to communicate meaning in a theatrical performance (AO1).

A Theatre Studies student at Aberystwyth University manipulates two puppets in a production of *Riddley Walker*.

You might never have made or used a puppet before. There are many good reasons, however, to consider puppetry as a practical option for Component 2 or 3 of your Drama course.

* Puppets can be used creatively to communicate messages in a 'safe' way.

* They enable engaging and imaginative storytelling.

* You can have fun making puppets and bringing them to life. Your audience will be amused by them too.

* Puppets can characterise animals and fantasy figures more easily than human actors might be able to.

* You might want to be part of a performance, but prefer to be a puppet **animator** rather than an actor.

* Puppets are a highly effective way of bringing humour and audience interaction to a performance.

* Puppets can be simple to make and operate or more complex and sophisticated. The choice is yours.

TASK 5.2

Discuss with a learning partner:
- Which reason for using puppet design appeals to you most?
- How convinced are you to consider puppet design for your practical design work. Why?

Chapter 5 Practical Guide to Puppet Design 109

FOCUS
The rich diversity and history of puppetry.

An ornate Thai shadow puppet made from stained and punctured leather.

ASSESSMENT CHECK
Your research will develop your knowledge and understanding of how drama and theatre is developed and performed (AO3).

Puppets at a water theatre in Hanoi. These simple wooden rod puppets have their origins in the flooded paddy fields of 11th-century Vietnam.

THE CULTURAL AND HISTORICAL IMPORTANCE OF PUPPETS

There is evidence that puppets have a longer history in drama than human actors do, with traditions that stretch back for many centuries. Most ancient cultures developed their own style of puppetry to tell stories, conduct rituals and to inform and entertain people. To this day, traditional puppets retain a significant cultural role throughout the world.

Storytelling
As narrator or as character, puppets have taken a role in the telling of tales since ancient times. The earliest puppets we know about were being used in India in the second century BCE. These were **shadow puppets** used to 'illustrate' ancient stories of humans and demons.

Around 350 years ago were the early appearances of the character who becomes Punch in the **puppet-booth** seaside shows that are still seen today.

Regional cultures
Culturally, the use of puppets for entertainment often grew from environmental conditions or local traditions.

Kathputli puppet shows are native to Rajasthan. Historically, these provided moral and social education as well as entertainment.

Photo: John Webb

A traditional Kathputli theatre, with simple but elaborately costumed string puppets, in Jaipur.

Chapter 5 — Practical Guide to Puppet Design

Health and politics

Puppets have frequently been used to 'speak' messages across the world. They are particularly helpful when dealing with sensitive issues or during times of oppression when puppets can get away with 'saying' things that people might find difficult.

In South Africa, for example, Gary Friedman's community theatre Puppets for Democracy was established to help educate people in the mechanics of voting in the first democratic elections in 1994. It was very important that people understood that their vote would be secret and fair.

DESIGN TIP
Visit www.vam.ac.uk/articles/a-history-of-puppets-in-britain for information and inspiration about the history of puppets in Britain.

Photo: Nan Melville (New York)

Nelson Mandela on the campaign trail, being interviewed by Clarence Keyter, a rod-and-glove combination puppet.

Photo: Gisèle Wulfsohn

Gary Friedman's outreach programme Puppets Against Aids also helped to communicate health information, allay fears and present the facts about a taboo subject, such as here in Cape Town.

Prime Minister Margaret Thatcher was a memorable glove-and-rod puppet in the satirical television programme *Spitting Image*.

'Major', a glove puppet, rehearsing with a musician for a performance at Cumberland Infirmary, Carlisle. Notice how the **focus** of the puppet is clearly on the musician.

TASK 5.3

1. Find out about a puppet theatre company from your culture or from one that interests you.
   - What is the name and location of the puppet company?
   - Does it exist to entertain and/or to educate?
   - Is the company linked to a particular tradition or culture?
   - What style(s) of puppet does the company use?
2. Can you find images of its puppets? Create a slide presentation to share with your class.

DESIGN TIP
Visit www.campquality.org.au to see the friendly puppet characters the charity Camp Quality uses to bring laughter and comfort to children facing cancer.

Chapter 5   Practical Guide to Puppet Design

FOCUS

How to identify the type of puppet that will best suit the needs of your production.

A sculpture in Omsk, Russia, of Harlequin with his glove puppet Petrushka.

ASSESSMENT CHECK

Making informed choices will help you to:
- explain the process of refining your initial ideas and intentions
- select materials that show characterisation and understanding of puppet types.

An expressive Miss Piggy reveals one of her rods!

DESIGN TIP

Some glove puppets also use rods to operate the arms. These are **hand-and-rod puppets** and are how the Muppets were created.

TYPES OF PUPPET

Puppets can be made from all sorts of materials and can be crafted into a great variety of shapes and sizes. They can convey human, animal and fantasy characters, expressing and provoking a full range of emotions.

Glove, hand and sock puppets

Glove puppets have been in existence for a very long time. The earliest ones were probably made and used in ancient Egypt where they were made from ivory and clay.

They are cheap to make and easy to use and carry around, so glove puppets have a strong tradition in street theatre across the world.

Working a glove puppet

To operate a glove or **hand puppet**, you might use the index finger (or index and middle fingers) to **manipulate** the head, with the thumb and middle (or ring) finger within the arms of the puppet.

Glove puppets can simply reach to the wrist or can have a longer body with legs attached. In that case, the forearm of the animator will be concealed. Glove puppets with long bodies and feet that hang down beyond the hand are great fun.

Television entertainer Rod Hull and his puppet Emu join in the fun on a Clacton beach. Emu got up to a lot of mischief that Hull would not have been able to without him! (The arm across Emu's body is false.)

TASK 5.4

Create a sock puppet in about ten minutes.
1. Grab a sock (long ones will cover your arm and give you more to decorate, but it doesn't really matter).
2. Put your hand into the foot and form a mouth.
3. Use a pen to mark positions for the eyes and nose.
4. Glue or stitch on eyes (buttons work well).
5. Add a felt nose or tongue, and use pipe cleaners, wool, pompoms for hair, ears and so on if you wish. (See the example on page 116.)
6. Give your puppet a name and introduce them to somebody in the room.

Rod puppets

Rod puppets have been used since ancient times and are known to have been particularly important in Indonesia, Japan and China. They are also the most commonly used type in shadow puppetry.

Generally, rod puppets are manipulated from below through the use of wooden or metal sticks (rods). This type of puppet works particularly well on stage if it is jointed in some way to create a range of realistic gestures.

Rod puppets can be supported on simple stands so the animator is free to concentrate on the movement of head and limbs. Rods can also be attached in a wide variety of places to achieve the desired type of movement. Some basic puppets can be operated with a single rod. Others need more than one person to animate them. If the head of a rod puppet can move, this greatly increases its expressiveness.

In this touching scene from *War Horse*, the young foal Joey is helped to graze by three animators.

The long rods of this traditional Chinese puppet allow the **puppeteer** to operate the character from below.

TASK 5.5

Make a quick rod puppet (person, fish, snake, monster… your choice!)
1. Draw the outline of a character on a piece of card.
2. Decide which parts of the puppet should move (legs and/or arms, for example).
3. Cut out all the parts.
4. Use paper fasteners to connect all parts of the puppet together.
5. Paint and decorate the puppet.
6. Use tape to attach a rod to the back of each main moving part. (For a long puppet such as a snake or dragon, you could fan-fold the main body and have one rod for the head and another for the tail.)
7. Work with at least one other person to create a conversation or short scene.

Visit www.redtedart.com for details of how to make this Day of the Dead puppet and a range of other puppets.

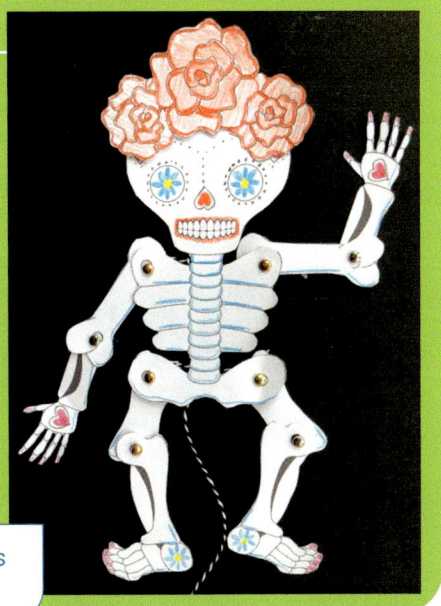

© Maggy Woodley / Red Ted Art

Chapter 5 Practical Guide to Puppet Design 113

Marionettes

This type of puppet is suspended on strings. **Marionettes** might have originated in Egypt. They were certainly in use as early as 2000BC. They can be operated successfully with a minimum of five strings or threads, which are usually attached to a wooden frame.

The puppets themselves can be made from a wide range of materials, including wood, papier mâché and cloth.

Although marionettes can be complex and expensive to produce, effective ones can be made simply from card and string.

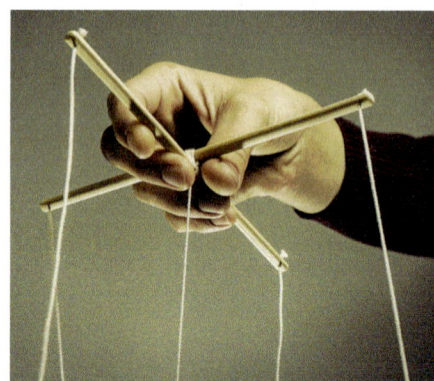

Thunderbirds are go! A fan enjoys operating a Scott Tracy marionette.

By tilting and moving the frame and by pulling individual strings, the puppeteer can give the marionette a great range of movement.

Shadow puppets

These puppets are defined by the way they are presented to the audience: shadows of the puppet shapes appear on a screen.

The image is produced by shining a light from behind the screen with the puppet between it and the light. The size of the shadow shrinks and sharpens as the puppet is placed closer to the screen and further from the **light source**.

Originally, the light source was the Sun, a burning torch or a candle. These days an electric bulb or theatre lantern provide safer alternatives.

The impact that shadow puppets can make is enormous compared with the cost and effort involved. Just some simple cardboard scenery, for example, could be added to enhance the setting.

Shadow puppets can be very expressive and are full of impact.

Little Red Riding Hood's rod shadow puppet being chased by the Wolf.

A Thai shadow puppet artist at work. These puppets are beautifully decorated even though it is often only their shadows that are seen on the other side of the screen.

114 Chapter 5 Practical Guide to Puppet Design

> **TASK 5.6**
>
> Working as a small group or a whole class, set up your own shadow puppet theatre.
>
> 1 Gather the materials that you will need, including:
>   - a pale sheet or large piece of cloth for the screen, and something to hang it over
>   - a light source, such as a large torch or a stage lantern
>   - shapes to create the shadows such as glove and/or simple cardboard rod puppets, interesting objects such as teapots, your own hands or bodies.
>   - some card scenery to lean against the screen.
> 2 Tell a simple story or retell a fairy tale that can be narrated or **voiced** by your puppets.

Back/rucksack puppets

Puppets that can be worn on the back of an animator have great scope for impact. This is partly because they can be a very large size. The metal frame of a rucksack is used to support the puppet. This is likely to be extended upwards with the use of additional metal or wooden rods. This usually leaves the wearer's arms free to operate the puppet's limbs and so on, but additional animators are sometimes needed too.

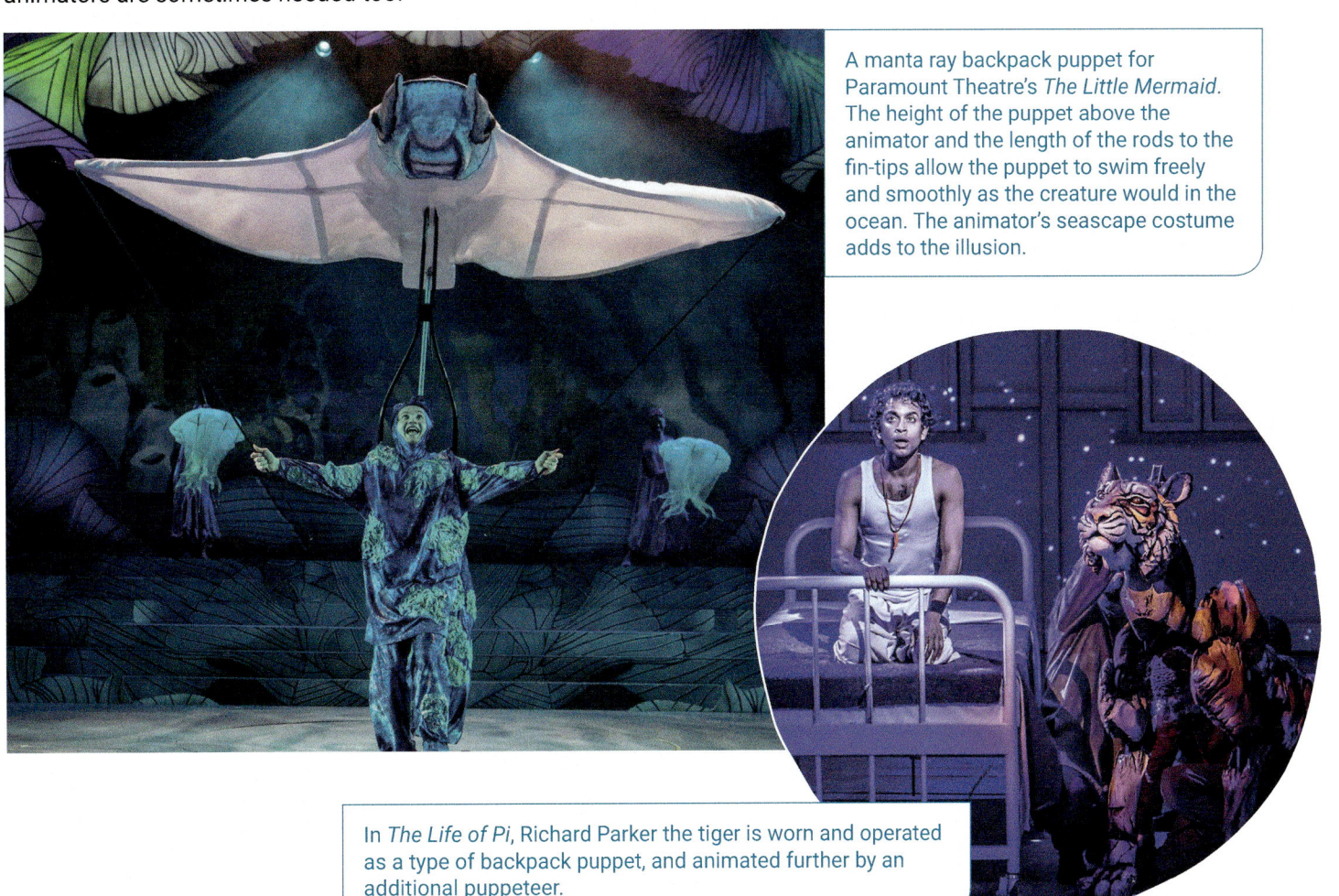

A manta ray backpack puppet for Paramount Theatre's *The Little Mermaid*. The height of the puppet above the animator and the length of the rods to the fin-tips allow the puppet to swim freely and smoothly as the creature would in the ocean. The animator's seascape costume adds to the illusion.

In *The Life of Pi*, Richard Parker the tiger is worn and operated as a type of backpack puppet, and animated further by an additional puppeteer.

Chapter 5 Practical Guide to Puppet Design

FOCUS

Deciding what sort of puppet will best suit your purposes.

ASSESSMENT CHECK

Your research here will help you to realise a puppet that shows understanding of:

- structural design, size, shape, scale; functionality, performer manipulation skills and intentions of the performance
- a variety of puppet types.

DESIGN TIP

To see the War Goose puppet in action, visit https://youtu.be/Q3lQJNFF0q0.

This sock puppet is simply made but has excellent character definition.

DESIGN TIP

The 'voice' of the puppet will add a great deal of information about its character. Consider pitch, tone, pace and expression.

WHICH TYPE OF PUPPET SHOULD I DESIGN?

The success of a puppet can be largely dependent on two factors.

A clearly defined character

When an actor creates a character, they have many complex tools at their disposal, including subtle use of voice, movement and facial expression. A puppeteer is almost certain to be more limited, which is why careful decisions need to be made in order for characterisation to be effective. Some puppets have greater capacity for varied facial expressions. Hand puppets are a good example of this as their mouths can often be opened.

In general, eye placement is crucial to giving any type of puppet personality. You should always experiment with their placement before they are attached or painted. If you want your puppet to be able to 'look' at you or the audience, the eyes need to be clearly visible. You should also consider the size of the eyes and how close together they are.

Audience appeal

Audience appeal is closely related to having a clearly defined character. Its focus is on the ability of the puppet to draw audience engagement. Many puppets rely on their movement to create audience appeal. The goose in *War Horse*, for example, plays a comic role which depends on the skill of its animator as much as on its design and construction. The speed with which this wheeled rod puppet moves alongside the action of actors on the stage is essential to its appeal.

Puppets may also have audience appeal because of their beauty, size or ability to interact.

Audience members meet a puppet fukuiraptor from Erth's Dinosaur Zoo at the Southbank Centre.

116 Chapter 5 Practical Guide to Puppet Design

How to choose your puppet

In choosing what type of puppet to make and use, you need to consider the potential strong points and weaknesses of each style, including practicalities.

Puppet type	Benefits	Challenges
Glove puppet	• Simple to make and use. • Excellent for picking up and holding things. • Interacts well with the audience.	Usually around 30cm long, glove puppets won't suit if you want a large puppet.
Rod puppet	• Easy to make and use. • Versatile in terms of form. • One rod can hold a number of small paper puppets, such as birds. • Several rods can allow sophisticated animation. • Possible to interact with the audience. • Excellent in shadow puppetry.	Complex puppets might need more than one person to operate them.
Marionette	Can be very graceful and create a range of gestures.	• Can be harder to make. • Need plenty of practice to make movements fluid. • Strings can become tangled.
Shadow puppet	• Ideal for creating 'other worlds'. • A great style to use if a character has a long journey. • Useful for large groups of characters, such as an army.	• Requires a screen and a light source, which needs to be created carefully if space is limited. • Very limited scope for audience interaction.
Back pack/ rucksack puppet	• Ideal for parades and carnivals and where there is plenty of space onstage. • Excellent for creating height and large-scale impact.	• Can be weighty and awkward. • Sometimes difficult to put on and take off. • Requires a spacious performance area. • Outside, wind can make them hazardous to wear.

In selecting the type of puppet to design, you should be thinking about creating a puppet that is easy to 'read' and effective for the audience. You need to think about:

- the size and configuration of your acting area
- the positioning of the audience
- your aims and intentions for the puppet.

Ask yourself if the audience members need to have an emotional engagement with the puppet. If so, how will you manage that in terms of design and pupeteer operation?

DESIGN TIP

Puppet types can be combined to make them more versatile. For example, a glove puppet could have rods to move its legs.

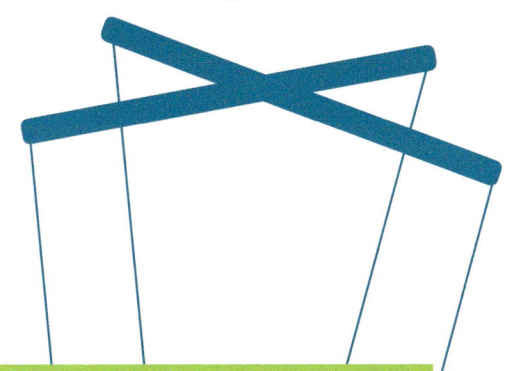

TASK 5.7

1. Imagine you are designing a puppet for a devised piece of theatre about looking after pets. You want the puppet to interact with the audience of primary school children. Use the table above to help you decide what type of puppet to design.

2. Draw an annotated sketch of your design, including the size of your puppet.

Chapter 5 Practical Guide to Puppet Design

FOCUS
Where to find information and inspiration for your own puppet design.

ASSESSMENT CHECK
This section will support you in explaining your research findings and how you developed and refined your ideas.

RESEARCH FOR PUPPET DESIGN

Even if you are creating a simple puppet, you should still research to make sure that your design:

- is a suitable type for the performance space. There is no point designing a shadow puppet, for example, if there is not enough room for a screen or the stage configuration is in the round.
- meets the needs of the production. Some puppets lend themselves to audience interaction better than others.
- is suitable for the character. If your puppet needs to 'speak', you might feel that a glove puppet is better than a marionette.
- can be manipulated effectively and used efficiently. Most people would struggle to get a rucksack puppet on and off quickly on their own.
- expresses a clear personality with audience appeal. You should research which type of 'eyes' will best communicate your intention for the puppet you are designing.
- Check through the table on page 117.

Where can I find the information I need?

Visit...
- Museums might have puppets from particular eras. Paintings can be inspiring in puppet design.
- Your local library can order specialist books for you.
- If there is a puppet theatre company nearby, get in touch. Nothing beats first-hand contact with puppets and the people who make and animate them.

Watch...
- Contemporary and 20th-century television programmes are a valuable resource for puppet designers. They show how puppets can be voiced, as well as how movement adds to characterisation. Older programmes can often be found on specialist channels and online.
- Look for special features on how puppets are made and operated in shows such as *War Horse*, *Avenue Q* and *The Lion King*.

Search...
- Video clips and instructions of how to make puppets.
- Images of particular types of puppet.
- Websites of puppet theatre companies.
- Interviews with puppet makers.

A puppet designer at work.

Rod puppets in the CBBC animated series *Strange Hill High*.

TV star glove puppet Basil Brush hosts an awards ceremony.

DESIGN TIP
Keep downloaded and bookmarked online resources in a research folder on your computer.

Chapter 5 Practical Guide to Puppet Design

HOW TO DOCUMENT YOUR PUPPET DESIGN

All types of theatre designer must be able to show their design ideas long before the puppets, costumes, set, lighting and sound are actually created.

You do not need to be good at art to draw your designs and they do not have to be pretty. Your sketches should, however, be clear and detailed.

- Sketch your puppet design front on and in profile (a side view).
- Create a transparent version that shows the structure of the puppet and/or how it is animated. Give the outline of the puppet and then its inner workings.
- Annotate the sketch with information about the materials you will use, including costume. Add details of size and colour.
- If you have space, give brief reasons for your choices. You might, for example, choose a light construction material or an item of clothing that suggests the puppet's personality.

HEALTH AND SAFETY IN PUPPET DESIGN

Many of the health and safety consideration for set and costume design on pages 75 and 95 are likely to apply to puppet design too.

For your own puppet, you need to consider, in particular:

- materials and construction methods (careful and proper use of tools, avoiding wood splinters and so on)
- the health and comfort of the animator (puppet weight, ease of manipulation, allergies)
- how you will make sure there is no risk to performers and audience members (stability of puppet, no sharp edges).

TASK 5.9

Study the documents you created for task 5.8. Make sure you have considered health and safety fully and make any necessary changes.

FOCUS
Increasing your confidence in drawing clear and informative designs.

ASSESSMENT CHECK
Improving the quality of your presentation will help you to communicate your artistic intentions.

TASK 5.8
Think of a puppet you would like to design. Draw three sketches: front, side and transparent with explanatory annotations.

DESIGN TIP
Plenty of detail in your drawn design will be a very useful addition to your devising log for Component 2. Similarly, your examiner will gain a clear idea of your artistic intentions in Component 3.

FOCUS
Considerations for keeping yourself, your group members and your audience safe.

ASSESSMENT CHECK
The expectation that your puppets are designed and made safely comes under AO2. For both Components 2 and 3, you must adopt the latest safe working practices.

FOCUS
Selecting materials and construction methods with which to realise your puppet design.

ASSESSMENT CHECK
By now, you are making appropriate choices that show understanding of a puppet's:
- structural design, size, shape, scale; functionality
- construction materials, colour, texture, shape, costume, potential for characterisation.

LOOK HERE
Pages 112–117 will help you decide what kind of puppet to make.

CREATING YOUR PUPPET FOR THE STAGE

What can I use to make my puppet?
You can use almost any material and method to create your puppet. The main things you need to consider are:

- What **scale** of puppet does the production demand? A shadow puppet, for example can be made to appear larger by moving it closer to the light source. A backpack puppet will make an impact due to its large size. Neither will be able to go into the audience, however, in the way that a glove puppet can.
- Does the puppet need to be light? A bird at the end of a thick wire will probably only be able to stay in the air if it is made of paper and feathers. In contrast, weights in the feet can be very effective when, for example, a marionette is walking.

Paper and cardboard
These can be cut and folded to create lightweight and versatile puppets and puppet parts such as wings, noses and ears. They tend to be flimsy, however, and can be damaged easily.

Polystyrene
This material is a good, quick alternative to papier mâché when it comes to making solid items that are still light. Balls and egg shapes are easy to find and cheap to buy. You can carve them into the shapes of heads, hands, feet and so on, then paint them and glue on wool, feathers, fabric and so on.

Cloth

Fabric is excellent for puppet making. Different types, weights and quantities of fabric create markedly different results.

- Stuffed children's tights make excellent legs.
- Felt doesn't fray and is useful for glove puppets, facial features, ears and so on.
- Scraps of fabric can be used for stuffing.
- Pieces of lightweight fabric can be used for clothing. 
- Fake fur is ideal for animal puppets.
- Cloth accessories such as scarves and shoes help to bring out the character.
- Avoid highly patterned prints for the body of a puppet, as it can be confusing to 'read'.

The heads and features of these stick puppets are made from sponges cut to shape.

LOOK HERE
'Key process – sewing' on pages 92–93 will support your practical work.

Haberdashery and craft items

These items are excellent for making limbs, features and accessories for your puppet:

- Lengths of ribbon
- Pipe cleaners
- Fabric glue
- Sticky tape
- Balls of wool
- Feathers
- Buttons
- Plastic and glass eyes.

Wood

Lightweight wood, such as lengths of dowel and strips of plywood are useful for creating frames, rods and, possibly, limbs.

Characterisation

Don't underestimate the importance of your puppet's eyes. The type and where you position them can make the difference between a convincing puppet with a recognisable character and a 'dead' one. Glass eyes have the most 'depth' and realism. If you want your puppet to 'look' at the audience, try placing them quite close together and fairly close to the mouth. Always experiment with eye positions before fixing them!

TASK 5.10

Create a simple puppet of your choice using the advice in this section and in the chapter as a whole.

Chapter 5   Practical Guide to Puppet Design

FOCUS
Operating the puppet for maximum effect.

ASSESSMENT CHECK
You need to design and realise a puppet with a well-defined character and audience appeal and understand performer manipulation skills.

ANIMATING PUPPETS

Bringing your puppet to life

Manipulating the puppet is part of its realisation and is essential in defining character and building a relationship with the audience. Each type of puppet will need a different kind of animation.

* Study your puppet carefully. What type of character do you think it has? What voice and movements are suggested?

* Closely observe the animal or type of person behind your creative intentions for the puppet. This will help you to develop movements that are believable and engaging.

* Find an upright position for your puppet that looks right. The angle will vary slightly depending on the position of the puppet's eyes. Don't allow it to tilt sideways.

* Develop a **rhythm** for your puppet. How does it move? At what pace?

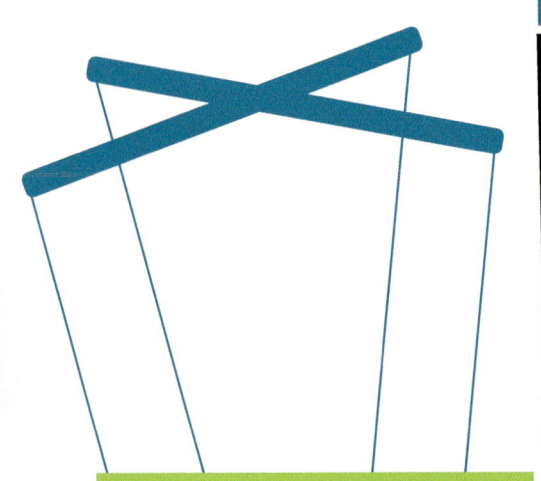

In *Ajijaax on Turtle Island*, this whooping crane pair greet each other at their nest. Having two operators for each puppet means that the cranes can make a wide range of movements, helping their realism and characterisation.

* Get used to moving its head up and down and from side to side if it can. Allow it to 'look' at something and experiment with the idea of getting it to take a closer look without actually travelling.

* Use a bobbing motion to make your puppet appear to walk or run. Practise making it move at different speeds.

* Never let your puppet droop or lose its animation on stage. It needs to be able to listen and watch even when it is not speaking. It should probably never be totally still.

TASK 5.11

1. Practise animating your puppet (or coaching the person who will manipulate it in performance) in some of the following situations:
   * Waiting for a bus
   * Getting angry when a bus drives past your stop
   * Falling asleep when you shouldn't
   * Catching a snowflake or a cold
   * Noticing the audience.
2. Perform your animation for your class or group. Try to make improvements based on their feedback.

Chapter 5   Practical Guide to Puppet Design

Giving your puppet a voice

If your puppet 'speaks', try the advice given on the right.

Leslie Caron in conversation with her puppet companion, in *Lili* (1953).

* Only the lower jaw of the puppet needs to move, as this is close to human speech movement.
* Aim to make the movements of the puppet's mouth as real as possible.
* A small movement of the lower jaw should be made for each syllable.
* Keep the puppet's mouth at least slightly open when it is talking.
* Always look at the puppet's face when it is 'speaking', so that you can see the effect and direct the audience's attention to the puppet.
* Watch and listen to people or relevant animals to help you find the right tone, pitch and style of voice to bring out the desired characteristics in your puppet. This is known as **voicing** the puppet.

Harry Melling tries to reason with his demonic hand puppet in *Hand to God*.

TASK 5.12

Using only your bare hands, have a 'puppet' conversation with a partner. Your conversation can be about whatever you wish, but why not discuss your feelings about 'the authorities' (the people who are animating them – ie, you!).

FOCUS
Your last opportunity to check that your design is working well in practice.

ASSESSMENT CHECK
In rehearsals, you will demonstrate your knowledge and understanding of how drama and theatre is developed and performed (AO3).

You also reflect, analyse and evaluate (AO4), and test that your design shows an understanding of the performer/audience relationship.

DESIGN TIP
Try not to interrupt the rehearsal unless there is a health and safety issue.

TECHNICAL AND DRESS REHEARSALS FOR PUPPET DESIGNERS

The rehearsal schedule works towards a technical ('tech') and then a dress rehearsal ('dress'). These are the rehearsals that draw everything together.

As puppet designer, you will either animate the puppet or sit in the audience area for the final rehearsals. Have your notebook to hand and check that your puppet is meeting your artistic intentions.

Technical rehearsal

The tech is when technicians and designers can make sure they have everything in place. It will probably be the first opportunity to put all the production elements (performers, puppets, lights, sound, costumes and set) together. If you encounter some typical problems, try the suggestions below.

Potential problems	Possible solutions and timings
An element of the puppet does not look right or work properly. There might be an issue with sightlines for shadow puppetry, for example.	Assess how to make the alteration. Can the screen be moved, for example? Try to implement changes before the dress rehearsal.
An animator is having difficulties with some aspect of a puppet's manipulation. Perhaps it does not move fluidly.	Work with the **manipulator** (or have more practice if that is you) to improve the puppet in performance.
A puppet does not look as good as you had hoped under some of the lighting states.	Note down which scenes are causing the problem. Talk to the lighting designer before the dress rehearsal and see if you can come to a compromise in the intensity or colour of lighting.

After the technical rehearsal, check that the animator and the performers (plus the director if there is one) are happy with the puppet in performance. If not, try to solve any issues and arrange for an extra, puppet-based rehearsal as soon as possible.

Dress rehearsal

The 'dress' is the final, timed, **run** before the performance. Now that technical issues have, hopefully, been addressed, the performers can run through the production uninterrupted.

Again, watch from the audience area with a notebook unless you are the animator. Either move around yourself or ask someone else to look out for the following:

- Have changes from the tech been made successfully?
- Are sightlines working well?

If there are still issues, revisit your notes and the table above. Work with your colleagues to tackle problems. Make final tweaks as necessary.

124 Chapter 5 Practical Guide to Puppet Design

EVALUATING YOUR PUPPET DESIGN

Once you have used the Signposted sections to be clear about what evaluation is and the best way of approaching it, you can focus on assessing the success of your puppet design, as in the brief example below.

> *Using shadow puppetry to create the fight was a very effective choice because it looked as though a lot of people were involved due to the use of four light sources projecting multiple shadows of just three people behind the screen. I was also pleased that the sightlines worked very well. One part of my design that was particularly successful in supporting our artistic intentions was the use of shadow rod puppets to create the moment when the girl sees the vision of her grandfather...*

Examining the detail of your design

Whenever you evaluate, you should make at least three different points. These points should be illustrated with specific examples. Each time, you should also explain your reason for a particular value judgement. You should describe anything that could have gone better.

It is very important to compare your finished puppet design against your artistic intentions. Check your notes and make sure you include the success of this aspect in your evaluation.

Peter and his grandfather in *Peter and the Wolf* by Sue Small at Foxes Ridge. The shadow puppets have jointed arms and the creator added scenery to the set.

FOCUS
Placing a value judgement on drama.

ASSESSMENT CHECK
In Component 2, you will analyse and evaluate the realisation of your creative intentions. In the written exam you might evaluate a professional puppet designer's work.

SIGNPOST
First, read the evaluation guidance on page 78.

LOOK HERE
More examples of evaluation can be found in Chapter 6 of this book.

TASK 5.13

1. Copy and complete this table (some examples have been included). The notes will provide a solid basis for your evaluation writing.

Puppet design evaluation

Design element	Moment in the play	Evaluation	Reason for evaluation
Screen	Throughout the shadow puppetry sections.	Effective in performance.	The positioning of the screen and the light sources enabled excellent sightlines.
Rod puppets	The vision of the grandfather.	Successful in supporting artistic intentions.	The scene was moving because of the detailed look and actions of the shadow grandfather. The relationship between the actor in front of the screen and the grandfather puppet behind it communicated their closeness to the audience.
Use of actors in shadow	The fight scene.	Powerful and exciting.	The way the fight took place through shadow-work was full of impact for the audience. This was partly due to the distancing effect of not seeing actual people and from the increase in numbers created by using multiple light sources.

2. Expand your notes into three paragraphs of evaluative writing.

Chapter 5 Practical Guide to Puppet Design

PUPPET VOCABULARY

Animation The act of bringing an inanimate object to life, such as in cartoons and with puppetry.

Animator A person who manipulates a puppet, bringing it to 'life'.

Audience appeal In a similar way to creating a defined character, the success of a puppet relies largely on its ability to encourage the engagement of the audience.

Backpack puppet A puppet which is worn on the back of the animator. This allows them to be very large and/or tall.

Focus The direction of a puppet's gaze or attention – for example on an object or another character.

Glove puppet A puppet that is worn over the hand.

Hand-and-rod puppet A hand puppet with added rods to allow the arms, for example, to move.

Hand puppet: A puppet that is held or worn on the hand.

Light source Anything that emits light, such as a torch or stage lantern.

Manipulate To move something or make something happen.

Manipulator Another word for animator; a person who operates the puppet.

Marionette A puppet whose head, limbs and body are suspended on strings or wires.

Puppet booth: A tent-like structure within which the puppeteer operates the puppets and is not seen by the audience (as used in Punch and Judy shows).

Puppeteer: A person who performs with puppets.

Rhythm: The typical speed and movement of a puppet.

Rod puppet A type of puppet which is often held above the animator and is controlled with thin strips of wood or metal.

Run Either a rehearsal of the whole play or the number of times a play will be performed (for example, *The Crucible* has a three-week run at this theatre).

Scale The size of one thing crelative to something else.

Shadow puppet A puppet that is designed to cast shadows rather than be seen in actuality.

Shadow puppetry A form of puppetry where a light source is placed behind a screen and a shadow puppet is placed between the two.

Voicing: Creating the speaking voice for a puppet. This will usually be produced by the puppet animator.

COMPONENT 1: UNDERSTANDING DRAMA

Chapter 6

Introduction to design in the written exam	128
Section A: Theatre roles and terminology	132
Section B: Study of the set play	137
Section C: Live theatre evaluation	137
Lighting design in the set play (Section B)	138
Lighting design in live theatre (Section C)	144
Sound design in the set play (Section B)	148
Sound design in live theatre (Section C)	154
Set design in the set play (Section B)	157
Set design in live theatre (Section C)	161
Costume design in the set play (Section B)	164
Costume design in live theatre (Section C)	168
Puppet design in the set play (Section B)	172
Puppet design in live theatre (Section C)	175

FOCUS
- Preparing for the written exam.
- Understanding what the examiner is looking for.

Masks help to characterise the Moon and the Sun in this movement performance.

DESIGN TIP
Remember that a harmonious world is skilfully and collectively created by every person involved in a production. Understanding this is the key to success in Component 3.

LOOK HERE
The Practical Guide to Design chapters at the beginning of this book will help you with the knowledge and understanding of how different theatrical elements can create impact and convey meaning.

INTRODUCTION TO DESIGN IN THE WRITTEN EXAM

The written exam requires every student to have a detailed understanding of **all** aspects of theatre included in the GCSE Drama course. For some questions, you will be able to choose whether you focus on performance or design. At other times, there will be no choices.

Studying and analysing drama

What must I be able to do?
In general terms, you need to have and demonstrate:
- a thorough and extensive knowledge of the set play you are studying and of the live performance you have seen
- knowledge of all the creative aspects of staging a theatre production, including the various roles of the people who put together a performance
- knowledge and experience of creating a piece of theatre, which will help to make your writing clear
- the ability to comment meaningfully and confidently about how the extract **could** be staged and about how the performance you saw **was** staged.

Specifically in relation to theatre design, you **must** answer:
- 1-mark questions about theatre roles, stage positioning and stage configuration (Section A)
- a 4-mark question (Section B) on an aspect of design relating to the set play (for example, a costume or set you would design in relation to the given extract).

There are also questions where you can **choose** to write about theatre design rather than performance.
- In Section B, there will be a 20-mark question about any single element of design (puppetry, set and so on) relating to your set play (a performance question is given as an alternative).
- In Section C, you will have the choice to write about either performance or one of two design elements (such as set or lighting) relating to the live performance. This is a 32-mark question.

How should I think about my writing in the exam?
For Section B, it would be useful to focus on the idea that you are staging a performance as part of a real team that must work creatively together and make the best choices to communicate ideas to the audience. This should help your written response have detail and depth.

Similarly, you watch the work of a creative team in the performance you see for Section C, and analyse and evaluate the impact of it. Again, it helps to remember that these are people who made choices throughout the process of getting the production on the stage. Did they make good decisions? What were they and how did they impact on you as an audience member?

Why should I consider answering optional design questions?
If you have enjoyed working practically on design elements for Component 2 or 3, the written exam gives you the opportunity to show what you have learned. You can also include annotated sketches or diagrams in your answers. This allows you to convey knowledge, creativity and understanding with fewer words.

Sharing your skills and knowledge of design in the written exam

You have developed your knowledge and skills in a range of disciplines, such as costume and set design, during the course. If you have worked practically on lighting, sound, costume, set or puppetry, you will be able to use those skills and knowledge very productively in the written exam. You will need to prepare thoroughly, however, in order to apply them to the set play.

Even if you have not opted for design in Components 2 and 3, you will have appreciated the use of costume, lights, set and sound. This might have been in performances you have been part of as well as ones you have seen.

You are unlikely to be an expert at every performance and design discipline. You should, however, have sufficient knowledge and specialist vocabulary to make insightful comments about techniques and designs and how they enhance the artistic intentions of a scene or moment.

You certainly need to have a good level of knowledge for all the design elements that exam questions could be about. You will be asked to explain, interpret, analyse and evaluate design from the perspective of an audience member or a designer.

> **DESIGN TIP**
>
> Revisit and update the table in Task 6.1 at regular intervals. In this way, you will be in a good position to decide which optional design questions you might want to answer in the exam.

TASK 6.1

You will not be **required** to write about design elements in great depth, but there will be choices for questions that carry a large number of marks and which therefore require greater depth and detail.

Ask yourself how confident you are in your drama skills and knowledge. Complete your own version of this table.

Drama skill	Good / OK / Not so good	Strengths and weaknesses
Costume design	🙂	✓ Helped to create my own costume for devised piece. ✚ Need to know more technical terms to analyse costume in the live production seen.
Set design	😃	✓ Designed set for scripted piece and can make a model box and draw a ground plan. ✚ Need to create a design for set text and analyse the set from the live production seen.
Lighting design	😠	✓ Know how effective lighting can be. ✚ Need to understand different types of lantern and technical terms. ✚ Explore lighting design for set play and live show.
Sound design	😃	✓ Have explored sound design for the set text and analysed sound from the live production seen. ✚ Make notes for live production and consider how director would think about sound for set text.
Puppet design	😐	✓ Have taken part in a workshop. ✚ Explore suitability of puppetry for my play.
Performance	🙂	✓ Acted in some pieces and understand about voice and movement. ✚ Focused on lighting recently, so need to remind myself of technical terms linked to performing.

Using your practical experience, knowledge and understanding

To succeed in the written exam, it is essential to prepare for it throughout your course.

Different roles and elements in drama

The main theatre elements for production and design are lighting, sound, set, costume and puppetry, but you might be asked more specifically about, for example, props and stage furniture or staging. These might overlap with other design elements, for example:

- Staging might include the use of set on a specific type of stage.
- Props and stage furniture might form part of a set design.
- Personal props, such as a phone, pen or spectacles, might form part of the costume design for certain characters.

A Curious Incident of the Dog in the Night-Time at the Gielgud Theatre.

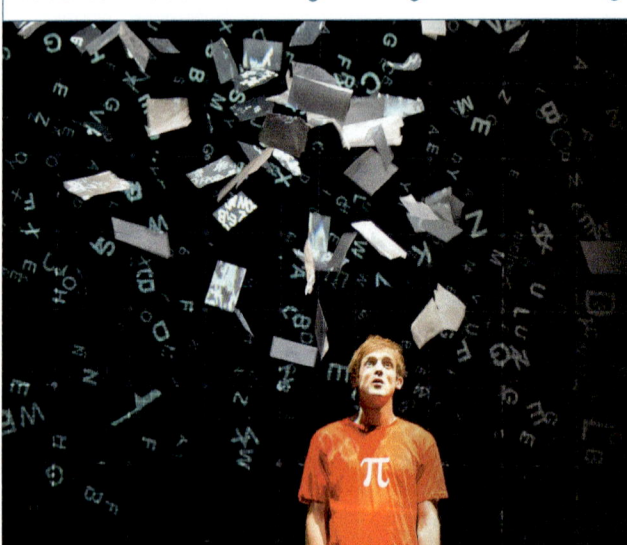

- Do more than simply take part in drama lessons. Step back and really think about what is happening. Keep a project notebook to record your thoughts. You could have separate sections for performance and the different design elements.
- Use the knowledge and experience that you have gained to examine all elements of drama.
- Take an interest in all the elements of drama. For example, talk to the performers if you are the costume or lighting designer, and so on.
- Keep a glossary of technical terms you come across and try to use them in lessons and in your writing so that they become really familiar.
- Carry out as many tasks as you can from the Practical Guide to Design chapters at the beginning of this book.

TASK 6.2

Start a drama journal or scrapbook and add to it every week. Use the ideas above and include sketches, images and mood boards to keep yourself interested. (Search on Pinterest for some useful examples.)

Take inspiration from the fact that your journal will be invaluable when it comes to revising for your exam and the mock exams you take during your course.

DESIGN TIP

You could make notes in your set play, but remember that only clean – unannotated – copies can be taken into the exam.

Your experience from the whole course will help you

It would be a mistake to think of the exam as a big new element that takes place at the end of your course. Instead, try to think of it as an opportunity to show what you have learned over the years you have studied and been interested in drama.

Chapter 6   Component 1: Understanding Drama

Recognising artistic intentions and practical processes

Professional theatre makers are skilled in their fields. Similarly, you have developed your own knowledge and skills in a range of disciplines during your Drama course. You might have focused on acting and have learned a great deal about voice, movement and characterisation. Alternatively, you might have developed your skills as a designer, or studied both design and performance.

Either way, the devised and scripted performances you work on involve all of your group aiming to communicate a common artistic intention. If you work practically on lighting, sound, costume or set, you will have an opportunity to use those skills and knowledge very productively in the written exam. If not, you can develop your knowledge of the design elements by doing some design work as part of your exam preparation.

The devising log is a major piece of written work for your devised theatre piece for Component 2. For Component 1, you are again writing from a very practical viewpoint:

- How would **I** perform or design an extract from my set play?
- How would **I** create impact for my audience within this crafted world?
- How do the performers and designers of live performances I have seen use their skills to create impact?

The naturalistic aspects of set and costume design in *Be More Chill* mean that the audience easily recognises the high school location. It combines these, however, with bold colours and high-tech lighting that give it a modern sense of quirkiness appropriate to the characters and themes.

A Midsummer Night's Dream at the RSC's Swan Theatre in Stratford-upon-Avon. Designers and performers work together harmoniously to convey meaning and create atmosphere.

Preparing for the exam

When revising for the design questions in the exam:

- use the specialist language glossaries in this book when you are writing – including your notes and any annotations – or reviewing your writing
- study your set play in detail and make notes on design ideas that spring to mind or that you notice in the stage directions
- consider how you would use design to stage your set play
- make notes using specialist language about all the design options for the live performance you are writing about
- develop your ability to **interpret**, **analyse** and **evaluate**.
- make use of any design experience you have gained outside your course, such as in amateur theatre or further reading.

Chapter 6 Component 1: Understanding Drama

FOCUS
- Theatre roles and stage positions.
- The demands of different staging configurations and their influence on designers.

ASSESSMENT CHECK
Your knowledge of theatre roles, stage configurations and stage positions is examined in Component 1.

In Components 2 and 3, you should:
- consider the performer/audience relationship
- understand the use of performance space and spatial relationships.

Learning about the implications of staging configurations and positions is a key element of AO3.

SECTION A: THEATRE ROLES AND TERMINOLOGY

These multiple-choice questions are designed to test your knowledge of theatre roles, stage configurations and stage positioning. These questions are not difficult to revise for, and you should aim to answer them quickly.

Key theatre roles and their contribution to a production

Playwright

Writes the script of the play.

Director

Develops a 'concept' or key theme for the production before rehearsals start. Works with the designers to develop the creative characteristics and technical aspects of the production. Rehearses the performers to develop their performances.

Performer

Realises a role or creates a performance, appearing on stage in front of the audience.

Understudy

Studies a performer's role in order take over if required.

Lighting designer

Designs the lighting states and effects for a performance, taking into account the theatre's technical facilities. The result is a lighting plot (see page 29).

Sound designer

Designs the sound for the performance and creates a sound plot and cue sheet (see pages 52–53) as well as deciding whether amplification is required.

Set designer

Designs the set and chooses set dressings. Uses sketches and other design materials and supervises the creation of the set.

Costume designer

Designs what the performers wear on stage, and ensures that the costumes fit correctly, taking into consideration the style and period of the production.

Puppet designer

Designs the puppets required for a production, considering how they will be operated during the performance.

Technician

Sets up and operates technical equipment during the performance, for example lights and sound boards.

Stage manager

Responsible for all aspects back stage. Oversees the crew, lists of props, scene changes and other technical aspects. Creates the **prompt book** and calls the cues, as well as arranging the rehearsal schedule.

Theatre manager

Responsible for running the theatre, including supervising the front of house and box office teams.

Stage positioning

Stage positioning is the terminology used to describe different areas of the stage. This diagram shows the stage in a typical end-on configuration.

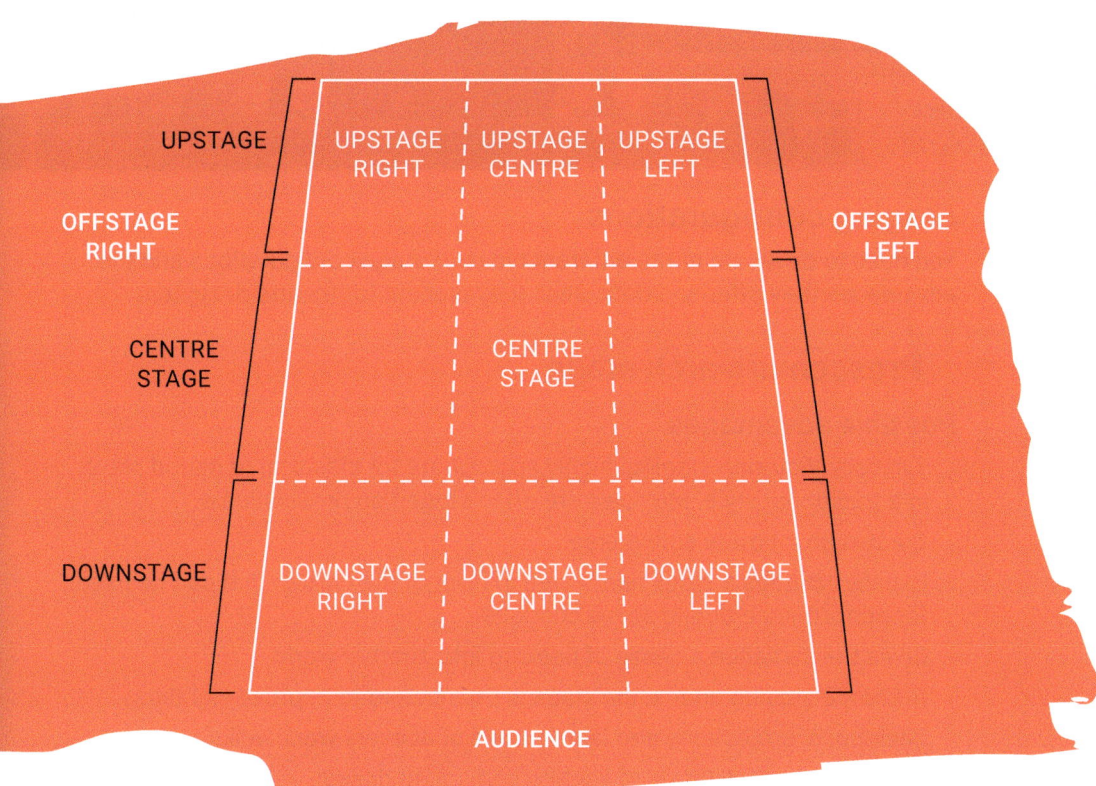

	UPSTAGE RIGHT	UPSTAGE CENTRE	UPSTAGE LEFT	
UPSTAGE				
OFFSTAGE RIGHT				OFFSTAGE LEFT
CENTRE STAGE		CENTRE STAGE		
DOWNSTAGE	DOWNSTAGE RIGHT	DOWNSTAGE CENTRE	DOWNSTAGE LEFT	

AUDIENCE

DESIGN TIP

The help you remember right and left and up and down on stage, imagine you are an actor centre stage, facing the audience. Downstage right, for example, is on your right, down towards the audience.

Stage space and spatial relationships

All types of theatre designers need to create their designs with close regard to the relationship between acting areas and audience. This relationship will partly depend on how a stage or performance area is arranged.

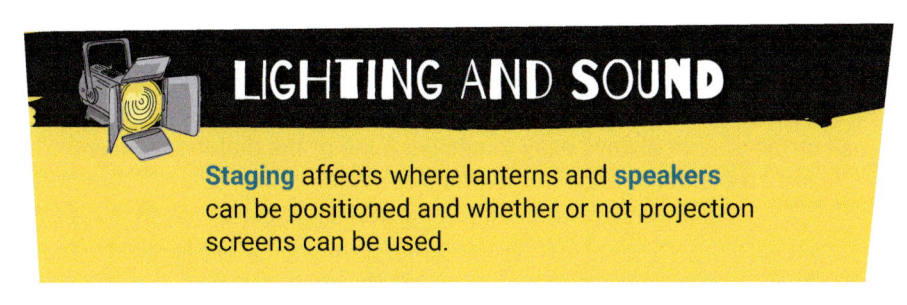

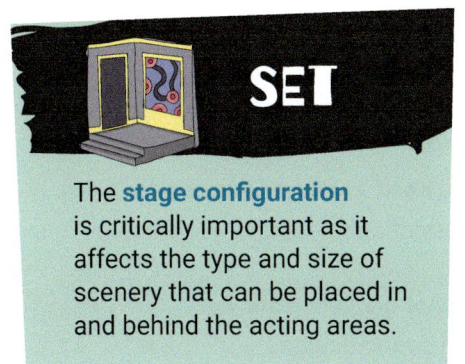

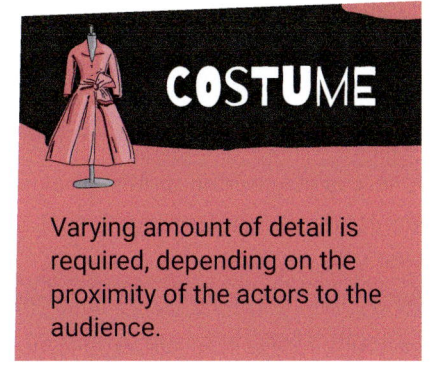

LIGHTING AND SOUND

Staging affects where lanterns and **speakers** can be positioned and whether or not projection screens can be used.

SET

The **stage configuration** is critically important as it affects the type and size of scenery that can be placed in and behind the acting areas.

COSTUME

Varying amount of detail is required, depending on the proximity of the actors to the audience.

PUPPETRY

The stage configuration plays a significant part in choosing puppet types. **Shadow puppets** will be very difficult to produce in theatre in the round, for example.

Chapter 6 Component 1: Understanding Drama 133

The proscenium arch gives a picture-frame effect above and on each side of an end-on stage.

Staging configurations

You need to be aware of the different types of stage configurations and the advantages they offer and difficulties they present for theatre designers.

Proscenium arch stage

Possible advantages

- Typically Victorian staging: highly appropriate for classical or period plays in a traditional style. Musicals are often staged on prosceniums.
- Creates an intimate acting area.
- Usually includes a small apron area in front of the curtain that can be used for performance during scene changes.
- Gives the audience a sense of peeking into another world.
- Audience seating and/or the stage is often **raked** to improve sightlines.
- Backdrops, projections and large pieces of scenery work well.
- Straightforward in terms of lighting and sound design.
- Detail in costume and set is not crucial as the audience is at a distance.
- Footlights work well and offer additional lighting angles.

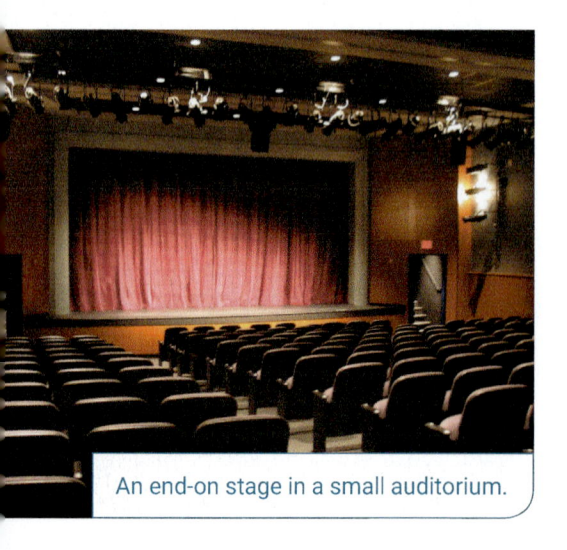

Potential problems

- Sightlines are problematic as the side panels of the arch might obscure parts of the stage for some of the audience.
- Pillared seating areas can also reduce visibility for the audience.
- If the stage is raked, anything on wheels must be wedged or have brakes.
- Many auditoriums have raised circles, which means that some of the audience is distant and almost above the acting area.
- Small props are not always easy to see because of the distance between the acting area and the back of the **stalls** or circle.
- Often involves seating part of the audience in raised circles, which means some viewers are a long way from and almost above the acting area while the front row of the stalls is very close. Sound and lighting must be carefully balanced to compensate for this.

End-on stage

Possible advantages

- A neutral stage configuration that lends itself to many periods and styles.
- Similar to proscenium arch in that a distinct and separate world can be created.
- Backdrops, projections and large pieces of scenery work well.
- Straightforward in terms of lighting and sound design.

An end-on stage in a small auditorium.

Potential problems
- The distance between the back of the audience and the acting area can be lengthy.
- If the stage is raked, anything with wheels will need to be wedged or have brakes.
- If seating is not raked, sightlines can be a problem.
- Details in costumes and small props might not be seen clearly.

Thrust stage

Possible advantages
- The large apron provides an acting area close to the audience, which helps the audience to feel involved.
- Props and costumes can be detailed.
- The main stage can incorporate large pieces of scenery, projection and backdrops.
- Useful for using different levels, as many thrust aprons include a step.

Potential problems
- Sightlines can be very complex. Audience members on the side banks of seating, for example, will struggle to see action on their side of the main stage.
- No scenery or tall pieces of furniture can be placed on the apron.
- Side-lighting the apron can be problematic as the audience could be dazzled: steep angles are needed.

Timothy Mackabee's award-winning design for *The Odd Couple* at Dallas Theatre Center.

Traverse stage

Possible advantages
- The acting area is close to the audience, creating a more intimate relationship.
- Props and costumes can be detailed.
- The two ends of the acting area can incorporate large pieces of scenery, projections and backdrops, creating different 'worlds' or locations.

Potential problems
- No scenery or large pieces of furniture can be placed on the traverse itself.
- Side lighting can be problematic as the audience can get dazzled: steep angles are needed.
- Costumes need to be detailed at the back too.
- Having audience members directly opposite each other can be distracting.

The Railway Children at King's Cross Theatre.

The New Vic Theatre, Newcastle-under-Lyme.

The Dukes Lancaster promenade performance of *A Midsummer Night's Dream*, with Andy Serkis as Lysander. This took place in a local park. Locations included woodland, lawns and next to (and even on) a lake.

TASK 6.3

Devise a game for your classmates based on theatre roles, stage configurations and/or stage positioning. This could take the form of:
- a multiple-choice quiz
- Bingo (You would read out responsibilities or benefits/challenges and players would mark the role or stage configuration. Each card could, for example, have six random roles or configurations.)
- a guessing game where one person would act out the role or stand in a particular stage position and the rest of the class would identify it
- an imaginative game that you invent yourself.

Theatre in the round

Possible advantages
- The acting area is closer to the audience, which helps the audience to feel involved.
- This configuration allows directors and designers to use the space imaginatively.
- Having performers enter and exit through the corner aisles (close to the audience) can be exciting.
- Props and costumes can be detailed.

Potential problems
- No scenery or large pieces of furniture can be used.
- Lighting is problematic as the audience can be dazzled: steep angles are needed.
- Costumes need to be detailed at the back too.

Promenade theatre

This type of staging is unique. It involves the audience walking (a promenade) from one location to another with the actors. Locations are often outdoors, or in large buildings such as warehouses.

Possible advantages
- Very exciting for both audience and performers.
- Creates a 'we're all in this together' atmosphere.
- Suits productions with outdoor locations.

Potential problems
- The weather!
- Challenging for all design options.
- Considerable health and safety risks.

Chapter 6 Component 1: Understanding Drama

SECTION B: STUDY OF THE SET PLAY

The idea of 'interpreting practically' implies that you can imagine it on the stage. You will be assessed on the extent of your **knowledge** of the extract and the play as a whole and how that interacts with your **understanding** of how it could be staged. These critical judgements will also be used in Section C when you write about a live performance.

You will be working with the guidance of your teacher on a particular text for this section of the exam, where you will be given an extract of the play along with a series of questions about how you would perform and stage it.

This involves the key skills of interpretation and analysis. The two concepts are closely linked as it is your close study and knowledge (**analysis**) that will lead you to put forward choices (**interpretation**) of aspects of the play.

TASK 6.4

1. Choose a design option that you are interested in developing.
2. Pick an extract from your set play that has plenty of scope for that design role.
3. - For **set**, **puppetry** or **costume**, draw some sketches to interpret the extract in an exciting way.
   - For **lighting** or **sound**, think about the locations, period and atmosphere you could create.
   - For **lighting**, put together a mood board using the guidance in Chapter 1.
   - For **sound**, jot down some diegetic and non-diegetic sound effects that you would like to hear, perhaps with some music choices.

ASSESSMENT CHECK

These questions in the exam assess AO3: 'Demonstrate knowledge and understanding of how theatre is developed and performed.'

The notes here will help you to:

- demonstrate knowledge and understanding of the characteristics and context of the play
- explore ideas for how the play might be interpreted practically.

SECTION C: LIVE THEATRE EVALUATION

In this section of the written exam, you will answer one question about a show you have seen. (This cannot be a performance of your set play.)

There are three questions to choose from. One will be performance based; the other two will be about single design elements.

TASK 6.5

1. Work in your group to re-create, roughly, how the stage looked for a memorable scene. Use levels, objects and furniture to stand in for pieces of set.
2. On your 'stage', create a freeze-frame for a key moment in the scene.
3. Take it in turns to 'come out' of the freeze-frame and describe the costumes, sound and lighting for that moment.
4. If possible, photograph the freeze-frame. Include it in your journal with annotations about set, sound, costume and lighting. If puppetry was involved, you should include that too.

Annotated sketches can easily sum up set and costume design, for example.

ASSESSMENT CHECK

This question tests your knowledge and understanding of how theatre is developed and performed for AO3 and your skills in analysing and evaluating the work of others for AO4.

Blue Stockings costume.

DNA set design.

FOCUS

How to write as if you are a lighting designer.

ASSESSMENT CHECK

Section B assesses AO3: 'Demonstrate knowledge and understanding of how theatre is developed and performed.'

These notes will help your knowledge and understanding of design and of the set play.

LIGHTING DESIGN IN THE SET PLAY (SECTION B)

If you have only worked practically as a performer, the design questions might seem rather daunting. This book is here to support you and increase your knowledge and confidence.

Thinking as a lighting designer for the set text

Do you watch television and films? Have you been to a music concert?

If yes, you will be able to harness your subconscious knowledge of how lighting can be used creatively.

Next time you go to a concert or watch a film, notice where the designer has gone beyond the use naturalistic lighting. Try to concentrate on the mood or meaning being enhanced. This might mean watching out for the use of colour, angle and pace of lighting transitions. Alternatively, it might simply mean noticing how bright or dim the lighting is, or how dramatic shadows are being produced.

You will not know in advance what extract you will be given, but you will know which play it will be from.

To start you off, can you think of three ways you could explore the text? Anything that helps you to become familiar with the text on the page and in performance is worth spending time on. The best way to revise, however, is to create lighting designs yourself.

Why is it useful to create a lighting design for the set text?

LOOK HERE

'Introduction to lighting design' on pages 14–15 will develop your thinking.

DESIGN TIP

Using specialist design language is one of the most important things you can learn to do.

- Working with your design practically will make it memorable when it comes to the written exam.
- If you are new to lighting, you will gain practical knowledge and technical language that could be useful in the exam and in real life.
- It is also fun!

What early decisions about lighting need to be made?

Once you are familiar with the whole play, ask yourself:

- Will non-naturalistic lighting work with the production style?
- What do I want to communicate to the audience?
- What is the context of the play?
- Are special effects needed?
- How else can I enhance the artistic intentions and mood and atmosphere? Gobos? Colour?

> **LOOK HERE**
>
> 'Introduction to design in the written exam', pages 128–131, has several tasks and lots of advice. Read it carefully and complete Task 6.2 in particular, relating it to lighting design.

Creating a mood board

Mood boards help a designer to think about style, atmosphere, colour and artistic intentions in terms of impact and meaning. It could be digital or produced on paper or card.

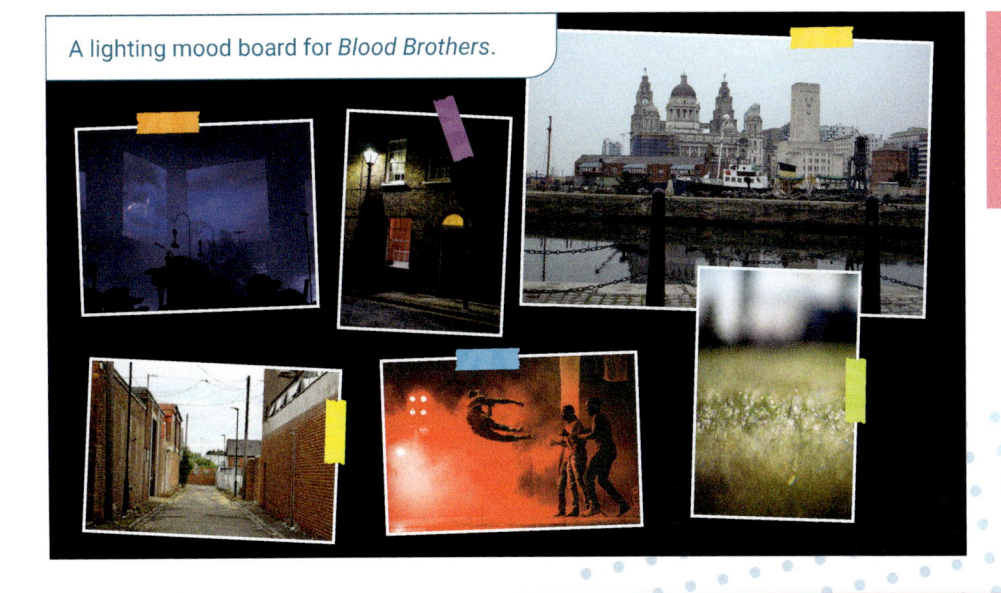

A lighting mood board for *Blood Brothers*.

> **TASK 6.6**
>
> With a partner, discuss what lighting effects the creator of this mood board might produce.

> **TASK 6.7**
>
> 1. To begin your own mood board, quickly think of at least eight adjectives for the play. Words for *Blood Brothers*, for example, might include: *funny, heartbreaking, moving, musical, bright, narrated*.
> 2. Gather images that match your adjectives in some way.
> 3. Move on to think about suitable nouns, such as *conflict, childhood, secrets, poverty, 1960s, 1980s, Liverpool*, and gather images for them with the same 'feel' as those for your adjectives.
> 4. Now think about how to organise these images onto the page. They could overlap or be grouped in ways that inspire you.
> 5. You could also add pictures or actual items showing colours and textures, such as metal and wood.
> 6. With a partner, discuss lighting effects suggested by your mood board.

Chapter 6 Component 1: Understanding Drama

Careful lighting that considers colour, intensity and use of shadow creates atmosphere. Here, this is enhanced with a smoke effect.

Planning your lighting design

TASK 6.8

1. Research and make notes on the social, historic, political and economic contexts of the set text you have studied.

   The 39 Steps, for example, is set in 1935, in the build-up to the Second World War. The play is both a comic melodrama and a gentle parody of the thrillers of that period. *Blood Brothers* is set in Liverpool between the 1960s and 1980s. It uses music and comedy to address social inequality and the role of women.

2. Use your research to complete your own version of the table below. (An example has been given using *Blood Brothers*.)

	How lighting could communicate meaning, context and atmosphere
Locations: • Liverpool • Street • Mrs Johnstone's kitchen • Fairground • Bus • Countryside • School.	• Lighting used naturalistically to create locations. For example, a projection of the Liverpool skyline. • Many locations appear in quick succession. Intensity of lighting will help to focus the audience. Use of spotlights to create small lit areas on the stage. • Practical effects in the kitchen, for example, to suggest light from table lamp.
Contexts: • 1960s to early 1980s Liverpool • Contrast between poverty and privilege.	• Bright city lights on projection contrast with dimmer, colder lighting on the side streets – street lamps?
Style/mood/atmosphere: • Naturalism • Non-naturalism • Comedy • Tragedy.	• Shadows could be created to add dark drama by using footlights. • Brighter, warmer lighting would help the atmosphere during moments of humour.

TASK 6.9

1. Select a section of your set text that offers plenty of opportunities for interesting lighting and transitions.
2. Make a list of the lighting effects that you want to create.
3. Read sections in Chapter 1 to help you make notes about how you could create those effects.

TASK 6.10

Taking your mood board and the table above as a guide, begin to make some decisions about your design (as much as you can so far).
- What will the stage configuration be? Where will the audience sit? (This has a crucial effect on where you position the lights.)
- How will locations be suggested?
- What are the main moods and atmospheres?
- How might you fit in with the colour palette of set and costume?

Exam practice

You need to practise how you will respond in the written exam itself. If you have prepared well, it should not be too daunting.

You need to be ready to write confidently and fairly rapidly as soon as you have understood the questions and decided which one to answer. Completing the tasks in this section will help you.

Question B.1

The first question you will answer in Section B requires you to suggest a possible design for your set play and might look like the one below.

Your teacher will be able to give you similar questions and extracts from the set play you are studying so that you can practise writing your own answers.

> You are designing lighting for a performance of this extract [the start of Act 2, when Proctor returns to his house after working in the fields]. The lighting must reflect the context of *The Crucible*, set in a Puritan community in the late 17th century. Describe your design ideas for the lighting. [4 marks]

DESIGN TIP
Briefly include design details with reasons for your choices. You must comment on the context as set out in the question.

TASK 6.11
Using the B.1 mark scheme, put the extract from a student answer below into a band from 1 to 4. Share your ideas with a partner and come to a joint decision on which band best fits the example.

For this scene, my lighting design will be entirely naturalistic. The fireplace will be fitted with a practical effect of a red LED light that can be operated by the actors. A pale orange light will shine onto the fireplace from a low angle in the wings. It will be a Fresnel with a barn door on it, which will allow light to spill beyond the fireplace itself and cast warm light onto the face of whichever character is near it. At that time, the fireplace was the heart of the puritans' simple homes.

The wash of light that covers the stage will use straw coloured filters to suggest the fact that it is early evening in springtime. The key light for this effect will be at the back of the stage positioned to shine in to the room as if it is the setting sun. As the scene moves on, I will decrease the intensity of this lighting from 50% to 30% to suggest that night is falling. An oil lamp (which is correct for the context) containing a flickering LED light will be on the table ready to be 'lit' by the actors towards the end of the scene.

LOOK HERE
'Angles, colour and intensity', pages 20–23, and 'Research for lighting', page 27, offer inspiration and advice on achieving lighting effects.

'Types of stage lantern', pages 16–17, will help you with technical language.

DESIGN TIP

You might find it helpful to memorise a few filter colours that would be suitable for your set play.

Lee Filters colour temperature set of gels.

Richard Ede as Hannay tries to make his escape across travel-trunk stepping stones in this high-action scene from *The 39 Steps*.

Question B.5

The final question in Section B carries 20 marks and is optional in the sense that you could answer B.4, which is a performance question, instead.

TASK 6.12

1 Highlight and check your understanding of the key words in this question:

> You are a designer working on one aspect of design for this extract [Act 1, Scene 14 of *The 39 Steps*]. Describe how you would use your design skills to create effects which support the action. Explain why your ideas are appropriate for:
> - this extract
> - the play as a whole.
>
> [20 marks]

2 Label the example answer below with:

F – **F**ocus on the question

Ex – Supporting **ex**ample

T – Appropriate **t**echnical language

I – **I**deas that fit the extract and the play.

3 Use the mark scheme to decide on a band and then a mark out of 20.

I would use lighting to suggest the location, period, setting and atmosphere of the scene and the play as a whole. Scene 14 takes place at the crofter's cottage at midnight. It is an interior location, but natural and artificial light coming through the window is also important in enhancing the action and atmosphere of the scene. Assuming that there is a proscenium arch configuration, I would use a profile spot with a colour filter (183 Moonlight Blue) and position it in the wings as a side light. The intensity would be around 30% to allow Hannay to be seen but to also suggest a slightly cloudy moonlight and the angle would allow the light to shine through the window towards Hannay's bed. The window would have thin curtains so that moonlight and the light from the headlights of the police arriving at the start of the scene would be visible.

The special effect of the sweeping headlights would be produced by two AML spots in the wings which are pre-programmed to make the swinging effect that is needed.

Once Margaret is in the room with Hannay, I would use three-point lighting to fade in (to 40%) a wash made up of Fresnel lanterns using Lee filters 154 (Pale Rose). This colour adds warmth to the stage which is in keeping with the relationship between Hannay and Margaret. This relationship was shown in the previous scene where I would use the same colour filters for continuity. The colour also suggests the type of lamplight which would have been available in the 1930s.

I would raise the intensity of the lighting state to 60% when the crofter enters to reflect the energy he brings into the room and focus the audience away from the intimate relationship between Hannay and Margaret. The key light would come from the side of the stage where Margaret and the crofter enter to suggest that the light is coming from the hallway.

At the end of the scene where Margaret is left alone at the window, I would return to the moonlight effect; its coldness of colour echoing Margaret's feeling at Hannay's departure.

Other moments in the play where I would use the moonlight effect include Scenes 10 and 11, where Hannay is on the moors. At this point in the play I would use a fog machine to create the mist. This would work well with the blue light which would be reflected by the fog effect, enhancing the eerie atmosphere.

The 39 Steps is a melodrama and I would generally want to use exaggerated lighting to add to the effect. A good example of this is in Scene 3 where I would use a snap transition from the total darkness at the beginning of the scene to instant 70% white light as Hannay switches the standard lamp on. This would startle the audience who would get a glimpse of the room and the characters before the light is switched off. The 'street lighting coming through the window' would suggest the typical neon of 1930s London and be created using Lee filter 525 Argent Blue which has a cool atmosphere and suggest the menace which is outside in the streets.

TASK 6.13

Test yourself.

1. Choose an extract from your set text of around 80 lines.
2. Try the question in Task 6.12 under exam conditions. Allow yourself no more than 25 minutes.

DESIGN TIP

You are expected to include technical detail because you are writing from the viewpoint of someone with a lot of subject knowledge. Try to use appropriate technical terms.

FOCUS
How to evaluate a lighting design.

ASSESSMENT CHECK
Section C assesses AO3 and AO4. These pages help you to:
- demonstrate knowledge and understanding of how drama and theatre is developed and performed
- investigate and identify how successfully theatre makers communicated meaning to an audience (analysis)
- assess the merit of approaches used and formulate judgements (evaluation).

DESIGN TIP
A show programme is likely to be a useful source of information.

DESIGN TIP
The way lighting worked with sound and set or contributed to atmosphere and context would be valuable information to include in your exam.

LIGHTING DESIGN IN LIVE THEATRE (SECTION C)

In this part of the exam, you could give detailed explanations and an evaluation of the lighting design in a performance you have seen. You should justify your opinions with examples that include a 'number of precise details.' You are also aiming to use technical language.

Preparation for a lighting design question

Look in the show programme, theatre marketing material and online for information about the lighting designer. Major productions and tours often have images, information and reviews online. Photographs in particular will help to remind you of details of the lighting and how they complemented other elements of the performance.

Remember that you were a member of the audience. The exam will ask you to comment on the impact lighting had on the audience. Share your responses with your classmates, but aim to write about your own viewpoints in the exam. You are expected to make a critical evaluation.

Made in Dagenham at the Adelphi Theatre.

TASK 6.14

1. Study any notes about the lighting that you made after seeing the performance.
2. Draw a quick sketch of the set, with lighting special effects added.
3. Annotate it with details of the lighting that created impact or otherwise contributed to meaning and mood. What do you remember about the lighting, and why?
4. Discuss the lighting with other people in your class. Pooling your memories is valid and the discussion will help you to recall the experience of seeing the production.

Evaluation as a skill

TASK 6.15

Read 'Evaluating your lighting design' carefully and complete Task 1.18, using examples from the live performance. Remember that you are evaluating someone else's lighting design, rather than your own.

Evaluating lighting

The exam question will ask you about a design element of the production as a whole: it will not specify which moments to write about. So, evaluate the moments that stood out for you as examples of effective lighting.

TASK 6.16

1. If you can, find a copy of the script for the live performance you are writing about. Browse through it until you find a section where you remember lighting having an impact on you.
2. Try to remember the lighting at key points in this section. These could be as short as a single moment or as long as a whole scene or more. Consider transitions between lighting states.
3. Write at least two paragraphs of critical judgement, which include:
   - subject-specific language, such as *intensity, transitions, colour gels, automated lights*, and so on
   - how lighting enhanced style and helped to create settings
   - how the use of lighting changed the look of the set and the effect that had on atmosphere and meaning
   - evaluation supported by detailed examples, such as, 'The use of… was powerful because…' and 'I was impressed by… because it made me feel/think…'
4. Swap your writing with someone else's for feedback. You could use the bullet points above as a checklist.

SIGNPOST

'Evaluating your lighting design' on page 37 gives guidance on evaluative writing about lighting.

DESIGN TIP

Try as many exam-type questions as you can. Your teacher should be able to set you suitable questions. When you feel ready to practise under exam conditions, keep only your 500 words of notes with you. Give yourself a maximum of 20 minutes to complete your answer.

Note the effective use of lighting in *Anything Goes* (at the Ahmanson Theatre, Los Angeles). What is the effect of putting lights behind the portholes? The couple downstage are lit from the front. How does their appearance differ from the couples on the platforms?

Chapter 6 Component 1: Understanding Drama 145

Working with an example answer

The mark scheme is a valuable tool when you are preparing for the written exam. The following task will allow you to assess a sample answer and then practise one of your own.

TASK 6.17

1. Highlight the key words in the following example question:

> Describe how lighting was used to support the action in the production. Analyse and evaluate how successful the lighting was in helping to communicate the action of the production to the audience. You should make reference to:
> • types of lighting • colour and intensity of the lighting • any special effects. [32 marks]

2. Now check your understanding of these key words, using a glossary if necessary.

3. Annotate the example answer on the facing page (about *A Curious Incident of the Dog in the Night-Time*). Look for:

    F – **F**ocus on the question

    Ex – **Ex**ample to support argument or point

    T – Appropriate **t**echnical language

    U – **U**nderstanding and knowledge of lighting design in relation to the performance

    E – **E**valuation in terms of how successful the lighting was.

4. Use the AO4 mark scheme to decide on a band and a mark out of 20. (The remaining 12 marks relate to AO3.)

An example from Paule Constable's lighting design for *The Curious Incident of the Dog in the Night-Time*.

The designer, Paule Constable, has developed a magical lighting design from the original staging in the round at the National Theatre to the proscenium staging I saw at the Lowry.

The lighting can only be described in relation to the set, which is basically a box. It represents Christopher's brain. How Christopher's brain works is a main theme of the play.

The floor and the three sides of the box are made of something that can be pixelated, so lighting happens alongside the images that appear on all of the surfaces. Moving projections add to the overall effect of looking into a box full of moving images and light.

One of the simplest special lighting effects was the use of small par cans within the moveable white cubes, which were used as seats, for example. These threw white light onto the faces of nearby actors at moments such as when Christopher found the letters from his mother. Their relationship is another central theme. This cold and stark uplighting cast me suddenly into Christopher's feelings and helped me to share his shock. Because the lighting wasn't balanced from other sources, it had a very eerie effect. Simple special effects in lighting can be as powerful as spectacular ones.

Nearly all of the lighting was cold white to reflect Christopher's mathematical, ordered brain functions. This simple choice had a huge impact on the look of the production and supported the action.

The pace of lighting changes was key to making the special effects work seamlessly. At moments, profile spots pinpointed individual actors as they were mentioned by the narrator. These were clean and tightly focused and snapped rather than faded in, which felt very exciting. The lighting contributed to the pace of the show, which suggested the speed of Christopher's brain.

It was the same when we were submerged into Christopher's vision of the stars or maths equations. Projections, pixelated lighting and a low-intensity whitewash of light (used to make the performers visible) were co-ordinated to take us into Christopher's head. The timing of the lighting transitions was crucial and the cues were precise. The overall effect was mesmerising.

Slower, more reflective scenes used lighting for a different atmosphere, such as when Christopher's mum appears for the first time as a memory. Although Christopher is shown in the usual white spotlight, his mother is bathed in a warmer, straw-coloured, softly focused spotlight. This helped me to understand Christopher's warm memories of his mother. By contrast, the use of downlighting to create a clear box of light around Christopher at the flat showed his sense of being imprisoned and uncomfortable there.

My favourite use of lighting was Christopher's journey to the railway station. The ambient lighting pulsed while moving projections of street names and the paths he was following appeared and disappeared very precisely. I was swept up in the journey as all my senses were captivated.

TASK 6.18

Test yourself.

1. Based on the live performance you have chosen, answer the question in Task 6.17.

   Use the AO3 and AO4 mark schemes and other tasks in this chapter to guide you.
2. If possible, ask another student or your teacher to mark your answer. Can you make improvements based on their comments?

DESIGN TIP

Include as much detail as possible in your answers. Highlight your evaluative judgements by using terms such as 'effective' and 'powerful impact'.

FOCUS

How to write as if you are a sound designer.

ASSESSMENT CHECK

Section A assesses AO3: 'Demonstrate knowledge and understanding of how theatre is developed and performed.'

These notes will help your knowledge and understanding of design and of the set play.

LOOK HERE

'Introduction to sound design' on pages 40–41 will develop your thinking.

DESIGN TIP

Using specialist design language is one of the most important things you can learn to do.

SOUND DESIGN IN THE SET PLAY (SECTION B)

If you have only worked practically as a performer, the design questions might seem rather daunting. This book is here to support you and increase your knowledge and confidence.

Thinking as a sound designer for the set text

Do you listen to music? Do you watch television and films?

If yes, you will be able to harness your subconscious knowledge of how sound can be used creatively.

Next time you listen to music or watch something that goes beyond the use of dialogue in terms of sound, concentrate on the meaning and atmosphere being enhanced. This might mean listening out for the diegetic and non-diegetic sounds in a film or identifying the dominant emotion or atmosphere in a piece of music.

You will not know in advance what extract you will be given, but you will know which play it will be from.

To start you off, can you think of three ways you could explore the text? Anything that helps you to become familiar with the text on the page and in performance is worth spending time on. The best way to revise, however, is to create sound designs yourself.

Why is it useful to create sound design for the set text?

- Working with your design practically will make it memorable when it comes to the written exam.
- If you are new to sound design, you will gain practical knowledge and subject-specific language that will be useful in the exam and in real life.
- It is also fun!

If you decide to complete your sound design, you will create the documentation that would enable your sounds to be successfully operated during a performance.

Steppenwolf's production of *The Crucible*. What sound effects and music – if any – might be suitable for this scene?

Chapter 6 Component 1: Understanding Drama

What early decisions about sound need to be made?

Once you are familiar with the whole play, ask yourself:

> **Will non-diegetic sound work with the chosen style of the production?**
> (A purely diegetic and naturalistic design would only include the sounds that the actors would hear.)

> **What period of time is the production to be set in? How could I use sound to enhance this?**

Creating a mood board

Mood boards help a designer to think about style, atmosphere, sound and artistic intentions in terms of impact and meaning. It could be digital or produced on paper or card.

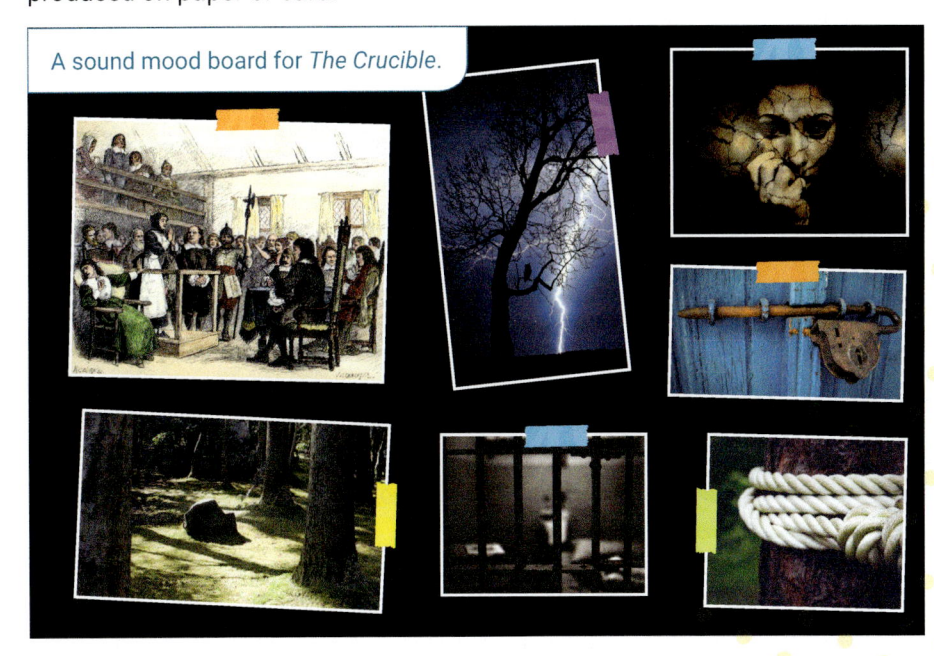

A sound mood board for *The Crucible*.

TASK 6.19

With a partner, discuss what sound effects the creator of this mood board might produce.

TASK 6.20

1. To begin your own mood board, quickly think of ten adjectives for your set text. Words for *The Crucible* might include: *frightening, dark, secret*, and so on.
2. Gather images that match your adjectives in some way.
3. Move on to think about suitable nouns, such as *witchcraft, persecution, McCarthyism, puritans, farmsteads*, and gather images for them with the same 'feel' as those for your adjectives.
4. Now think about how to organise these images onto the page. They could overlap or be grouped in ways that inspire you.
5. You could also add pictures or actual items showing colours and textures, such as bark, rope and wood.
6. With a partner, discuss what sound effects are suggested by your mood board.

DESIGN TIP
Underscoring and soundscapes can add an extra dimension to sound design.

DESIGN TIP
You will need to comment on the original context of the play in the exam. Consider the period in which the play is set when you answer question B.1 in particular.

What music and sound effects would you use in this scene from *The 39 Steps*? (Village Theatre, Issaquah, Washington.) How could you ensure your choices are in harmony with set and lighting design as well as the mood of the scene in terms of action and characterisation?

Revising sound design in the set text

TASK 6.21

1 Research and make notes on the social and historical contexts of the set text you have studied.

Blood Brothers, for example, is set over quite a long time period – from the early 1960s to the early 1980s – and is located in Liverpool. *The 39 Steps* is set in England and Scotland between the First and Second World Wars.

2 Use your research to complete your own version of the table below. (Examples have been given using *The 39 Steps*.)

	How sound design could enhance settings, themes, context and atmosphere
Settings: • Music Hall • Crofter's cottage • The moors • The train • Hannay's flat.	• Diagetic sounds such as the train and the wind. • The applause of the music hall. • 1930s music.
Themes: • Love • Nationalism • Spying • Chases and escapes	• Exaggerated cliffhanger soundscape. • The tempo of the music and effects will also support the different themes. Slow for romantic moments; faster for excitement and danger.
Context: Mid-1930s Britain.	• Music from the period will help put the play into context. • The radio's announcer's voice should be recorded with some reverb to convey the sound of the older recording studios.
Genre/mood/ atmosphere: • Farce • Melodrama • Humour.	• Underscoring to add romantic or thrilling atmosphere. • Exaggerated sounds that are clichéd. • Loud volume for exciting or funny moments.

TASK 6.22

Taking your mood board and the table above as a guide, begin to make some decisions about your design (as much as you can so far).

- What will the stage configuration be? Where will the audience sit? (This effects where you will place your speakers.)
- How will locations be suggested?
- How will the time period of the play be indicated?
- What are the main moods and atmospheres?
- How much non-diegetic sound might you want?
- Do you need your sounds to fit in with changes in lighting?

Chapter 6 Component 1: Understanding Drama

TASK 6.23

1. Select a section of your text that offers plenty of opportunity for interesting sounds and music.
2. Make a list of the sound effects that you want to create and the type of music you think would add the right atmosphere.
3. Read sections in Chapter 2 to help you make notes about how you could find and cue those effects.
4. Set up a computer folder that contains your effects and music.
5. Play your chosen sounds to classmates. Use their feedback to evaluate your work.

TASK 6.24

1. Try creating a source sheet and cue sheet for your extract.
2. If you can, work with actors to perform the extract, so that you can operate the sound yourself.

A production in the round, like *The Crucible* at Cleveland Playhouse, presents interesting opportunities and challenges for a director, designers and performers.

Exam practice

You need to practise how to respond in the written exam. If you have prepared well, it should not be too daunting.

You need to be ready to write confidently and fairly rapidly as soon as you have understood the questions and decided which one to answer. Completing the tasks in this section will help you.

Question B.1

The first question in Section B asks you to suggest a possible design for your set play. It might look like the one below.

Your teacher can give you similar questions and extracts from the play you are studying so that you can practise your own answers.

TASK 6.25

Read the question below, and then the sample response on the following page. Use the B.1 mark scheme to put the response into a band. Share your ideas with a partner and come to a joint decision on which band best fits the example.

The extract referred to is from Scene 9 of *The 39 Steps* – on the train ('He kisses her passionately' to the end of the scene).

> You are designing sound for a performance of this extract. The sounds must reflect the context of *The 39 Steps*, set in England and Scotland in 1935. Describe your design ideas for sound. [4 marks]

LOOK HERE

'Introduction to design in the written exam', pages 128–131, has several tasks and plenty of advice. Read it carefully and complete Task 6.2 in particular, relating it to sound design.

DESIGN TIP

Briefly include design details with reasons for your choices. You must comment on the context as set out in the question.

For this extract, I would use sound design to help create the illusion that the action aboard the train is real. Sound is particularly important because the staging is very non-naturalistic and the audience would need realistic sound to help make the scene as tense and thrilling as it is intended to be.

An important element of realism will come from the type of train sounds that I would use. As the play is set in the 1930s, the Edinburgh train that Hannay is aboard would have been steam powered. This means that there would be the clattering of the wheels on the line and the occasional sound of hissing steam. I would mix a track of recorded sound using online sources to powerfully suggest the sound of the train in motion. The volume would change at points. For example, I would reduce the volume to very low when the 'romantic music is playing' (a 1930s melody) to avoid splitting the attention of the audience. It would also need to be quiet enough for the actors' voices to be heard. When Hannay opens the door of the train to leap out, I would turn the train soundtrack up high and also introduce a track of wind rushing by to show that Hannay is in great danger. Later in the extract, when the communication cable is pulled, the frantic screeching of the brakes trying to pull the train to a halt would be almost deafening. The effect of the sound would only work well if the actors rehearsed with it to get the timing of their movements in sync with the sound.

I am imagining that it is staged in the round.

Question B.5

The final question in Section B carries 20 marks and is optional. (You could answer B.4 instead, which is a performance question.)

TASK 6.26

1. Highlight and make sure you understand the key words in this question:

> You are a designer working on one aspect of design for this extract. Describe how you would use your design skills to create effects which support characterisation. Explain why your ideas are appropriate for:
> • this extract • the play as a whole. [20 marks]

2. Label the example answer on the facing page with:

   F – **F**ocus on the question

   Ex – Supporting **ex**ample

   T – Appropriate **t**echnical language

   I – **I**deas that are appropriate to the extract and the whole play.

3. Use the mark scheme to decide on a band and then a mark out of 20.

The following response is about *The Crucible* (Act Three, from 'Danforth: Look at me' to 'Mary Warren: Abby, I'm here!').

> *I would use sound design to help the audience's journey through the extract. I am imagining that it is staged in the round.*
>
> *Silence is an important aspect and I would use it at the start of the scene to allow the dialogue to build its own tension. Another of the many points in the play when I would use silence is in the scene between Proctor and Elizabeth (start of Act 2). The silence would help to convey how strained their relationship is at this point in the play.*
>
> *For the extract, when Elizabeth says 'No sir!', I would fade in a piece of music that is a theme for Elizabeth and John's relationship: a section of Shostakovich's Symphony Number 10 — played on the clarinet. It has a slightly haunting feel. It seems to sum up the warmth that is buried in their relationship with a sense of regret running through it. As it underscores some dialogue, I would play it at a low volume level (−15 dB).*
>
> *Using music as a thread that runs through the play enhances the audience's understanding that the character or character relationship is the focus. The same theme for Elizabeth and Proctor would be used at several points, including the very end of the play as 'the new sun is pouring in upon her face'. Here, the volume would come in quietly (−5dB) and fade up to 5dB over 5 seconds before fading out completely in time with the lights fading to blackout.*
>
> *In the extract, the sound effect of the door closing as Elizabeth is removed would be a recorded source and I would add a little echo to help create the feeling that she and John will not see each other again. The music track would fade out under 'She only thought to save my name!' This would allow for the change in pace and focus as Hale's speech begins.*
>
> *The next sound cue would come with Abigail's 'weird, wild, chilling cry'. I would snap in a drone sound mixed with the sound of crows and the Shostakovich piece at a low level. This multi-layered soundscape should heighten the audience's experience of the moment.*
>
> *This time, the volume would rise to 0dB as the actors' voices rise during this moment of hysteria. The sound effect would help the audience to sense the fear in Danforth and the girls. I would have speakers above the acting area pointing at the four audience seating areas and on the back walls behind them. I want the audience to be fully immersed in the scene.*
>
> *I would briefly reduce the volume of the soundscape to −5dB when Mary Warren jumps to her feet and pleads 'Abby!' I want to mark this as the moment when Mary becomes involved in the girls' hysteria. Throughout the play, the volume and the speed of transitions would be key. I would position myself at various audience points during the technical rehearsal to check the volume levels.*

TASK 6.27

Re-create the soundscape described in this example answer by opening three separate tabs and playing crows cawing, the symphony and a drone sound at the same time. How effective do you think it is?

TASK 6.28

Test yourself.

Write your own response to a similar question based on an extract from your set play.

DESIGN TIP

You are expected to include technical detail because you are writing from the viewpoint of someone with a lot of subject knowledge. Try to use appropriate technical terms.

Richard Armitage and Anna Madeley share a quieter moment as Proctor and Elizabeth at the Old Vic.

ASSESSMENT CHECK

Section C assesses AO3 and AO4. These pages help you to:

- demonstrate understanding of how drama and theatre is developed and performed
- investigate and identify how successfully theatre makers communicated meaning to an audience (analysis)
- assess the merit of approaches used and formulate judgements (evaluation).

DESIGN TIP

A programme from the performance is likely to be a useful source of information.

DESIGN TIP

The way sound worked with lighting or contributed to atmosphere and context would be valuable information to include.

SOUND DESIGN IN LIVE THEATRE (SECTION C)

In this part of the exam, you could give detailed explanations and an evaluation of the sound design in a performance you have seen. You should justify your opinions with examples that 'include a number of precise details.' You are also aiming to use technical language.

Preparation for a sound design question

Look in the show programme, theatre marketing material and online for information about the sound designer and the sound itself. Major productions and tours often have images, information and reviews online. Photographs in particular might help to remind you of details of the sound and how it complemented other elements of the performance. You might also be able to find interviews with sound designers.

Remember that you were a member of the audience. The exam will ask you to comment on the impact that sound had on the audience. Share your responses with your classmates, but aim to write about your own viewpoints in the exam. You are expected to make a critical evaluation.

Christopher Shutt with his Tony Award for the sound design in *War Horse*.

TASK 6.29

1. Study any notes about the sound design that you made after seeing the performance.
2. Make some simple sketches based on your notes and images you find.
3. Annotate them with details of sound and music that created impact or otherwise contributed to meaning and mood. What do you remember about the sound, and why?
4. Discuss the sound with other people in your class. Pooling your memories is valid and the discussion will help you to recall the experience of the production.

Evaluation as a skill
Evaluating sound design
The exam will ask you about design in the production as a whole: it will not specify which scenes to write about. So, evaluate the moments that stood out for you as examples of how sound was used effectively.

> **SIGNPOST**
> 'Evaluating your sound design' on page 61 gives guidance on evaluative writing about sound.

TASK 6.30
1. If you can, browse of the script for the live performance to find a section where sound had an impact on you.
2. Try to remember the sound at key points in this section. Consider soundscapes and the mixing of sound effects, as well as the use of music.
3. Write at least two paragraphs of critical judgement, which include:
   - technical language, such as *volume*, *soundscape*, *live*, *recorded*
   - how sound contributed to the style of the production
   - atmosphere or meaning that sound enhanced for the audience
   - evaluations supported by details, such as, 'The... was powerful because...' and 'I was impressed by... It made me feel/think...'
4. Swap your writing with someone else's for feedback.

TASK 6.31
1. Read 'Evaluating your sound design' carefully and complete the task.
2. Remember that you are evaluating someone else's set design, rather than your own. Use examples from the live performance.

Working with an example answer
These tasks will help you to analyse an answer before trying one of your own.

TASK 6.32
1. Highlight and make sure you understand the key words in this question:

> Describe how sound was used to support the style of the production. Analyse and evaluate how successful the sound was in helping to communicate the style of the production to the audience. You should make reference to:
> • type of sound • sound effects • volume, amplification and direction.   [32 marks]

2. Annotate the example answer on the following page with:

   F – **F**ocus on the question

   Ex – **Ex**ample to support argument or point

   T – Appropriate **t**echnical language

   U – **U**nderstanding and knowledge of sound design in relation to the performance

   E – **E**valuation in terms of how successful the sound was.

3. Use the AO4 mark scheme to decide on a band and a mark out of 20. (The remaining 12 marks relate to AO3.)

Joey faces down the tank in *War Horse*.

> **DESIGN TIP**
>
> Include as much detail as possible in your answers. Highlight your evaluative judgements by using terms such as 'effective' and 'powerful impact'.

TASK 6.33

Test yourself.

1. Answer the same question, about the live performance you have chosen.

    Use the mark schemes and other tasks in this chapter to guide you.

2. If possible, ask another student or your teacher to mark your answer. Can you make improvements based on their comments?

> **DESIGN TIP**
>
> Try as many exam-type questions as you can. To practise under exam conditions, give yourself a maximum of 40 minutes to complete your answer.

The sound designer of War Horse, Christopher Stutt, has developed a varied design that uses live and recorded sound to enhance the style, meaning and atmosphere of this exciting and moving production on a proscenium stage. The style of the play can be best described as epic, period storytelling. Diverse locations and experiences had to be conveyed in an aural landscape.

Many outdoor, diegetic sounds were used. Recorded, naturalistic sounds added a depth of atmosphere to the countryside scenes. The specially composed music was greatly enhanced by the sounds of birds and integrated perfectly with the other design elements, particularly lighting. The warm colours of the lights combined very well with the sounds that evoked summer mornings.

One of the sound design highlights was created using recorded sound. It was the moment when the tank comes onto the stage. Special speakers were worn by the performers operating the tank. Recorded sounds of a tank engine were amplified from these speakers at a very loud volume, which gave me an overwhelming sense of the horror that the horse and characters must have felt. Speakers at the sides of the stage intensified the sound on stage and all around the auditorium, which pulled us powerfully into the action.

The volume of music and sound effects varied depending on the dialogue. During ensemble scenes, such as the horse sale and when Joey is pulling the plough, the radio mics of the principal players were louder than the ensemble cast who were then free to create the background 'babble' of voices without drowning out dialogue. The designer and technicians must have spent time in each theatre on the tour to check that sound levels were correct.

Live sound was introduced when the performers used their voices to create, for example, the sounds of Joey. His snorting, whinnying and so on were synchronised with the puppeteers' movements. Recorded sounds could have been used, but the live sounds had much more life and power. Each of the three puppeteers had separate radio microphones, and then the sound was mixed and transmitted live in the form of one sound by the sound engineer. I think this contributed significantly to our sense of the horses being alive.

A chilling example of this sense of the horses being real is when Joey is caught in barbed wire. I felt terribly involved and quite upset during this moment. Fortunately, the same techniques created opposite emotions, such as when Albert and Joey are alone together and their communication with each other was wonderfully uplifting. This expert use of sound allowed the audience to be totally involved in the world of the story.

SET DESIGN IN THE SET PLAY (SECTION B)

If you have only worked practically as a performer, the design questions might seem rather daunting. This book is here to support you.

Thinking as a set designer for the set text

You will not know in advance what extract you will be given, but you will know which play it will be from.

To start you off, can you think of three ways you could explore the text? Anything that helps you to become familiar with the text on the page and in performance is worth spending time on. The best way to revise, however, is to create set designs yourself.

What do you think the set should look like?

Once you are familiar with the play, begin to imagine how the set might look.

It is often useful to study the original designs for the play. The designer will have had an excellent understanding of the playwright and director's artistic intentions and the circumstances of its production.

Why is it useful to document a set design that is unlikely to be built?

- Ground plans and sketches will show your skills and present a clear idea of your design. These are often quick to produce.
- You can annotate your drawing, which will also be quicker than writing a prose description.
- A model box would allow you to explore how practical a design is. You can move things around and see how it would look.
- Working with a design practically will make it memorable.
- If you are new to set design, you will gain practical knowledge and useful subject-specific language.
- It is also fun!

FOCUS
How to write as if you are a set designer.

ASSESSMENT CHECK
Section A assesses AO3: 'Demonstrate knowledge and understanding of how theatre is developed and performed.'

These notes will help your knowledge and understanding of design and of the set play.

DESIGN TIP
Using specialist design language is one of the most important things you can learn to do.

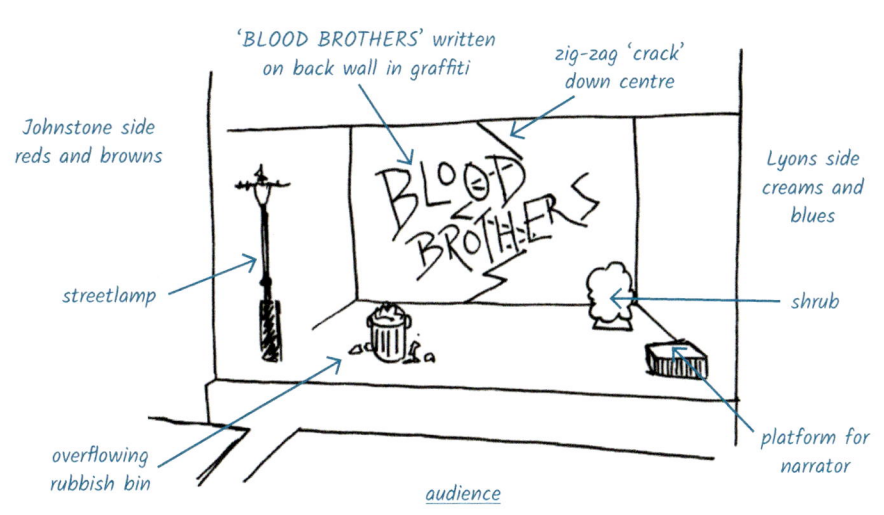

Labelled sketch annotations:
- 'BLOOD BROTHERS' written on back wall in graffiti
- zig-zag 'crack' down centre
- Johnstone side reds and browns
- Lyons side creams and blues
- streetlamp
- shrub
- overflowing rubbish bin
- platform for narrator
- audience

This labelled sketch of a set for *Blood Brothers* provides a lot of information in a few words!

TASK 6.34

1. Draw some rough sketches of possible designs for your set text and decide which works best.
2. When you have a sketch that you are happy with, follow the instructions on page 70 to create a ground plan.
3. You could also create a 3D model, using the guidance on pages 71–72.

LOOK HERE
There is another example of a set design sketch on page 69.

DESIGN TIP

You don't need to build your set design, but you could construct a simple one if you are rehearsing sections of the text in lessons.

TASK 6.35

1. To begin your own mood board, quickly think of five adjectives for your set text. Words for *Hansel and Gretel* might include *playful, funny, hungry, dark*.
2. Gather images that match your adjectives in some way.
3. Move on to think about suitable nouns, such as *chickens, forest, witch*, and gather images for them with the same 'feel' as those for your adjectives.
4. Now think about how to organise these images on the page or screen, grouping them in ways that inspire you.
5. You could add pictures or real items showing colours and textures, such as bark or wire.

DESIGN TIP

Deciding on a stage configuration (end on, in the round, and so on) is a vital early step.

Creating a mood board

Mood boards help a designer to think about style and atmosphere and artistic intentions in terms of impact and meaning.

A set design mood board for *Hansel and Gretel*.

Planning your set design

TASK 6.36

1. Begin your own version of this table with factual, stylistic and atmospheric clues that could influence set design choices.

Stage configuration:			
Historical period	Locations/s	Genre and style	Atmosphere/s

2. Now make some decisions about your design.
   - Will the set be permanent, changed for different scenes, or composite (all locations on stage at the same time)?
   - How will locations be suggested?
   - Will your set be naturalistic or abstract?
   - What colour palette will you use?
   - What textures and materials would work well?
   - What should be on the floor of the acting area?

Exam practice

You need to write confidently and fairly rapidly as soon as you have understood the questions and decided which one to answer. If you have prepared well, it should not be too daunting. Completing the tasks in this section will help you.

Question B.1

The first question in Section B asks you to suggest a possible design for your set play. It might look like the one below.

Your teacher can give you similar questions and extracts from the play you are studying so that you can practise writing your own answers.

> You are designing a setting for this extract [the start of Act 3, where Puck and a Fairy meet and then Titania and Oberon argue]. The set must reflect the original ancient Athens setting of *A Midsummer Night's Dream*. Describe your design ideas for the setting. [4 marks]

DESIGN TIP
Briefly include design details with reasons for your choices. You must comment on the context as set out in the question.

TASK 6.37

Using the B.1 mark scheme, put the student answer below into band 1 to 4. Share your ideas with a partner and come to a joint decision on which band best fits the example.

> *I would design my set as promenade performance in a local park. The audience would sit in a semi-circular configuration on cushions or picnic chairs they carry with them. The various entrances and exits required would utilise the trees, shrubs and rocky outcrops that can be found in the park. I would have two ornate semi-derelict Greek statues constructed from lightweight but robust materials on metal and wood plinths. These would be secured USL and USR of the main performance area. The plinths would be 60cm high, stepped up in 20cm stages. They would suggest the original setting as well as allow the actors to use levels. Oberon, for example, could step higher to show his power on the line 'Am I not thy lord?'*
>
> *The statues themselves would suggest Diana (goddess of hunting and the moon) and Aphrodite (goddess of love and beauty). These would fit the theme and plot. The colour palette would suggest the marble of the ancient Greek period and blend with the natural surroundings of the park.*

Question B.5

The final question in Section B carries 20 marks and is optional. (You could answer B.4 instead, which is a performance question.)

TASK 6.38

1. Highlight the key words in the following example question:

> You are working on one aspect of design for this extract [*Blood Brothers* Act 1, from where the twins become blood brothers to Edward's exit]. Describe how you would use your design skills to create effects which support the action. Explain why your ideas are appropriate for:
> - this extract
> - the play as a whole. [20 marks]

2. Now check your understanding of the key words, using a glossary if necessary.

3. Label the answer on the following page with:

   F – **F**ocus on the question

   Ex – Supporting **ex**ample

   T – Appropriate **t**echnical language

   I – **I**deas suitable for the extract and the whole play.

4. Then use the AO3 mark scheme to decide on a band and then a mark out of 20.

I am designing the set for Blood Brothers on a proscenium arch stage.

For this extract I would use a backdrop of the city of Liverpool including tall buildings, such as the Liver Building, at the top of the backdrop and council houses on the lower levels. This would reflect the cultural differences in the extract and the play as a whole. It would also locate the play in of 1960s Liverpool. The LED lights which illuminate parts of the backdrop would be switched on for the council houses, as this is where the extract is set.

I would design a naturalistic set for the street where Mickey lives, and include levels such as a low wall where the boys could sit as they inspect Sammy's dead worms. The wall could also act as a screen so that Sammy might, for example, appear from behind it with his cap gun. The wall would be a lightweight but sturdy construction of metal and plywood which the boys could walk along at moments such as when Mrs Johnstone enters. She would see Edward standing up there and it would be clear that she is totally focused on him alone. The wall would be positioned on a diagonal downstage left so as to avoid interrupting sightlines. Another moment in the play where this level would be useful is later in Act I when Mrs Johnstone cradles Edward who is crying because he is leaving the city. She would sit on the wall and hold him against her, giving the audience the strong impression of the mother who wants to protect the son she has been separated from.

The colour palette would be largely naturalistic and combine with the textures (of the deep red bricks for example) to create the council housing. The brickwork would be painted onto large flats to create the house fronts and a wall upstage centre. Monochrome graffiti would be painted onto it. This would look harsh against the red brickwork and give the impression of a run-down area.

The floor-covering for my design would be dark grey vinyl. The neutral colour would work well for every scene. In this extract, the boys would be able to chalk on it and then rub it off as if they were chalking on a pavement. At other points in the play, the floor would reflect the colours of the lights such, as when red light is used during the death scene.

DESIGN TIP

You should include technical detail because you are writing from the viewpoint of someone with a lot of subject knowledge. Try to use technical terms. Adding a sketch or ground plan could save you time.

TASK 6.39

Test yourself.

1. Choose an extract from your set text of around 80 lines.
2. Write your own response to the question used in Task 6.38. Use the AO3 mark scheme and your experience of identifying important skills in the same task to guide you.

SET DESIGN IN LIVE THEATRE (SECTION C)

In this part of the exam, you could give detailed explanations and an evaluation of the set design in a performance you have seen. You should justify your opinions with examples that include a 'number of precise details.' You are also aiming to use technical language.

Preparation for a set design question

Look in the show programme, theatre marketing material and online for information about the set designer. Major productions and tours often have images, information and reviews online. Photographs in particular might help to remind you of details in the set and how they complemented other elements of the performance.

Remember that you were a member of the audience. The exam will ask you to comment on how the set supported the style or action of the play. Share your responses with your classmates, but aim to write about your own viewpoints in the exam. You are expected to make a critical evaluation.

TASK 6.40

1. Study any notes about the set that you made after seeing the performance.
2. Make some simple sketches based on your notes and images you find.
3. Annotate them with details of the set that created impact or otherwise contributed to meaning and mood. What do you remember about the set, and why?
4. Discuss the set with your classmates. Pooling your memories is valid and the discussion will help you to recall the experience of seeing the production.

Evaluation as a skill

TASK 6.41

1. Read 'Evaluating your set design' carefully and complete Task 3.12.
2. Complete Task 3.13 with examples from the live performance you have seen. Remember that you are evaluating describing and someone else's set design, not your own.

Set design evaluation

The exam question will ask you about a design element of the production as a whole: it will not specify which scenes to write about. So, describe and evaluate moments that stood out for you as examples of how the set was used to good effect.

ASSESSMENT CHECK

Section C assesses AO3 and AO4. These pages help you to:
- demonstrate understanding of how drama and theatre is developed and performed
- investigate and identify how successfully theatre makers communicated meaning to an audience (analysis)
- assess the merit of approaches used and formulate judgements (evaluation).

DESIGN TIP

A programme from the performance is likely to be a useful source of information.

SIGNPOST

'Evaluating your set design' on pages 78–79 gives guidance on evaluative writing about sets.

LOOK HERE

Look over Chapter 3 to help you with technical language and the period accuracy of your sketches.

DESIGN TIP
Consider including one or two annotated sketches in your notes for the exam.

TASK 6.42

1. If you can, find a copy of the script for the live performance you are writing about. Browse through it until you find a section where you remember the set having an impact on you.
2. Try to remember what the set looked like at key points in this section. These could be as short as a single moment or as long as a whole scene or more.
3. Write at least two paragraphs of critical judgement, which include:
   - subject-specific language, such as *flats*, *gauze*, *trucks* and so on
   - how lighting changed the look of the set and the effect of that
   - the way the set was used by the actors and the effect of that
   - atmosphere or meaning that was enhanced for the audience
   - evaluations supported by detailed examples, such as, 'The use of… was powerful because…' and 'I was impressed by… because it …'
4. Swap your writing with someone else's for feedback. You could use the bullet points above as a checklist.

Working with an example answer

The mark scheme is a valuable tool when you are preparing for the written exam. The following tasks will allow you to assess a sample answer and then practise one of your own.

TASK 6.43

1. Highlight the key words in this question:

   > Describe how the set was used to support the style of the production. Analyse and evaluate how successful the set was in helping to communicate the style of the production to the audience. You should make reference to:
   > • the appearance of the set • any changes in the set • how it was used by the actors.
   > [32 marks]

2. Now check your understanding of these key words, using a glossary if necessary.
3. Annotate the answer below, on the following page with:

   F – **F**ocus on the question

   Ex – **Ex**ample to support argument or point

   T – Appropriate **t**echnical language

   U – **U**nderstanding and knowledge of set design in relation to the performance

   E – **E**valuation in terms of how successful the set was.
4. Use the AO4 mark scheme to decide on a band and then a mark out of 20. (The remaining 12 marks relate to AO3.)

What symbolic meaning is conveyed by the collapse of the Victorian part of the set in this scene from the end of *An Inspector Calls*? How does this link to the destruction in the wartime section? (Original design by Ian MacNeil.)

TASK 6.44

Test yourself.

1. Based on the live performance you have chosen, answer the question in Task 6.43.

   Use the AO3 and AO4 mark scheme and other tasks to guide you.
2. If possible, ask another student or your teacher to mark your answer. Make improvements based on their comments.

DESIGN TIP

Try as many exam-type questions as you can. Your teacher should be able to set you suitable questions. When you feel ready to practise under exam conditions, give yourself a maximum of 40 minutes to complete your answer.

The extraordinary set for An Inspector Calls was designed by Ian MacNeil more than 20 years ago and it is truly unique and memorable. It combined the naturalistic style of the play with some really quirky non-naturalistic features, particularly the way that the Birlings' house is constructed on stilts.

The raked cobbled stage in a proscenium configuration suggested a style of production that spans the 1912 period of time when the play is set and the 1945 period when it was written. The cobbled street has an old, yet timeless feel as you still find cobbled streets in the north of England today.

The world outside the Birlings' Edwardian house is in the style of 1940s northern towns. The only large props here are a telephone box and a streetlamp. Telephone boxes weren't around in 1912 and so this piece of set design is important in establishing the two time periods existing alongside each other. It is also functional, as Mr Birling uses it at the end of the play to call the police. This is an example of how the set design forces the family out into the real world where they don't want to be.

Under the streetlamp is where we first see the Inspector, which is quite symbolic because we link him with the truth, which is like light in the darkness. This image of Inspector Goole is similar in style to 1940s film thrillers, especially when the footlights cast shadows behind him.

The atmosphere of the world outside the house is grim, which is maybe why the designer chose to have what looks like real rain falling on stage. This was one of my favourite things about the staging because it was so clever and really supported the idea that poor people live miserable lives.

The other thing that was incredible was the Birlings' house which had hydraulics built into it so that it could swing open and also tilt up. It was a real surprise when the scene with the young couple on the balcony ended with them going inside and the house opening like a doll's house. This part of the set design really suited the style of the piece because it showed how the Birlings like to stay in their own cosy world and ignore the world outside. It is the Inspector who forces them out into the world as the truth of their lack of care for others is put to them. The colour palette of the inside of the house is full of rich purples and golds which is a great contrast to the dark grey used outside the house. I think that the colour inside the house and the use of set dressings like the tablecloth and the cut glass and silver strongly enhance the sense of the huge difference between the lives of the wealthy and the lives of ordinary, poorer people. When the house tilts up at the end of the play and all of the Birlings' fine things tip out onto the street, the set is being used to show that the Birlings (and people like them) don't have the safe and steady lives they think they deserve.

Upstage was a huge cyclorama which had a projection on it of a sky filled with clouds. During the play, the sky turned to different colours which had a significant impact on the atmosphere. It also made me feel as if the action included me too because it was so big and sometimes had such a realistic feeling to it. I can hardly imagine seeing a more exciting set.

FOCUS

How to write as if you are a costume designer.

ASSESSMENT CHECK

Section B assesses AO3: 'Demonstrate knowledge and understanding of how theatre is developed and performed.'

These notes will help your knowledge and understanding of design and of the set play.

Photo: Robert Day

Heather Agyepong as Sephy and Billy Harris as Callum wear similar check patterns in Pilot Theatre's *Noughts & Crosses*.

DESIGN TIP

Using specialist design language is one of the most important things you can learn to do.

COSTUME DESIGN IN THE SET PLAY (SECTION B)

If you have only worked practically as a performer, the design questions might seem rather daunting. This book is here to support you and increase your knowledge and confidence.

Thinking as a costume designer for the set text

You will not know in advance what extract you will be given, but you will know which play it will be from.

To start you off, can you think of three ways you could explore the text? Anything that helps you to become familiar with the text on the page and in performance is worth spending time on. The best way to revise, however, is to create costume designs yourself.

How do you think the costumes should look?

TASK 6.45

1. Research and make notes on the historical, social, political and economic contexts of the set play you have studied.

   Noughts & Crosses, for example, was written in 2007. The play is set in an alternative 21st-century Britain.

2. Use your research to complete your own version of the table below. (Examples have been provided using *Noughts & Crosses*.)

Character	Garments	Accessories	Link to contexts
Sephy	• Tailored, knee-length dress in pale blue cotton • Navy school blazer with pale blue trim • Pale blue leather pump-style flat shoes.	• Smart, navy blue rucksack.	Sephy is a Cross – she is part of the wealthy ruling class. The quality and styling of her costume reflects this.
Callum	• Orange jumpsuit/overall of coarse, heavy cotton. Loose enough to cover school uniform underneath • White shirt and navy trousers under the overalls.	• Worn black trainers. • Simple black canvas rucksack.	• Callum is a Nought – he is part of the underclass. • The orange jumpsuit should remind the audience that he is a second class, anonymous Blank to most of the Crosses. • His trainers and bag are a reminder that he is poor.

164 Chapter 6 Component 1: Understanding Drama

TASK 6.46

1. Search the internet for costume images appropriate to your set play. Familiarise yourself with key costume features relating to the period, including fabrics and fashions, and the social and cultural conditions of the play's main characters.
2. Select an extract of about 80 lines that inspires you in terms of its costume possibilities.
3. Decide whether the style would be naturalistic or non-naturalistic.
4. Choose two characters from the extract. Complete a table like this for their costume features.

Character	Period and culture	Fabric/colour choices	Garments	Make-up, accessories, hair and headwear, shoes

5. Sketch each character and annotate it to include detail.
6. Show and explain your designs to another member of the class and answer any questions they have.

LOOK HERE

'Introduction to design in the written exam', pages 128–131, has several tasks and plenty of advice. Try Task 6.2 in particular.

DESIGN TIP

Briefly include design details with reasons for your choices. You must comment on the context as set out in the question.

Exam practice

You need to practise how to respond in the written exam. If you have prepared well, it should not be too daunting.

You need to be ready to write confidently and fairly rapidly as soon as you have understood the questions and decided which one to answer. Completing the tasks in this section will help you.

Question B.1

The first question in Section B requires you to suggest a possible design for your set play. It might look like the one on the right.

Your teacher will be able to give you similar questions and extracts from the set play you are studying so that you can practise your own answers.

> You are designing a costume for Mrs Lyons to wear in a performance of this extract [Act 1, where Mickey calls on Eddie]. The costume must reflect the context of *Blood Brothers*, set in Liverpool in the early 1970s. Describe your design ideas for the costume.
>
> [4 marks]

TASK 6.47

Using the B.1 mark scheme, put the student answer below into band 1 to 4. Share your ideas with a partner and come to a joint decision on which band best fits the example.

> In this extract I would costume Mrs Lyons in a straight knee-length skirt and a short-sleeved blouse. The skirt would be made of navy polyester – a popular fabric of the time. The pale pink blouse would have very small buttons. She would also drape a long-sleeved white cardigan around her shoulders. This combination is appropriate for a middle-class woman at home in the early 1970s. She would wear pale blue eye make-up and pale pink lipstick because, even at home, Mrs Lyons would want to look respectable for herself and for her husband. Her hair would have a centre parting with grips holding it at each side, which was a 'sensible' look at that time.
>
> Mrs Lyons' character appears to be an upright, everyday mother who doesn't have to go out to work. However, the audience know she is hiding a terrible secret. I would give her a single string of pearls to wear. This would allow the actress to fiddle with them nervously when she comes back from making Mickey leave.

Question B.5

The final question in Section B carries 20 marks and is optional. (You could answer Question B.4 instead, which is a performance question.)

TASK 6.48

1 Highlight the key words in the following sample question about Act 3 of *The Crucible* (when Elizabeth has been brought from the cells to explain why she fired Abigail).

> You are a designer working on one aspect of design for this extract. Describe how you would use your design skills to create effects which support the action. Explain why your ideas are appropriate for:
> - this extract
> - the play as a whole. [20 marks]

2 Now check your understanding of those words, using a glossary.

3 Read and annotate the student response on the following page with:

   F – **F**ocus on the question, including context

   Ex – **Ex**ample to support argument or point

   T – Appropriate **t**echnical language

   I – **I**deas appropriate to the extract and the play as a whole.

4 Use the AO3 mark scheme to decide on a band for the response, and then a mark out of 20.

In this image of Irene Allen as Elizabeth Proctor, her hair is uncombed and matted. Her face and hands are scratched and streaked with dirt. Her dress is still buttoned up, but it is torn, creased and soiled. These details of costume and make-up clearly reveal the suffering that Elizabeth is going through and indicate her degraded, vulnerable state. (Designed by Michael Taylor for Edinburgh Lyceum.)

Chapter 6 Component 1: Understanding Drama

I have chosen a naturalistic design for The Crucible in its stated context of the 1690s.

I want my costumes to show Elizabeth and Proctor's journey as characters. Having been imprisoned for some time in squalid conditions, Elizabeth would wear a distressed, broken-down version of her original costume. Her coarse cotton dress is blue to reflect the coolness of her personality, but it would now be torn and dirtied. Her apron would be gone, to symbolise the loss of her role as a housewife, but she will retain a sullied version of her white puritan collar: the fact that she is a devout Christian will be evident. Her hair will be loose and tangled, and her bonnet gone. She might attempt to secure her hair in the neck of her dress. She would be embarrassed to have her hair uncovered during this Puritan period. In Acts 1 and 2, she would wear a plain brown cap.

She will be barefoot to show her vulnerability, whereas, in earlier parts of the play, she would wear long woollen stockings and flat, brown leather lace-up shoes. I will use the brown and black shades of a bruise wheel to add 'dirt' to exposed skin. I will use redder shades to reveal the damage done to her wrists by the heavy handcuffs.

Proctor will also wear a degraded version of his original costume. The leather jerkin will be retained to reflect his physical and emotional strength, but his breeches and rough wool shirt will be torn, soiled and bloodied. He has been tortured, so, his face and hands will be bloodied and bruised. I will have ensured that the actor has no allergies to make-up products. I would mix fake blood with coffee granules to give an authentic textured effect and maintain some shine to the 'damaged' areas of skin so that the marks show up brutally under the intensity of the stage lights. Proctor's work boots will be split and misshapen, encouraging the actor to move with a shuffling gait, demonstrating his pain. The aim is to enhance the audience's empathy with the character. Earlier in the play, Proctor's boots are worn, but cared for, as they are very important to a famer.

In contrast, Danforth's costume will be pristine throughout. The texture of his black breeches and doublet will be smooth and fine, to suggest his wealth. I would choose a good-quality cotton with a sateen finish. His black slip-on shoes will be highly polished to reflect his pious attention to detail. In keeping with his Puritan faith, there will be little embellishment to his costume, but I would add a buckle to his tall felt hat to show his sense of superiority. He will have a fine white cotton shirt and starched white cravat. The audience should interpret Danforth's character as being 'holier than thou'.

DESIGN TIP

You are expected to include technical detail because you are writing from the viewpoint of a designer with subject-specific knowledge and skills. Try to use appropriate technical terms. You might find it helpful to add an annotated sketch.

TASK 6.49

Test yourself.

Now write your own response to a question similar to that in Task 6.48, based on an extract from your own set play.

ASSESSMENT CHECK

Section C assesses AO3 and AO4. These pages help you to:

- demonstrate understanding of how drama and theatre is developed and performed
- investigate and identify how successfully theatre makers communicated meaning to an audience (analysis)
- assess the merit of approaches used and formulate judgements (evaluation).

DESIGN TIP

The way costumes worked with lighting or contributed to atmosphere and context would be valuable information to include in your written exam.

DESIGN TIP

A show programme is likely to be a useful source of information.

LOOK HERE

Use Chapter 4 to help you with technical language and period accuracy of your sketches.

COSTUME DESIGN IN LIVE THEATRE (SECTION C)

In this part of the exam, you could give detailed descriptions and an evaluation of the costume design in a performance you have seen. You should justify your opinions with examples that include a 'number of precise details.' You are also aiming to use technical language.

Preparation for a costume design question

Look in the show programme, theatre marketing material and online for information about the costume designer. Major productions and tours often have images, information and reviews online. Photographs in particular will help to remind you of details in the costumes and how costumes complemented other elements of the performance.

Remember that you were a member of the audience. You will need to comment on the effect the costumes had on you. Share your different responses with your classmates, but aim to write about your own viewpoints in the exam. You are expected to make a critical evaluation.

TASK 6.50

1. Study any costume notes you made after seeing the performance and put them together with production photographs you have found.
2. Use these to draw your own simple sketches of key characters.
3. Annotate them to pick out particular details that created impact or were otherwise important. What do you remember about them? Why? What effect did they have on the audience? Did they contribute to characterisation, context, style or themes?
4. Discuss costuming with other people in your class. Pooling your memories is valid and the discussion will help you to recall the experience of seeing the production.

Evaluation as a skill

Evaluating costume design

The exam will ask you about a design element of the production as a whole: it will not specify which moments to write about. So, describe and evaluate examples of how costumes were used effectively.

TASK 6.52

1. If you can, find a copy of the script for the live performance you are writing about. Browse through it until you find a section where you remember the costumes having an impact on you.
2. Try to remember what the costumes looked like at key points in this section. These could be a single moment or a whole scene.
3. Write at least two paragraphs of critical judgement, which include:
   - subject-specific language, such as *colour palette, style, silhouette, texture, fit* and so on
   - the effect lighting had on the appearance of the costumes
   - how atmosphere or meaning that was enhanced for the audience
   - evaluations supported by detailed examples, such as, 'The use of… was powerful because…' and 'I was impressed by… because it made me feel/think…'
4. Swap your writing with someone else's for feedback. You could use the bullet points above as a checklist.

TASK 6.51

Read carefully 'Evaluating your costume design' on page 105 and complete Task 4.15 with examples from the live performance. Remember that you are evaluating someone else's costume designs, rather than your own.

SIGNPOST

'Evaluating your costume design' on page 105 gives guidance on evaluative writing about costumes.

Working with an example answer

The mark scheme is a valuable tool when you are preparing for the written exam. The following tasks will allow you to assess a sample answer and then practise one of your own.

TASK 6.53

1. Highlight and make sure you understand the key words in this question:

   > Describe how the costume was used to support the characterisation of the production. Analyse and evaluate how successful the costumes were in helping to communicate the characterisation of the production to the audience. You should make reference to:
   > • fabrics/accessories • colour/texture • shape/fit.   [32 marks]

2. Annotate the example answer on the following page with:

   F – **F**ocus on the question

   Ex – **Ex**ample to support argument or point

   T – Appropriate **t**echnical language

   U – **U**nderstanding and knowledge of costume in the performance

   E – **E**valuation in terms of how successful the costumes were.

3. Use the AO4 mark scheme to decide on a band for the response, and then a mark out of 20. (The remaining 12 marks relate to AO3.)

DESIGN TIP

Try as many exam-type questions as you can. Your teacher should be able to set you suitable questions. When you feel ready to practise under exam conditions, give yourself a maximum of 40 minutes to complete your answer.

Chapter 6   Component 1: Understanding Drama   169

The drab, stained costumes and faces of Cosette and Eponine contrast with the well-fitting, brightly patterned, delicately embroidered dress of Fantine and her softly curled hair.

The whole production of Les Misérables at the Sondheim Theatre was extraordinary. Andreane Neofitou designed dozens of breathtaking costumes for the ensemble cast of this famous musical, which not only looked stunning, but enhanced our understanding of the characters and their journeys faultlessly.

For example, when we first see Cosette as a child, she is dressed in a loose-fitting, grey, ragged dress with a stained apron and a cap typical of a poor child in early 19th-century France. The choice of what appeared to be coarsely textured natural fabric was also very accurate for the period and the context of Cosette's poverty. Her feet were bare and special effects make-up in greys, reds and browns had been applied to her feet, face and arms to create the impression that she was dirty, bruised and underfed. Her hair was loose and had been lightly backcombed and powdered so that it appeared tangled and unwashed. The costume itself was heavily 'broken down' to suggest how neglected the child was as well as how hard she was working. This obviously created empathy toward Cosette from the audience.

By contrast, the clothes that had been designed and created with great detail for the adult Cosette reflected the way that her life had been turned on its head. Her wedding dress was in the style of the early 1830s, with a boat neck, large puffed sleeves and a full-length veil. It had lace details on the bodice and a skirt that was heavily pleated at the waist. I imagine that there was a netted underskirt as it was tight fitting at the bodice and extremely full in the skirt. Although it appeared to be white, I believe it was ivory or off-white silk. The way that the dress appeared under the coloured lights suggested that the fabric wasn't bright white as it would have absorbed more colour or seemed blue. In terms of characterisation, Cosette's costume helped the actress to radiate the joy of her marriage as the audience loved watching Marius waltz her around the stage as her skirt swirled around her.

The many costumes clearly presented the time period as well as helping to conjure up the various locations such as the factory and the barricades.

As all of the performers apart from Valjean play more than one character (in some cases quite a few), and the costumes played a very important part in establishing these characters. Partly this was a matter of style and fit. Some of the ensemble actresses wore layers of costumes including different-coloured long woollen stockings that could be removed easily for quick changes. The attention to such details was exceptional. As a bottom layer the actresses must have worn boned, lace up corsets and underskirts which could be worn with a range of different skirts and accessories to create the look for various characters. When playing a poor character such as the factory workers, aprons, scarves and shawls concealed the fitted items of costume underneath which was a very effective way of multi-rolling.

For the men, tight breeches for the military roles would have been covered with loose trousers held up with suspenders or rag belts. The uniforms they wore helped to convey their rank and were trimmed in great detail, using bright gold epaulettes and braiding that looked fantastic under the lights.

Colour was used in a creative as well as an authentic way. For example, the convicts were all clothed in coarse orange/brown shirts which reminded me of prison colours. The numbers that were sewn onto their shirts was another example of careful detail to ensure that the audience knew exactly what their role was. The colours of the French flag ran through the production with red and blue being a frequently used combination. A long version of the flag itself was used as a sash.

Even without the amazing set, music and performances, the production was magnificent, and the costumes, for me, were the best thing of all.

TASK 6.54

Test yourself.

1. Based on the live performance you have chosen, answer the question in Task 6.53.

   Use the AO3 and AO4 mark schemes and other tasks to guide you.

2. If possible, ask another student or your teacher to mark your answer. Make improvements based on their comments.

DESIGN TIP

Include as much detail as possible. Be sure to highlight your evaluation by using appropriate terms such as 'effective' and 'powerful impact'.

FOCUS

How to write as if you are a puppet designer.

ASSESSMENT CHECK

Section B assesses AO3: 'Demonstrate knowledge and understanding of how theatre is developed and performed.'

These notes will help your knowledge and understanding of design and of the set play.

DESIGN TIP

Using specialist design language is one of the most important things you can learn to do.

Puck overlooks the troupe of puppet performers in BYU's *A Midsummer Night's Dream*.

LOOK HERE

'Introduction to design in the written exam', pages 128–131, has several tasks and lots of advice. Read it carefully and complete Task 6.2.

PUPPET DESIGN IN THE SET PLAY (SECTION B)

Thinking as a puppet designer

If you have only worked practically as a performer, the design questions might seem rather daunting. This book is here to support you.

Some plays lend themselves more than others to the exciting use of puppetry. If you decide that your set play could unleash your creativity, the tasks in this chapter will guide you.

Puppetry revision for the set text

You will not know in advance what extract you will be given, but you will know which play it will be from.

TASK 6.55

1. Research and make notes on the historical, social, political and cultural context of the original setting for the play you have studied. *The 39 Steps*, for example, is set in 1930s Britain.

2. Use your research to complete your own version of the table below. (An example has been provided using *The 39 Steps*.)

Character/object	Puppet possibilities	Notes and link to context, style, genre
Biplanes	Rod shadow puppets	The pair of biplanes would appear in Scene 15 when Hannay is chased by them. I would use a backlit screen. Closer to the light, the puppets will look bigger. I would start with them close to the screen and move them back towards the light to suggest they are getting closer to him. The planes would be 2D front-on puppets, made of stiff card. They fit the broad style.
Hannay hanging from the Forth Bridge	• Shadow bridge with shadow Hannay? • Glove puppet with rod-controlled arms?	My shadow puppet plan would use a fixed card Forth Bridge, side-on view, and a rod puppet of Hannay. Rods would be attached to his back and to each arm, which would be jointed so he could hang on with both arms and then one. Alternatively, a glove-puppet Hannay could hold on to the bridge with arms on rods. The legs would be lightly padded and weighted to make them swing as the puppet is moved. The bridge could be created with a blanket suspended between two stepladders. The blanket could conceal the puppeteers.

Revising puppet design

How do you think the puppets should look?

> **TASK 6.56**
>
> 1. Select an extract of about 80 lines that inspires you in terms of puppet possibilities.
> 2. Decide whether the style would be naturalistic or non-naturalistic.
> 3. Choose one or two puppets from the extract. Complete a table like this to organise your thoughts about important details.
>
> | Puppet name | Type | Scale | Materials needed for puppet | Additional garments and accessories |
> |---|---|---|---|---|
> | | | | | |
> | | | | | |
>
> 4. Sketch each puppet and annotate it to identify and explain details.
> 5. Show and explain your designs to a classmate.

The 'real' Hannay is chased by rod-puppet biplanes in this shadow theatre scene from *The 39 Steps*.

Exam practice

You need to practise how to respond in the written exam. If you have prepared well, it should not be too daunting. You need to be ready to write confidently and fairly rapidly as soon as you have understood the questions and decided which one to answer. Completing the tasks in this section will help you.

Question B.5

The final question in Section B carries 20 marks and is optional. (You could answer B.4 instead, which is a performance question.)

> **TASK 6.57**
>
> 1. Highlight and make sure you understand the key words in this question:
>
> > You are a designer working on one aspect of design for this extract [Act 1, from 'Hansel and Gretel blow...' to 'There are too many mouths to feed']. Describe how you would use your design skills to create effects which support the action. Explain why your ideas are appropriate for:
> > - this extract
> > - the play as a whole. [20 marks]
>
> 2. Read the example answer on the following page and label it with:
>
>   **F** – **F**ocus on the question
>
>   **Ex** – Supporting **ex**ample
>
>   **T** – Appropriate **t**echnical language
>
>   **I** – **I**deas suitable to the extract and whole play.
>
> 3. Use the AO3 mark scheme to decide on a band and a mark out of 20.

DESIGN TIP

Be aware that Question B.1 will not ask you specifically about puppet design.

DESIGN TIP

Visit The Fetch Theatre's website at www.thefetch.co.uk for inspirational puppet and mask design ideas. You could go to one of their performances – or that of another touring company – if they are in your local area.

DESIGN TIP

You are expected to include technical detail because you are writing from the viewpoint of a designer with subject-specific knowledge and skills. Try to use appropriate technical terms. You might find it helpful to add an annotated sketch.

TASK 6.58

Now write your own response to a question similar to that in Task 6.57, based on an extract from your own set play.

I would use puppets to create the characters of the two chickens Dianne and Maureen as well as the crows that circle at the start of the extract. The crows are important in setting the atmosphere for the onset of famine for the family. I would put five simply made puppets onto heavy wire. Their bodies would be made from cardboard tubes and their wings from black paper so that they will flap as they move. They would have white button eyes, card beaks and black feathers attached to the paper wings and tails.

They would be animated by a puppeteer who would have a length of doweling onto which each of the different length wires would be attached at intervals. Held like bicycle handlebars that could be tilted, raised and lowered, the crows would be seen circling the stage, bobbing as the heavy wires moved up and down. The effect of the crows would be enhanced by a recorded sound effect.

The two chickens would be hand and rod puppets which there would need to be two versions: one when they are fat, and one for this extract, where they are described as scrawny. I would create the puppets from pieces of brown, black and yellow fur fabric. They would be stuffed with discarded fabric and garments for the larger areas and toy stuffing for the smaller ones. I would add felt wings and beaks and make the feet from pipe cleaners. The puppets would be given individual characters by placing their eyes in different positions and using different-coloured body fabric. I would also dress them differently, with Diane in a brightly printed cotton apron and Maureen in a head scarf, which would help the animators to characterise them as housewives. The animators would have observed real chickens to make their movements correct. It is important to keep the chickens 'alive'. They can never be allowed to just droop and become lifeless, so they move slightly and 'watch' the action of the play while they are on stage, just as actors stay in character throughout.

In the earlier section of the play they will move more quickly as they are not hungry and will be more lively and 'cheerful'. As well their movements, voicing the chickens will vary from scene to scene. The animators will find their voices just as actors do by developing their separate characteristics and experimenting. The chickens are humorous characters so this will be reflected in their characters, perhaps giving them different accents. I would also encourage the actors to find ways of including a clucking sound and a flustering, bustling quality to their movements. To make this work fully, I would attach a rod to the puppet's beak so that each animator would be able to move the puppet head with one hand while the other hand is inside the puppet itself. I would go into rehearsals and help them learn to use the puppets well.

PUPPET DESIGN IN LIVE THEATRE (SECTION C)

In this part of the exam, you could give detailed explanations and evaluations of puppet design in a performance you have seen. You should justify your opinions with examples that include a 'number of precise details.' You are also aiming to use technical language.

Preparation for a puppet design question

Look in the show programme, theatre marketing material and online for information about the puppets used and the designer/makers. Major productions and tours often have images, information and reviews online. Photographs in particular will help to remind you how the puppets looked and were operated as well as how they complemented other elements of the performance.

Remember that you were a member of the audience. The examiners will expect you to comment on the effect that the puppets had on the audience. Share your different responses to the show with your classmates, but aim to write about your own viewpoints in the exam. Remember that you are expected to make a critical evaluation.

TASK 6.59

1. Study any puppetry notes you made after seeing the performance. Put them together with production photographs you have found.
2. Use these to draw your own simple sketches of key puppets.
3. Annotate these to pick out particular details that created impact or were otherwise important. What do you remember about the puppets? Why? What effect did they have on the audience? Did they contribute to genre, style or mood? Why do you think the theatre company included puppets in their performance?
4. Discuss the use of puppets with other people in your class. Pooling your memories is valid and the discussion will help you to recall the experience of seeing the production.

TASK 6.60

1. Read 'Evaluating your puppet design' on page 125 and complete Task 5.13.
2. Remember that you are evaluating someone else's puppet designs, rather than your own. Complete the task using examples from the live performance you saw.

Practise evaluating puppets

The exam question will ask you about a design element of the production as a whole: it will not specify which moments to write about. So, describe and evaluate the moments that stood out for you as examples of how puppets were used effectively.

ASSESSMENT CHECK

Section C assesses AO3 and AO4. These pages will help you to:

- demonstrate knowledge and understanding of how drama and theatre is developed and performed
- investigate and identify how successfully theatre makers communicated meaning to an audience (analysis)
- assess the merit of approaches used and formulate judgements (evaluation).

SIGNPOST

'Evaluating your puppet design' on page 125 gives guidance on evaluative writing about puppetry.

DESIGN TIP

A programme from the performance is likely to be a useful source of information.

LOOK HERE

Remember to use Chapter 5 of this book to help you with subject-specific language and period accuracy of your sketches.

DESIGN TIP

The way puppets interacted with performers and the audience would be valuable information to include in your written exam.

This rod puppet from Little Angel Theatre is full of character. Visit https://littleangeltheatre.com for online puppet shows and puppet-making activities.

DESIGN TIP

Try as many exam-type questions as you can. Your teacher should be able to set you suitable questions. When you feel ready to practise under exam conditions, keep only your 500 words of notes with you. Give yourself up to 20 minutes to complete your answer.

TASK 6.61

1. If you can, find a copy of the script for the live performance you are writing about. Browse through it until you find a section where you remember the puppets having an impact on you.
2. Try to remember what the puppets looked like at key points in this section. These could be as short as a single moment or as long as a whole scene or more.
3. Write at least two paragraphs of critical judgement, which include:
   - subject-specific language, such as rod puppet, scale, character, animator and so on
   - how the use of lighting changed the look of the puppets and the effect of that
   - how atmosphere or meaning was enhanced for the audience
   - evaluations supported by detailed examples, such as, 'The use of… was powerful because…' and 'I was impressed by… because it made me feel/think…'
4. Swap your writing with someone else's for feedback. You could use the bullet points above as a checklist.

Working with an example answer

The mark scheme is a valuable tool when you are preparing for the written exam. The following tasks will allow you to assess a sample answer and then try one of your own.

TASK 6.62

1. Highlight the key words in the following example question:

   > Describe how puppets were used to support the style of the production. Analyse and evaluate how successful the puppets were in helping to communicate the style of the production to the audience. You should make reference to:
   > • type of puppet • characterisation • scale. [32 marks]

2. Now check your understanding of these key words, using a glossary if necessary.
3. Annotate the example answer on the following pages with:

   F – **F**ocus on the question

   Ex – **Ex**ample to support argument or point

   T – Appropriate **t**echnical language

   U – **U**nderstanding and knowledge of costume design in relation to the performance

   E – **E**valuation in terms of how successful the puppets were.

4. Use the AO4 mark scheme to decide on a band for the response, and then a mark out of 20. (The remaining 12 marks relate to AO3.)

The Lion King in Taipei.

The puppetry in The Lion King was extraordinary in the range of puppets and how they were animated. The production is groundbreaking in terms of its style. The original designer, Julie Taymor, brought the culture and beauty of the savanna plains to the stage in a unique and powerful way.

From the moment the lights came up, we were totally captivated.

In the first scene, where Simba's birth is celebrated, many different animals were on stage. The giraffes were animated by performers whose legs and arms were on tall stilts, with head-pieces over a metre tall. With the bending of the actors' bodies (the arm stilts are longer than the leg ones) and the head-pieces held upright, their silhouettes looked very realistic. I've learned that puppets aren't just things that you use with your hands.

When I watched The Lion King it took me a while to work out how the magic was being created because costume, make-up, masks, performers and puppetry were working really closely together.

The way that the character of Scar is put together is a good example. The carbon-fibre head looks like it is wooden, but is actually very light, which is important because the performer must be able to express the character freely with his body and face. The audience is meant to see the actor's face as well as the puppet head of Simba. The puppet head was able to tilt and project forward which was important to his cruel character.

This blending of actor and puppet is a duel or double event. It felt like the best of both worlds — the expression of the actor and the puppet design at the same time. Sometimes the puppet and the puppeteer become separate, as when Mustafa removes his mask and puts it on the stage.

The scale of the puppet heads had to roughly match the size of the performer for the double event to be successful while, at other times, an animator could be concealed inside each leg of the elephant.

Chapter 6   Component 1: Understanding Drama

> **DESIGN TIP**
>
> Include as much detail as possible. Be sure to highlight your evaluation by using appropriate terms such as 'effective' and 'powerful impact'.

The Lion King was also an ensemble piece: most of the cast played more than one role and had to be very versatile. The types of puppet included shadow, hand-held, worn, rod, headwear, robotic, on their own or combined with other types. All the types worked perfectly together because the shape and characters of the animals were so different.

Every puppet matched the needs of the play. It was also great when that you could believe in the story at the same time as figuring out how each animal was being created. For example, Timon the puppet's feet are attached to the actor and his arms are operated with rods. It is very playful and the humour suits the character's personality.

My favourite puppet was the only hand-held puppet that I saw. Zazu the hornbill had masses of personality. The way that he was voiced by the actor worked in real harmony with the visuals. Zazu's actor wore a blue suit with a fluffy white cravat, which reminded me of the sky – the hornbill's home. His suit had dinner-suit 'tails' and he wore a bowler hat, which suited Zazu as one of Mustafa's officials.

At the same time that he was performing as Zazu, the actor was operating the puppet. I think there must have been a Slinky spring or flexible hose within the bird's neck, which allowed it to extend and pull back, adding lots of expression. The fact that Zazu's eyes had three different positions operated by the left hand of the actor, while the right hand sat inside the puppet and operated the wings was an exceptional feat. I completely forgot that I was looking at a puppet: he was so real.

We could not see all the individual details of the puppets from a distance, but we could tell that the materials were chosen very carefully to appear organic, which fits in with the Pride Lands and creates harmony with Mustafa's mane being made of straw.

I could have watched the play a dozen times and still seen something new being done with puppets. It was exciting, beautiful and really inspiring.

TASK 6.63

Test yourself.

1. Answer the question on page 176, about the show you saw.
   Use the AO3 and AO4 mark schemes and other tasks to guide you.
2. If possible, ask another student or your teacher to mark your answer.
   Then make improvements based on their comments.

COMPONENT 2: DEVISING DRAMA – A PRACTICAL GUIDE

Chapter 7

Your design challenge	180
How your design for the devised piece will be assessed	182
Responding to stimuli	183
Agreeing on your artistic intentions	184
Genre, style, structure, form, character and language	186
Working positively as a group	190
Production meetings	191
Using rehearsals to develop and refine your designs	192
Final rehearsals	194
Lighting Design for the Devised Piece	**195**
Section 1: Response to a stimulus	196
Section 2: Development and collaboration	198
Reviewing sections 1 and 2	200
Producing and documenting your lighting design	201
Section 3: Analysis and evaluation	202
Sound Design for the Devised Piece	**203**
Section 1: Response to a stimulus	204
Section 2: Development and collaboration	206
Reviewing sections 1 and 2	208
Producing and documenting your sound design	209
Section 3: Analysis and evaluation	210
Set Design for the Devised Piece	**212**
Section 1: Response to a stimulus	213
Section 2: Development and collaboration	215
Reviewing sections 1 and 2	217
Producing and documenting your set design	218
Section 3: Analysis and evaluation	219
Costume Design for the Devised Piece	**221**
Section 1: Response to a stimulus	222
Section 2: Development and collaboration	224
Reviewing sections 1 and 2	226
Producing and documenting your costume design	227
Section 3: Analysis and evaluation	228
Puppet Design for the Devised Piece	**230**
Section 1: Response to a stimulus	231
Section 2: Development and collaboration	233
Reviewing sections 1 and 2	235
Producing and documenting your puppet design	236
Section 3: Analysis and evaluation	237

FOCUS
How to devise with your group and design at the same time.

ASSESSMENT CHECK
You need to take an equal part in developing and communicating your group's artistic intentions with a clear and practical design that adapts in response to rehearsals. This will help you towards AO1.

LOOK HERE
See page 183 for details of different stimuli and how you might use them.

YOUR DESIGN CHALLENGE

The essence of devising

DEVISE Plan or invent (a complex procedure, system, or mechanism) by careful thought.

"Devised theatre is 'a process in which the whole creative team develops a show collaboratively. From actors to technicians, everyone is involved in the creative process.'"
(John Walton, theatre director)

As a designer, you will work with your group to develop form, content, style and genre and a harmonious world that has impact for an audience. Within this group dynamic, you will focus on your design element.

The process of devising

Devising drama has **collaboration** and **inventiveness** at its heart. You will work closely as a group to generate ideas that can be developed into a finished piece of theatre.

You will start from an inspiring **stimulus**. From there, you will experiment and gradually decide on:

- content, including a theme or message that you want to explore
- genres and performance styles, such as comedy, naturalism, dystopian theatre, physical theatre
- the structure, for example a linear series of improvisations, or movement backwards and forwards through time.

180   Chapter 7   Component 2: Devising Drama – A Practical Guide

When can I start designing?

Your design work will emerge from the **dramatic intentions** of your group, inspired by the stimulus. You will soon find opportunities to make design an important and interesting part of the finished piece.

As the group moves through the devising process, you should be involved in each other's work. This is a **group** endeavour, and collaboration is essential for harmony in the final performance.

DESIGN TIP

Never overlook the importance of the devising log. Record your thoughts, designs, analysis and evaluations at every stage of the devising process.

TASK 7.1

Once your group has made some decisions about content (what the piece will be about), you can develop your design ideas. Begin a table like this to get you started:

Stimulus:

Artistic intention	Style and genre	Structure	Design ideas	
To highlight climate change as a major threat.	• Mainly naturalistic. • Gritty drama.	Episodic – set in the future with flashbacks to today.	Set	• Levels to suggest power in flashback scenes and different areas for hot and cold climates • Plastic items such as bags and bottles (pollution and climate change) • Monochrome colours to tie in with costume and lighting.
			Lighting	• Contrasting colour palettes (to show very hot and cold environments). • Special spotlight to pick out monologues. • Special 'flashback' lighting state.
			Costume	• 'Disposable' white overalls for scientist character (suggests world is becoming uninhabitable). • Contrasting warm and thin clothing worn for alternate scenes (unstable climate). • Muted monochromes (hints at severity of situation).
			Sound	Special soundscape for flashback scenes – could be voices arguing about climate change with an abstract tense sound effect.
			Puppetry	Polar bear glove-and-rod puppet – add a distinct character with audience appeal – a disappearing Arctic.

LOOK HERE

Pages 184–185 will help you to pin down your artistic intentions.

Chapters 1 to 5 will guide you through the design process.

Pages 192–193 will help you to refine ideas in rehearsal and continue the collaboration.

FOCUS

A breakdown of what you need to produce for the devised piece and how marks are divided over the two parts.

ASSESSMENT CHECK

Your design in performance is assessed for AO2: 'Apply theatrical skills to realise artistic intentions in live performance.'

Your devising log will be assessed on your ability to:

- 'Create and develop ideas to communicate meaning for theatrical performance' (AO1)
- 'Analyse and evaluate their own work and the work of others' (AO4).

DESIGN TIP

Images can be used to support your devising log in all three format options. These will not themselves add to the word count, but written annotations and labels will.

DESIGN TIP

It is very important that you cover every bullet point in the table.

HOW YOUR DESIGN FOR THE DEVISED PIECE WILL BE ASSESSED

The performance and the devising log

This component, which covers your devised piece of drama, is worth 80 marks and makes up 40 per cent of your GCSE. You will be assessed on your ability to:

- create and communicate meaning
- realise artistic intention in devised drama.

Your design for the devised piece is assessed in two ways:

Your design in the performance of a devised piece (20 marks)

Design role	What you need to produce
Lighting	**One** lighting design. This must show a range of lighting effects/states and cues/transitions designed to meet the demands of the devised piece.
Sound	**One** sound design. This must show a range of sound effects and cues/transitions designed to meet the demands of the piece.
Set	**One** set design. This must be for one setting, showing dressings and props designed to meet the demands of the devised piece.
Costume	**One** costume design for **one** performer. This must show clothing and accessories (and hair and make-up if applicable) designed to meet the demands of the devised piece.
Puppetry	**One** puppet design. This must be a complete puppet designed to meet the demands of the devised piece.

Your devising log (60 marks)

Format: all design options	What you need to do and demonstrate and explain
Your devising log should consist of: • 15 pages of 2500 words, accompanied by annotated photographs, sketches, drawings or cue sheets as required **or** • 1500 words accompanied by 12 minutes of audio-visual recording **or** • 15 minutes of audio-visual recording.	**Section 1: Response to a stimulus** (AO1, 20 marks) • Your initial response to the stimuli and the chosen stimulus • Ideas, themes and settings in response to the stimulus • Your research findings • Your own dramatic aims and intentions • The dramatic aims and intentions of the pieces as a whole. **Section 2: Development and collaboration** (AO1, 20 marks) • How you developed and refined your ideas and the group's • How you developed and refined the piece in rehearsal • How you developed and refined your own theatrical skills • How you responded to feedback • How you as an individual used your refined ideas in the final piece. **Section 3: Analysis and evaluation** (AO4, 20 marks) • How far you developed your theatrical skills • The benefits you brought to the group and how you positively shaped the outcome • The overall impact you had as an individual • Areas for development in future devising work.

Chapter 7   Component 2: Devising Drama – A Practical Guide

RESPONDING TO STIMULI

First thoughts

All drama devisers use stimuli to feed their theatre-making process. Your teacher will offer stimuli that give you plenty of scope as starting points for devised drama. These could be images, texts or themes, for example. Your teacher will also set you tasks for exploring the stimulus. This exploration will begin to fire individual and group responses in the form of:

- personal experiences
- experiences of people you know
- stories you have heard and read about
- social and cultural similarities and differences (such as the way people from different backgrounds might think about the stimulus.

To begin with, try to let your minds roam freely from your initial experience of the stimulus. You could use:

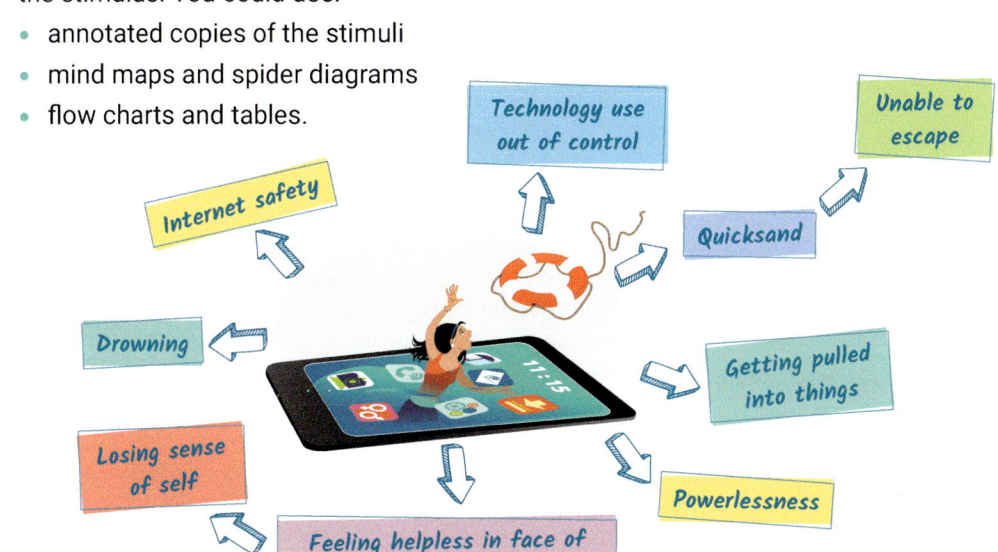

- annotated copies of the stimuli
- mind maps and spider diagrams
- flow charts and tables.

> **FOCUS**
> Ways to think about different stimuli in your role as a group member and designer.

> **ASSESSMENT CHECK**
> Under AO1, you use stimuli to create and develop a performance piece from inception to performance.
> Your devising log must cover your initial response to the stimuli and what the intentions of the piece were.

Ideas that excite

Once you start sharing ideas, take particular notice of those that excite you or other people in your group. These are the ones that are producing strong social and personal reactions. If they interest you, they are likely to interest your audience. Do remember, though, that ideas will change and develop as you begin to work with them creatively.

> **DESIGN TIP**
> Note the importance of charting all the stages of your design and devising work in detail.

TASK 7.2

Spend some time at home thinking about the stimulus and then report back to your group. Use a table like this to organise your ideas. (An example has been provided for you, using the image above.)

Stimulus: Cartoon of young person 'drowning' in smartphone	
Themes, messages, issues	Ideas that come from the stimulus and themes
• Internet safety. • Gaming as a distraction from the real world.	• Movement piece. • Sinister music or sound effects. • Monologues from people affected by too much gaming.

> **DESIGN TIP**
> For now, don't push your role as designer to the front of your mind. Respond to the stimulus's overall potential for drama instead.

Chapter 7 Component 2: Devising Drama – A Practical Guide 183

FOCUS

How to pin down the aims and objectives of your devised drama.

ASSESSMENT CHECK

This process helps you to:

- communicate and realise your intentions
- consider the impact that you can make on an audience
- explore ideas that you want to communicate
- collaborate and come to decisions.

Make sure your discussions address the focus of AO1: 'Create and develop ideas to communicate meaning for theatrical performance.'

DESIGN TIP

Revisit your ideas board often while agreeing your artistic intentions. Update it by removing, adding and regrouping ideas.

AGREEING ON YOUR ARTISTIC INTENTIONS

What are artistic intentions in a devised piece?

When you perform or design from a playscript, the content (narrative, characters, setting and so on) are already in place. Your artistic intentions will be how you interpret that script for an audience.

In **devised** theatre, by contrast, your artistic or dramatic intentions relate to what you want to tell the audience. You might begin with a message or question that springs from your stimulus, for example:

- What can society do to avoid climate catastrophe?
- Why is a sense of community important?
- How can we use social media platforms more positively?

FOLLOWING WARM TRAILS

This metaphorical idea encourages you to trust your instincts when developing ideas. Look for signs that a particular route on the devising trail will lead you to an excellent devised piece. If an idea excites several members of the group, you are probably onto a good thing.

How can our group decide on its aims and objectives?

TASK 7.3

Work together to test some of the group's ideas through drama activities such as improvisations. Make notes on successful points that move you closer to agreeing your artistic intentions.

TASK 7.4

An ideas board is a useful way of bringing ideas together and specifying aims and objectives. More than just a list of ideas, look to include on your board (you could use a pin-board, whiteboard or a large sheet of cardboard):

- the stimulus, its title, or a description of it
- themes, messages and questions that arise from the stimulus
- descriptions, photographs or sketches of dramatic explorations you have found inspiring
- news headlines and articles, for example, that have prompted ideas
- images that have captured your imagination
- initial design ideas – keep that part of your brain firing!

Deciding on your artistic intentions

In addition to generating and sharing ideas, you need to analyse and evaluate this creative process. This will help you to make decisions and assess why they are the best choices.

Time will be limited. Settling on the aims and objectives for your piece should be a relatively quick aspect of the creative process. If your group starts to feel stuck, try the following task.

TASK 7.5

1. One at a time, each member of the group takes one item from the ideas board and puts it on the floor or table.
2. Give yourselves two minutes to arrange the items in priority order. If there is indecision or argument, collect items for further review.
3. Study the result. Sensitively analyse and evaluate the group's decisions and confirm your artistic intentions.

Wording artistic intentions

Once you have agreed on what your artistic intentions are, try the following task as a way of writing them down.

TASK 7.6

1. As a group, write a short paragraph that sums up the theme or message you want to share with your audience.
2. Highlight the most important key words.
3. Use these key words to write a brief, clear aim for your theatre piece.

The following table provides a couple of examples.

The general idea (theme)	The clear artistic intentions	
Climate change is **threatening our world**. **We** can all do something to **help**, but it's not enough. **Governments** need to work together and **make big changes quickly**. Young people should be listened to – some of us have joined **protests** because we feel so strongly about **our future**.	Aim	To highlight climate change as a major global threat.
	Key messages	• Young people should be encouraged to protest. • Everyone should contribute. • Governments need to work together to tackle the problem urgently.
Social media sites are **useful** ways of staying in touch with friends and sharing ideas. But they can be **dangerous** because they allow **bullying** and extremism. They encourage people to **stay at home** rather than actually being with friends. There are important things to do to **stay safe online**. We want to share this with younger students.	Aim	To help Year 7 students to get the best from social media.
	Key messages	• Avoid personal details – use privacy settings. • Don't get involved in bullying or discrimination: report it instead. • Stay in touch with friends and have fun, but **be** with people too.

ASSESSMENT CHECK
These tasks will help you work together to develop and refine your own ideas and those of the group.

LOOK HERE
Pages 192–193 will help you to maintain your creative intentions during rehearsals.

DESIGN TIP
Remember that you can adapt the wording of your intentions during the rehearsal process.

Chapter 7 Component 2: Devising Drama – A Practical Guide

FOCUS
Exploring different styles of devised theatre and coming to decisions about your own.

ASSESSMENT CHECK
You should analyse and evaluate your decisions about how the content of your piece is communicated. Considering why choices are made will help you towards AO4.

GENRE, STYLE, STRUCTURE, FORM, CHARACTER AND LANGUAGE

Genre and performance style

Think about the genre (or category) of your piece, and the style/s in which you might present it. Applying or exploring the genres, styles and methods of key practitioners can enhance your work. You could consider, for example:

- comedy
- melodrama
- tragedy
- commedia dell'arte
- naturalism
- epic theatre
- documentary
- physical theatre

Which genres allow you to communicate your artistic intentions in effective and interesting ways?

Naturalistic set and costumes in *Elmina's Kitchen*.

A piece could combine different genres and styles. Dark comedy, for example, tackles serious themes, but in amusing, thought-provoking ways.

Designers, genre and style

Designers play an important role in establishing genre. At the most basic level, all design elements communicate light and dark in some way. Designs for a game-show genre, for example, could include formal costumes for the presenter, bright lighting, a repeated jingle and a raised platform and podiums as part of the set.

Style-wise, a naturalistic set design will seem far more real and instantly recognisable than one for a non-naturalistic piece. The same is likely to be true for naturalistic sound, costume and lighting. Silhouette and fabric choice will be important in establishing the period, for example. In this case, lighting and sound designers would be unlikely to use many non-naturalistic effects as they could clash with the main style.

Structure and form

Structure is the 'shape' of the performance, or the way it is built. Narrative structures include:

- linear
- cyclical
- episodic
- narrative.

You might not be able to decide on your structure until you have spent some time exploring your piece. A structure might emerge rather than being a conscious early decision. Similarly, the best form for the piece or a section might be decided as you go through the process.

Designers, structure and form

A designer needs to think about structure as soon as it is chosen. A linear piece, for example, might need changes of costume to support the sense of time passing. In a cyclical piece, the repetition of lighting states could help the audience to recognise a return to a location or situation. Lengthy scene changes, by contrast, would disrupt a fast-moving, episodic piece.

Designers should support the forms used. Set, sound and lighting can all enhance the use of split stage scenes, for example. If mime or movement sequences are involved, costumes need to allow the performers can move freely. Sound effects and music, as well as set design, are highly important for these scenes as well.

This split stage in *The Book Collector* emphasises the contrast and separation between the dark, heavy library and the light, airy bookshop. It communicates meaning about the characters as well as placing the scene and contributing to audience understanding of the narrative.

Character and language

Although you might think of costume as being the most important design aspect for characterisation, it should be supported by all designers. Music can help to present a character's emotions, and lighting could sharpen our attention on a character. Set can also reflect, for example, a character's sense of freedom or restriction.

At first glance, language might not seem to have a great deal to do with design. But a character who uses formal language is likely to wear more formal clothing. Words could form part of a set design. Song lyrics should also be carefully chosen to suit the language of the piece.

CASE STUDY: CYBERBULLYING

Starting from the stimulus of a news article about increasing incidents of bullying, a group of Year 10 students set about devising a YPT docudrama on the theme of cyberbullying. They aimed for an audience of Year 7 students, whom they saw as being particularly vulnerable.

The group researched statistics, watched anti-bullying videos and shared their own experiences. They then improvised a few scenarios. They realised that it was much easier to understand the effects of cyberbullying than the reasons why young people get drawn into it. This led to further research and new improvisations.

One of the group had opted for sound design and began work on diegetic and non-diegetic sounds.

As well as the diegetic sounds of phone buttons, ringtones and notifications, the designer developed two underscores of ambient sounds. These supported characterisation by reflecting the feelings of the victim and the main perpetrator. These emerging soundtracks were used in rehearsals, where they helped to shape the devised piece.

The structure became a cyclical story of the bully. Scenes looked at her younger life and how she gradually came to understand the misery of her victim. Sound effects were an integral part of the piece.

CASE STUDY: LIES

Yevgeny Yevtushenko's poem 'Lies' was adopted as a devised performance stimulus. It begins:

> *Telling lies to the young is wrong.*
> *Proving to them that lies are true is wrong.*
> *Telling them that God's in his heaven*
> *and all's well with the world is wrong.*
> *The young people know what you mean.*
> *The young are people.*

Yevgeny Yevtushenko

TASK 7.7

1. Work with your group to complete a table like this to summarise advantages and disadvantages – for you – of different genres and styles. (Examples have been included to start you off.)
2. You could complete similar tables to help you consider genre, style and structure.

Genre	Strengths for our group	Challenges for our group	Notes
Physical theatre	• Suits our non-naturalistic style. • Some performers feel very comfortable with this style. • Interesting for lighting – lots of scope for SFX.	• Not everyone has experience of this style. • Costume design might be limited? • Is it too difficult for our audience to 'read' our artistic intentions?	• Could mix physical theatre with docudrama. • Follow Frantic Assembly techniques.
Comedy	• Suits non-naturalistic style. • Adds audience appeal and interest.	• Can be difficult to accomplish successfully.	Communicates character.

CASE STUDY: BEAUTY AND THE BEAST

A small group devised a modern version of *Beauty and the Beast* as a largely physical performance. Their artistic intentions concentrated on the physical and emotional repercussions of substance abuse.

The only piece of set was a white wooden frame, the size of a doorframe. It was used to represent a door, a window, a picture frame and a cage. It was supported and moved by the performers, which made it very versatile.

Costumes were simple – mostly black – and stretchy to support the form and minimalist style.

The lighting designer made a highly significant contribution to characterisation and the non-naturalistic style. A range of cover washes enhanced the atmosphere. Transitions between lighting states were sometimes very slow, to give the impression of time passing. At other times, he used snap transitions for moments of shock or sudden change. In addition, tight white spotlights were used during monologues.

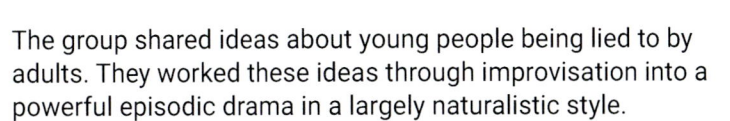

The group shared ideas about young people being lied to by adults. They worked these ideas through improvisation into a powerful episodic drama in a largely naturalistic style.

They chose to differentiate between harmless pretences, such as the tooth fairy, and lies that could be damaging. Using a range of forms, including advert and duologue, scenes focused on politicians, family and other authority figures lying to young people and the effects of this.

In end-on staging, the set created levels and 'hidden' areas with a clever arrangement of existing stage **rostra blocks**. Two levels were placed upstage centre to increase the proximity of those in authority to young people. The spaces under the stage blocks created locations such as a bedroom. The set strongly supported the episodic narrative.

DESIGN TIP

Play to the strengths of your group. Remember that you can combine theatrical forms. For example, a naturalistic narrative could include one or more scenes of physical theatre.

FOCUS
Advice on avoiding or recovering from group-work problems.

ASSESSMENT CHECK
Together, you should 'engage with the process of collaboration, rehearsal and refinement' and 'work collaboratively within a group to realise artistic intentions.'

DESIGN TIP
Analise your collaborative involvement. Is it thorough and supportive?

KEEPING COMMUNICATION OPEN

WORKING POSITIVELY AS A GROUP

The importance of good communication

Teachers have to consider many things when they form groups for practical work. Not everyone will be happy with the resulting make-up of their group, but the ability to work collaboratively is a valuable skill needed here, and for life.

Most importantly, good communication is essential for creating good theatre.

> **TASK 7.8**
>
> As a group, share thoughts of examples in life of excellent communication. Be specific and try to assess what skills are being used.
>
> For example, a particular teacher might be really effective at communicating their subject. This could be to do with their skills in bringing the subject to life, their enthusiasm, and the way they make students feel that their ideas are listened to.
>
> Alternatively, you might think about pedestrian crossings, where clear visual and aural cues are given to pedestrians and drivers. Bumps near the edge of the pavement also help sight-impaired pedestrians. Excellent communication in terms of design!

Building a positive group environment

Negative dynamics are a common problem in group work, with a range of causes. The chart below offers some ideas for improving your group's ability to get along socially and make practical progress.

> **TASK 7.9**
>
> Use the points below to evaluate a recent group session. Ask yourself:
> - What are my qualities as a group member?
> - How could I improve my contribution to the group?
> - Do I offer ideas and consider others' ideas too?

- Have a clear objective for the session, for example to gather ideas of how the stimulus can be explored through drama.
- Highlight the positive things people say and do.
- Take turns to speak. If necessary, have an object that can be held by the speaker, and pass it on frequently.
- Listen sensitively and carefully when others are speaking. Don't just wait for your turn to speak.
- Encourage everyone to talk. Go around the circle every few minutes so that everyone has a chance to contribute. Keep it positive.
- Try to be objective about difficulties. Focus on what has gone wrong rather than on an individual. Try to limit comments to those that help the objective of the meeting.
- Ask a teacher for support early on if communication is not going well.
- Always avoid blaming one person. Communication is a shared activity!

PRODUCTION MEETINGS

AGENDA PERFORMANCE PROBLEMS
CHALLENGES PROGRESS DATES TIME
LIST COLLABORATION DESIGN DEADLINES
PLAN COSTUME PRIORITY SOURCE
TECHNICAL LIGHTING
COMMUNICATION EVALUATION SET
POSITIVITY COLLABORATE SOUND
IMPORTANT CHECK STRATEGY SOLUTION
ANALYSIS

The design and performance elements of your group might often be working separately. You will need regular times to meet and check overall progress. The benefits of having regular meetings with a set agenda are:

- The agenda can be short and the meeting focused.
- All designers have a chance to give and get peer feedback.
- Deadlines and schedules can be set and checked.
- Issues can be raised and support organised.
- Notes from the meeting will help to keep your devising log detailed and let you show progression.

As you are likely to be a small group without a director, having a representative from the performing group is a good idea. Minutes of the meeting can be shared with the rest of the group.

Agenda
- Progress report.
- Sharing of research and sketches etc (for each designer).
- Schedules and deadlines.
- Issues.
- Date of next meeting.

Highlight and make notes on your agenda of what is discussed during the meeting. Include any changes to the piece that are being made and any actions you need to take. Use these notes as a checklist.

Just me?

If you are the only designer for your devised group, you should still have brief production meetings with the performers. Deadlines need to be met and it is in everyone's interests to maintain progress towards a harmonious performance.

If you need to, ask fellow group members to support with particular design elements. For example, could one or two performers operate some basic lighting or sound equipment for you when they are not on stage?

FOCUS
Bringing the design elements together and tracking progress.

ASSESSMENT CHECK
Overcoming challenges shows collaborative involvement and analysis of your personal contribution to the creative process.

Along with rehearsals, regular meetings should help you to take into consideration the performer/audience relationship.

DESIGN TIP
File old agendas to help in compiling your devising log.

FOCUS
Working together to develop the devised piece.

ASSESSMENT CHECK
You should demonstrate your engagement with the process of collaboration, rehearsal and refinement. Keep in mind that you are working towards AO1: 'Create and develop ideas to communicate meaning for theatrical performance.'

SIGNPOST
Make sure you have tried Task 7.1 on page 181. Remember that it is a starting point. Your ideas will develop and change.

LOOK HERE
'Your design challenge' on pages 180–181, and the appropriate practical design chapter, will support you further.

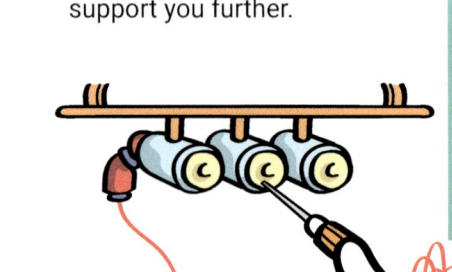

USING REHEARSALS TO DEVELOP AND REFINE YOUR DESIGNS

Focus on your design specialism

As the performers start to rehearse, you will need to turn your attention to designing.

TASK 7.10

As a way of clarifying your thoughts, begin your own version of the following journal. Add to it as you go along to help your analysis and evaluation.

Group details: 5 performers plus Lighting, Costume, Set: Total 8		
Artistic intentions	Notes on style, forms, genre, structure	Set design notes
To explore the importance of community, locally, nationally, internationally. • Gain a better awareness of what 'community' means. • Understand the value of being part of a community. • See what happens when communities are broken up or divided.	7 Oct Main style: Non-naturalistic YPT. Forms: Ensemble, movement, duologue, freeze-frames. Genre: Social drama / YPT. Structure: Episodic.	7 Oct Use image or symbol (invented) on fabric - flag? Suggests togetherness - performers could use dramatically to connect, wrap, be a barrier? 12 Oct Circular - perform in the round? Create semi-circular shape using curved cyclorama - project onto it? 23 Oct Levels for dramatic interest? Small steps? Could show people helping others up? Sightlines? 25 Oct Colour - monochrome to allow for strong coloured lighting and give a neutral feel? Bursts of colour with the flag idea? Talk to Costume!

Remember your health and safety responsibilities, and ask for help!

192 Chapter 7 Component 2: Devising Drama – A Practical Guide

Ongoing research

Your design work will progress quite rapidly as long as you 'feed' your creativity. This is continuous research, of which rehearsals are an important part. These ideas should keep you going.

- What inspiration do you find in the themes and messages of your artistic intentions?
- Keep an eye on the news. Are there topical examples of issues that relate to your artistic intentions?
- What do the form and style suggest in terms of design? (Perhaps particular sounds or visual ideas.)
- Are there other plays related to your artistic intentions? They could be useful for design ideas. For bullying, for example, you could look at *DNA* by Dennis Kelly or *The Terrible Fate of Humpty Dumpty* by David Calcutt.
- Be in rehearsals as much as possible. An improvised scene might lead you to a new underscore or different lighting effect.

TASK 7.11

Keep a detailed record of your research and response to rehearsals (use the table in Task 7.10) for your devising log. Save images (or links to them). Keep in mind the 'how and why' of your design.

Developing your design alongside performers and other designers

It is critical that you collaborate with the rest of your group. This will be a balance between presenting your ideas and responding to ideas that others bring. Together, you need to arrive at a harmonious world on the stage. Here are some ways to work collaboratively during rehearsals:

ASSESSMENT CHECK

The research and rehearsal processes will help you to:
- develop and refine your ideas and those of the group
- respond to feedback.

It is essential that you collaborate in order to meet AO4: 'Analyse and evaluate your own work and the work of others.'

LOOK HERE

The case studies on pages 188–189 are examples of design developments during rehearsals.

Use the guidance on page 190 to help with offering and receiving suggestions and making changes.

DESIGN TIP

You should write about collaboration in Section 2 of your devising log.

- Keep returning to your artistic intentions.
- Hold them at the front of your mind.
- Spend time in rehearsals.
- Notice what performers are doing.
- See if your design needs to be guided or adapted by a particular aspect of the performance.
- Spend a few minutes before each rehearsal with any other designers.
- Share plans supportively and check that all design elements are in harmony.
- Feed performers with your developing design ideas.
- Take in mood boards or design items as appropriate.

Chapter 7 Component 2: Devising Drama – A Practical Guide

FOCUS

How to run and use the key rehearsals in the final days before performance.

ASSESSMENT CHECK

By the time of final rehearsals, you will be contributing positively to the overall effect of the performance. This point is your opportunity to refine your initial ideas and intentions into a final devised piece.

LOOK HERE

Guidance on the technical and dress rehearsals in Chapters 1 to 5 will take you through the rehearsal process.

NOTE

This chapter assumes that you are writing your whole devising log. If you are taking a different approach, make detailed notes, spider diagrams and so on to support your final presentation.

FINAL REHEARSALS

Now that your group's devised piece is nearly ready to be performed, it is time to check the effect of your work in full collaboration with the rest of the group.

Any production needs final technical and dress rehearsals before the actual performance. With a devised piece, it pays to put in an extra stage…

Pulling all the elements together

LIGHTING
SOUND
SET DESIGN
COSTUME DESIGN
PUPPET DESIGN

For a devised piece, you might work with visual and aural cues as much as with your script, and some of the performance might be polished improvisation. You will need to be extremely familiar with the piece if your production is going to reach the necessary level of harmony. The following task will help costume and sound designers, in particular, but could also raise valuable points for lighting, set and puppetry.

TASK 7.12

Once the performers are able to do a run of the whole piece, you should watch it at least twice. Do it in costume and with the set, but without lights or sound. This allows you to concentrate on the action without having to operate light or sound.

Take detailed design notes in a table like this.

Moment in the piece	Event or line before the moment (*standby cue* for light or sound)	What should happen	Notes
Raising the flag above their heads	Performers move to top levels.	Switch to sfx (2).	Rehearse before the tech if possible.
Raising the flag above their heads		Costume cape should fall to the floor.	Talk to performer.

Make sure you leave plenty of time for final rehearsals, and any last-minute design changes, in order to achieve a polished performance.

Chapter 7 Component 2: Devising Drama – A Practical Guide

LIGHTING DESIGN FOR THE DEVISED PIECE

The requirements of your lighting design

Your lighting design will emerge from your role as a member of a devising group. It will be marked in terms of your ability to effectively use a wide range of skills in an inventive way. Your lighting should 'locate' the action and characters, help to create mood and atmosphere and suit the chosen genre, structure and style of the piece. It needs to communicate your group's artistic intentions and have an impact on the audience.

The examiners are hoping to see lighting designs that:
- make a highly positive, creative contribution to the devised performance
- clearly establish a location and time of day and enhance the mood or atmosphere of the piece.
- effectively use special effects such as shadows, flashes, UV and gobos.

The examiners warn against lighting designs that:
- are overly simple and rely heavily on general washes
- include poor cross fades and snaps
- include lengthy blackouts.
- suggest little collaboration with the group.

The devising log

The log is your opportunity to explain how you have engaged fully with the process of devising from the viewpoint of group member and lighting designer. You will chart the process from beginning to end, detailing your understanding of all the skills you have used and the decisions you have made.

Your ability to work with your group to bring its artistic intentions to reality is important along with analysis and evaluation of your successes and the challenges you have faced along the way.

Your devising log should:
- include detailed cue sheets and notes
- identify equipment used
- show clear understanding of the needs of the piece
- provide evidence of collaboration.

You should avoid working in isolation. It is extremely important that all designers collaborate closely with the rest of their group throughout the devising process.

DESIGN TIP
See your lighting design and your devising log as two parts of the same whole. They must be worked on at the same time.

SIGNPOST
Chapter 1 supports your lighting design work and guides you through the entire process of designing, rigging and operating lighting. Use it here alongside the guide at the beginning of this chapter.

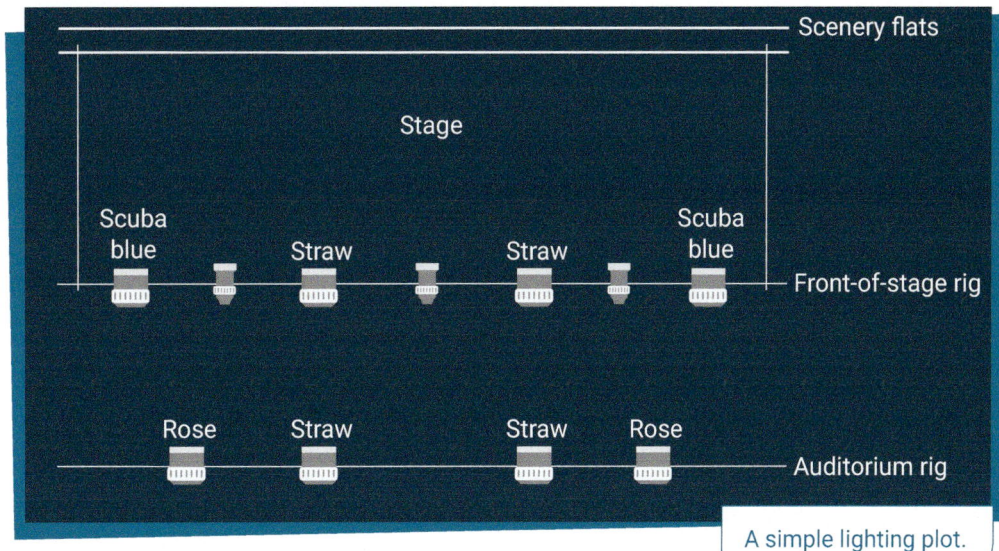

A simple lighting plot.

LOOK HERE
See page 182 for a breakdown of the devising log's contents.

FOCUS
Approaching the first section of your log.

ASSESSMENT CHECK
AO1 asks you to create and develop ideas that communicate meaning.

This section begins your process of documenting the practical creation and development of ideas, with a focus on the stimulus and your response to it.

SIGNPOST
The following sections at the beginning of this chapter will help you to start the devising log:
- Your design challenge
- Responding to stimuli
- Agreeing on your artistic intentions.

SECTION 1: RESPONSE TO A STIMULUS

The early stages: your chosen stimulus

It is valuable to comment very briefly on more than one stimuli, but you should focus on the stimulus your group chose to work with. Include a detailed explanation in Section 1 about the initial ideas, themes and settings you considered and the research you carried out individually and as a group.

You need to explain:
- your initial response to the stimuli presented by the teacher and the stimulus you chose
- the ideas, themes and settings you have considered in response to the stimulus you chose
- your research findings
- your own dramatic aims and intentions and those for the piece as a whole.

TASK 7.13

1. Read the draft log extract on the facing page. Then select **two** of the following pieces of advice to help the writer add useful detail:
- Mention the other stimuli before explaining why you chose this one.
- Include the song lyrics.
- Explain the themes, ideas and settings suggested by the stimulus.
- Write about the group's artistic intentions for the piece and how these relate to the song.
- Explain why you chose to be a lighting designer.

2. Share your answers with a partner. Do they agree?

I was the lighting designer for our devised performance. Our stimulus was the song 'Titanium' by David Guetta featuring Sia. It is an urban dance track and has a very energising feel. The lyrics are about being strong and resilient.

From my chemistry lessons and online research, I understood that titanium is a silvery grey metal that is strong and tough and doesn't corrode easily. In terms of lighting design, I'm immediately thinking of hard-edged profile spots, high intensity and possibly gobos. The metal itself suggested bright, clean, sharp lighting. I researched different-coloured filters and found some, such as deep lavender and electric lilac, that would create the sense of drama I wanted. I tested these colours using par cans and profile spotlights, discovering that the electric lilac created a strong blast of colour which I went on to use in the movement pieces because they really defined the performers. The stimulus itself (the song) had the same kind of energy as the lighting, which worked well. I told other people in my group about the metal and it raised some excitement, so we decided to explore the idea of strength and resilience further. In particular, we were interested in young people who didn't give up easily.

I carried out some major research. I had the theme of strength and resilience from our stimulus, but needed to find out what was going to happen in the play. I suggested that we come back to the next lesson with examples.

Our exploration of inspirational strong young people was effective, as it threw up some very interesting characters including:

Malala Yousafzai, the Nobel Peace prize-winner who fought for girls to go to school in Pakistan.

Greta Thunberg, the Swedish teenager who campaigns about climate change.

Jesy Nelson, the singer from Little Mix who suffered cyberbullying and made a documentary to try to help others.

Musharaf Asghar, a student from the television series *Educating Yorkshire* who has a severe stammer, but learned to speak publicly with help from his teachers.

The Thai football team who were trapped in an underground cave for two weeks, but stayed positive.

I knew that this would give me plenty of scope for naturalistic and non-naturalistic lighting effects.

TASK 7.14

1. Look through the sections listed in the Signpost. Collect completed tasks and extra notes. Remind yourself of the Section 1 bullet points.
2. Mention the stimuli you were presented with, then write about the stimulus you chose. Give a detailed account of the thoughts and feelings it provoked in you as an individual.
3. Write a short paragraph about how your own and the group's thinking about the stimulus came together. What themes, ideas and settings did you discuss? You could annotate a picture or include mind-maps or spider diagrams.
4. Write about your research and how it influenced your lighting ideas.
5. Describe your group's artistic intentions, explaining what you want the audience to think and feel. Refer to the stimulus. What are your own artistic intentions for the lighting design?
6. Read through your text to check that it covers all the Section 1 bullet points and that the word count is about right (700 to 800 words).

DESIGN TIP

Proofread as you go along. As well as spelling and punctuation, check that you are keeping to the point and using specific examples.

LOOK HERE

These pages will be helpful:
- Genre, style, structure, form, character and language, page 186,
- Types of stage lantern, pages 16–17
- Understanding your lighting resources, pages 18–19.

FOCUS

Reflecting on the development and refinement of ideas, theatrical skills and collaboration.

ASSESSMENT CHECK

AO1 asks you to create and develop ideas that communicate meaning. You will be creating a design that contributes positively to the performance.

SIGNPOST

The following sections will be particularly helpful in making key decisions about your lighting and its development.

- Angles, colour and intensity, pages 20–23
- Special effects in lighting, pages 24–25
- Research for lighting, page 27
- Working positively as a group, page 190
- Using rehearsals to develop and refine your design, pages 192–193.

DESIGN TIP

Keep your notes from group sessions. Use them to remind yourself of the research and explorations that have taken place.

SECTION 2: DEVELOPMENT AND COLLABORATION

This section of your log needs to be driven by the devising process. In other words, you should chart significant moments in the development of your work and explain how they shaped your lighting design. This will involve the development of the devised piece as a whole.

Your log should cover:

- your growing knowledge of what makes an effective lighting design
- how your lighting ideas enhanced and supported the devised piece
- how you collaborated with the group to improve your design and the piece as a whole.

Take some time to focus on the collaboration that you are undertaking. How are you feeding and being fed by the group? What challenges are you attempting to overcome?

You should analyse the way that you worked with other people in your group. This includes overcoming difficulties as well as the times when ideas and group work flowed easily.

TASK 7.15

Work with a partner to read the example below and answer the following questions:

1. Why is this example better than the one on the previous page?
2. How could the writer make further improvements?

I found it easiest to develop my lighting design on my own because I could work at my own pace. I have learned, however, that it is best to go to rehearsals often. The performers changed what they were doing a lot and I needed to keep up with them. This was obvious one day when they started to work on a movement piece. I went away and developed a lighting state involving AMLs, which I thought would add excitement to the scene.

I was also able to test out some of my ideas in the rehearsal room and see if the rest of the group liked what I was working on. For example, I experimented with a number of coloured gels for the non-naturalistic monologues that the performers had introduced. They said that they found that the use of a cold, dramatic colour enhanced their ability to get into role. In the end I opted for quite a strong gel (Electric Lilac) to produce a slightly mysterious, hard-edged profile spotlight.

I was lucky that we have quite a lot of lighting resources, such as eight LED par cans and four automated moving profile spotlights. This meant that there were a lot of possibilities for variety in my lighting design. As we worked in the round, I would only have been able to produce very simple lighting if we didn't have a good amount of equipment and a suitable lighting rig. The height and the position of the rig made it possible to avoid dazzling the audience or the performers.

I needed lighting states for a range of locations, including a cave, which was an interesting challenge. At first, I thought I could use a low-intensity blue wash

TASK 7.16

1. Look through the three sections from Chapter 1 listed in the Signpost. Keep the completed tasks and any extra notes in front of you.
2. Use them to write at least two paragraphs about how you are developing a lighting design and how your knowledge of effective lighting has grown.
3. Explain how you applied this knowledge to produce a lighting design. Include:
   - your independent work
   - a list of the equipment you used
   - any special effects you considered.
4. Write a further paragraph or two about how you collaborated with the rest of your group to improve your lighting design. Think about:
   - feedback you received and how it influenced your design
   - how interaction with the rest of the group, including performers, affected your design
   - problems you faced and how you overcame them
   - successes and their effect on the overall piece.
5. Identify how your work was presented in the final performance. How were your lighting skills used?
6. Check your writing and keep track of the word count (roughly 800 words).

DESIGN TIP

It is helpful to include lighting details, such as the names (and numbers) of colour filters. Many of these can be found online.

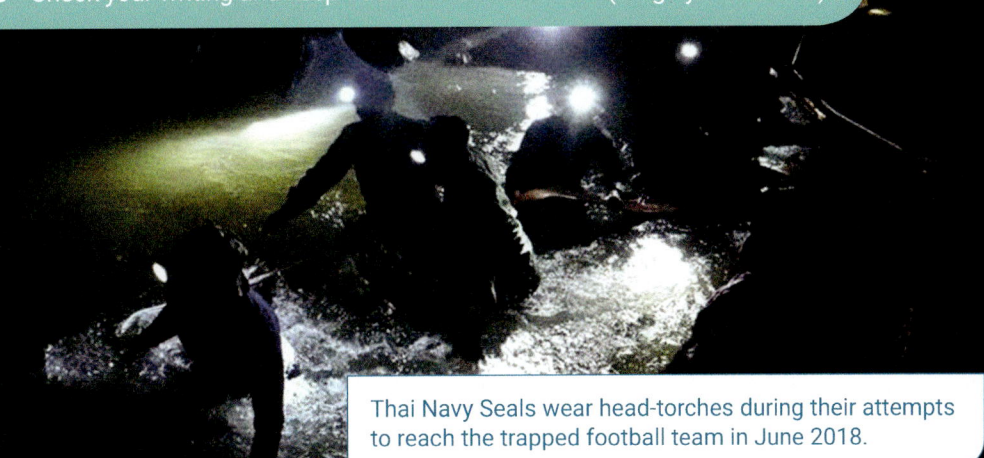

Thai Navy Seals wear head-torches during their attempts to reach the trapped football team in June 2018.

to create atmosphere. In rehearsals, however, it looked more like an outdoor space. I tried altering the position of the fresnels and introducing some soft-edged profiles in a deeper colour (Palace Blue) to create shadows, but this did not produce the lighting state I wanted.

One of the photographs of the Thai football team showed the boys in a beam of light that must have been shone onto them by rescuers. It also showed the boys using torchlight. I came up with a new plan that would have much more impact for the audience. I asked the performers to experiment with using low-strength torches in their improvisation. Other than that, the acting area was completely dark. Suddenly, I was getting the effect that we were looking for.

When the performers saw the circle of light on the boys in the photograph, they decided to end the improvisation with the moment that the first rescuers' lights hit them. For that I used the automated moving profile in a bright, cold colour (Hampshire Frost) that they could respond to as if in shock. Movement wise, I experimented with swiping the light upwards from the floor to suddenly 'catch' the boys.

FOCUS
- Making sure you give enough detail.
- Checking and improving your work so far.

ASSESSMENT CHECK
You should be giving plenty of specific examples and using drama terminology.

DESIGN TIP
Remember to refer to your design ideas throughout your devising log.

REVIEWING SECTIONS 1 AND 2
Reviewing your devising log

TASK 7.17

1. Read through your devising log. Use this chapter and the assessment guidance for each section to see that you have not drifted away from the key points. Check:
   - Can I improve any sentences by adding examples?
   - Should I include more drama vocabulary? (Use the glossary at the end of Chapter 1.)
2. Go through all your notes as well as re-reading what you have already written. You will improve your devising log considerably if you do this task thoroughly!

TASK 7.18

Use the following questions to remind you of significant events you might not have mentioned so far.

- Have I worked with other designers? How did their work affect mine, and vice versa?
- What have I learned from my research?
- Have there been any discoveries during rehearsals? How were they important to my lighting design?
- What improvements have I made to my design? How and why did I make them?
- Have I given and received feedback? How did this influence the work?
- Am I using suitable technical language?

TASK 7.19

Use your responses to the questions above to improve Sections 1 and 2. Include subject-specific language and add one or two detailed examples.

PRODUCING AND DOCUMENTING YOUR LIGHTING DESIGN

What should I produce for my final lighting design?

You should present:

- cue sheets, rigging diagrams or grid plans and a lantern schedule
- the realisation of your lighting in the devised performance.

You also need to supervise the rigging, focusing, programming (if applicable) and the operating of your design if you are not doing these yourself.

Producing your design

Your lighting in performance should be inventive and effective. Your lighting must also support the communication of creative intent to the audience, with consistent attention to design considerations that enhance the production value including mood and atmosphere.

It is vital that you have considered all aspects of your group's artistic intentions and the specific points required by your course. You must also ensure that you keep a close eye on safety issues.

TASK 7.20

Fill in your own version of the following table before you finalise your design.

My range of skills: How does my lighting design…	
…reflect my **artistic intentions** and those of my group?	Theme of inner strength and resilience enhanced by use of strong, motivating lighting states.
…avoid **health and safety** hazards?	• Electric cables taped down. • Focusing avoids dazzle for audience and performers. • Safety cables in use.
…enhance **mood** and **atmosphere**?	• Coloured gels. • Pace of transitions.
…show **inventiveness** and make an impact on the audience?	Wide range of special effects.
…show **collaboration** with performers and other designers?	• Practical effect involving torches used by performers. • Co-ordination on timing rehearsed with sound designer. • Continuous research in rehearsals.

FOCUS

Documenting the completion of your lighting design.

ASSESSMENT CHECK

You need to show how your final design looks and the extent to which you actualised it on the stage. You will be assessed on:

- the inventiveness of your work
- the level and range of theatrical skills
- your success in realising your artistic intentions.

Your finished lighting will demonstrate AO2: 'Use theatrical skills to realise artistic intentions in live performance.'

SIGNPOST

Chapter 1 will guide you through the completion, rigging and plotting of your design. Make sure that you have worked through it before setting your lights ready for the performance.

LOOK HERE

Pages 28–29 will help you with the technical drawings and documents that you need. These can be included in your devising log as an appendix.

FOCUS
How to write in detail about your design in performance and reflect on your learning.

LOOK HERE
'Evaluating your lighting design', page 37, will help you with this section of your log.

SECTION 3: ANALYSIS AND EVALUATION

Until the performance has taken place, you will not be in a position to finish your devising log. When you are, you need to identify and investigate (analyse) and assess the merit of the different approaches used (evaluate).

You should analyse and evaluate:
- how far you developed your theatrical skills
- the benefits you brought to the group and the way in which you positively shaped the outcome
- the overall impact you had as an individual.

You should also appraise areas for development in future devising work (those aspects that did not go as well as you had hoped).

TASK 7.21

Write 700 to 800 about your lighting that are detailed and evaluative. Base it on the table in Task 1.18, your notes and the bullet points above. You could structure it like this:

- How effectively did you develop your skills during the devising process? Give examples.
- Use evaluative language to give your design an overall judgement. Effective? Powerful? Successful?
- Give three specific examples of moments that had impact or enhanced atmosphere or helped to convey meaning. If something did not go to plan, you should analyse what happened and why. What areas would you develop further another time?
- Refer to your artistic intentions for the piece. How did your lighting support those intentions and the production as a whole?

Editing

When you have completed your log and included the required diagrams, proofread it and assess it against the mark schemes. Have you included analysis of the devising process and evaluation of the choices made?

You must also check the word count, as you need to keep below 2500 words, including annotations.

TIPS FOR REDUCING YOUR WORD COUNT
- Avoid repeating yourself. Which section does your point fit in best? Don't include it again elsewhere.
- Remove anything unnecessary. Don't waste words that won't gain marks.
- Give enough detail, but avoid waffling!
- See if some sentences could be made shorter by rephrasing.

TIPS FOR INCREASING YOUR WORD COUNT
- Repeat the tasks on page 200.
- Can you add detailed annotations to your drawings?
- In Section 1, add details of your research.
- Add at least one more example in Section 3 of a moment in the performance where your design was used successfully, or could have been better.
- Take feedback from an audience member. Include their comments, along with your own responses.

Chapter 7 Component 2: Devising Drama – A Practical Guide

SOUND DESIGN FOR THE DEVISED PIECE

The requirements of your sound design

Your sound design will emerge from your role as a member of a devising group. It will be marked in terms of your ability to effectively use a wide range of skills in an inventive way. Your sound design should create mood and atmosphere and suit the chosen genre, structure and style of the piece. It also needs to communicate your group's artistic intentions and have an impact on the audience.

The examiners are hoping for sound designs that:
- support the action and clearly communicate meaning for the audience
- establish location and period and inventively enhance the devised performance
- are technically secure
- include suitable 'intro' and 'outro' music.

The examiners warn against sound designs that:
- are underscored too loudly
- rely too heavily on music and are repetitive and lacking creativity
- are added on to the performance rather than being integral to it.

The devising log

The log is your opportunity to explain how you have engaged fully with the process of devising from the viewpoint of group member and set designer. You will chart the design process from beginning to end, detailing your understanding of all the skills you have used and the decisions you have made.

Your ability to work with your group to bring its artistic intentions to reality is important, along with analysis and evaluation of your successes and the challenges you have faced along the way. Your devising log should:
- include sketches and equipment lists
- show thorough understanding of the technicalities of live, recorded and directional sound
- show the development of ideas and clear understanding of the needs of the piece
- provide evidence of collaboration.

You should avoid working in isolation. It is extremely important that all designers collaborate closely with the rest of their group throughout the devising process.

DESIGN TIP
See your sound design and your devising log as two parts of the same whole. They must be worked on at the same time. This could involve taking detailed notes or writing the log as you go along and reviewing it at the end of the process.

SIGNPOST
Chapter 2 provides practical guidance for your sound design work and guides you through the entire process of designing, mixing, plotting and operating sound effects.

LOOK HERE
See page 182 for a breakdown of the devising log's contents.

DESIGN TIP
You have 2500 words for the whole devising log, including your annotations on your sketches and plans. A minimum of 2300 is best. You could alternatively opt for an audio-visual recording, or a combination of a recording with a written piece.

FOCUS
Approaching the first section of your log.

ASSESSMENT CHECK
AO1 asks you to create and develop ideas that communicate meaning.

This section begins your process of documenting the practical creation and development of ideas, with a focus on the stimulus and your response to it.

SIGNPOST
The following sections at the beginning of this chapter will help you to start the devising log:
- Your design challenge
- Responding to stimuli
- Agreeing on your artistic intentions.

SECTION 1: RESPONSE TO A STIMULUS

The early stages: your chosen stimulus

It is valuable to comment very briefly on more than one stimuli, but you should focus on the stimulus your group chose to work with. Include a detailed explanation in Section 1 about the initial ideas, themes and settings you considered and the research you carried out individually and as a group.

You need to explain:
- your initial response to the stimuli presented by the teacher and the stimulus you chose
- the ideas, themes and settings you have considered in response to the stimulus you chose
- your research findings
- your own dramatic aims and intentions and those for the piece as a whole.

TASK 7.22

The example on the facing page is the start of a sound design devising log.

Although the writer makes some good points, they are not fully responding to the Section 1 bullet points.

1. Select **two** of the following pieces of advice to help the writer add useful detail.
   - Write about all the stimuli you were shown.
   - Explain the themes, ideas and settings that the chosen stimulus suggested to you and the group.
   - Add a paragraph or two about the research you did, how it linked to the stimuli and influenced your sound design.
   - Explain why you chose to be a sound designer.
   - Explain your personal artistic intentions for sound in the piece.
2. Share your answers with a learning partner. Do you agree?

The *Persistence of Memory* by Salvador Dali.

TASK 7.23

Annotate the painting.
- What do you see?
- What does the painting make you think and feel?
- What ideas for sound does it suggest?

Chapter 7 Component 2: Devising Drama – A Practical Guide

I was the sound designer for our devised performance. We also had a lighting designer and three performers. Our stimulus was Salvador Dali's painting *The Persistence of Memory*. It intrigued us more than the other stimuli, such as a newspaper article about cyberbullying.

The painting is a surrealist work that includes soft, flowing clocks in a strange landscape with ants crawling over a pocket watch. My first response was that it is a very weird picture, but interesting. It seemed to have a mixture of nature and man in it. The title is interesting too because memory is about time, which links to the clocks. Persistence is about keeping going. I suppose some memories do persist, but what about the things we forget?

Later, an interesting idea grew in response to the painting because one of the group has a grandparent with dementia. He talked about how difficult it was. For Joyce (Mo's gran), memory is not persistent at all. Sometimes, she doesn't even know who he is. At other times she remembers things from when she was young, but not what she had done that day.

My group liked the idea of memory. Someone spoke about the way the clocks are kind of limp and stretched as if time doesn't pass at the same rate.

We decided that we would devise our piece around the idea of memories and the way that time can seem to go more slowly or more quickly when you are doing different things.

As sound designer, I started to think about the effect of a clock ticking and slowing it down or speeding it up to suggest time passing at different rates.

One of the first things we did was to improvise our earliest memories. We discovered that they were nearly all linked to strong emotions such as fear, pain or joy. We knew that could be useful for our performance. At first, we thought we could act them out and ask the audience which emotions they contained. However, we rejected this idea after a while because we weren't sure we wanted an interactive style and we thought it would be too obvious. I suggested that we use sound design to highlight the emotions and show the scenes as a sort of physical theatre dumb show. We agreed it was a more sophisticated idea that could be more effective.

TASK 7.24

1. Look through the sections in the Signpost. Collect completed tasks from Chapter 2 and any additional notes.
2. Mention the stimuli you were presented with, then write about the stimulus you chose. Give a detailed account of the thoughts and feelings it provoked in you as an individual.
3. Write a short paragraph about how your own and the group's thinking came together. What themes, ideas and settings did you discuss? You could annotate a picture or include mind-maps.
4. Write about your research and how it influenced your sound design ideas.
5. Describe your group's artistic intentions, explaining what you want the audience to think and feel. Refer to the stimulus. What are your own artistic intentions for the sound design?
6. Read through your text to check that it covers all the bullet points above and that the word count is about right (700 to 800 words).

LOOK HERE

'Research for sound design', pages 44–45, will be helpful.

Page 211 has some useful evaluation sentence starters.

DESIGN TIP

Remember to discuss your research and how it influenced your designs.

DESIGN TIP

An important element of analysis is explaining which ideas or designs you rejected and why.

FOCUS
Reflecting on development and refinement of ideas, theatrical skills and collaboration.

ASSESSMENT CHECK
AO1 asks you to create and develop ideas that communicate meaning. You will be creating a design that contributes positively to the performance.

SIGNPOST
The following sections will be particularly helpful in making key decisions about your sound design:
- Sourcing, creating and mixing sounds, pages 46–49
- Special sound effects, pages 50–51
- Working positively as a group, page 190
- Using rehearsals to develop and refine your design, pages 192–193.

SECTION 2: DEVELOPMENT AND COLLABORATION

This section of your log needs to be driven by the devising process. In other words, you should chart significant moments in the development of your work and explain how they shaped your sound design. This will involve the development of the devised piece as a whole.

Your log should cover:
- your growing knowledge of what makes an effective lighting design
- how your lighting ideas enhance and support the devised piece
- how you collaborated with the group to improve the piece.

Spend some time on your collaboration. How are you feeding and being fed by the group? What challenges are you attempting to overcome?

TASK 7.25
1. Collect completed tasks from Chapter 2 and any additional notes.
2. Use them to write at least two paragraphs about how your knowledge of effective sound design has grown.
3. Explain how you applied this knowledge to produce a sound design. Include:
   - your independent work
   - a list of the equipment you used
   - how you considered live, recorded and directional sound.
4. Write a further paragraph or two about how you collaborated with the rest of your group to improve your lighting design. Think about:
   - feedback you received and how it influenced your design
   - how interaction with the rest of the group, including performers, affected your design
   - problems you faced and how you overcame them
   - successes and their effect on the overall piece.
5. Identify how your work was presented in the final performance. How were your sound skills refined and used?
6. Check your writing and keep track of the word count (roughly 800 words).

TASK 7.26
1. Read the following example, looking out for analysis of collaboration as well as specific examples of growing skills and how they led to the development of the piece.
2. Work with a partner to find:
   - two examples of collaboration
   - two examples where the student analyses how problems were overcome
   - an example of how live sound were used and one example of complex recorded sound
   - one example of how directional sound was used
   - an example of the way developed skills were used in the performance.

Early on, the lighting designer and I sat down to share our ideas. We were very keen to make sound and lighting complement each other, which meant working together quite a lot. This worked out particularly well when we thought about moments in the piece that could be enhanced by fast-paced sound and lights.

We went to watch the scenes in rehearsal, where time was passing slowly or quickly depending on the experiences of the characters. The performers found our comments helpful and their work gave us ideas for light and sound.

A good example of how everyone's work was developed through this collaboration was a scene set in a school detention. As a group, our artistic intention was for this scene to communicate the boring, slightly surreal experience of sitting in silence for an hour with nothing to do.

The dripping clocks in our stimulus *The Persistence of Memory* and our stylistic choice to use a mixture of naturalism and non-naturalism resulted in improvisations where characters' memories were being briefly acted out within the detention setting. The performers experimented with slow-motion movement, but found it quite difficult to synchronise their timing.

I had already been thinking about using the sound of a ticking clock, so I set a metronome to a slow speed. The rhythm helped the actors to time their movements as well as adding to the surrealism of the scene. The lighting designer enhanced this by experimenting with colours and transition speeds. A short video was made of our improvisation so that we knew we would be able to re-create it another time.

Although I could have recorded the sound of the metronome, I decided to use it live in performance. This was achievable as I was able to use its gauge to reproduce the same pace every time.

I included several non-diegetic soundscapes and effects to enhance atmosphere and support our artistic intentions. A good example was in the scene where the lady with dementia was with her grandson. I researched the probable effects of dementia and put together a soundscape which included both naturalistic and non-naturalistic sounds. I used the sound of children playing (from her distant memories) and added a slow metronome effect and a distorted drone sound to create some of the confusion she was experiencing.

To create this complex mix of sounds, I created each of the three sound effects individually and ensured they had the sound qualities I wanted. The metronome was recorded live, whereas the other two effects were sourced from the internet. When recording the sound of children playing, I varied the volume so that it faded in and out continuously from very quiet to about 40%. I also added reverb to the drone effect to increase atmosphere. Once I was happy with each of the effects, I experimented with mixing them together. I played with the balance in terms of volume levels and was reasonably pleased in the end. I positioned speakers on opposite sides of the stage to create a sense that the sound was coming from two different directions.

I also experimented with adding a piece of 1940s swing music, but it felt as though there was too much going on so I used the music track to transition into the scene instead.

This is a good example of how I refined my work for in the actual performance.

FOCUS
- Making sure you give enough detail.
- Checking and improving your work so far.

ASSESSMENT CHECK
Your teachers want to give you as many marks as possible for your devising log. You can help them by giving plenty of specific examples and using drama terminology.

DESIGN TIP
Look through the student-style examples for the other design elements in this chapter. They might inspire some new ideas.

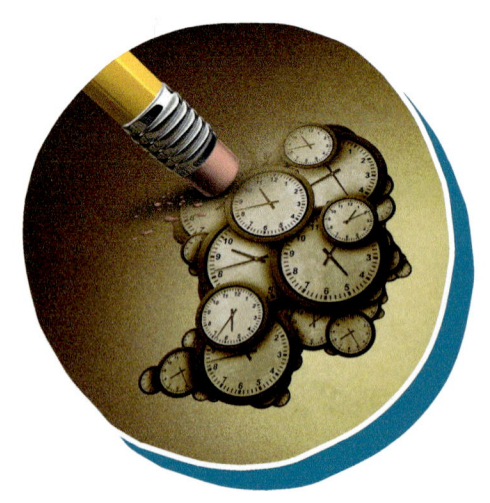

REVIEWING SECTIONS 1 AND 2
Reviewing your devising log

TASK 7.72
1. Read through your devising log. Use this chapter and assessment guidance for each section to see that you have not drifted away from the key points. Check:
   - Can I improve any sentences by adding examples?
   - Could I add plans or a mood board?
   - Should I include more drama vocabulary? (Use the glossary at the end of Chapter 2.)
2. Go through all your notes as well as re-reading your devising log so far. You will improve your log considerably if you do this thoroughly.

TASK 7.28
Use the following questions to remind you of significant events you might not have mentioned so far.

- Did I experiment with mixing sound? What were the results?
- What problems did I need to overcome? How did I achieve this?
- What did I learn and use from my research and rehearsals? What did I change and why?
- Have I given and received feedback? How did this influence the work?
- How did I use different styles and types of sound?
- What health and safety issues did I take into account?
- Did I experiment with live sound? How and why?
- What did I produce that contributed significantly to mood and atmosphere?

208 Chapter 7 Component 2: Devising Drama – A Practical Guide

PRODUCING AND DOCUMENTING YOUR SOUND DESIGN

What should I produce for my final sound design?

You should present:
- cue sheets that detail all the effects used
- a plan showing speaker positions.

You also need to supervise the operation of the sound design in performance and the creation and recording of material (if not doing these yourself).

Producing your design

Your finished sounds should be engaging and effective for the audience. They must also support the communication of your creative intent. Check that you have considered details that enhance meaning, mood and atmosphere.

TASK 7.29

Fill in your own version of this table before you finalise your design:

How does my sound design...	
...reflect my **artistic intentions** and those of my group?	• Theme of persistence of memory. • The clock effects enhance the theme. • Music evokes particular periods. • Soundscape helps to raise questions around memory.
...avoid **health and safety** hazards?	• Sound levels checked. • Cables taped down.
...enhance **mood** and **atmosphere**?	Atmospheric effects and music enhance performance.
...show **inventiveness** and make an impact on the audience?	• Carefully chosen effects in addition to music. • Gradual volume changes/fades.
...show **collaboration** with performers and other designers?	• Close work with performers improved the piece. • Used sound effects during rehearsals. • Worked closely with lighting designer.

It is worth saying that you will need to make your sound design reasonably complex to attain high marks. Ideally, you will go beyond the minimum requirements and:

- mix sounds to create a soundscape
- experiment with live, recorded and directional sound
- consider using special effects such as echo and reverb, even if you decide not to use them in the end
- remember the power of silence – don't use sound just for the sake of it
- select music carefully
- pay attention to pre-set and post-show music, as well as scene transitions.

FOCUS

Documenting the completion of your sound design.

ASSESSMENT CHECK

Your teacher needs to know how your final design sounds and the extent to which you actualised it in the performance. You will be assessed on:

- the inventiveness of your work
- the level and range of theatrical skills
- your success in realising your artistic intentions.

SIGNPOST

Chapter 2 will guide you through all aspects of creating your design.

TASK 7.30

Check your own writing so far. Can you improve it by adding details or removing repetition?

LOOK HERE

'How to document your sound design' on pages 52–53, will help you with the evidence you need.

FOCUS
How to write in detail about your design in performance and reflect on your learning.

LOOK HERE
'Evaluating your sound design', page 61, will help you here. Make sure you fill in the table in Task 2.22.

SECTION 3: ANALYSIS AND EVALUATION

Until the performance has taken place, you will not be in a position to finish your devising log. When you are, you need to identify and investigate (analyse) and assess the merit of the different approaches used (evaluate).

You should analyse and evaluate:
- how far you developed your theatrical skills
- the benefits you brought to the group and the way in which you positively shaped the outcome
- the overall impact you had as an individual.

You should also appraise those areas for development in future devising work (the aspects that did not go as well as you had hoped).

> **TASK 7.31**
>
> The example below is from the final section of a sound designer's devising log.
>
> 1. Find phrases that show the student evaluating how far they developed skills during the devising process.
> 2. Find phrases that show the student evaluating the contribution of sound to the final performance.
> 3. Highlight evidence of how well sound in performance matched intentions. For example, was the sound design successful in supporting the structure of the piece?
> 4. Find a phrase that shows the student has considered future development they would like to make.
> 5. On a scale of 1 to 5 (1 is 'not at all' and 5 is 'outstanding'), how detailed do you think the student is in their evaluation.

During the devising period, I learned a great deal about sound design. For example, I had not worked with live sound before and feel much more comfortable with it now. I also developed skills in mixing sound to create soundscapes.

I received a lot of positive feedback after the performance. Audience members said the sound was really atmospheric, which had been one of my major aims from the beginning. They thought the transition sound effects were helpful in holding the piece together and loved the sound in the detention scene because it made a big difference to creating the effect that time was going really slowly.

Two scenes were singled out for particular praise by a member of staff who saw the final performance. One was the scene with the dementia character. I was told that the scene became very moving because the soundscape evoked the strong feelings that both characters in the scene were experiencing. I was very pleased to hear this because we set out to explore complex emotions and situations in that scene. We were successful in achieving our aims and my sound design was an important part of that.

LOOK HERE
If you are struggling to make your log fit the desired word count, try the tips on page 202.

The other scene that was commented on by the member of staff in relation to sound was about a young child who became lost on a ship. It came from an early memory of one group member, and we aimed to show how time can feel that it is moving very quickly. For this scene, it was important to suggest location and I used some diegetic sea and boat effects mixed with the metronome set to a fast speed. This scene also worked successfully with the lighting, which was mainly blue and cold. I was told that the scene actually raised the heart-rate of some of the audience and I was very proud of that achievement as we had wanted to convey fear.

I learned a great deal from designing the sound for our devised piece, particularly linked to mixing sound to create soundscapes. Although I think I could have improved the volume of the sound in one or two places, I think my design was very successful overall.

TASK 7.32

Write 700 to 800 words about your sound design that are detailed and evaluative. Base it on the table in Task 2.22, your notes and the bullet points above. You could structure it like this:

- How effectively did you develop your skills during the devising process? Give examples.
- Use evaluative language to give your design an overall judgement. Effective? Powerful? Successful?
- Give three specific examples of moments that were inventive or enhanced atmosphere or helped to convey meaning.
- If something did not go to plan, you should analyse what happened and why. What areas would you develop further another time?
- Refer to your artistic intentions for the piece. How did your sound support those intentions and the production as a whole?

Phrases containing judgement vocabulary will help you to evaluate. For example:

> **The... was effective because...**
> **... was successful/powerful because...**
> **A moment that made me proud was... because...**

Editing

When you have completed your log, proofread it and assess it against the mark schemes.

You must also check the word count, as you need to keep below 2500 words, including annotations.

DESIGN TIP

See your set design and your devising log as two parts of the same whole. They must be worked on at the same time.

SIGNPOST

Chapter 1 provides practical guidance for your set design work and guides you through the entire process of designing and supervising the construction of a set.

LOOK HERE

See page 182 for the structure of the devising log and what it should contain.

SET DESIGN FOR THE DEVISED PIECE

The requirements of your set design

Your set design will emerge from your role as a member of a devising group. It will be marked in terms of your ability to effectively use a wide range of skills in an inventive way. Your set should 'locate' the action and characters, help to create mood and atmosphere and suit the chosen genre, structure and styles. It needs to communicate your group's artistic intentions and have an impact on the audience.

The examiners are hoping to see set designs that:

- clearly communicate meaning for the audience
- inventively support the action in the performance space
- might use projected images or set dressings to establish location and period
- might create different spaces if required
- might provide opportunities for **stage business** (such as opening the curtains).

The examiners warn against set designs that:

- are overly simple
- rely heavily on the use of chairs (they can make set changes very noisy, for example)
- lack creativity.

The devising log

The devising log is your opportunity to explain how you have engaged fully with the process of devising from the viewpoint of group member and set designer. You will chart the design process from beginning to end, detailing your understanding of all the skills you have used and the decisions you have made.

A set design sketch, with several levels, for *West Side Story*.

Your ability to work with your group to bring its artistic intentions to reality is important, along with analysis and evaluation of your successes and the challenges you have faced along the way.

Your devising log should:

- include sketches and ground plans
- show the development of ideas
- show clear understanding of the needs of the piece
- provide evidence of research and collaboration.

You should avoid working in isolation. It is extremely important that all designers collaborate closely with the rest of their group throughout the devising process.

SECTION 1: RESPONSE TO A STIMULUS

The early stages: your chosen stimulus

It is valuable to comment very briefly on more than one stimuli, but you should focus on the stimulus your group chose to work with. Include a detailed explanation in Section 1 about the initial ideas, themes and settings you considered and the research you carried out individually and as a group.

You need to explain:

- your initial response to the stimuli and the stimulus you chose
- the ideas, themes and settings you have considered in response to the stimulus you chose
- your research findings
- your own dramatic aims and intentions and those for the piece as a whole.

TASK 7.33

The example on the following page is the beginning of a sound design devising log.

Although the writer makes some good points, they are not fully responding to the Section 1 bullet points.

1. Select **two** of the following pieces of advice to help the writer add useful detail.
   - Write about all the stimuli you were shown.
   - Explain the themes, ideas and settings that the chosen stimulus suggested to you and the group.
   - Add a paragraph or two about the research you did, how it linked to the stimuli and influenced your sound design.
   - Explain why you chose to be a sound designer.
   - Explain your personal artistic intentions for sound in the piece.
2. Share your answers with a learning partner. Do you agree?

TASK 7.34

1. Look through the sections listed in the Signpost. Collect completed tasks and extra notes.
2. Mention the stimuli you were presented with, then write about the stimulus you chose. Give a detailed account of the thoughts and feelings it provoked in you as an individual.
3. Write a short paragraph about how your own and the group's thinking came together. What themes, ideas and settings did you discuss? You could annotate a picture or include mind-maps.
4. Write about your research and how it influenced your set design ideas.
5. Describe your group's artistic intentions, explaining what you want the audience to think and feel. Refer to the stimulus. What are your own artistic intentions for the set design?
6. Read through your text to check that it covers all the bullet points above and that the word count is about right (700 to 800 words).

FOCUS
Approaching the first section of your log.

ASSESSMENT CHECK
AO1 asks you to create and develop ideas that communicate meaning.

This section begins your process of documenting the practical creation and development of ideas, with a focus on the stimulus and your response to it.

SIGNPOST
These sections at the beginning of the chapter will be your resource for starting the devising log:
- Your design challenge
- Responding to stimuli
- Agreeing on your artistic intentions.

LOOK HERE
See pages 188–189 for a summary of the group's ideas for the poem discussed in the response.

DESIGN TIP
Remember to:
- directly link your comments to the stimulus
- show how your research influenced your design.

We were presented with a number of stimuli, including a photograph of two people facing each other with their fingers crossed behind their backs. The idea of hiding the truth seemed to be the theme behind all the stimuli we were asked to consider.

Our chosen stimulus was a poem called 'Lies' by Yevgeny Yevtushenko. It was written in 1952 and calls upon adults to tell young people the truth.

I believe that the poem has great potential for drama, but, at first, I didn't have any particular inspiration for the setting. Part of the problem was that the stimulus implies that there are many situations where lying happens. Homes, schools, on television… For research, I looked at a number of plays which have lies as one of their themes. *Hamlet*, *The Crucible* and *Curious Incident*… came to mind. I noticed that they are all set in quite specific time periods. The poem 'Lies' wasn't like that. I decided to make my design modern to connect the audience strongly to the theme.

I started to think about a recognisable set that could also represent a range of locations. For example, I looked at using levels in a modern way that could still represent power, and about bars or barriers of some kind. Perhaps a composite set with non-naturalistic elements used in different ways would work. I looked at the roads near my house. Scaffolding is interesting because it makes levels and I was also interested in temporary fencing. I discovered that I could borrow these from a local firm. Four would make a square or a short alleyway. As our piece was episodic, I felt that I needed to create a versatile set. These ideas fitted well with the stimuli, which talks about 'obstacles', for example.

My own artistic intentions for the set were to use items of stage furniture, such as these barriers, to physically show the emotional barriers that lies can create.

I like the fact that the theme of adults lying to young people is quite challenging and can be emotional. There are different types of 'untruths' to do with family and the world. In my own case, for example, some serious information about my dad's health was kept from me for quite a long time. I understand why, but would have rather known straight away.

Our dramatic intentions were to create a piece about the problems caused when young people are not told the truth. We also had a specific objective around the line from the poem, 'Tell them the difficulties can't be counted'. Humans have immense challenges to face, like climate change. These are issues that we need to talk about and understand. Do we want to be told that we don't need to worry, or do we need to know the details so that we can be aware of our potential future and act on it? This idea was clear from the line in the poem 'Forgive no error you recognise.'

Luckily, all of our group felt very strongly about the artistic intention. This was particularly true once we decided to focus on the damage that lies can do. We decided to drop this 'harmless' untruths once we realised that they were a diversion from what we really wanted to talk about.

From 'Lies' by Yevgeny Yevtushenko

The young people know what you mean. The young are people.
Tell them the difficulties can't be counted,
and let them see not only what will be
but see with clarity these present times…
Forgive no error you recognise,
it will repeat itself, increase,
and afterward our pupils
will not forgive in us what we forgave.

SECTION 2: DEVELOPMENT AND COLLABORATION

This section of your log needs to be driven by the devising process. In other words, you should chart significant moments in the development of your work and explain how they shaped your set design. This will involve the development of the devised piece as a whole. Remember that you are seeking to create a design that 'contributes positively to the overall effect of the performance and communicates intended meaning for an audience.'

Your log should cover:

- your growing knowledge of what makes an effective set design
- how your set design ideas enhanced and supported the devised piece
- how you collaborated with the group to improve your design and the piece as a whole.

Take some time to focus on the collaboration that you are undertaking. How are you feeding and being fed by the group? What challenges are you attempting to overcome?

Note how the student-style example on the following page shows knowledge and understanding of production elements and the use of stage space and spatial relationships. The designer is also making appropriate judgements and interpreting content and style.

FOCUS
Reflecting on the development and refinement of ideas, theatrical skills and collaboration.

ASSESSMENT CHECK
AO1 asks you to create and develop ideas that communicate meaning. You will be creating a design that contributes positively to the performance.

SIGNPOST
The following sections will be particularly helpful in making key decisions about your set and its development.

- Research for set design, page 67
- Understanding your resources, page 73
- Working positively as a group, page 190
- Using rehearsals to develop and refine your design, pages 192–193.

TASK 7.35

1. Look through the sections from Chapter 3 in the Signpost. Keep the completed tasks and any extra notes handy.
2. Use them to write at least two paragraphs about how you knowledge of effective set design has grown and how you have applied this knowledge to produce a lighting design. Include:
   - your independent work
   - sketches, ground plans and mood boards
   - notes on different locations you considered.
3. Write a further paragraph or two about how you collaborated with the rest of your group to improve your set design. Think about:
   - feedback you received and how it influenced your design
   - how interaction with the rest of the group, including performers, affected your design
   - problems you faced and how you overcame them
   - successes and their effect on the overall piece.
4. Identify how your work was presented in the final performance. How were your set design skills used?
5. Review your writing and keep track of the word count (roughly 800 words). Check that you have used set-specific words to describe collaboration and significant moments in the design process.

The group decided that it wanted the audience to be close to the action. This led us to consider staging our piece in the round. I knew that this would present sightline challenges. For example, creating levels is difficult because high rostra will block the view of parts of the acting area for some of the audience. It is also difficult to use flats except in the corner aisles. The performers listened to myself and the lighting designer making an argument for end-on staging and eventually agreed with us. This was a significant moment for the whole group, but for me in particular, as I was not able to move forward with my set design until the stage configuration was agreed.

My set design began to take shape as I came across the word 'deception' as an alternative to 'lies'. This felt more subtle and suggests *hiding* the truth. When I looked at literature with that theme, plays by Shakespeare came up, including *Othello*, *Hamlet* and *Romeo and Juliet*. I shared this with the group, and they thought they might use short extracts from these plays. This would help them use a wide range of language in the performance. I began to think about how I could support this language use.

I found this production image and liked the idea of using quotes on a run of flats. We knew we wanted non-naturalism in terms of style and I thought that having flats that were thematically linked, along with levels and barriers, made a meaningful and versatile set.

These are the quotes I chose to use:

'O, what a tangled web we weave, when first we practise to deceive.' (Walter Scott, 'Marmion')

'False face must hide what the false heart doth know.' (*Macbeth*)

'Integrity is the lifeblood of democracy. Deceit is a poison in its veins.' (Edward Kennedy)

At first, I thought about writing on the flats with marker pens and spray paint. When I tested it on cardboard, however, it looked messy and wasn't easy to read. I discovered it would be better to paste large photocopies of the quotes onto three flats that we already had in school. I would paint the flats white, and use black and red lettering.

In a production meeting we decided that monochrome and red will be our colour palette. The monochrome aspects would be suitable for using coloured lights. The costume designer was keen to use red accents to suggest the danger of lies.

One day, in rehearsals, I noticed that the performers were making all their entrances and exits from the sides of the stage and that it looked clumsy. I changed my design to make large gaps between the flats to help the performers enter and exit from the back of the stage.

By working together, we were on the way towards a very harmonious world for the stage. I continued my research by visiting rehearsals regularly. I helped the actors to use three tables to represent the flats so they could start to work with the positions of entrances and exits.

We used stage blocks to create two small sections of different heights. To begin with, I thought that the positioning of these blocks would work DSR and CSL because it would add variety. However, when the actors were working with them it created some sightline problems, so I changed their positions to DSR and DSL.

As part of finalising my design, I carefully considered health and safety. Most importantly, I securely braced and weighted the three flats. They were made fire retardant by using a top layer of watered-down PVA. As the actors needed to climb up onto the levels safely, I made each rise 9 inches, which is not too big a stride. I also checked with the costume designer to find what footwear the actors would be wearing to make sure there was no risk of them slipping. The barriers were light to lift and had wide bases so that they were stable.

Collaboration with other designers and performers ensured that the set was co-ordinated in terms of colour palette and that it was creative and practical in performance.

TASK 7.18

1. Use the bullet points for this section, plus the AO1 mark scheme for Component 2, to put this example into a band.
2. Share your thinking with a partner.
   - Why have you agreed or disagreed?
   - Pick out evidence from the example to justify your reasoning.
3. Can you come to an agreement and decide on a mark?

REVIEWING SECTIONS 1 AND 2

Reviewing your devising log

TASK 7.37

1. Read through your devising log. Use this chapter and assessment guidance for each section to see that you have not drifted away from the key points. Check:
   - Can I improve any sentences by adding examples?
   - Should I include more drama vocabulary? (Use the glossary at the end of Chapter 2.)

Go through all your notes as well as re-reading what you have already written. You will improve your devising log considerably if you do this thoroughly.

TASK 7.38

Use the following questions to remind you of significant events you might not have mentioned so far.
- What problems did I need to overcome? How did I achieve this?
- What did I learn and use from my research and rehearsals? What did I change and why?
- Did I hit an obstacle? What did I do?
- Has there been a moment when I felt particularly pleased or proud? What was it and what was the effect that pleased me?
- Have I given and received feedback? How did this influence the work?
- Am I using suitable technical language?
- What health and safety issues did I take into account?
- Have I included sketches and draft plans?

FOCUS
- Making sure you give enough detail.
- Checking and improving your work so far.

ASSESSMENT CHECK
Your teacher wants to give you as many marks as possible for your devising log. You can help them by giving plenty of specific examples and using drama terminology.

DESIGN TIP
Remove waffle. Include brief, precise details of your design ideas.

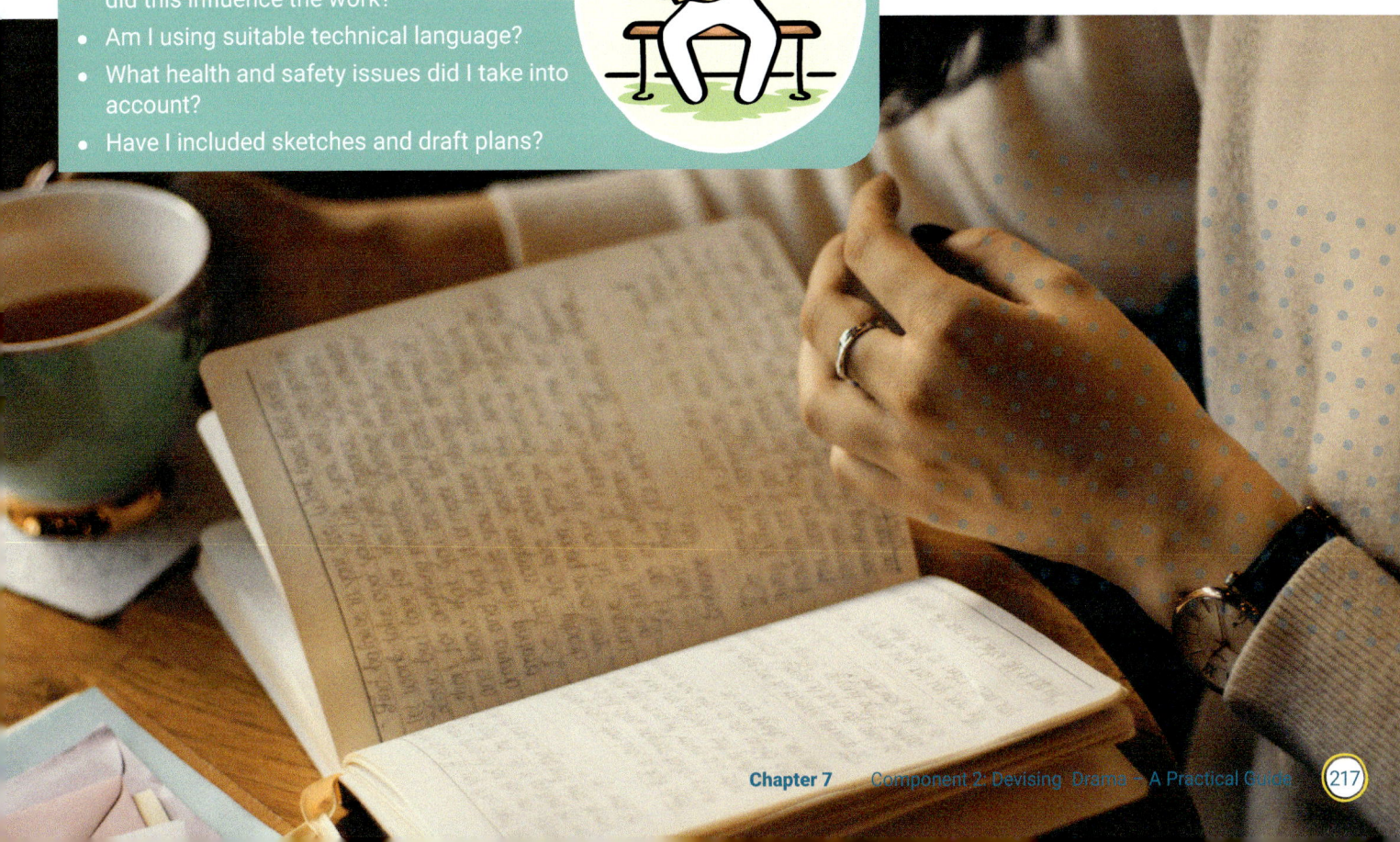

FOCUS

Documenting the completion of your set design.

ASSESSMENT CHECK

Your teachers need to know how your final design looks and the extent to which you actualised it on the stage. You will be assessed on:

- the inventiveness of your work
- the level and range of theatrical skills
- your success in realising your artistic intentions.

Your finished set will demonstrate AO2: 'Use theatrical skills to realise artistic intentions in live performance.'

LOOK HERE

Pages 69–72 will help you with technical drawings. Annotate them so that they are very clear.

DESIGN TIP

The ground plan needs to be drawn to scale, unlike the more artistic drawings.

PRODUCING AND DOCUMENTING YOUR SET DESIGN

What should I produce for my final set design?

You should present:

- drawings of the final design to be realised in the performance space including relevant props and set dressings
- a ground plan of the performance space, including entrances and exits, audience positioning and any stage furniture
- sketches of early designs to illustrate the development of your designs

You also need to have supervised the construction, painting, hiring or finding of the scenic elements required for your design.

Making your design

Your finished set should be engaging and inventive and effective for the audience. It must also support the communication of your creative intent. Check that you have considered design details that enhance production values, including, mood and atmosphere.

TASK 7.39

Fill in your version of the following table before you construct your set.

How does my set design…	
…reflect my **artistic intentions** and those of my group?	• Theme of lies carried in quotes on flats. • Levels to suggest power and barriers (to truth).
…avoid **health and safety** hazards?	• Barriers light to lift. • Non-slip surfaces. • Flats securely weighted and fire retardant. • Height of levels not too great.
…enhance **mood** and **atmosphere**?	• Metal barriers suggest captivity. • Serious/harsh tone.
…show **collaboration** with performers and other designers?	• Levels and entrances between flats allow characters to eavesdrop. • Performers found practice items useful in rehearsal. • Co-ordinated choice of colour palette with lighting and costume. • Combination of costume and set is safe.
…show inventiveness and make an **impact** on the audience?	• Powerful impact because set is uncluttered. • Symbolic and practical elements like the barriers, flats and levels. • Details help to communicate meaning. • Use of colour is engaging.

SECTION 3: ANALYSIS AND EVALUATION

Until the performance has taken place, you will not be in a position to finish your devising log. When you are, you need to identify and investigate (analyse) and assess the merit of the different approaches used (evaluate).

You should analyse and evaluate:

- how far you developed your theatrical skills
- the benefits you brought to the group and the way in which you positively shaped the outcome
- the overall impact you had as an individual.

You should also appraise those areas for development in future devising work (the aspects that did not go as well as you had hoped).

Check that you have commented on all the areas in the Section 3 bullet points. Make sure that you evaluate the development of your skills during the devising process as well as the final performance. Also, note areas for improvement.

Phrases containing judgement vocabulary will help you to evaluate. For example:

- **The... was effective because...**
- **... was successful/ powerful because...**
- **A moment that made me proud was... because...**

FOCUS
How to write in detail about your design in performance and reflect on your learning.

LOOK HERE
'Evaluating your set design', pages 78–79, will help you with this section of your devising log. Make sure you fill in the table in Task 3.13.

TASK 7.40

Discuss the following student-style example with a partner.
- What evaluative language has the writer included?
- Have they included detailed examples to back up their statements?

> I have learned a huge amount through the process of designing a set for our piece. One important thing I discovered was that a set design develops over time, through research and overcoming difficulties. When I started to work with 'deception' as a synonym for 'lies', my design began to include more creative elements, such as the flats with the quotes on them.
>
> My final design was effective in creating a harmonious world in collaboration with the other designers and the performers. An example was when the lights turned red. As the set was mainly monochrome, the colour change had a powerful impact. The character was standing on a raised level in a white coat when she realised that the lie she told a child had been a mistake. She stepped down and sat on the floor. My set helped to show her mood and convey her regret. This also fitted our artistic intention of exploring the effect of withholding the truth from young people.
>
> Another scene that made me proud of my contribution included the line 'O, what a tangled web we weave when first we practise to deceive.' This was one of the quotes that I had pasted, in black, onto a white flat. The connection between the set and the speech was effective as it emphasised that one lie tends to lead to another. This use of set also supported the language used in the piece.
>
> I intended to achieve a set that would support the episodic structure of our piece. I think I was particularly successful because of the speed with which the set could be rearranged. It meant that the flow of the performance was not interrupted. As the actors were multi-rolling, the flats helped them to make minor costume changes out of sight.
>
> The gaps between the flats were effective as they allowed the performers to enter and exit smoothly. At one point, this was used dramatically. The character who had not been told about his father's illness stood in the 'doorway' and overheard the truth. I was pleased that my set helped this moment to be powerful.
>
> Overall, my set design was very successful. The only thing I might have improved would have been the quality and size of the lettering on the flats. However, I had very good feedback from the audience, and the rest of my devising group were very excited by the impact the piece (including my set) had.

Editing

When you have completed your devising log and attached extra documents, proofread it and assess it against the AO1 and AO4 mark schemes. Make sure you have included analysis of the process and evaluation of your choices.

Check the word count is below 2500 words, including annotations.

TASK 7.41

Write a few paragraphs (700 to 800 words) about your set that are detailed and evaluative. Base them on the table in Task 3.13, your notes and the bullet points on the previous page. You could structure it like this:

- How effectively did you develop your skills during the devising process? Give examples.
- Use evaluative language to give your design an overall judgement. Effective? Powerful? Successful?
- Give three specific examples of moments that were inventive or enhanced atmosphere or helped to convey meaning.
- If something did not go to plan, you should analyse what happened and why. What areas would you develop further another time?
- Refer to your artistic intentions for the piece. How did your set support those intentions and the production as a whole?

TIPS FOR REDUCING YOUR WORD COUNT

- Avoid repeating yourself. Which section does your point fit in best? Don't include it again elsewhere.
- Remove anything unnecessary. Don't waste words that won't gain marks.
- Give enough detail, but avoid waffling!
- See if some sentences could be made shorter by rephrasing.

TIPS FOR INCREASING YOUR WORD COUNT

- Repeat the tasks on page 217.
- Can you add detailed annotations to your drawings?
- In Section 1, add details of your research.
- Add at least one more example in Section 3 of a moment in the performance where your design was used successfully, or could have been better.
- Take feedback from an audience member. Include their comments, along with your own responses.

COSTUME DESIGN FOR THE DEVISED PIECE

The requirements of your costume design

Pastel costumes (designed by Roger Kirk) in *42nd Street* give a feeling of softness and sophistication.

Each costume design will emerge from your role as a member of a devising group. It will be marked in terms of your ability to effectively use a wide range of skills in an inventive way. Your costume should 'locate' the period and characters, help to create mood and atmosphere and suit the chosen genre, structure and styles of the piece. It needs to communicate your creative intent and have an impact on the audience.

The examiners are hoping to see costume designs that:
- show excellent understanding of how the costume can support the performer and the piece as a whole
- are inventive and successful within a small budget
- are complete in terms of costume, make-up and accessories.

The examiners warn against costume designs that:
- focus on make-up with little or no design in the garments
- are overly simple or lack creativity.

The devising log

The log is your opportunity to explain how you have engaged fully with the process of devising as a group member and costume designer. You will chart the process from beginning to end, detailing your understanding of all the skills you have used and the decisions you made.

Your ability to work with your group to bring its artistic intentions to reality is important, along with analysis and evaluation of your successes and the challenges you have faced along the way. Your devising log should:
- show the development of ideas
- show clear understanding of the needs of the piece
- indicate how research has been used
- provide evidence of collaboration.

Avoid working in isolation. It is extremely important that all designers collaborate closely in their group throughout the devising process.

DESIGN TIP
See your costume designs and your devising log as parts of the same whole. They must be worked on at the same time.

SIGNPOST
Chapter 4 provides practical guidance for your costume design work and guides you through the entire process of designing, sourcing and creating costumes. Use it here alongside the practical guide at the beginning of this chapter.

LOOK HERE
See page 182 for a breakdown of the devising log's contents.

FOCUS
Approaching the first section of your log.

ASSESSMENT CHECK
AO1 asks you to create and develop ideas that communicate meaning.

This section begins your process of documenting the practical creation and development of ideas, with a focus on the stimulus and your response to it.

SECTION 1: RESPONSE TO A STIMULUS

The early stages: your chosen stimulus

It is valuable to comment very briefly on more than one stimuli, but you should focus on the stimulus your group chose to work with. Include a detailed explanation in Section 1 about the initial ideas, themes and settings you considered and the research you carried out individually and as a group.

You need to explain:

- your initial response to the stimuli presented by the teacher and the stimulus you chose
- the ideas, themes and settings you have considered in response to the stimulus you chose
- your research findings
- your own dramatic aims and intentions and those for the piece as a whole.

TASK 7.42

1. The example on the following page is the start of a costume design devising log. Use the Section 1 bullet points and the AO1 mark scheme to put it into a band. Is there enough detail?
2. Share your thinking with a partner.
   - Why have you agreed or disagreed?
   - Pick out evidence from the example to justify your reasoning.
   - Can you come to an agreement and decide on a mark?
3. What areas for improvement would you suggest?

TASK 7.43

What words and phrases could you add as a response to this stimulus photograph?

A detail from a stimulus photograph that shows a range of circus performers, including acrobats and a ringmaster.

222 Chapter 7 Component 2: Devising Drama – A Practical Guide

I chose to be the costume designer. There was also a lighting designer and four performers. The stimuli we were shown seemed to have 'relationships' in common. One was the song 'Family Portrait' by Pink. It's a heartfelt piece about a daughter who wants her family to stay together, which I thought had a very strong storyline. However, I thought it might lead to a rather obvious devised piece with contemporary, naturalistic costume, so I wasn't drawn to it.

The stimulus we chose was this photograph of circus performers. They are balancing, juggling and presenting their skills. It had the feel of the final sequence of a show. As a designer, I was inspired by the costumes' well-worn, slightly shabby appearance while also being colourful and richly textured.

I researched the history of circus costumes and discovered that performers used to make their own outfits from anything they could find. Our budget was small, so I thought that I could put my costume together from lots of sources.

Although it was easy for me to be excited by the circus theme as a costume designer, the group as a whole found the stimulus rather difficult to respond to. Unlike the Pink song, it didn't have a clear storyline. On the other hand, it gave us scope for inventiveness. The setting of a circus was one which we all warmed to because of famous troupes such as Cirque de Soleil.

I suggested that we brainstorm the photograph which led to interesting words and phrases such as:

- Hard work
- Skill
- Tiredness
- A face for the public.

This last point was interesting and gave me and the group a sense of what was on show and what was being hidden, which felt like a warm trail.

At this point, each performer chose a character from the photograph and created a freeze-frame, which was thought-tracked by the rest of the group. We discovered that what they said and did was very different from what they were thinking. I know that this is something that many people do.

Three of the performers in our group do dance or gymnastics, which drew us using of these skills in the circus setting. I knew that my design would need to take the physicality into account, so I focused on the use of stretch fabric when developing my ideas.

It took us quite a while to arrive at the intentions for the piece, but we finally worded it like this:

Aim: To create an entertaining piece of largely physical theatre that discusses people's private and public lives.
Objective: To explores contrasts in terms of onstage and backstage relationships.

I think that most people have a public persona to some extent and this idea had plenty of dramatic potential.

TASK 7.44

1. Look through the sections listed in the Signpost. Collect completed tasks and any extra notes. Remind yourself of the Section 1 key points.
2. Write a few paragraphs describing the stimulus and responses to it.
3. Note your group's artistic intentions and how you arrived at them.
4. Add any sketches or costume ideas you had at this early stage.
5. Include information about your research how it influenced your thinking about costume.
6. Read through your paragraphs to check that they cover the key points and the word count is around 700 to 800.

TASK 7.45

1. Check your own Section 1 against the AO1 mark scheme. Can you make at least three improvements?
2. As well as checking spelling and punctuation, check that you are keeping to the point and using specific examples.

LOOK HERE

'Introduction to costume design' on pages 82–83 might help with Task 7.44.

FOCUS
Reflecting on the development and refinement of ideas, theatrical skills and collaboration.

ASSESSMENT CHECK
AO1 asks you to create and develop ideas that communicate meaning. You will be creating a design that contributes positively to the performance.

SECTION 2: DEVELOPMENT AND COLLABORATION

This section of your log needs to be driven by the devising process. In other words, you should chart significant moments in the development of your work and explain how they shaped your costume design. This will involve the development of the devised piece as a whole, remembering that you are seeking to create a design that 'contributes positively to the overall effect of the performance and communicates intended meaning for an audience'.

Your log should cover:

- your growing knowledge of what makes an effective costume design
- how your costume ideas enhanced and supported the devised piece
- how you collaborated with the group to improve your design and the piece as a whole.

TASK 7.46

The example below is the second section of the costume design devising log from the previous page.

1. Use the Section 2 key points and the AO1 mark scheme to put it into a band.
2. Share your thinking with a partner.
   - Why have you agreed or disagreed?
   - Pick out evidence from the example to justify your reasoning.
   - Can you come to an agreement and decide on a mark?

As time went on, we experimented with different sorts of physical theatre, influenced by, for example, Frantic Assembly's chair duets and Queen's song 'The Show Must Go On'. This resulted in an emotional scene that became the climax of the piece. It developed my understanding that my costume would need to allow plenty of movement. Stretch fabric was desirable and garments without lycra, for instance, would need to have ease in terms of fit.

Another factor was that one of the performers was uncomfortable with physical theatre. We spent rehearsal time making sure that this aspect of her performance was as confident and polished as possible. I often gave her feedback, which was appreciated.

Her costume (she played the Ring Mistress) was one that I chose to design. This was partly because I could introduce an element of tailoring, while allowing for a full range of movement. I also wanted to make sure that the performer had a well-fitting costume that would boost her confidence as well as supporting character, style and atmosphere. It could help her get into the role.

To suit the style of our piece, I wanted an element of steampunk-meets-circus in my designs. I also wanted the costume to be easily adapted to suit backstage scenes as well as the onstage ones. I decided that the costume would have stretch items, such as leggings and a T-shirt, with an over-garment of a jacket that had a steampunk feel in a fit that was loose enough to enable of movement.

The costume I decided on was an altered cherry-red jacket with black and gold embellishments. I found it in a charity shop and restyled it with a friend's help. Under the jacket, the actress wore black leggings and T-shirt. Her make-up and hair were bold, with back-combing adding height to her hair.

A significant moment in the devising process occurred when I understood that the available budget was limited. I returned to my earlier research in which I had discovered that many 19th-century performers put together their own costumes. I began to think about ways that I could adapt second-hand clothing and so work cheaply.

I found that ballet net was quite cheap and comes in a range of colours. It was also easy to work with as it doesn't fray or need hemming. I experimented with adding it to charity shop garments to produce flamboyant costume ideas.

All the performers found it very helpful being able to rehearse in elements of costume. Their feedback helped me to make minor changes to ensure that they could all move safely and easily. I also took the lining out of the red coat to make it less bulky and allow more movement.

SIGNPOST

The following sections will be particularly helpful in making key decisions about your costumes and their development.

- Colour and fabric for the stage, pages 86–89
- Health and safety in costume design, page 95
- Working positively as a group, page 190
- Using rehearsals to develop and refine your design, pages 192–193.

TASK 7.47

1. Look through the sections in the Signpost. Collect completed tasks and notes.
2. Use them to write at least two paragraphs about how your knowledge of effective costume design grew.
3. Explain how you applied this developing knowledge to produce a costume that met the needs of the devised piece. Include:
   - your independent work
   - drawings, mood boards, photos, fabric swatches
   - health and safety considerations.
4. Write a further paragraph or two about how you collaborated with the rest of your group to improve your costume design. Think about:
   - feedback you received and how it influenced your design
   - how interaction with the rest of the group, including performers, affected your design (you might have noticed, for example, that the character had a particular personality trait, such as anxiety, that you could enhance for the audience)
   - problems you faced and how you overcame them
   - successes and their effect on the overall piece.
5. Identify how your work was presented in the final performance. How were your costume skills used?
6. Check over your writing and keep track of the word count (roughly 700 to 800 words).

DESIGN TIP

Check that you have analysed the process as well as responded to the key points for the section.

FOCUS
- Making sure you give enough detail.
- Checking and improving your work so far.

ASSESSMENT CHECK
Your teacher wants to give you as many marks as possible for your devising log. You can help them by giving plenty of specific examples and using drama terminology.

DESIGN TIP
Remove waffle! Include brief, precise detail.

REVIEWING SECTIONS 1 AND 2

Reviewing your devising log

TASK 7.48

1. Read through your devising log. Use this chapter and assessment guidance for each section to see that you have not drifted away from the Check:
   - Can I improve any sentences by adding examples?
   - Should I include more drama vocabulary? (Use the list at the end of Chapter 4.)
2. Go through all your notes as well as re-reading what you have written so far. You could improve your devising log considerably if you do this thoroughly.

TASK 7.49

Use the following questions to remind you of significant events you might not have mentioned so far.
- What did I learn from my research?
- Did I hit an obstacle? What did I do?
- Has there been a moment when I felt particularly pleased or proud? What was it and what was the effect that pleased me?
- Have I given and received feedback? How did this influence the work?
- Can I say more about genre, structure, character, form and style?
- Am I using suitable technical language?
- How else did I contribute in rehearsals? What was the effect?
- What health and safety issues did I take account?
- Do I have sketches, swatches, images of mood boards and so on?
- Have I considered design details that enhance production values, including characterisation?

TASK 7.50

Use your responses to the questions above to improve the first two sections of your log. Aim to include more subject-specific language and add one or two detailed examples.

226   Chapter 7   Component 2: Devising Drama – A Practical Guide

PRODUCING AND DOCUMENTING YOUR COSTUME DESIGN

What should I produce for my final costume designs?

You should present:
- a final costume design, including accessories, hair and make-up if appropriate, with fabric samples if this helps to explain your design
- earlier design sketches to show the development of your work
- the realisation of the costume design in the devised performance (in other words, the actual costume worn, which matches your final drawings).

You also need to have supervised the construction of the designed costume if you have not made it yourself.

Making your design

This is the moment where you finish the job of constructing and pulling together the garments, accessories, hair and make-up.

Remember that your finished costume should be engaging and inventive and effective for the audience. It must also support the communication of your creative intent.

TASK 7.51

Fill in your version of the following table before you construct either of your final costumes.

How does my costume design…	
…reflect the **artistic intentions** of my group?	Costumes transform easily on stage from backstage to onstage wear. This fits with our artistic intention of contrasting relationships.
…avoid **health and safety** hazards?	• Avoid trailing items. • Ensure freedom of movement. • Non-slippery footwear.
…enhance **mood** and **atmosphere**?	Colours and textures of circus, flamboyant styling including hair and make-up.
…show **inventiveness** and make an **impact** on the audience	Transforming the charity-shop jacket into a flattering ring mistress coat.
…show **collaboration** with performers and other designers?	• Co-ordinated use of colour palette with lighting designer. • Working together to ensure there were four costumes (for all performers). • Providing costume items early enough in rehearsal for plenty of practice.

FOCUS
Documenting the completion of your costume design.

ASSESSMENT CHECK
You will be assessed on:
- the inventiveness of your work
- the level and range of theatrical skills
- your success in realising your artistic intentions.

Your finished costume will demonstrate AO2.

LOOK HERE
'How to document your costume design', pages 98–99, will help you with the technical drawings.

Acrobat / trapeze artist
- Pink hair
- Silver rhinestones?
- Purple net ruffles
- 'Natural' tights
- Snug pumps (Or bare feet?)

DESIGN TIP
Make sure you annotate your drawings so that the details are clear.

Chapter 7   Component 2: Devising Drama – A Practical Guide

FOCUS

How to write in detail about your design in performance and reflect on your learning.

LOOK HERE

'Evaluating your costume design', page 105, will help you with this section.

DESIGN TIP

Check that you have included hair, make-up and mask drawings (if relevant), as well as clothing designs.

SECTION 3: ANALYSIS AND EVALUATION

Until the performance has taken place, you will not be in a position to finish your devising log. When you are, you need to identify and investigate (analyse) and assess the merit of the different approaches used to make judgements (evaluate).

You should analyse and evaluate:

- how far you developed your theatrical skills
- the benefits you brought to the group and the way in which you positively shaped the outcome
- the overall impact you had as an individual.

You should also appraise those areas for development in future devising work (the aspects that did not go as well as you had hoped).

TASK 7.52

Write three or four paragraphs about your costume design that are detailed and evaluative. Base this on the table in Task 4.15, your notes and the bullet points above. You could structure it like this:

- How effectively did you develop your skills during the devising process? Give examples.
- Use evaluative language to give your design an overall judgement. Effective? Powerful? Successful?
- Give three specific examples of moments that were inventive or enhanced atmosphere or helped to convey meaning.
- If something did not go to plan, analyse what happened and why. What areas would you develop further another time?
- Refer to your artistic intentions for the piece. How did your set support those intentions and the production as a whole?

The example on the following page could help you with the structure.

Check that you have commented on all the areas in the Section 3 bullet points. Make sure that you evaluate the development of your skills during the devising process as well as the final performance. Also, note areas for improvement.

I learned a great deal about designing costumes during the devising process. I was worried about my drawing ability, but realised that detailed annotations can make up for a lack of artistic skill on paper. I also learned the importance of collaborating with other designers and the performer I was designing for. A good example of this was how I negotiated the use of colour with the lighting designer which really improved the whole look of the piece.

I had a budget of £20 and was thrilled that I was able to produce dynamic, good-quality costumes by sticking to my strategy of working with pre-loved garments which I adapted and embellished.

Our audience told us that the piece was exciting and entertaining, which is exactly what we set out to achieve.

One of the moments in the performance that had a lot of impact involved the actor who played the Ring Mistress. She really owned the stage. Her posture was upright and her gestures were broad and powerful. She said that the costume had really helped her, and audience members commented on the impact of her costume and how it strengthened her character. I am very proud of that. Removing the bulky lining of the coat was successful in that the actor was able to move fluently in the physical theatre sequences. Restyling the coat to make it more fitted and with a short swallow-tail was highly effective. The tails were short enough not to be trodden on and added the formality required.

In the backstage sections of the piece, the actress swapped her coat for a broken-down red cardigan. I chose the colour for visual continuity; a reminder of her onstage role. The fact that the cardigan was rough, pilled acrylic with stretched cuffs and a few holes succeeded in supporting the character. I used a cheese grater to raise the surface and produce the holes. I stretched the cuffs by pulling them while the garment was wet. The fact that it was second hand made it easier to produce this look.

The actress changed her posture when she wore the cardigan by rounding her shoulders and slouching a little, which emphasised the difference between her on- and offstage personalities. Her hairstyle could be flattened for the backstage scenes. Again, this powerfully reinforced the differences in her personality.

In future, I would like to develop my own sewing skills so that I could confidently make costumes from scratch. I believe that it would have been better if I had customised the T-shirt my performer wore. Adding my own embellishments could have been very effective.

Editing

When you have completed your devising log and included the drawings required, proofread it and assess it against the AO1 and AO4 mark schemes.

Check the word count too, as you need to keep under 2500 words, including annotations.

LOOK HERE

For tips on reducing or increasing your word count, see page 202.

PUPPET DESIGN FOR THE DEVISED PIECE

The requirements of your puppet design

Your puppet design will emerge from your role as a member of a devising group. It will be marked in terms of your ability to effectively use a wide range of skills in an inventive way. Your puppet should help to 'locate' the period and style and help to create mood and atmosphere. It also needs to communicate your group's artistic intentions and have an impact on the audience.

The examiners are hoping to see puppet designs that:

- demonstrate excellent understanding of how the puppet can support the piece as a whole
- have been thoroughly researched
- show careful consideration of materials and construction principles
- are used extensively in the performance by an animator who is well rehearsed.

The examiners warn against puppet designs that:

- are not used effectively in the performance
- are overly simple or cannot be seen clearly.

The devising log

The log is your opportunity to explain how you have engaged fully with the process of devising from the viewpoint of group member and puppet designer. You will chart the process from beginning to end, detailing your understanding of all the skills you have used and the decisions you have made.

Your ability to work with your group to bring its artistic intentions to reality is important, along with analysis and evaluation of your successes and the challenges you have faced along the way.

Your devising log should:

- show the development of ideas
- include images and annotations
- use and show extensive research
- provide evidence of collaboration.

You should avoid working in isolation. It is extremely important that all designers collaborate closely with the rest of their group throughout the devising process.

> **DESIGN TIP**
> See your puppet design and your devising log as two parts of the same whole. They must be worked on at the same time.

Bexley the bear, designed and made by Alex Milledge for the international company Brymore Productions. He has rods on his hands and a 'handle' at the back to operate his head. Alex says about him: 'Bexley is made of a mixture of recycled, found and new materials. He has a body made of sponge so that he is friendly and squashy for children to touch and engage with.'

> **SIGNPOST**
> Chapter 5 of this book provides practical guidance for your puppet design work and supports you through the entire process of designing, creating and animating puppets. Use it here alongside the practical guide at the beginning of this chapter.

There is no limit to the inventiveness of puppet designers! Alice is watched by the Cheshire Cat made by the Puppet Kitchen.

SECTION 1: RESPONSE TO A STIMULUS

The early stages: your chosen stimulus

It is valuable to comment very briefly on more than one stimuli, but you should focus on the stimulus your group chose to work with. Include a detailed explanation in Section 1 about the initial ideas, themes and settings you considered and the research you carried out individually and as a group.

You need to explain:

- your initial response to the stimuli presented by the teacher and the stimulus you chose
- the ideas, themes and settings you have considered in response to the stimulus you chose
- your research findings
- your own dramatic aims and intentions and those for the piece as a whole.

TASK 7.52

1. Look through the sections listed in the Signpost, right. Collect completed tasks and any extra notes. Remind yourself of the Section 1 bullet points.
2. Mention the stimuli you were presented with, then write about the stimulus you chose. Give a detailed account of the thoughts and feelings it provoked in you as an individual.
3. Write a short paragraph about how your own and the group's thinking about the stimulus came together. What themes, ideas and settings did you discuss? You could include mind maps, spider diagrams or an annotated copy of the stimulus, for example.
4. Write about the research you began, springing from the stimulus material. Explain how it influenced your puppet design ideas.
5. Describe your group's artistic intentions, explaining what you want the audience to think and feel. Refer to the stimulus. What are your own artistic intentions for puppet design?
6. Read through your text to check that it covers all the Section 1 bullet points and that the word count is about right (700 to 800 words).

TASK 7.53

Read the example extract on the following page. It would probably be placed within the top two bands by an examiner. Why do you think this is?

FOCUS

Approaching the first section of your log.

ASSESSMENT CHECK

AO1 asks you to create and develop ideas that communicate meaning.

This section begins your process of documenting the practical creation and development of ideas, with a focus on the stimulus and your response to it.

SIGNPOST

The following sections at the beginning of this chapter will be your resource for starting the devising log:

- Your design challenge
- Responding to stimuli
- Agreeing artistic intentions.

DESIGN TIP

Proofread as you go along. As well as spelling and punctuation, check that you are keeping to the point and using specific examples.

LOOK HERE

Introduction to puppet design, page 108, will help with Task 7.52.

Girl with a Balloon by Banksy.

Begging for Change by Meek.

The Flying Buttresses. Photo © Lindsey Harris

Zelva the giant tortoise robot enjoys a stroke from her co-creater Rupert Parry.

I took on the role of puppet designer for our devised piece.

We were shown a range of images by street artists, including Banksy. Some of them used colour; some were black and white. Some included text; others were simply pictures. However, they were all thought provoking. Our group chose *Girl with a Balloon* and Meek's *Begging for Change* because they were both very moving and had complicated ideas in them even though they appeared quite simple. The double meaning in the word 'change' is very clever and made me think about the fact that everybody needs money to survive and that some people have to beg in order to stay alive. The image suggests that this isn't fair and I agree with that. In terms of settings, although streets are an obvious location, these themes and the situations suggested by the stimuli happen all over the world.

As a puppet designer, I liked the idea that my puppet could play a real part in the artistic intentions of the devised piece. I started to explore the different ways that puppets can be used and came across The Flying Buttresses' animatronic tortoise, Zelva, which is really interactive and helps children learn to approach animals properly. I decided that I would like to create an animal puppet that could be central to our devised piece.

In Banksy's balloon image, I felt sorry for the little girl, but there isn't really any hope that she will get the balloon back. Our initial ideas around this image focused on the importance of having hope when there doesn't seem to be any. The theme of climate change arose from this because it seems that there is so little time to stop it getting worse. We were also struck by the figure being a child, which made me think about the phrase 'children are our future'. The group started to discuss the theme of change. The stimulus of the homeless man is calling for change and the girl with the balloon is in a suddenly changing situation that she doesn't like.

Our research, and the way our ideas developed, led us towards a piece for younger children. The world they live in is changing incredibly fast in both good ways (medical and technological) as well as bad ways (environment and mental health, for example) so we arrived at our dramatic intention which would be to create a Young People's Theatre piece.

Its aim would be to get a younger audience thinking about change:

- What things do they want to change?
- What can they change?
- How can we cope with changes that we can't control and don't like?

I explained to the group that I could create a puppet who, like Zelva, would interact with the audience and help link scenes together.

While I was researching climate change, I came across a report about Iguanas in Florida that fall out of trees because they get too cold and lose their grip. People help to warm them up and they recover. I took this as inspiration. I thought that a glove-puppet form for the head and a rod for the tail could work well.

I also thought that it would be possible to give the puppet plenty of personality and introduce humour into the performance.

LOOK HERE

Visit www.illuminate.com for an annotated version of this student text.

TASK 7.54

Check your own Section one against the bullet points and the AO1 mark scheme. Can you make at least three improvements?

SECTION 2: DEVELOPMENT AND COLLABORATION

This section of your log needs to remain driven by the devising process. In other words, you should chart significant moments in the development of your work and explain how they shaped your puppet design. This will involve the development of the devised piece as a whole.

Your log should cover:

- your growing knowledge of what makes an effective puppet design
- how your puppet ideas enhanced and supported the devised piece
- how you collaborated with the group to improve your design and the piece as a whole.

Take some time to focus on the collaboration that you are undertaking. How are you feeding and being fed by the group? What challenges are you attempting to overcome?

You should analyse the way that you worked with other people in your group. This includes overcoming difficulties as well as the times when ideas and group work flowed easily.

FOCUS
Reflecting on the development and refinement of ideas, theatrical skills and collaboration.

ASSESSMENT CHECK
You will be creating a design that contributes positively to the performance and communicates intended meaning for an audience.

SIGNPOST
The following sections will be helpful in making key decisions about your puppet:

- Types of puppet, pages 112–115
- Why choose puppets?, page 109
- How to document your puppet design, page 119
- Using rehearsals to develop and refine your designs, pages 192–193.

TASK 7.55

The example on the following page is the second section of the puppet design devising log from the previous page.

1. Read it through, then use the Section 2 bullet points and the AO1 mark scheme to put it into a band.
2. Share your thinking with a partner.
   - Why have you agreed or disagreed?
   - Pick out evidence from the example to justify your reasoning.
   - Can you come to an agreement and decide on a mark?

TASK 7.56

1. Look through Chapter 5 and the beginning of this chapter. Keep the completed tasks and notes with you.
2. Use them to write at least two paragraphs about how your knowledge of effective puppet design has grown.
3. Explain how you applied this knowledge to produce a puppet that met the needs of your piece. Include:
   - your independent work
   - sketches and photos
   - how you developed the puppet's personality and gave it audience appeal
   - your thoughts about how the puppet would be animated.
4. Write a further paragraph or two about how you collaborated with the rest of you group to improve your puppet design. Think about:
   - feedback you received and how it influenced your design
   - how interaction with the rest of the group, including performers, affected your design
   - problems you faced and how you overcame them.
   - successes and their effect on the overall piece
5. Identify how your work was presented in the final performance. How were your puppet skills used?
6. Check your writing and keep track of the word count (roughly 700 to 800 words).

As I started to experiment with different designs for my puppet, I began to think that a rod puppet might work better than a mixture of rod and glove. It would have one rod at the head and another near the tail. I saw some examples of rod puppets that were manipulated from above and could scuttle along the ground.

I also thought that it could have a 'home base' on a branch near the front of the acting area, which would increase its appeal and be highly visible.

I wanted my puppet to have plenty of movement like a real lizard. I found a crocodile dog toy to adapt, and called my puppet Iggy. At 55cm long, it seemed like a good size to animate and be easily seen.

To construct the puppet, I made a slit in the body and stuffed it with soft-toy filling. I hit a problem when I found that the puppet was too stiff to move fluidly, so I removed some stuffing to make it more flexible in the tail and neck.

I tested this out in rehearsals. We hoped that Iggy would link the scenes together by 'talking' to the audience. I got some very useful feedback from the performers who said that Iggy still looked like a crocodile. They also said that I was hunched over while I was manipulating him, which looked awkward. It also meant that it was hard to hear the voice for Iggy.

So, I made the metal rods longer and practised animating him in a more upright posture, which worked well. I had quite a 'lazy' American drawl for Iggy's voice and it definitely worked better when I was less bent over. I improved the voice too by watching videos of southern American accents, settling on Alabama. A Florida accent would have been more accurate, but the Alabama accent seemed to allow more personality.

Most importantly, I shortened the puppet's head and sewed more scales onto his face and body. He looked much more like an Iguana after that.

My puppet became really important in the piece because our intention to get younger students thinking about change could have been rather 'heavy'. The scene where Iggy describes how he got too cold and fell out of a tree involved a performer finding him and covering him with a scarf to warm him up. It was one of the earliest scenes we improvised and Iggy and the performer built up a warm, humorous relationship that we thought would have audience appeal. Iggy then gets into a 'conversation' with the audience about how change makes them feel. This led to scenes of events, such as moving house, that we hoped would help children understand that good things can come from change, especially if you talk about how you feel.

We also had scenes that encouraged children to think about what they would like to change about the world. For example, Iggy moved around the space looking for (pre-placed) rubbish that he needed help with because he couldn't pick it up himself.

We had to collaborate in many ways to make the performance work. For example, we did a lot of work on how to always look at Iggy rather than me when having a conversation. Iggy was on his branch for most of the time so that he was at head height.

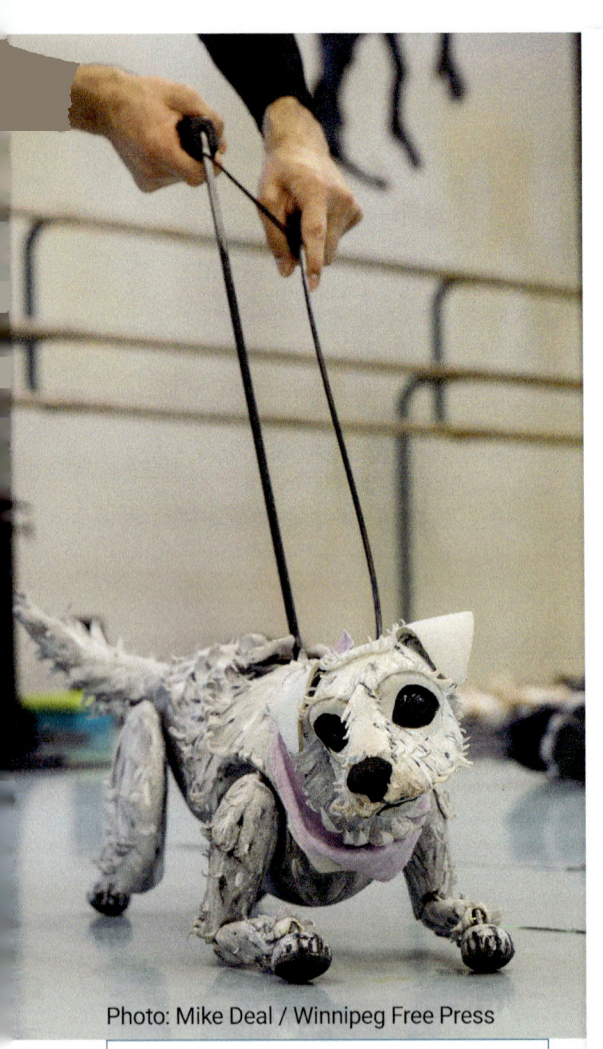

Photo: Mike Deal / Winnipeg Free Press

Toto in rehearsal for Royal Winnipeg Ballet and Cincinnati Ballet's *The Wizard of Oz*.

DESIGN TIP

Proofread as you go along. As well as spelling and punctuation, check that you are keeping to the point and using specific examples.

DESIGN TIP

Keep your notes from group sessions. Use them to remind yourself of the research and explorations that have taken place.

REVIEWING SECTIONS 1 AND 2
Reviewing your devising log

TASK 7.57

1. Read through the first two sections of your devising log. Use this chapter and the assessment guidance for each section to see that you have not drifted away from the key points. Check:
   - Can I improve any sentences by adding examples?
   - Should I include more drama vocabulary? (Use the glossary at the end of Chapter 5.)
2. Go through all your notes as well as re-reading what you have already written. You will improve your devising log considerably if you do this task thoroughly.

TASK 7.58

Use the following questions to remind you of significant events that you might not have mentioned so far.
- What problems did I need to overcome? How did I achieve this?
- Did I change my ideas? What did I change and why?
- How did I make sure that my puppet had a personality?
- What feedback did I give or receive? How was it helpful?
- Have I taken health and safety into account?
- How did I make sure that my puppet would have audience appeal?

FOCUS
- Making sure you give enough detail.
- Checking and improving your work so far.

ASSESSMENT CHECK
Your teacher wants to give you as many marks as possible for your devising log. You can help them by giving plenty of specific examples and using drama terminology.

DESIGN TIP
Remove waffle. Include brief, precise detail.

FOCUS

Documenting the completion of your puppet design.

ASSESSMENT CHECK

Your teacher needs to know how your final design looks and the extent to which you actualised it on the stage. They will assess you on:

- the inventiveness of your work
- the level and range of theatrical skills
- your success in realising your artistic intentions.

Your finished puppet will demonstrate AO2: 'Use theatrical skills to realise artistic intentions in live performance.'

DESIGN TIP

If there are any last improvements to be made to your puppet, now is the time to make them.

PRODUCING AND DOCUMENTING YOUR PUPPET DESIGN

What should I produce for my final puppet design?

You should present:

- annotated drawings of the final design
- sketches of your earlier designs to show the development of your work.

You also need to have supervised the construction of your puppet if you did not make it yourself.

Making your design

Your finished puppet should be inventive and effective. It must also support the communication of creative intent to the audience, with consistent attention to design considerations that enhance the production value including mood and atmosphere.

It is vital that you have considered all aspects of your group's artistic intentions and the specific points required by your course. You must also ensure that you keep a close eye on safety issues.

TASK 7.59

Fill in your own version of the following table before you construct the final version of your puppet.

How does my puppet design...	
...reflect my **artistic intentions** and those of my group?	Iggy is central to our ideas about exploring aspects of change with a younger audience.
...avoid **health and safety** hazards?	• There are no pins or sharp objects in the puppet. • I made sure I could operate him without putting strain on my back or arms.
...enhance **mood and atmosphere**?	Iggy adds humour and warmth to the piece.
...show **collaboration** with performers and other designers?	Action on feedback made sure that the inclusion of a puppet would be successful.
...show **inventiveness** and make an impact on the audience?	Feedback reassures me that Iggy has a real character and people seem to like him.

FOCUS

How to write in detail about your design in performance and reflect on your own learning.

SECTION 3: ANALYSIS AND EVALUATION

Until the performance has taken place, you will not be in a position to finish your devising log. When you are, you need to identify and investigate (analyse) and assess the merit of the different approaches (evaluate).

You should analyse and evaluate:

- how far you developed your theatrical skills
- the benefits you brought to the group and the way in which you positively shaped the outcome
- the overall impact you had as an individual.

You should also appraise those areas for development in future devising work (those aspects that did not go as well as you had hoped).

TASK 7.60

Write 700 to 800 words about your puppet design that are detailed and evaluative. Base this on the table in Task 5.13, your notes and the bullet points on the left. You could structure it like this (also look at the example on the following page):

- How effectively did you develop your skills during the devising process? Give examples.
- Use evaluative language to give your design an overall judgement. Effective? Powerful? Successful?
- Give three specific examples of moments that were inventive or enhanced atmosphere or helped to convey meaning.
- If something did not go to plan, analyse what happened and why. What areas would you develop further another time?
- Refer to your artistic intentions for the piece. How did your puppet design support those intentions and the production as a whole?

LOOK HERE

'Evaluating your puppet design', page 125, will help you with this section of your devising log. Make sure you fill in the table in Task 5.13.

TASK 7.61

1. Use the Section 3 bullet points and the AO4 mark scheme to put the example into a band.
2. Share your thinking with a partner.
   - Why have you agreed or disagreed?
   - Pick out evidence from the example to justify your reasoning.
   - Can you come to an agreement and decide on a mark?
   - What advice would you give the writer that might help them improve their work?

DESIGN TIP
Check that you have included annotated sketches, fabric swatches and photographs.

LOOK HERE
If you are struggling to make your devising log fit the desired word count, try the tips on page 202.

I developed my skills in puppet design hugely over the course of the devising process. It was my first experience of working on puppetry. I would definitely do it again. By refining various elements, I was able to create a puppet with audience appeal and a real character. I think part of this was my choice to base the puppet on a real situation (iguanas falling out of trees). From my research, I was able to imagine the personality of an iguana troubled by climate change, but with an element of humour that the audience could engage with.

Feedback from the audience of Year 7 students was really positive. Some wanted to 'meet' Iggy after the performance, which was great fun for all of us. Technically, I did things like altering the position of his eyes so that he could 'look' directly at people, which was very engaging.

In the performance itself, I was particularly proud of the impact my puppet had on the audience. The moment when Iggy asked for volunteers to help him pick up litter produced lots of offers from the audience. This was one of the ways I knew he was successful. At another point, I animated Iggy's fall from the branch in slow motion and made sure that he didn't seem badly hurt when he landed, by having him 'snore'. This got plenty of laughs, which is what we wanted at that point, as well as appreciation for our character who discovered him and warmed him up.

I had not realised how engaging a fairly simple puppet could be. Our piece was about working for change and dealing with changes that can't be stopped. The performers had several scenes where they multi-rolled. Iggy linked them with bits of narration and audience interaction.

We were told that our piece was very creative and inventive. The puppet added something unique to our piece.

There are, however, things that I would do differently another time. I would have sewn Iggy from scratch out of cotton that I could have painted, rather than the material the toy crocodile was made of, which was harder to work with. I would also have chosen wooden rather than metal rods. Although the metal ones were fairly sturdy, I think I would have got more movement into the puppet with more solid rods.

Check that you have commented on all the key points. You should also make sure that you evaluate the development of your skills during the devising process as well as in the final performance. Also note areas for further development (things you could have improved).

Editing

When you have completed your devising log and included the necessary drawings, proofread it and assess it against the AO1 and AO4 mark schemes.

Check the word count too, as you need to keep under 2500 words, including annotations.

COMPONENT 3: DESIGNING FOR TEXTS IN PRACTICE

Chapter 8

How your design skills will be assessed	240
Six Steps to Lighting Design for Texts in Practice	**242**
1 Working on your own with the script	242
2 The design brief meeting and rehearsals	244
3 Revisiting the script	245
4 Confirming your lighting designs	246
5 The final design meeting	247
6 The completed lighting design	248
The Statement of Dramatic Intentions for lighting design	249
Six Steps to Sound Design for Texts in Practice	**250**
1 Working on your own with the script	250
2 The design brief meeting and rehearsals	252
3 Revisiting the script	253
4 Confirming your sound designs	254
5 The final design meeting	255
6 The completed sound design	256
The Statement of Dramatic Intentions for sound design	257
Six Steps to Set Design for Texts in Practice	**258**
1 Working on your own with the script	258
2 The design brief meeting and rehearsals	260
3 Revisiting the script	261
4 Confirming your set designs	262
5 The final design meeting	263
6 The completed set design	264
The Statement of Dramatic Intentions for set design	265
Six Steps to Costume Design for Texts in Practice	**266**
1 Working on your own with the script	266
2 The design brief meeting and rehearsals	268
3 Revisiting the script	269
4 Confirming your costume designs	270
5 The final design meeting	271
6 The completed costume design	272
The Statement of Dramatic Intentions for costume design	273
Six Steps to Puppet Design for Texts in Practice	**274**
1 Working on your own with the script	274
2 The design brief meeting and rehearsals	276
3 Revisiting the script	277
4 Confirming your puppet designs	278
5 The final design meeting	279
6 The completed puppet design	279
The Statement of Dramatic Intentions for puppet design	280

FOCUS
- Advice on what examiners expect to see on their visits to schools.
- Details of the assessment criteria and how to meet them.

DESIGN TIP
You must choose the same specialism for both extracts.

LOOK HERE
Review page 10 for how each design role should be applied in Component 3.

Explanation and guidance for the central concept of artistic intentions are given on pages 184–185.

There is specific guidance on the Statement for each role following each set of six steps.

DESIGN TIP
You do not need to finish this document until just before the examiner comes into your school, but you should prepare notes for it and collect your work-in-progress as your design develops.

HOW YOUR DESIGN SKILLS WILL BE ASSESSED

In this component, you will 'learn how to contribute to text-based drama in a live theatre context for an audience'. It is assessed by a visiting examiner. For the scripted extracts, the examiner will look at two types of evidence of your design skills:

- your Statement of Dramatic Intentions, which is not formally assessed
- the two designs you produce – one for each extract from the chosen text. (Each extract is marked out of 20. Together, they account for 20 per cent of the total marks for your Drama GCSE.)

The Statement of Dramatic Intentions

This is your explanation of what you intend for your design in performance. It guides the examiner's understanding of your design and the process you have been through.

You need to write about 150 words that detail:

- your intentions for the piece
- what you want your audience to experience.

You can attach diagrams, sketches, plans and cue sheets to support your design ideas.

The designs in performance

AO2 is the objective for the finished designs: 'Apply theatrical skills to realise artistic intentions in live performance.' Your designs should therefore demonstrate the application of your knowledge about how to develop and create finished designs for the extracts.

The examiner will be looking very carefully for the way design is used during the performance of both extracts. As the extracts are assessed separately, you might must create a noticeably different design for each extract. [run on] You are expected to show a range of skills and effects.

You are assessed on your ability to:

- interpret texts
- create and communicate meaning
- realise artistic intention in text-based drama.

The examiner will be looking very carefully for the way design is used during the performance of both extracts. They will be noting the:

- overall contribution to performance made by your design
- range of theatrical skills demonstrated in your design
- effectiveness with which you deploy your design skills
- appropriateness of your interpretation to the play as a whole, as shown through your design
- sensitivity to the context of the play you display through your design
- success in achieving your artistic intent, as evidenced by your design when considered against your Statement of Dramatic Intentions.

SIGNPOST

You will get the most out of this chapter if you refer closely to the guidance and tasks in the relevant Practical Guide to Design chapter at the beginning of this book.

DESIGN TIP

Make sure that you are in touch with what is going on in rehearsals throughout the process. It is sure to influence the way your design develops.

DESIGN TIP

Use a notebook or secure folder. Loose bits of paper get lost or become disorganised.

The performers in their muted period costumes are dominated by the back projection in this scene from *1984* at Nottingham Playhouse.

Chapter 8 Component 3: Designing for Texts in Practice 241

FOCUS
- The lighting design process from page to stage.
- How to interpret, analyse and evaluate as you experiment with different designs, select those that are most successful and realise your designs.

ASSESSMENT CHECK
Your lighting should:
- contribute positively to the performance and communicate meaning
- help to establish location, time, mood or atmosphere
- use a range of lighting effects and lighting states
- show you can select appropriate equipment and position it in order to realise the intended design
- show an understanding of how to apply rigging, positioning and angling.

You must also adopt the latest safe working practices.

SIGNPOST
Chapter 1 will help you with every aspect of your practical lighting work.

DESIGN TIP
It is your lighting **design** that is assessed. Although you are expected to operate the lighting equipment when possible, this is not part of the assessment.

SIX STEPS TO LIGHTING DESIGN FOR TEXTS IN PRACTICE

STEP 1
Working on your own with the script

As soon as you know that you are designing the lighting, start your independent work. This is likely to be at the same time as rehearsals begin.

You will need to look at the script with the eyes of a lighting designer. Think about the genre, style, context and locations you will need to enhance. Your teacher should be able to tell you what the stage configuration will be.

1. Read the whole play (or a detailed summary). As you go through, use a table like the one below to note details that could influence your choices.

Play: *Sparkleshark* by Philip Ridley				
Genre: Social drama				
Staging configuration	Location/s	Historical, social and cultural contexts	Themes/ messages	Style, moods and atmosphere
In the round.	Rooftop of block of flats.	• Contemporary (modern day) • Youth culture.	• Friendship • Bullying.	• Mixture of naturalism and non-naturalism • Comedy • Fantasy.

2. Carefully read each extract. Highlight, and mark brief annotations on:
   - locations – specific (such as a rooftop) and more general (city, for example), and whether they are interior or exterior
   - weather/season and time of day
   - shifts in mood and atmosphere
   - the need for a special lighting state, such as colours for a fantasy scene
   - any questions that crop up.

   See the example on the following page.

3. Make more detailed notes from your table, above. Use your annotations to begin a chart like the following.

Locations	Interior/exterior	Time of day (or night)	Weather/season
• Street • Kitchen.	Forest (p27).		

Shifts in mood or atmosphere	Special lighting state	Direct address or other non-naturalistic feature	Questions/ideas
	Opening fridge (p5, l11).		

242 Chapter 8 Component 3: Designing for Texts in Practice

LIGHTING

'Hansel and Gretel' has the structure of a <u>nightmare</u>. A few domestic objects – buckets, a knife, a blanket, a plate, a jug, an axe – create both the <u>house</u> and the <u>forest</u> and appear in the <u>Witch's house</u>. The Mother also reappears, grotesque, as the Witch. A chorus of three is always present, and active. [...] The story is one of starvation, terror and catharsis. The rhythms of speech are taut and violent, containing the fearful tensions and, finally, joyous release of the drama.

House interior (1a)

Father It was no more than once upon a time when a poor woodcutter lived in a <u>small house</u> at the <u>edge of a huge, dark forest</u>. Now, the woodcutter lived with his wife and his two young children – a boy called Hansel and a little girl called Gretel. [...] <u>Night after hungry night</u>, he lay in bed next to his thin wife, and he worried so much that he tossed and he turned and he sighed and he mumbled and moaned and he just couldn't sleep at all. [...]   *Q Build*

Q Build up father

Is this a special, eg spot? Or is there other action here?

And as he fretted and sweated <u>in the darkness</u>, back came the bony voice of his wife; a voice as fierce as famine. [...]

   Outside. Bright light.   *Location 1b*

There was <u>bright, sparkling moonlight</u> outside and the <u>white pebbles</u> on the ground <u>shone like silver coins and precious jewels</u>. Hansel bent down and filled his empty pockets with as many pebbles as he could carry. [...]

   Inside.   *Location 1a returning*

'Don't worry, Gretel, you can go to sleep now. We'll be fine, I promise.' And he <u>got back into bed</u>.

Q Sunrise state

Mother At <u>dawn, before the sun had properly risen</u>, their mother came and woke the two children. [...]   *Q Location 2 - Forest*

Father Then the whole family <u>set off along the path to the forest</u>. [...]

Mother 'You stupid boy, that's not your kitten. It's just <u>the light of the morning sun glinting</u> on the chimney. Now come on.' [...]

   The family go <u>deeper into the dark heart of the forest</u>.   *Time passing*

Gretel The forest was <u>immense and gloomy</u>. [...]   *Darkening*

Hansel Hansel and Gretel collected a big pile of firewood and when it was <u>set alight</u> and the <u>flames were like burning tongues</u>, their mother said: *SFX*

Mother 'Now lie down by the fire and rest.'

Locations:

1) <u>House</u>   (a) <u>interior</u> – 2 spaces?
2) <u>Forest</u>   (b) <u>exterior</u> – night, bright moonlight dawn
3) <u>Witch's house</u>

(SFX)   – <u>Fire</u> – They light it: Practical
           – Battery and bulb?
           <u>OR</u> Staging – Footlights? Unit within set?

STEP 2

The design brief meeting and rehearsals

Now that you have an understanding of the script and have started to think about lighting design, arrange a meeting with your group. Take your script and notebook and any lighting ideas you might already have. If you have a set, sound, puppet or costume designer, they should be there too.

You will not be able to finalise your lighting designs until there is agreement on:

- the staging configuration (Is it in the round, traverse, end on?)
- a rough idea of the set design
- the style and setting of the performance (Is it naturalistic or stylised? Do you need a practical special such as a table lamp, for example? If so, what period does it need to suit?)

LOOK HERE

Details on making a mood board for lighting can be found on page 139.

During the meeting

1. Share your thoughts so far about lighting. Show any sketches or mood boards and invite feedback. Try to deal with any criticism positively: very few designers are likely to get it all right first time.
2. Listen carefully to others and give similar sensitive feedback.
3. Make sure you discuss the following questions.
    - Do we have issues from Step 1 that can be answered in this meeting? If not, how and when can they be addressed?
    - Are we beginning to move towards a shared artistic vision for the performance? What do we imagine it looks like?
    - How will we communicate our ideas to each other? Can we create a shared resource bank for notes and images as we work independently? (This could be a folder on your school's intranet or a service such as Dropbox, which many professional theatres use.)
    - What shall we work on before we next meet? What do we want to achieve by when?
4. Make detailed and well-organised notes of the discussions and any decisions made. You could put them under the heading 'Design Brief Meeting' in your notebook.
5. Agree on a date for the next design meeting.

STEP 3
Revisiting the script

This step is another stage you can complete independently. You should, however, be continuously checking in on rehearsals, as developments might influence your design. Similarly, other designers and the performers will benefit from your updates.

1. Add details to your script annotations and ideas tables, based on what you learned at the design brief meeting. Your new knowledge of the staging and possible set design, for example, might allow you to think more clearly about locations, lighting states and use of colour. Similarly, a shared sense of dramatic intention for the performance might prompt you to consider moods that you would like to enhance at particular moments.

   Be clear on how your designs could enhance your dramatic intentions. Make sure your lighting designs are clearly influenced by those intentions.

2. Sketch the acting area and mark areas with the positions for different locations that you might want to light separately. Collaborate with the set designer to ensure that you have covered all the areas that need to be lit. These might include specific 'rooms', outdoor sites or a space on the stage that is used for monologues, for example.

   Once you have identified the areas, you can use them in different ways. For example, you could subtly highlight one area by increasing intensity. This will lead the audience's focus to, for example, the children who are listening on the other side of the door. Or, you could light just one area of the stage and leave the rest in darkness.

3. Are there special effects that need to be planned for? How could you use lights to create moonlight, for example, or fire or bright sunlight? Do you need to plan for a spotlight for a narrator or for a monologue?

4. Create a key to use on your script that links to notes or sketches in your notebook. These could be asterisks, numbers or a letter Q, for example, to indicate a lighting change (see Step 1). An arrow down the side of a script extract could show where you intend to build or decrease the intensity of a lighting state.

5. Carefully consider space, using it to its best potential. This includes lighting the stage in a way that encourages interesting spatial interactions. For example, you could light an area in the auditorium to use for a monologue.

6. Continue to note down any questions that emerge.

ASSESSMENT CHECK

During this review of the script, you will be working on AO2: 'Apply theatrical skills to realise artistic intentions in live performance.'

LOOK HERE

See page 29 for a lighting plot for *Hansel and Gretel*.

'Understanding your lighting resources', pages 18–19, and 'Research for lighting', page 27, will be helpful here.

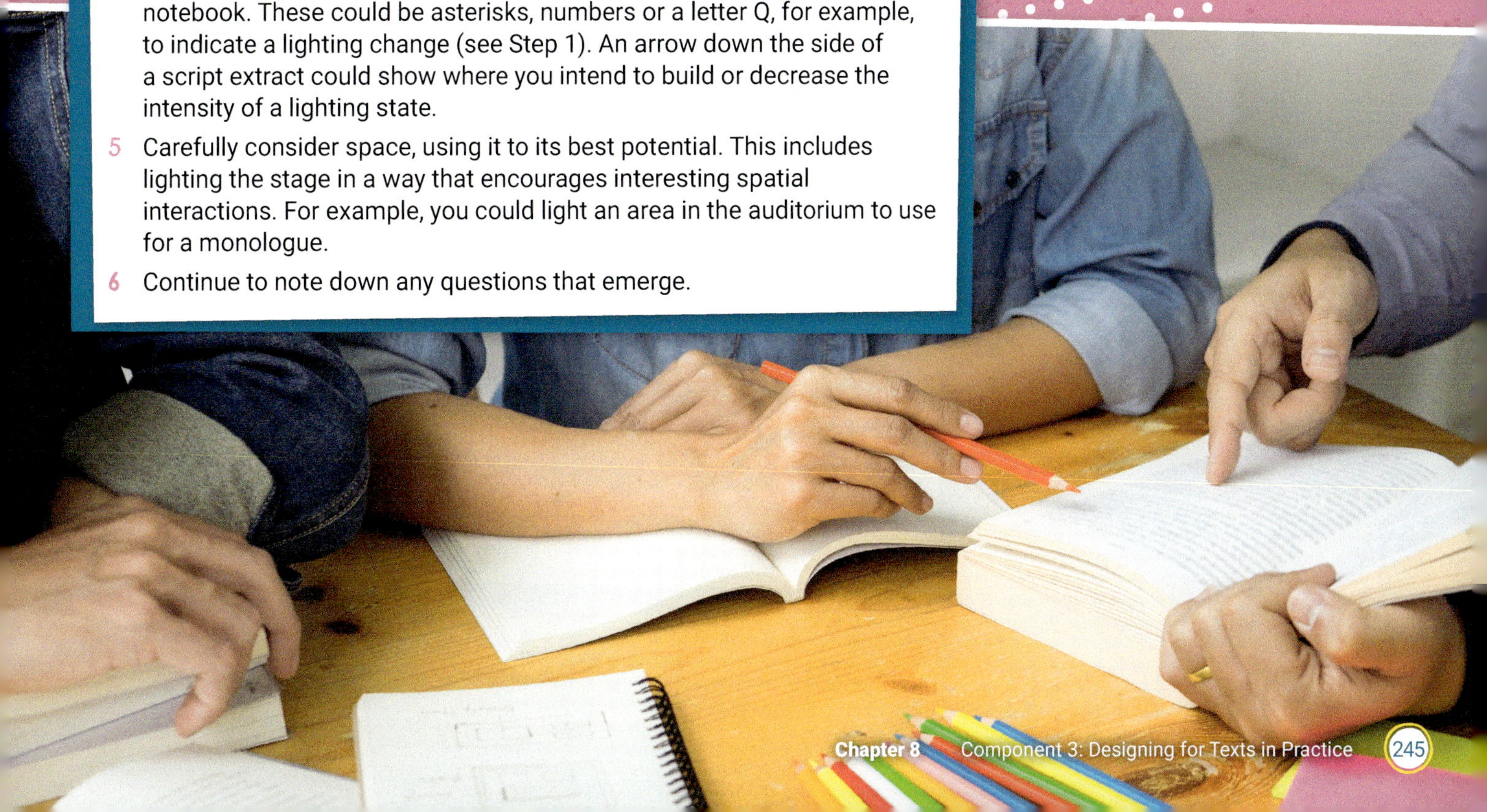

ASSESSMENT CHECK

In reviewing and selecting your designs, you are helping to ensure that your personal interpretation exhibits appropriateness to the play as a whole (AO2). At the same time, you will develop good habits for AO4: 'Analyse and evaluate your own work.'

SIGNPOST

Chapter 1 provides important information on creating lighting designs.

DESIGN TIP

AO4 is tested in the written exam, but this step will give you excellent practice in the key skills of analysis and evaluation.

STEP 4

Confirming your lighting designs

For your lighting designs to be agreed at the final design meeting, they need to be at the final design stage themselves.

Rehearsals will be well underway now. You should take your final design ideas into the rehearsal room and check if there are any new developments that affect you. An extra lighting state might be needed if the performers have introduced a flashback, for example. Do you still have time to include this in your design?

1. Revisit the tasks on pages 18–19 before you finalise your lighting designs on paper. Now is also the time to look back at 'Research for lighting', page 27. What additional items, such as colour gels or gobos, are included in your design?

2. If you are thinking of using special effects, experiment with the equipment to create them. Test their practicality and impact before committing them to the final design.

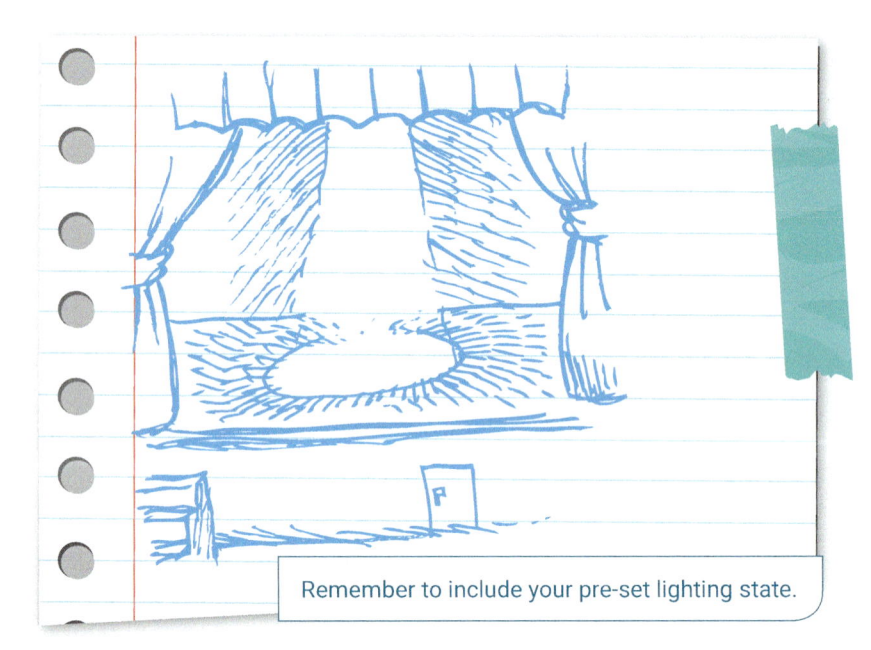

Remember to include your pre-set lighting state.

3. Check with the other designers that all the designs are compatible, both artistically and in terms of keeping performers and audience safe. Complete the checklist below.

Extract:					
Period, mood, style and genre?	Supports dramatic intentions?	Compatible with set design?	Compatible with costume?	Any notes on use of space and health and safety	Notes on special effects, colour, types of lantern, etc.
Y/N	Y/N	Y/N	Y/N		

STEP 5
The final design meeting

Hold a last design meeting. In professional theatre, the stage manager, production manager and other specialists would also be present.

This is the meeting where everything is agreed, including budgets. As a designer, you should not buy or make anything final, or start putting special effects together, until the designs have been signed off.

1. Bring the finished plans of your designs to be signed off. The documentation could include a rigging diagram, sketch of acting area(s) with lighting locations marked, your annotated script, plus any notes. Through discussion, confirm the final designs.

   In terms of collaboration, this is the final chance to check that your designs harmonise with other designers' work. You need to complement set, costume and puppetry, in particular.

2. Don't be afraid to ask questions and raise concerns. It is vital that you leave this meeting ready to realise your designs.

DESIGN TIP

Help your group to envision the world of the stage. Make sure that you bring with you enough detail about your designs, including, for example, gobos that you want to use.

3. Complete a table like this one during or straight after the meeting. (An example has been started for you.)

Extract:		
Agreed lighting design (including changes)	**Agreed budget**	**Notes**
All fine, but add an extra special effect for the monologue.		

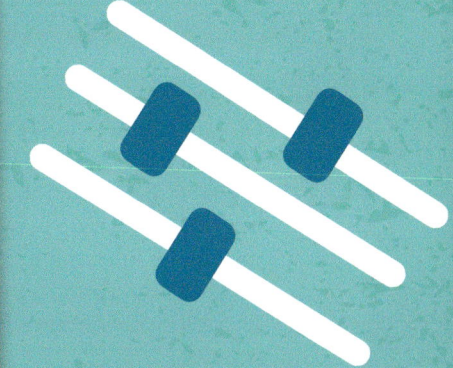

Chapter 8   Component 3: Designing for Texts in Practice   247

STEP 6
The completed lighting design

Clever use of lighting creates an oversized shadow and a sinister atmosphere in this scene from The Woman in Black.

Finally, you can set up your lighting ready for the performance.

You will supervise the rigging and focusing, so be sure to arrange suitable times for these tasks with your human resources.

Preparation

The last thing you want is to get to the day of rigging and focusing only to discover that something is missing. This checklist should help.

- ○ Rigging diagrams – checked and accurate.
- ○ If some lanterns are already rigged, do I know which ones are to be moved and where to?
- ○ Lanterns clean and ready to be rigged.
- ○ Sufficient cables in place or ready to be attached.
- ○ Safety equipment ready (eg, heat-resistant gloves and security cables).
- ○ Performance space booked/reserved for rigging.
- ○ Ladders or scaffolding tower located and booked in.
- ○ Lighting desk/board ready for focusing process.

Actualising

1. Make sure you know the date of the technical rehearsal. Have your lighting designs operable and tested in good time.
2. Check that all lanterns are rigged and focused in good time and that your plan and cue sheet are finished and clear.
3. Once your lighting is rigged and focused, allow plenty of time for the operation of your lighting cues to be practised.

LOOK HERE
Refer to Chapter 1 for guidance on rigging, plotting and operating.

DESIGN TIP
Remember to evaluate your designs at each stage. How successfully are they matching your intentions in terms of concept, interpretation and communication of meaning?

THE STATEMENT OF DRAMATIC INTENTIONS FOR LIGHTING DESIGN

Your lighting will be seen in the performance. In addition, you need to explain how your lighting design fits the intentions of the scripted piece. This statement allows the examiner to match your lighting designs to your dramatic intentions. You should write about 150 words for each extract.

Including the information so briefly can be tricky, but focus on how your design interprets the extract. Remember to cover these points:

- What is your central lighting design idea in the key extract?
- How have you interpreted this extract through your lighting design?
- What are you hoping to communicate to the audience?

One way of doing this could be to look back at the final task from Step 1 and include a version of it in your explanation. Add notes to show how you interpreted the extract through lighting. For example:

Extract 1: interpretation		
Interior location: Small house at the edge of forest (p13). A lighting state that includes a straw-coloured spotlight positioned to suggest light coming through the window.	**Exterior location**: Forest (p15). Dappled-leaf-effect gobo on 2 profile spotlights.	**Atmosphere**: Moonlit night (p14). A cobalt blue filter on 3 of the fresnels.
Passing time: The forest gradually darkens (p15). Changing the intensity of the lighting state from 50% to 20% over about 50 seconds.	**Special lighting state**: Fire (p15). A battery and a red bulb activated by a performer.	

A further list or paragraph should explain what your lighting design should communicate to an audience, as in the example below.

Your cue sheets, annotated scripts and rigging diagrams should be attached to your Statement of Dramatic Intentions.

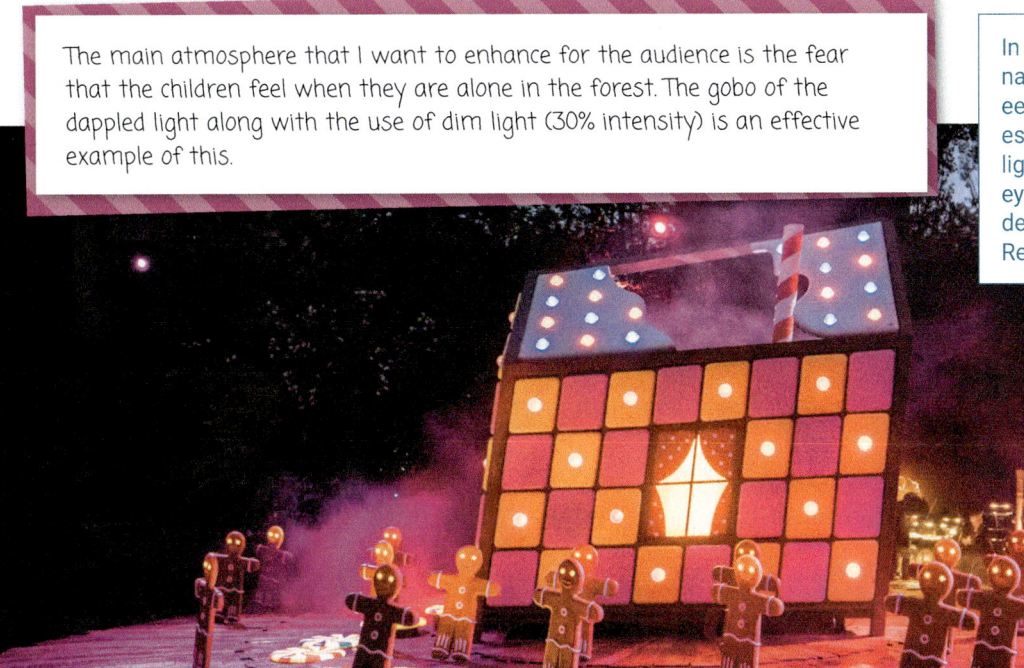

> The main atmosphere that I want to enhance for the audience is the fear that the children feel when they are alone in the forest. The gobo of the dappled light along with the use of dim light (30% intensity) is an effective example of this.

FOCUS
How to approach the explanation of your lighting design.

ASSESSMENT CHECK
Your supporting documents should show that you have developed skills in:

- realising artistic intention in text-based drama
- communicating intention to an audience

and can apply theatrical skills to realise artistic intentions in live performance (AO2).

DESIGN TIP
You will put your Statement into a template that your teacher will provide.

In this scene, a bright, non-naturalistic, pink wash gives an alien, eerie and somewhat sickly effect, especially in combination with the lights of the gingerbread men's eyes and house biscuits. (Lighting designed by Oliver Fenwick for Regent's Park Open Air Theatre.)

FOCUS

- The sound design process from page to stage.
- How to interpret the script, analyse and evaluate as you experiment with different designs, select those that are most successful and realise your designs as sounds in performance.

ASSESSMENT CHECK

Your sounds should:

- contribute positively to the overall performance and communicate meaning
- help to establish the location, period, time, mood or atmosphere
- show you can select the appropriate equipment to realise the intended sound design
- deploy different types of sound and sound effects as appropriate.

You must also adopt the latest safe working practices.

SIGNPOST

Chapter 2 will help you with your practical work.

DESIGN TIP

It is your sound **design** that is assessed. Although you are expected to operate the sound equipment when possible, this is not part of the assessment.

SIX STEPS TO SOUND DESIGN FOR TEXTS IN PRACTICE

STEP 1

Working on your own with the script

As soon as you know that you are designing sound, start your independent work. This is likely to be at the same time as rehearsals begin.

You will need to look at the script through the eyes of a sound designer. This means thinking about the genre, style, context and locations you will need to enhance. Your teacher should tell you what the stage configuration will be.

1. Read the whole play (or a detailed summary). As you go through, use a table like the one below to note details that could influence your sound design choices. (An example has been suggested.)

Play: *Romeo and Juliet* by William Shakespeare
Genre: Tragedy

Staging configuration	Location/s	Historical, social and cultural contexts	Themes/ messages	Style, moods and atmosphere
End on.	• Grand house: bedroom, balcony • Street.	• Modern-day setting. • Race: Capulets are white; Montagues black.	• Love • Romance • Grief/ sorrow • Racial tension.	• Naturalistic • Romance • Violence • Tragedy.

2. Carefully read each extract. Highlight and mark brief annotations on:
   - locations, and whether they are interior or exterior
   - key moments where music or a sound effect is important
   - weather/season and time of day
   - shifts in mood and atmosphere
   - a specified requirement for a sound cue
   - any questions that crop up.
3. Make more detailed notes from your initial table, above. Use your annotations to begin a chart like the following. (Some examples for *Hansel and Gretel* have been given for guidance.)

Locations	Interior/exterior	Time of day (or night)	Weather/season
House in the woods.	Forest (p27).	Moonlight.	Gloomy.
Shifts in mood or atmosphere	**Sound effect**	**Direct address or other non-naturalistic feature**	**Questions/ideas**
The flames were like burning tongues.	Owl.	Father narrates at the start of the extract.	Is a soundscape appropriate? Lots of scope for non-diegetic sound.

SOUND

Period? Victorian?   *Style?*

'Hansel and Gretel' has the structure of a <u>nightmare</u>. A few domestic objects – buckets, a knife, a blanket, a plate, a jug, an axe – create both the <u>house</u> and the <u>forest</u> and appear in the <u>Witch's house</u>. The Mother also reappears, grotesque, as the Witch. A chorus of three is always present, and active. [...] The story is one of starvation, terror and catharsis. <u>The rhythms of speech are taut and violent</u>, containing the <u>fearful tensions</u> and, finally, <u>joyous release</u> of the drama.

Reflect in sound design
<u>Diegetic</u>: Forest - Owl
- *Wind in trees*
- *Creaking*
- *Creatures - birds?*
- *Dripping brook?*
- *Blazing fire*
- *'Wild beasts'*

<u>Non-diegetic</u>: Discordant music in minor key - wind instruments - falling.
Soundscape:
- *Hunger, despair*
- *Creaking - samples*

Soundscape before lights up

Creaking

Owl

Father It was no more than once upon a time when a poor woodcutter lived in a <u>small house at the edge of a huge, dark forest</u>. Now, the woodcutter lived with his wife and his two young children – a boy called Hansel and a little girl called Gretel. [...] <u>Night after hungry night</u>, he lay in bed next to his thin wife, and he worried so much that he tossed and he turned and he <u>sighed</u> and he <u>mumbled</u> and <u>moaned</u> and he just couldn't sleep at all. [...]

And as he <u>fretted and sweated in the darkness</u>, back came the bony voice of his wife; a voice as fierce as famine. [...]   *Soundscape*

Father 'No, no, wife, I can't do that. How could I have the heart to leave young Hansel and Gretel in the forest? The <u>wild beasts</u> would soon sniff them out and eat them alive.' [...]

And when their father and mother had finally gone to sleep, Hansel got up, put on his coat, opened the back door, and crept out into the midnight hour.

<u>Outside</u>. Bright light.   *Location*

There was bright, sparkling moonlight outside and the white pebbles on the ground shone like silver coins and precious jewels. Hansel bent down and filled his empty pockets with as many pebbles as he could carry.

<u>Inside</u>. [...]

Mother At <u>dawn</u>, before the sun had properly risen, their mother came and woke the two children. [...]

The family go <u>deeper into the dark heart of the forest</u>.   *Volume*

Gretel The forest was <u>immense and gloomy</u>. [...]

Hansel Hansel and Gretel collected a big pile of firewood and when it was <u>set alight</u> and the <u>flames were like burning tongues</u>, their mother said: *Fire SFX*

Mother 'Now lie down by the fire and rest.'

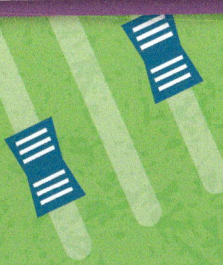

DESIGN TIP

In professional theatre, a white-card meeting might be held once the set designer has constructed a simple 3D version of the set in paper or card. Alternatively, there might be 2D sketches of the set and possibly some costume sketches.

LOOK HERE

Details on making a mood board for sound are on page 149.

STEP 2
The design brief meeting and rehearsals

Now that you have an understanding of the script and have some set design ideas, arrange a meeting with your group. Take your script and notebook and any ideas for sound that you might already have. If you have a set, lighting, puppet or costume designer, they should be there too.

You will not be able to finalise your designs until there is agreement on:

- the staging configuration (Is it in the round, traverse, end on?)
- the style and setting of the performance (Is it naturalistic or stylised?)
- whether it is set in a particular time period that music should reflect (Music you choose for a modern interpretation of *Romeo and Juliet*, for example, would be very different from a 16th-century version.)

During the meeting

1. Share your thoughts so far about sound design. Play any effects or music extracts you have found, and invite feedback. Try to deal with any criticism positively: very few designers are likely to get it all right first time.
2. Listen carefully to others and give similar sensitive feedback.
3. Make sure you discuss the following questions.
    - Do we have issues from Step 1 that can be answered in this meeting? If not, how and when can they be addressed?
    - Are we beginning to move towards a shared artistic vision for the performance? What do we imagine it looks like?
    - How will we communicate our ideas to each other? Can we create a shared resource bank for notes and images as we work independently? (This could be a folder on your school's intranet or a service such as Dropbox, which many professional theatres use.)
    - What shall we work on before we next meet? What do we want to achieve by when?
4. Make detailed and well-organised notes of the discussions and any decisions made. You could put them under the heading 'Design Brief Meeting' in your notebook.
5. Agree on a date for the next design meeting.

STEP 3
Revisiting the script

This step is another stage you can complete independently. You should, however, be continuously checking in on rehearsals, as developments might influence your design. Similarly, other designers and the performers will benefit from your updates.

1. Add details to your script annotations and ideas tables, based on what you learned at the design brief meeting. Your new knowledge of the style of the production might allow you to think more clearly about, for example, non-naturalistic soundscapes. Similarly, a shared sense of dramatic intention for the performance might prompt you to consider moods that you would like to enhance at particular moments.

   Be clear on how your designs could enhance your dramatic intentions. Make sure your sound designs are clearly influenced by those intentions.

2. Are there special effects that need to be planned for? How could you use sound to create the sense of night-time in a forest, for example?

3. Create a key to use on your script that links to notes or sketches in your notebook. These could be asterisks or numbers or a letter Q, for example, to indicate a change in sound. An arrow down the side of a script extract could show where you intend to build or decrease the volume of an effect.

4. Think carefully about the space and where, for example, to best place your speakers to create the best sound quality for the audience.

5. Continue to note down any questions that emerge.

ASSESSMENT CHECK

During this review of the script, you will be working on AO2: 'Apply theatrical skills to realise artistic intentions in live performance.'

LOOK HERE

Chapter 2 provides important information on creating sound designs.

ASSESSMENT CHECK

In reviewing and selecting your designs, you are helping to ensure that your personal interpretation exhibits appropriateness to the play as a whole (AO2). At the same time, you will develop good habits for AO4: 'Analyse and evaluate your own work.'

STEP 4

Confirming your sound designs

For your sound designs to be agreed at the final design meeting, they need to be at the final design stage themselves.

Rehearsals will be well underway now. You should take your final design ideas into the rehearsal room and check if there are any new developments that affect you. For example, you might need an additional piece of underscoring to enhance a moment of tension. Can you include this in your design?

1. Revisit the tasks in 'Sourcing, creating and mixing sounds', pages 46–48, before you finalise the sound designs on paper. Now would also be a good time to check that you have all the resources you need. Have you made your music choices, for instance? Do you know what will play as the audience come in and leave the performance space?

2. If you are thinking of using special effects, such as reverb or echo, use 'Special sound effects' on pages 50–51 to guide you. Experiment with building the effects that you want. Test their practicality, suitability and impact before committing them to the final design.

3. Check with the other designers that all the designs are compatible, both artistically and in terms of keeping performers and audience safe. Complete the checklist below.

Extract:

Period, mood, style and genre?	Compatible with other design elements?	Contributes to dramatic intentions?	Safety notes and use of space, speaker positions
Y/N	Y/N	Y/N	
Y/N	Y/N	Y/N	

DESIGN TIP

AO4 is tested in the written exam, but this step will give you excellent practice in the key skills of analysis and evaluation.

Chapter 8 Component 3: Designing for Texts in Practice

STEP 5
The final design meeting

Hold a last design meeting. In professional theatre, the stage manager, production manager and other specialists would also be present.

This is the meeting where everything is agreed, including budgets. As a designer, you should not buy or make anything final, or start putting special effects together, until the designs have been signed off.

1. Bring the finished plans of your designs to be signed off. The documentation could include a rough cue sheet, sketch of acting area(s) with locations of speakers marked, your annotated script, plus any notes. Through discussion, confirm the final designs.

In terms of collaboration, this is the final chance to check that your designs harmonise with the other designers' work. Lighting in particular needs to complement your designs.

2. Don't be afraid to ask questions and raise concerns. It is vital that you leave this meeting ready to realise your designs.
3. Complete a table like this one during or straight after the meeting.

Extract:		
Agreed design (including changes)	**Agreed budget**	**Notes**

LOOK HERE

You might find these sections useful at this point:
- How to document your sound design, pages 52–53
- Research for sound design, pages 44–45
- Directional sound, pages 54–55.

DESIGN TIP

Help your group to understand the style of your effects and music by having some available to play.

LOOK HERE

Chapter 2 offers plenty of support and guidance in terms of creating and finding sound effects and music, taking care of health and safety and so on.

SIGNPOST

Work through 'Plotting the sound design' (pages 56–57) first.

DESIGN TIP

Remember to evaluate your designs at each stage. How successfully are they matching your intentions in terms of concept, interpretation and communication of meaning?

STEP 6
The completed sound design

Finally, you can finish setting up and mixing your sounds ready for the performance.

Preparation

Once you have all your effects and music saved in a folder on a laptop or organised for other playback devices, you need to plot them.

Plotting

Plotting is the crucial stage where you get your cues in order and create the cue sheet.

An example cue sheet is given below. The cue sheet is an essential guide for whoever operates the sound for your production, whether or not you do this yourself. It gives the source, order, length and volume of each sound.

Extract 1

Sound cue sheet: Hansel and Gretel

Cue no and page no	Cue signal	Sound	Playback device (if more than one)	Level (dB)	Transition	Notes and timings
1 Pre-set	House open	Play music	CD player	-10		Pre-set from time house is open. Visual cue
2 p1	Visual: actors walk on	Music off		All out	Fade out	Over 10 seconds (in time with lighting)
3 p3	'Come over here!'	Soundscape 1	Laptop	+6	Fade up	Over 5 seconds gradual fade

Make sure that you know the date of the technical rehearsal. Have your sound designs plotted and practised in good time.

Once your sounds are set, allow plenty of time for your sound operator to practise your sound cues.

LOOK HERE

The notes on page 60 will help you to make use of rehearsals.

THE STATEMENT OF DRAMATIC INTENTIONS FOR SOUND DESIGN

Your finished sound will be heard in the performances. In addition, you need to explain how your sound design fits the dramatic intentions of the scripted piece. This statement allows the examiner to match your sound designs to your dramatic intentions. It should be about 150 words for each extract. Remember to attach cue sheets and diagrams.

Including the information so briefly can be tricky, but focus on how your design interprets the extract.

Try to cover these points:

- What is your central sound design idea in the extract?
- How have you interpreted this extract through your design?
- What are you hoping to communicate to the audience?

The example below is for an extract based on *Hansel and Gretel*.

> My central idea is to create a mixture of naturalistic and non-naturalistic sounds that will help the audience to understand the location, mood and atmosphere.
>
> My interpretation of the first extract is to satisfy the need to signpost the location of the forest through diegetic sound effects such as the owl and the crackling fire. However, I also want to create non-diegetic soundscapes so that the audience can experience the tensions between the mother and the children as well as their alarm at being left in the forest. To get the richness of sound necessary, I have mixed a number of effects and added reverb to make an eerie sound.
>
> I want the audience to get a powerful sense of atmosphere and for them to empathise with the children.

Gretel and Hansel at Manitoba Theatre for Young People. With a stark, simple, non-naturalistic set design such as this one, sound could be especially important for creating atmosphere and meaning.

FOCUS
How to approach the explanation for your sound design.

ASSESSMENT CHECK
Your supporting documents should show that you have developed skills in:

- realising artistic intention in text-based drama
- communicating intention to an audience

and can apply theatrical skills to realise artistic intentions in live performance (AO2).

DESIGN TIP
You will put your Statement into a template that your teacher will provide.

Chapter 8 Component 3: Designing for Texts in Practice 257

FOCUS

- The process of set design from page to stage.
- How to interpret, analyse and evaluate as you experiment, select and then realise your designs.

ASSESSMENT CHECK

Your set should:
- contribute positively to the overall performance and communicate meaning
- help to establish location, period, time, mood or atmosphere
- include appropriate materials and equipment
- show an understanding of stage configuration, performer/audience relationship, action, entrances/exits, scene changes, use of space, scale, levels
- include as appropriate dressings, furnishings, material, colour, texture, props.

You must also adopt the latest safe working practices.

SIGNPOST

Chapter 3 is designed to help you with every aspect of your practical work.

DESIGN TIP

It is your set **design** that is assessed. Although students are expected to construct the set when possible, this is not part of the assessment.

SIX STEPS TO SET DESIGN FOR TEXTS IN PRACTICE

STEP 1

Working on your own with the script

As soon as you know that you are designing the set, start your independent work. This is likely to be at the same time as rehearsals begin.

A non-naturalistic set design for Uchenna Dance's *Hansel and Gretel*. It is a very modern style that uses bold, primary colours, geometric shapes and click-together panels that recall children's building toys. This also makes the set versatile, as items can be put together differently to represent, for example, both the forest and the cottage.

You will need to look at the script through the eyes of a set designer. This means thinking about the genre, style, context and locations you will need to enhance. Your teacher should tell you what the stage configuration will be.

1. Read the whole play (or a detailed summary). As you go through, use a table like the one below to note details that could influence your set design choices. (An example has been suggested.)

Play: *Alice* by Lorna Wade				
Genre: Black comedy				
Staging configuration	Location/s	Historical, social and cultural contexts	Themes/ messages	Style, moods and atmosphere
Proscenium arch.	• Wonderland • Alice's living room • Alice's attic.	Contemporary (modern day).	• Family • Growing up • Dealing with grief.	• Fantasy and realism • Mixture of naturalism and non-naturalism • Comic moments.

2. Carefully read each extract. Highlight and mark brief annotations on:
   - locations – specific (such as an attic) and more general (Wonderland, for example)
   - key events and moments of action where an item of set is important
   - the economic and social situation of characters
   - special settings, including levels (these might be given in the script)
   - any questions that crop up.

258   Chapter 8   Component 3: Designing for Texts in Practice

3. Ask your teacher what style of production is most likely. You might be dealing with a highly naturalistic style, for example. From that information, what images pop into your head as you read? Draw some sketches to capture your ideas.

If you have time, make white-card models of your favourite designs.

4. Make more detailed notes from your table, above. These include the page and line number from the script, or a quotation. For example:

> **DESIGN TIP**
> Remember that there must be a separate design for each extract, if you are the set designer for both.

SET DESIGN

Keep these?
Scenery

Style: → Abstract? → Naturalistic?

p13: Are there beds in the cottage?

'Hansel and Gretel' has the structure of a nightmare. A few domestic objects – buckets, a knife, a blanket, a plate, a jug, an axe – create both the house and the forest and appear in the Witch's house. The Mother also reappears, grotesque, as the Witch. A chorus of three is always present, and active. [...] The story is one of starvation, terror and catharsis. The rhythms of speech are taut and violent, containing the fearful tensions and, finally, joyous release of the drama.

Location: in house
Silhouette?

Father It was no more than once upon a time when a poor woodcutter lived in a small house at the edge of a huge, dark forest. Now, the woodcutter lived with his wife and his two young children – a boy called Hansel and a little girl called Gretel. [...] Night after hungry night, he lay in bed next to his thin wife, and he worried so much that he tossed and he turned and he sighed and he mumbled and moaned and he just couldn't sleep at all. [...]

Bed? Boxes?

Levels?

And as he fretted and sweated in the darkness, back came the bony voice of his wife; a voice as fierce as famine. [...]

Where? Bedroom?

Hansel Now, Hansel and Gretel had been so hungry that night that they hadn't been able to sleep either, and they'd heard every cruel word of their mother's terrible plan.

Gretel Gretel cried bitter salt tears, and said to Hansel: 'Now we're finished.'

Hansel 'Don't cry, Gretel. Don't be sad. I'll think of a way to save us.'

And when their father and mother had finally gone to sleep, Hansel got up, put on his coat, opened the back door, and crept out into the midnight hour.

Level?

Location Outside. Bright light.

There was bright, sparkling moonlight outside and the white pebbles on the ground shone like silver coins and precious jewels. Hansel bent down and filled his empty pockets with as many pebbles as he could carry. [...]

Literal?

Along the path. Hansel keeps stopping and turning back. [...]

Spaced-out pebbles he collects?

The family go deeper into the dark heart of the forest.

Gretel The forest was immense and gloomy. [...]

Hansel Hansel and Gretel collected a big pile of firewood and when it was set alight and the flames were like burning tongues, their mother said:

Props? Scattered?

Mother 'Now lie down by the fire and rest.'

How do we create:
- forest
- house
- interior/exterior?
Revolving flats?
Composite?

Forest could be: imaginary
- hung fabric
- brooms/twigs
- flats
- scenery
- actors?

Flooring:
- Wooden, neutral – house and forest?
- Rush mats?
- Vinyl?

Chapter 8   Component 3: Designing for Texts in Practice   259

DESIGN TIP

In professional theatre, a white-card meeting might be held once the set designer has constructed a simple 3D version of the set in paper or card. Alternatively, there might be 2D sketches of the set and possibly some costume sketches.

STEP 2

The design brief meeting and rehearsals

Now that you have an understanding of the script and have some set design ideas, arrange a meeting with your group. Take your script and notebook and any sketches and models you have. If you have a costume, sound, puppet or lighting designer, they should be there too. Other designers (particularly lighting) won't get far with their work until they have some clarity about the set.

You will not be able to finalise your designs until you know the style of the production. This will tell you whether you are aiming for a representative set, or a naturalistic one that seeks to fully create the illusion of reality.

This design of the cottage for Glyndebourne Opera is more naturalistic, but note the use of soft cardboard more suitable for temporary boxes.

- Is it set in a particular time period?
- If there is to be a forest, for example, will there be literal representations of trees or something much simpler, such as strips of fabric hanging from the rigging? Or will trees be depicted by actors or simply imagined by the actors and audience?
- Will there be a composite set or will the stage be divided into different locations?
- Will buildings and rooms be physically on stage in some form? Will there be stage furniture? What form might it take?

During the meeting

1. Share your thoughts so far about set design. Show any sketches or models and invite feedback. Try to deal with any criticism positively: very few designers are likely to get it all right first time.
2. Listen carefully to others and give similar sensitive feedback.
3. Make sure you discuss the following questions:
   - Do we have issues from Step 1 that can be answered in this meeting? If not, how and when can they be addressed?
   - Are we beginning to move towards a shared artistic vision for the performance? What do we imagine it looks like?
   - How will we communicate our ideas to each other? Can we create a shared resource bank for notes and images as we work independently? (This could be a folder on your school's intranet or a service such as Dropbox, which many professional theatres use.)
   - What shall we work on before we next meet? What do we want to achieve and by when?
4. Make detailed and well-organised notes of the discussions and any decisions made. You could put them under the heading 'Design Brief Meeting' in your notebook.
5. Agree on a date for the next design meeting.

LOOK HERE

'Two styles of set design' on page 66 and 'Understanding your resources' on page 73 will be helpful at this point.

STEP 3
Revisiting the script

This step is another stage you can complete independently. You should, however, be continuously checking in on rehearsals, as developments might influence your design. Similarly, other designers and the performers will benefit from your updates.

1. Add details to your script annotations and ideas table, based on what you learned at the design brief meeting.

   Be clear on how your set design could enhance your dramatic intentions. Make sure your design is clearly influenced by these intentions.

2. Make any alterations to your draft designs as required. For example, does your colour palette need to change to fit in with the overall mood, or costume or lighting designs?

> You might have ideas for a modern, highly stylised *Hansel and Gretel*. Tall, thin trees could be made from long cardboard tubes or by hanging long strips of dark green and brown fabric, for example.

Are there special considerations that need to be planned for, such as interaction with furniture? An outdoor fire, for example, is required in Carol Ann Duffy and Tim Supple's version of *Hansel and Gretel*. You would need to work closely with the lighting designer to achieve something workable.

3. Carefully consider space. Your design needs to use the available space to its best potential. This includes leaving plenty of space for the actors to perform in, checking audience sightlines and making the set work well in terms of interesting spatial interactions through the use of levels, for example. Think about what set dressings and props will enhance your design.

4. Continue to note down any questions that emerge.

5. Explore what materials you need and where you might find them.

ASSESSMENT CHECK

During this review of the script, you will be working on AO2: 'Apply theatrical skills to realise artistic intentions in live performance.'

LOOK HERE

'Research for set design' on page 67 will be helpful here.

Chapter 8 Component 3: Designing for Texts in Practice

ASSESSMENT CHECK

In reviewing and selecting your designs, you are helping to ensure that your personal interpretation exhibits appropriateness to the play as a whole (AO2). At the same time, you will develop good habits for AO4: 'Analyse and evaluate your own work.'

DESIGN TIP

AO4 is tested in the written exam, but this step will give you excellent practice in the key skills of analysis and evaluation.

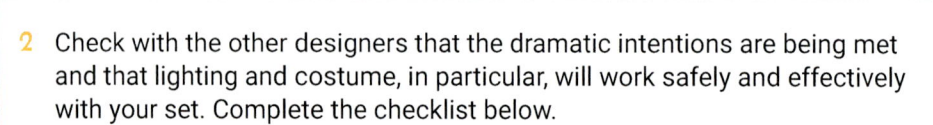

LOOK HERE

'How to document your set design' on pages 69–72 provides detailed guidance on plans, drawings and models.

'Sourcing materials for the set', page 74, and 'Creating your set design for the stage', page 76, will support you with constructing your sets.

STEP 4
Confirming your set designs

For your set to be agreed at the final design meeting, it needs to be at the final design stage itself.

Rehearsals will be well underway now. You should take your final design ideas into the rehearsal room and check if there are any new developments that affect you. For example, a character might need somewhere to hide on stage. Can you include this in your design?

1. Complete ground plans and sketches for each extract. While you do not have to make model boxes, you might find that they help you to examine how workable your set designs are. Whoever constructs your sets will also find them invaluable.

2. Check with the other designers that the dramatic intentions are being met and that lighting and costume, in particular, will work safely and effectively with your set. Complete the checklist below.

Extract:					
Period, mood, style and genre?	Practicalities including furniture and health and safety?	Supports artistic intentions?	Good use of space?	Compatible with other design elements?	Approximate costings
Y/N	Y/N	Y/N	Y/N	Y/N	

3. Check with your human resources that your designs are achievable in terms of construction and sourcing. For example, is there time to build the platform you want to put into your design? You need to be ready to build once your design is given the go-ahead.

Chapter 8 Component 3: Designing for Texts in Practice

STEP 5

The final design meeting

Hold a last design meeting. In professional theatre, the stage manager, production manager and other specialists would also be present.

This is the meeting where everything is agreed, including budgets. As a designer, you should not buy or make anything final until the designs have been signed off.

1. Bring the finished plans of your designs to be signed off. The documentation could include the ground plan, marked with entrances and exits, your annotated script plus any notes and models you have made. Through discussion, confirm the final designs.

    In terms of collaboration, this is the final chance to check that your designs harmonise with the other designers' work. Lighting and costume in particular have to complement your designs.

2. Remember that it is essential that the actors can move freely around the stage and set. This is a health and safety issue. You are also creating a world where the characters can live and breathe. The actors cannot inhabit a theatrical world if they are unable to function properly or maintain their characters fully.

3. Don't be afraid to ask questions and raise concerns. It is vital that you leave this meeting ready to realise your designs.

4. Complete a table like this one during or straight after the meeting. (An example has been started for you.)

Extract:		
Agreed set design (including changes)	**Agreed budget**	**Notes**
• As sketch and model boxes. • Change colour palette.	£50	Replace blue tones with amber ones.

Chapter 8 Component 3: Designing for Texts in Practice

SIGNPOST

Task 3.11 in 'Sourcing materials for the set' (page 74) will be very useful now if you haven't completed it already. Also look at 'Creating your set design for the stage' (page 76).

STEP 6
The completed set design

Finally, you can construct your set ready for the performance.

Preparation and construction

You will need to work very closely with the people building your set and helping you with materials, tools and equipment. Supervising the construction might involve basic assistance while things are being made or more actively helping to paint flats and so on.

Answer the questions below to help you produce your sets successfully and in good time.

- Are other items (including furniture and props) that need to be borrowed or bought being sorted in good time?
- What is the date of the technical rehearsal?
- Have I taken health and safety issues into account, including actors' entrances and exits?
- When will the set be put into the performance area?
- Are there any issues with items that need to be built, such as the late arrival of materials ordered for a platform? If so, chase them up.
- Are there additional stage dressings such as table cloths or cushions to be sourced?

LOOK HERE

Follow the guidance on page 75 for health and safety procedures.

DESIGN TIP

Refreshments are nearly always appreciated during builds!

Chapter 8 Component 3: Designing for Texts in Practice

THE STATEMENT OF DRAMATIC INTENTIONS FOR SET DESIGN

Your finished set will be seen in the performance. In addition, you need to explain how your set design fits the intentions of the scripted piece. This statement allows the examiner to match your set designs to your dramatic intentions. You should write about 150 words for each extract.

Including the information so briefly can be tricky, but you need to explain how your design interprets the extract. Remember to cover these points:

- What is your central set design idea in the key extract?
- How have you interpreted this key extract through your set design?
- What are you hoping to communicate to the audience?

You could also include a sketch or plan within your explanation, as below. Your final sketches and plans are required too.

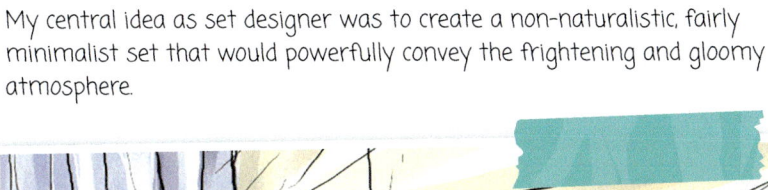

> My central idea as set designer was to create a non-naturalistic, fairly minimalist set that would powerfully convey the frightening and gloomy atmosphere.

> I used the colour red to communicate danger and contrasted this with white to suggest the children's innocence. I used blocks to create levels that worked for the trees and for levels in the woodcutter's cottage. The actors moved the blocks while in character. This communicated the sense of hard work which even the children had to endure. I wanted the audience to understand that they live in quite deprived circumstances, suggested when the mother only gives them a 'miserable mouthful of bread'.
>
> As part of my set design, I made heart shapes out of twigs and scattered white pebbles within them. Hansel picks up the pebbles at the start of the extract and the children pick up the twigs that form the heart shapes when they gather firewood later. This symbolised the breaking of their hearts when they are abandoned.

FOCUS
How to approach the explanation of your set design.

ASSESSMENT CHECK
Your supporting documents should show that you have developed skills in:

- realising artistic intention in text-based drama
- communicating intention to an audience

and can apply theatrical skills to realise artistic intentions in live performance (AO2).

DESIGN TIP
The statement should show how your designs match the intentions you set out with. Check this carefully.

DESIGN TIP
You will put your Statement into a template that your teacher will provide.

SIX STEPS TO COSTUME DESIGN FOR TEXTS IN PRACTICE

FOCUS
- The process of costume design from page to stage.
- How to interpret, analyse and evaluate as you experiment, select and then realise your designs.

ASSESSMENT CHECK
Your costumes, hair and make-up should:
- contribute positively to the overall performance and communicate meaning
- help to establish character, period, location, mood or atmosphere
- show an understanding of fabrics, textures, trimmings, accessories, colour, shape, fit, period, ethnic authenticity, movement constraints
- follow the latest safe working practices.

SIGNPOST
Chapter 4 is designed to help you with every aspect of your practical costume work.

DESIGN TIP
Remember that hair, masks and make-up are additional. They are important, but you will not receive good marks if you only work on hair and make-up.

STEP 1
Working on your own with the script

As soon as you know that you are designing a costume for each extract, start your independent work. This is likely to be at the same time as the performers begin rehearsals.

You will need to look at the script through the eyes of a costume designer. This means thinking about genre, styles and contexts. Your teacher should be able to tell you what the stage configuration will be.

1. Read the whole play (or a detailed summary). As you go through, use a table like the one below to note details that could influence your costume choices. (An example has been suggested.)

Play: *Dracula* by Bram Stoker/David Calcutt
Genre: Horror

Main characters	Location/s	Historical, social and cultural contexts	Themes/ messages	Style, moods and atmosphere
• Dracula • Jonathan • Mina • Lucy • Van Helsing	• Whitby • Dracula's castle.	• End of 19th century • Vampire stories.	• Fear • Love • The supernatural.	• Mainly naturalistic • Suspense • Horror.

2. Carefully read each extract. Highlight and mark brief annotations on:
   - locations – specific (such as the living room in a wealthy Victorian home) and more general (north-east coast of England, for example)
   - weather and time of year and time of day, as this will influence what a character would wear
   - the economic and social situations of characters
   - personality aspects that might affect characters' choice of clothing
   - a stated requirement for a special feature (pocket, bag, hat and so on)
   - any questions that crop up.

   See the example on the following page.

3. Make detailed notes from your table and then annotated sketches of possible designs. Your notes should take the form of the page and line number or quotation from the script and then your note. For example:

> p14: 'Hansel got up, put on his coat... filled his empty pockets with as many pebbles as he could carry...' Does he have nightwear, or is he in everyday clothes? Coat with big pockets could be a handed-down jacket from his father?

Chapter 8 Component 3: Designing for Texts in Practice

COSTUME

Style? – Germanic?
Period? – Victorian? Modern?
Times of famine, hunger, starvation
Freedom of movement

'Hansel and Gretel' has the structure of a nightmare. A few domestic objects – buckets, a knife, a blanket, a plate, a jug, an axe – create both the house and the forest and appear in the Witch's house. <u>The Mother also reappears, grotesque, as the Witch.</u> A <u>chorus</u> of three is always present, and active. [...] <u>The story is one of starvation, terror and catharsis</u>. The rhythms of speech are taut and violent, containing the <u>fearful tensions</u> and, finally, <u>joyous release</u> of the drama.

Woodcutter: Poor; works outdoors – manual
Outer clothes: Boots? Waistcoat? Belt? Pouch? Nightwear?
Wife: Thin; angular silhouette – a hard woman
Hansel: 8? Coat: Threadbare – with pockets – size?
Gretel: 6 or 7? Apron with pocket – size?

Father It was no more than once upon a time when a <u>poor woodcutter</u> lived in a small house at the edge of a huge, dark forest. Now, the woodcutter lived with his wife and his two <u>young children</u> – a <u>boy</u> called Hansel and a <u>little girl</u> called Gretel. It was hard enough for him to feed them all at the best of times – but these were the worst of times; times of <u>famine and hunger and starvation</u>. [...]

Night after hungry night, he lay in bed next to his <u>thin wife</u>, and he worried so much that he tossed and he turned and he sighed and he mumbled and moaned and he just couldn't sleep at all. [...]

Hansel Now, Hansel and Gretel had been so <u>hungry</u> that night that they hadn't been able to sleep either, and they'd heard every cruel word of their mother's terrible plan. [...]

And when their father and mother had finally gone to sleep, Hansel got up, put on his <u>coat</u>, opened the back door, and crept out into the midnight hour. [...]

Hansel bent down and filled his <u>empty pockets</u> with as many pebbles as he could carry. [...]

Mother Then she gave each of them a miserable mouthful of bread: 'There's your lunch; think yourselves lucky, and don't eat it all at once, because there's nothing else.'

Gretel Gretel put the bread in her <u>apron pocket</u>, because <u>Hansel's pockets were crammed with pebbles</u>.

Father Then the whole family set off along the path to the forest.

Where does the bread come from?

> **DESIGN TIP**
> It is your costume **design** that is assessed. You are expected to assemble the costume if possible, but this is not part of the assessment.

DESIGN TIP

In professional theatre, a white-card meeting might be held once the set designer has constructed a simple 3D version of the set in paper or card. Alternatively, there might be 2D sketches of the set and possibly some costume sketches.

STEP 2

The design brief meeting and rehearsals

Now that you have an understanding of the script and have some costume ideas, arrange a meeting with your group. Take your script and notebook and any costume sketches you have. If you have a set, sound, puppetry or lighting designer, they should be there too. A costume designer needs to consider potential movement restrictions of the set, for example.

You will not be able to properly develop your costume designs until you know:

- the style and setting of the performance (Is it naturalistic or stylised? Is it set in a particular time period? Do you need to create a typical Victorian gown, or are you setting the play in modern times?)
- which character(s) you will design for.

Your choice should give you plenty of scope for creativity and impact. It should allow you to contribute to characterisation and meaning. It must also set you a sufficient challenge. If you design costumes for both extracts, you might want to make the two designs quite different from each other.

Rough sketches for a contemporary costume design for *Hansel and Gretel*.

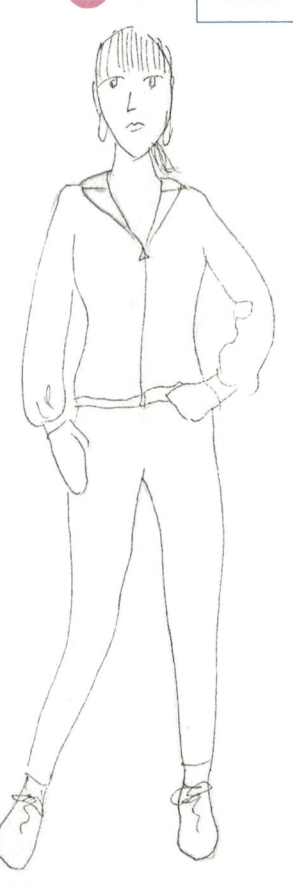

MOTHER

THE WITCH

During the meeting

1. Share your thoughts so far about costumes. Show any sketches or mood boards and invite feedback. Try to deal with any criticism positively: very few designers are likely to get it all right first time.
2. Listen carefully to others and give similar sensitive feedback.
3. Make sure you discuss the following questions.
   - Do I have questions from Step 1 that can be answered in this meeting? If not, how and when can they be addressed?
   - Are we beginning to move towards a shared artistic vision for the performance? What do we imagine it looks like?
   - How will we communicate our ideas to each other? Can we create a shared resource bank that we can put notes and images in as we work independently? (This could be a shared folder on your centre's intranet or a service such as Dropbox, which many professional theatres use.)
   - What shall we work on before we next meet? What do we want to achieve by when?
4. Make detailed and well-organised notes of the discussions and any decisions made. You could put them under the heading 'Design Brief Meeting' in your notebook.
5. Agree on a date for the next design meeting.

STEP 3
Revisiting the script

This step is another stage you can complete independently. You should, however, be continuously checking in on rehearsals, as developments might influence your design. Similarly, other designers and the performers will benefit from your updates.

1. Add details to your script annotations and ideas table, based on what you learned at the design brief meeting. Your new knowledge of the agreed style and historical period, for example, will allow you to develop your costume ideas.

    Similarly, a shared sense of dramatic intention for the performance might prompt you to consider enhancing atmosphere with a particular aspect of costume design. This could come from colour, shape and fabric choices.

    Be clear on how your design could enhance your dramatic intentions. Make sure your costume design is clearly influenced by these intentions.

More traditional versions of the Witch and the Mother.

2. Sketch a number of versions for your initial costume designs.
3. Are there special considerations, such as pockets, masks or wigs, that need to be planned for? For pockets, for example, you will need to know what they will hold so that you can make them the correct size. Make sure details like this are included in your preliminary sketches, along with footwear, headgear, accessories, make-up and masks as appropriate.
4. Carefully check the script for points where costumes might need to be changed. (These are often signposted in stage directions.)
5. Carefully consider space. This could mean shortening hemlines at the front to make steps easier. Alternatively, it could mean adding lots of detail to the back of a dress if the audience will see it frequently.

    It is essential that the actors can move freely around the stage and set. This is a safety issue. You are also creating a world where the characters can live and breathe. The actors cannot inhabit a theatrical world if they are unable to function properly or maintain their characters fully.
6. Continue to note down any questions that emerge.
7. Explore additional fabrics or accessories that might be needed and where they could come from.

ASSESSMENT CHECK

During this review of the script, you will be working on AO2: 'Apply theatrical skills to realise artistic intentions in live performance.'

ASSESSMENT CHECK

In reviewing and selecting your designs, you are helping to ensure that your personal interpretation exhibits appropriateness to the play as a whole (AO2). At the same time, you will develop good habits for AO4: 'Analyse and evaluate your own work.'

DESIGN TIP

AO4 is assessed in the written exam, but this step will give you excellent practice in the key skills of analysis and evaluation.

LOOK HERE

Pages 92–99 will help you to create and document your costume design.

STEP 4

Confirming your costume designs

For your costume designs to be agreed at the final design meeting, they need to be at final design stage themselves.

This means that you need to produce quality designs that are your best work. You don't need to be a great artist, but you do need to take time and care.

Rehearsals will be well underway now. You should take your final design ideas into the rehearsal room and check if there are any new developments that affect you. For example, a character might need an additional garment such as a cloak to hide something under. Can you include this in your design?

1. If you have a number of designs that you like, try to bring it down to two. Just one is ideal. Completing the table below should help you to decide which costume is the most effective. Remember that your design needs to contribute to meeting the creative intentions of the whole group.

Check with the other designers that colour palettes work together and that the costumes are appropriate to the proposed set and lighting, and any puppets. You must also keep performers safe.

Extract:					
Period, mood, style and genre?	Compatible with other design elements?	Suits social and economic background?	Suits personality/ character?	Suitable for the space and actor's comfort and safety?	Approximate costings, including accessories and make-up
Y/N	Y/N	Y/N	Y/N	Y/N	

2. Annotate your chosen sketch to help explain colour, fabric texture and finish.
3. Even if you will not be making your garment from scratch, it is useful to apply swatches to the design. These will help your fellow group members to see the 'look' you are aiming for.

THE WITCH

- RED CONTACT LENSES TO BE WORN.
- OFF CENTRE FASTENING ON COAT
- KEY FOR LOCKING UP CHILDREN
- SAME WOOL SKIRT AS MOTHER

MOTHER

- LEG OF MUTTON SLEEVES
- FLORAL FABRIC FOR THE HEAD SCARF
- OVERALL LOOK OF CLOTHES TO BE WELL WORN
- Wool Skirt

STEP 5
The final design meeting

Hold a last design meeting. In professional theatre, the stage manager, production manager and other specialists would also be present.

This is the meeting where everything is agreed, including budgets. As a designer, you should not buy or make anything until the designs have been signed off.

1. Bring your finished designs to be signed off. If you still have alternatives to be decided on, bring them for your colleagues to consider. Through discussion, confirm the final designs.

   In terms of collaboration, this is the final chance to check that your designs harmonise with the other designers' work. Set and lighting in particular have to complement your designs.

2. Check that there have been no changes to the set or the amount of physical movement used by the actor, as this could mean having to change aspects of your costume design.

3. Don't be afraid to ask questions and raise concerns. It is vital that you leave this meeting ready to realise your designs.

4. Complete a table like this one during or straight after the meeting. (An example has been started for you.)

Extract:		
Agreed costume design (including changes)	**Agreed budget**	**Notes**
As final drawings – design approved.	£20	Need to find cheaper fabric for cape.

DESIGN TIP

Help your group members to envision the world of the stage by making sure that you show the detail of your designs. As well as your designs, bring notes, fabric swatches and images of garments, hairstyles and make-up.

DESIGN TIP

Gather everything you need in one place and know where it all is! Add to your selection as you go along, including tools, accessories and make-up materials.

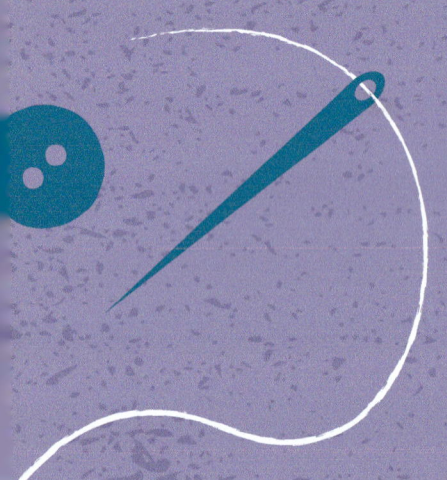

STEP 6
The completed costume design

Finally, you can make your costumes for the performance.

Preparation

Use your designs and budget to complete the following tables. (Some examples have been included to guide you.)

Extract:
Character:
Actor:

Costume item	Source	Estimated cost	Completed
Skirt	Alter existing one	none	
Apron	Charity shop?	£3	
Shoes	Actor's own	none	✓
Belt – with keys	Make	£2	
Make-up	Actor's and mine	none	✓

DESIGN TIP

Remember to evaluate your designs at each stage. How successful are they in contributing to characterisation, meaning and atmosphere?

LOOK HERE

The guidance on page 104 will help you with using rehearsals.

Actualising

1. Refer to Chapter 4 for help with sourcing, making, adapting and fitting. Remember that you need to supervise any making and alterations if you are not doing these yourself. Try to allow time for the actor to wear the costume in rehearsal to check that it works well for them in practice.
2. As you complete items of costume, add to or amend the table above.
3. Make sure you know the date of the technical rehearsal. You will need to have your costumes made and fitted in good time.

Chapter 8   Component 3: Designing for Texts in Practice

THE STATEMENT OF DRAMATIC INTENTIONS FOR COSTUME DESIGN

Your finished costume will be seen in the performance. In addition, you need to explain how your costume design fits the dramatic intentions of the scripted piece. This statement allows the examiner to match your costume designs to your intentions. You should write about 150 words for each extract.

Including the information so briefly is often tricky, but focus on how your design interprets the text. An annotated sketch of your design ideas could be useful. You could add notes to the sketch to explain how your interprets the extract or add a list of bullet points. For example (for seven-year-old Edward in *Blood Brothers*):

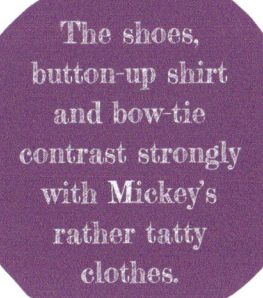

The smart white shirt, shiny shoes and bow-tie indicate that Edward is not dressed for playing outdoors.

The shoes, button-up shirt and bow-tie contrast strongly with Mickey's rather tatty clothes.

FOCUS
How to approach the explanation of your costume design.

ASSESSMENT CHECK
Your supporting documents should show that you have developed skills in:
- realising artistic intention in text-based drama
- communicating intention to an audience

and can apply theatrical skills to realise artistic intentions in live performance (AO2).

DESIGN TIP
You will to put your Statement into a template that your teacher will provide.

A further list or paragraph should explain what your costume should communicate to an audience. For example:

> The main point that I want the audience to understand is that Edward comes from a well-off family who are concerned with appearances. The way that Edward's hair has been so carefully neatened should help the audience to imagine the type of mother he has. Similarly, the choice of garments and accessories suggests a clean and well-ordered household. The red bow-tie adds a touch of class and suggests academic aspirations.

The Statement of Dramatic Intentions should show how your designs match the artistic intentions you set out with. Check this carefully. Along with your 150-word explanation, submit a list of costumes and accessories worn by your chosen character(s). This should include details of when and how they make any costume changes during each extract (for example, 'Edward takes off his tie').

SIX STEPS TO PUPPET DESIGN FOR TEXTS IN PRACTICE

FOCUS
- The process of puppet design from page to stage.
- How to interpret, analyse and evaluate as you experiment with, select and then realise your designs.

ASSESSMENT CHECK
Your puppet should:
- contribute positively to the overall performance and communicate meaning
- have a well-defined character and audience appeal
- consist of appropriate materials
- show understanding of structural design, size, shape, scale; functionality, performer skills and intentions
- show understanding of puppet types.

You must also adopt the latest safe working practices.

SIGNPOST
Use Chapter 5 to help you with your practical work.

DESIGN TIP
It is your puppet **design** that is assessed. You are expected to construct and/or operate the puppet(s) if possible, but this is not part of the assessment.

STEP 1
Working on your own with the script

As soon as you know that you will be designing puppets for the extracts, start your independent work. This is likely to be at the same time as the performers begin rehearsals.

You will need to look at the script through the eyes of a puppet designer. This means thinking about genre, types of puppet and the style of the piece. Your teacher should be able to tell you what the stage configuration will be. This will affect your decisions. For example, a shadow puppet will not be effective for theatre in the round.

1. Read the whole play (or a detailed summary). As you go through, use a table like the one below to note details that could influence your puppet choices. (An example has been suggested.)

Play: *A Christmas Carol* by Charles Dickens / Conor McReynolds / Richard Kidd
Genre: Ghost story

Main characters who might be suitable for puppets	Type of puppet	Historical, social and cultural contexts	Themes/ messages	Style, moods and atmosphere
• Tiny Tim • Jacob Marley • The ghosts.	• Glove and rod for Tiny Tim? • Backpack or rod puppet for Marley? • Ghost of the future could be a shadow puppet?	• Victorian England. • Characters strongly linked to wealth, poverty or the supernatural.	• Charity and compassion versus greed. • Christmas.	• Mixture of naturalism and non-naturalism. • Ghostly suspense.

2. Carefully read each extract. Highlight and mark brief annotations on:
    - characters – specifically ones that could be represented by a puppet (such as the ghosts)
    - the time of year and economic/social/cultural situations of potential puppet characters, as this will influence their posture and what they would wear
    - personality aspects of the characters that might affect the type and shape of puppet chosen
    - the extent to which a puppet character might interact physically with other characters and/or the audience as this will affect your choice of puppet type (a glove or rod puppet will work better than a shadow one for interaction)
    - any questions that crop up.

    See the example on the following page.

3. Make more detailed notes from your initial table, above, including page numbers and quotations.

4. Make simple, annotated sketches of possible puppet designs.

Toby Olié's impressive puppet for the Ghost of Christmas Yet to Come is operated by four animators. Its moveable arms and ability to bend and look at Scrooge give it great presence and believable characterisation. (Chichester Festival Theatre)

PUPPET

Sound effect to foreshadow Marley's entrance?

A bell gently rings in Scrooge's home. At first, he cannot locate the source of the noise, but as he finds it, a second bell starts to ring, and then a third, until a cacophony of noise dominates Scrooge's apartment.

What the devil is going on? What's this?

Rucksack puppet. Enters through audience.

The lights go out suddenly. The noise stops. A clanking noise replaces it, footsteps approaching, and the sound of heavy chains rattling.

Scrooge whimpers in the dark. ← *Audience interaction?*

What's going on? Hello? Is anyone there? Show yourselves!

The ghost of **Jacob Marley** enters. He is weighed down by thick, heavy chains. ← *Polystyrene?*
He stares into the eyes of **Scrooge**. *Flexible neck on rod?*

Radio mic with reverb?
Voice of animator – enhanced?

This … I mean … well, it's obviously … I … I don't believe it.

Marley Scrooge …

Scrooge I can't believe it … I won't believe it… I–

Marley Ebenezer Scrooge … *Puppet drawn to full height.*

Scrooge Speak not my name for I will not hear it! Not from you, for you are not real! You cannot exist if I refuse to believe what I see!

Marley You do believe.

Scrooge I do not! I've read about things like this. Apparitions brought on by stress … or … food poisoning! How do I know you are not just an undigested bit of beef, or an old potato?

Marley stares at **Scrooge**. *Lower head to Scrooge's level.*

Marley Do I look like a potato? *Arms on rod/s.*

Marley raises his arms in the air, and the bells chime louder than before […]

Scrooge watches **Marley** sit and follows suit. They stare at each other, **Marley** certainly looking the more relaxed of the two […] *Animator and puppet need to sit or kneel.*

DESIGN TIP

In professional theatre, a white-card meeting might be held once the set designer has constructed a simple 3D version of the set in paper or card. Alternatively, there might be 2D sketches of the set and possibly some costume sketches.

STEP 2
The design brief meeting and rehearsals

Now that you have an understanding of the script and have some puppetry ideas, arrange a meeting with your group. Take your script and notebook and any sketches you have. If you have a set, sound, costume or lighting designer, they should be there too.

You will not be able to properly develop your puppet designs until you know:

- the stage configuration (Some types of puppet suit certain stage configurations and not others.)
- the style and setting of the performance (Is it naturalistic or stylised? Is it set in a particular time period? You will be costuming any 'human' puppet and the costume needs to reflect the era and style.)
- which character(s) you will design for (This should be influenced by the puppet character's potential for enhancing the meaning and atmosphere of the extract.)

Think which characters would work successfully as puppets and consider which type of puppet would work best. Your choice should give you plenty of scope for creativity and impact. It should allow you to contribute to characterisation and meaning and set you a sufficient challenge.

During the meeting

1. Share your thoughts so far about puppets. Show any sketches and invite feedback. Try to deal with any criticism positively: very few designers are likely to get it all right first time.
2. Listen carefully to others and give similar sensitive feedback.
3. Make sure you discuss the following questions.
   - Do we have issues from Step 1 that can be answered in this meeting? If not, how and when can they be addressed?
   - Are we beginning to move towards a shared artistic vision for the performance? What do we imagine it looks like?
   - How will we communicate our ideas to each other? Can we have a shared resource bank for notes and images as we work independently? (This could be a shared folder on your school's intranet or a service such as Dropbox, which many professional theatres use.)
   - What shall we work on before we next meet? What do we want to achieve by when?
4. Make detailed and well-organised notes of the discussions and any decisions made. You could put them under the heading 'Design Brief Meeting' in your notebook.
5. Agree on a date for the next design meeting.

Chapter 8 Component 3: Designing for Texts in Practice

STEP 3
Revisiting the script

This step is another stage you can complete independently. You should, however, be continuously checking in on rehearsals as developments might influence your design. Similarly, the director and performers will benefit from your updates.

1. Add details to your script annotations and ideas table, based on what you learned at the design brief meeting. Your new knowledge of the agreed performance style, for example, will allow you to develop your puppet ideas. Similarly, a shared sense of dramatic intention for the performance might prompt you to consider enhancing atmosphere with a particular aspect of puppet design. This might come from type, size and costuming.

    Be clear on how your ideas could enhance your dramatic intentions. Make sure your puppet designs are clearly influenced by these intentions.

2. Develop sketches for the puppet designs.

3. Begin to gather materials for your puppets, and experiment with construction. Can you make a prototype of your puppet?

4. Carefully check the script for points where the puppet might be able to perform particular actions, including interacting physically with other performers or the audience. (These might be given in stage directions.)

    Are there special considerations, such as the need for your puppet to pick something up?

    Carefully consider space. Are there height restrictions to take into account? How does the chosen stage configuration influence your preferred puppet type?

    It is essential that the puppet and its animator can move freely around the stage and set. This is a safety issue for everyone on stage and in the audience.

5. Continue to note down any questions that emerge.

6. Explore fabrics or puppetry materials that might be needed, and research where they could come from. For example, can you source a metal-framed rucksack from a charity shop or start collecting dowels for rods?

7. If you will not be animating the puppet yourself, start to involve and educate the performer who will be.

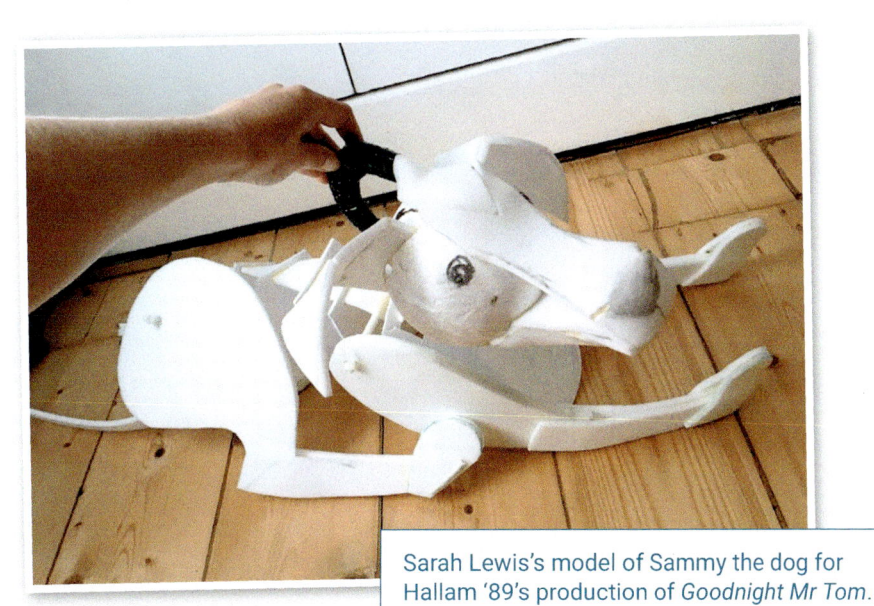

> Sarah Lewis's model of Sammy the dog for Hallam '89's production of *Goodnight Mr Tom*.

ASSESSMENT CHECK
During this review of the script, you will be working on AO2: 'Apply theatrical skills to realise artistic intentions in live performance.'

LOOK HERE
Chapter 5 will help you with this and all stages of practical puppetry.

ASSESSMENT CHECK

In reviewing and selecting your designs, you are helping to ensure that your personal interpretation exhibits appropriateness to the play as a whole (AO2). At the same time, you will develop good habits for AO4: 'Analyse and evaluate your own work.'

DESIGN TIP

AO4 is tested in the written exam, but this step will give you excellent practice in the key skills of analysis and evaluation.

LOOK HERE

Pages 119–121 will help you to create and document your puppet design.

STEP 4

Confirming your puppet designs

For your puppet designs to be agreed at the final design meeting, they need to be at final design stage themselves. This means that you need to produce quality designs that are your best work. You do not need to be a great artist, but you do need to take time and care.

Rehearsals will be well underway now. You should take your final design ideas into the rehearsal room and check if there have been any new developments that affect you. Your performer/animator might be working with a prototype puppet, for example. Is that working well? Do you need to make rods or gloves shorter or longer? Are there any other requirements that you have time to include in your design?

1. Complete the table below to check how effective your designs are. Remember that your design needs to contribute to the dramatic intentions of the whole group.

   Check with the other designers that colour palettes work together and that the puppet will suit the proposed set, lighting and costumes.

Extract:					
Period, mood, style and genre?	Compatible with stage configuration?	Suits dramatic intentions?	Suits personality/ character?	Suitable for the animator's comfort and safety?	Approximate costings
Y/N	Y/N	Y/N	Y/N	Y/N	

2. Annotate your design sketch to explain:
   - the materials used
   - how the puppet is constructed
   - how it will be operated.

Tom (Oliver Ford Davies) fully engages with his puppet dog Sammy in this production by Chichester Festival Theatre.

STEP 5
The final design meeting

Hold a last design meeting. In professional theatre, the stage manager, production manager and other specialists would also be present.

This is the meeting where everything is agreed, including budgets. As a designer, you should not buy or make anything until the designs have been signed off.

1. Bring your finished puppet designs to be signed off. Through discussion, confirm the final designs.

    In terms of collaboration, this is the final chance to check that your designs harmonise with the other designers' work. Set and lighting in particular need to complement your designs.

2. Check that there have been no changes to the set or the amount of physicality used by the animator, as this could mean having to change aspects of your puppet design.

3. Don't be afraid to ask questions and raise concerns. It is vital that you leave this meeting ready to realise your designs.

4. Complete a table like this one during or straight after the meeting. (An example has been started for you.)

Extract:		
Agreed puppet design (including changes)	Agreed budget	Notes
Change main fabric to allow more movement – design approved.	£20	Check availability or polystyrene chains.

DESIGN TIP

Help your other group members to envision your puppet on the stage by making sure that you bring enough detail about your designs with you. As well as your designs, bring notes, fabric swatches and any prototypes you have created.

STEP 6
The completed puppet design

Finally, you can make or finalise your puppet ready for the performance.

Preparation

Use your designs and budget checklists to ensure that you have all the necessary materials and tools for realising your final design.

Fix a suitable time for your animator to work with the puppet as it is completed. This will ensure that sizing and comfort are correct.

Actualising

Remember that you do not need to construct your final design, although it is probably better if you can.

Allow time for the animator to rehearse with the final puppet to check that it works well for them in practice.

LOOK HERE

The guidance on page 124 will help you with using rehearsals.

DESIGN TIP

Evaluate your designs at each stage. How successful are they in contributing to characterisation, meaning and atmosphere?

Chapter 8   Component 3: Designing for Texts in Practice

FOCUS
How to approach the explanation of your puppet design.

ASSESSMENT CHECK
Your supporting documents should show that you have developed skills in:
- realising artistic intention in text-based drama
- communicating intention to an audience

and can apply theatrical skills to realise artistic intentions in live performance (AO2).

DESIGN TIP
You will to put your Statement into a template that your teacher will provide.

THE STATEMENT OF DRAMATIC INTENTIONS FOR PUPPET DESIGN

Your finished puppet will be seen in the performance. In addition, you need to explain how your design fits the intentions of the scripted piece. This statement allows the examiner to match your puppet design to your dramatic intentions. You should write about 150 words for each extract.

Including the information so briefly is often tricky, but focus on how your design interprets the extract. See the example below.

Make sure you cover the following points:
- What is your main puppet design idea for the key extract?
- How have you interpreted this extract through your puppet design?
- What are you hoping to communicate to the audience?

One way of doing this could be to look back at the final task from Step 1 on page 274 and include a version of it in your explanation. Add notes to show how you interpreted the extract through puppet design.

In your statement, you should cover the affect you want the puppet to have on the audience and how that links to your dramatic intentions. For example:

> My dramatic intentions are to create an oversized puppet which will add an element of awe and power to the ghostly character of Jacob Marley. I will use lightweight 'chains' to enhance the important meaning that he is captured and weighed down by his bad deeds in life. I have chosen to add a flexible neck and long arms that will be controlled by rods.
>
> In the extract, the puppet will be manipulated down the aisles in our end-on stage configuration. When on stage, it will be able to lean over towards the audience. I want it to be intimidating, but I will direct the animator to avoid getting too close to any small children in the audience.

GLOSSARY

Accessories
Items such as bags, jewellery and small items that accompany garments.

Allergies
Adverse reactions in the body (for example to breathing or the skin) to certain products or ingredients.

AML (automated moving lantern)
Operated digitally, these lanterns can swivel and tilt.

Amplifier
A piece of equipment that produces the sound for the speakers, primarily used to increase volume.

Analyse
Examine in detail, thinking about parts in relation to the whole.

Animation
The act of bringing an inanimate object to life, such as in cartoons and with puppetry.

Animator
A person who manipulates a puppet, bringing it to 'life'.

Appliqué
A small colourful piece of embroidery – often a picture or pattern – sewn onto an item of clothing.

Artistic intentions
The creative theatrical aims of the production.

Atmospheric
A sound, for example, that creates a strong feeling or mood.

Audience appeal
In a similar way to creating a defined character, the success of a puppet relies largely on its ability to encourage the engagement of the audience.

Backcloth
A large piece of canvas or cloth which is often painted with a setting.

Backlight/backlighting
Lighting that comes from the back of the acting area.

Backpack puppet
A puppet which is worn on the back of the animator. This allows them to be very large and/or tall.

Back stitch
A closely worked stitch done by hand.

Barn door
A metal attachment that slides into the front of a lantern, with hinged flaps to control the beam.

Birdie
A miniature lantern ideal for hiding in small parts of a set or along the front edge of the stage.

Blackout
A moment when all the lights are dimmed, often suddenly.

Bruise wheel
Available from theatre make-up sellers, a palette of yellows, reds, browns and cream make-up, excellent for a range of special effects.

Channel
A number given to a lantern that corresponds to a number on the lighting board or desk.

Collaboration
Working with others towards a common aim.

Colour count
A record of the number of gels of each colour required.

Colour palette
A complementary set of colours that belong to a group, such as pastel or dark.

Constant sound
An uninterrupted sound.

Construction
Something that has been built (a set for example); the act of building.

Critical judgement
Analysing the merits and faults of something to decide its worth or success.

Cross-fade
Fading up one lantern or group while fading down another.

Cue
A moment when something happens, and what happens (such as 'Lights fade').

Cue sheet
A list of cues along with timings.

Cue to cue
Going through a play from one sound or lighting cue to the next, missing out the parts in between.

Darting
Sewing small, tapered folds into a garment to provide shape or otherwise alter the fit.

Diegetic sound
A sound that the characters would hear within their world, such as a phone ringing.

Digital
Using computer technology. Digital lighting desks, for example, are programmed using software.

Dimmer/Fader
A way of controlling the intensity (brightness) of the light. These are often manual or digital sliders.

Dimmer rack
The control centre for changing the intensity of each channel.

Downlight
A light that shines from above.

Drone
A constant sound that is often in the background. Drones are often used in non-naturalistic sound effects and are very good for creating atmosphere such as tension.

Echo
The effect that occurs when a sound bounces off surfaces.

Embellishments
Added extras such as lace, buttons, braids and so on; decorative details.

End on
A stage configuration that places the audience on one side of an open stage.

Evaluate
Give an opinion, a value judgement, backed up with examples and reasons.

Exterior (setting/location)
An outdoor space, such as a garden, street or outside a building.

Fabric choice
Considerations such as suitability and effect under lights.

Fade
A gradual increase or decrease.

Fader
A device to control the volume of a sound or the intensity of a light.

Fill light
Working with a **key light**, fill light is less intense (bright) and is often used to lessen shadows.

Filter/gel
A piece/sheet of coloured plastic/resin that fits at the front of a lantern to change the colour of the beam.

Finish
The surface of fabric – usually shiny or dull.

Flat
A tall, main piece of scenery that, as its name suggests, generally carries a 2D image.

> **Book flat**
> Two flats that are hinged along their 'spine'.
>
> **Free-standing flat**
> A braced, single flat that can stand anywhere on the set.
>
> **Run of flats**
> Two or more flats joined as a length to achieve a wall, for example.

Floating mic
A microphone positioned on the front of the stage.

Flood
A type of lantern that produces a wide spread of light; a broad cover of light.

Focus (lighting)
Adjust the angle and beam size of a lantern so that it lights the exact area required.

Focus (puppetry)
The direction of a puppet's gaze or attention – for example on an object or another character.

Freehand
Drawing something without a tracing or template to guide you.

French doors/windows
A pair of outward-opening doors often fully glazed, functioning as both windows and doors.

Fresnel
A type of lantern that is good for lighting large areas and which blends easily with other fresnels or spotlights to create a wash of light.

Furnishings
Set furniture (sometimes including curtains, rugs and so on).

Gauze
A loosely woven, transparent piece of fabric that can be front- or back-lit to produce different effects (sometimes called a **scrim**, which is made of a different type of fabric, but produces a similar effect).

Gel
See **Filter**.

General cover
Lanterns that provide overall lighting to the acting area.

Genre
A category or type of play (or other art), such as tragedy, comedy, period drama, that has distinctive stylistic or narrative features.

Glove puppet
A puppet that is worn over the hand.

Gobo
A metal cut-out plate that fits in front of a lantern and casts a shadow shape onto the stage (such as a tree outline, window frames and so on).

Hand-and-rod puppet
A hand puppet with added rods to allow the arms, for example, to move.

Hand puppet
A puppet that is held or worn on the hand.

Hanging mic
A microphone suspended above the performance area.

Illusion
Something that is not as it seems; something that is not real, but often gives an impression of reality.

In the round
A stage configuration in which the audience encircles the acting area.

Intensity
The brightness of lighting. Intensity is generally measured as a percentage (such as 60%).

Interior (setting/location)
An indoor space, such as a kitchen or a school hall.

Intermittent sound
A sound that is not constant; it comes and goes.

Interpret
Express your own ideas about intended meaning; your choice where there are a number of correct possibilities.

Key light
The main, strongest, most intense light, designed to copy the main light source (natural or artificial) in the real world.

Lamp
The technical name for a light bulb.

Lantern
The technical term for a **lighting fixture** that contains a bulb or lamp.

LED (Light Emitting Diode)
Lighting fixtures that use less energy and create less heat than other types of lantern. LEDs are the most popular type of fixture in professional theatres.

Light source
Anything that emits light, such as a torch or stage lantern.

Lighting desk/board/console
The means of operating the lighting, with channels, dimmers and faders.

Lighting fixture
A stage light unit.

Lighting plot
The diagram that shows where the lanterns are hung on the rigging.

Lighting state
The term used to describe the way a lantern or group of lanterns is used on the stage. For example, a particular lighting state could create a moonlit effect.

Live sound
A sound that is played directly for the audience.

Location
The place or setting where action takes place, such as a forest, a bedroom or a park.

Manipulate
To move something or make something happen.

Manipulator
Another word for animator; a person who operates the puppet.

Manual
Operated by hand as opposed to digitally.

Marionette
A puppet whose head, limbs and body are suspended on strings or wires.

Mass-produced
Made in great numbers, usually in a factory.

Mixer
A device that can change and combine sounds.

Model box
A 3D set design, often presented within a box of some sort.

Monochrome
Black, white and grey only.

Montage
A sequence or joining together of sounds to make a new piece of sound.

Natural
In terms of fabric – not man-made, such as cotton and wool.

Naturalistic
A set or lighting effect, for example, with characteristics of reality; having the appearance of a real place.

Non-diegetic sound
Sound that can be heard by the audience, but would not be heard by the characters (such as atmospheric music to encourage the audience to feel something).

Non-naturalistic
A set or lighting design, for example, that aims not to appear like reality.

Pace
The speed with which lighting or sound effects transition from one to the next.

Par can
A type of lantern that produces a very strong beam of light.

Pattern
A design printed onto or woven into fabric, including tartan, paisley, stripes. A paper pattern is the template pieces that guide sewers as they cut cloth out to make into garments.

Period (of history)
A specific time, era.

Pitch-shifting
Altering the pitch of a sound which, when mixed with other differently pitched versions of the same sound, makes it have a richer, thicker sound.

Playback device
The means through which recorded sound is played, such as a CD player or smartphone.

Plotting
The process of creating a cue sheet to show choices of what sound or light effect happens when (and where).

Practical effect
A lighting effect that is operated or worn by a performer.

Pre-set
Features of the drama onstage that are already in place before the audience enters.

Profile spotlight
A versatile lantern that can be used to create tight spots of light or bigger areas as required.

Promenade (theatre/staging)
Staging that involves the audience walking (a promenade) from one location to another with the actors. Locations are often outdoors, or in large buildings such as warehouses.

Props
Short for 'properties' (suggesting ownership): objects that would be owned by a character such as a torch, phone, set of keys.

Proscenium (arch)
A stage configuration where the audience are where the 'fourth wall' of a room would be – similar to end on, but with the addition of a picture-frame effect around the stage.

Puppet booth
A tent-like structure within which the puppeteer operates the puppets and is not seen by the audience (as used in Punch and Judy shows).

Puppeteer
A person who performs with puppets.

Radio mic
A microphone that is worn by a performer, often taped to the cheek.

Raked
Sloping. Raked seating is placed on an upwards slope away from the stage.

Realistic
A set, for example, that sets out to be like real life (naturalistic).

Recorded sound
Sound that is captured electronically, such as onto a computer file.

Rehearsal costumes
Practice clothes or shoes that bear some similarity to the final costume.

Representative
Something that represents (stands for) something else: for example, a non-naturalistic set that 'represents' and suggests rather than copies real life.

Reverb
The effect that occurs when sound waves hit surrounding surfaces and we hear the original sound plus its reflections. Adding reverb to a sound makes it longer and weightier.

Rhythm
The typical speed and movement of, for example, a puppet.

Rig
The bars that lanterns are hung on.

Rod puppet
A type of puppet which is often held above the animator and is controlled with thin strips of wood or metal.

Rostra blocks
Stage blocks, which can fit together, used to add height/levels.

Run
Either a rehearsal or read-through of the whole play, or the number of times a play will be performed (for example, The Crucible has a three-week run at this theatre).

Safety bond/cable/chain
The metal chain or cable that attaches the lantern to the rigging.

Scale
The size of something relative to something else.

Scenery
Parts of the set that represent locations or surroundings – on cloth or flats.

Seam
The joining of two pieces of fabric on the wrong side.

Set dressings
Accessories such as tablecloths, cushions and other decorative items.

Shadow puppet
A puppet that is designed to cast shadows rather than be seen in actuality.

Shadow puppetry
A form of puppetry where a light source is placed behind a screen and a shadow puppet is placed between the two.

Sidelight
Light that shines from the side of the stage, perhaps from the wings.

Silhouette
The outline shape of a costume, or the dark shape of a person or object against a lighter background.

Snap
A quick and sudden transition, such as from loud to silent or a **blackout**.

Sound desk
The means of operating the different sounds.

Soundscape
An effect made up of several sounds to give the impression of a city street, for example.

Source
Where the sound comes from, such as a computer file. Also used to describe the sound itself, such as a bell ringing.

Speaker
The device that transmits the sound. Its volume level can be altered.

Special effect
A lighting or sound effect that has a specific purpose, such as a colour wash to suggest a flashback.

Spotlight
A type of lantern that can create a tight circle of light or a larger, softer-edged one.

Stage business
Seemingly unimportant activity performed by an actor for dramatic effect.

Stage configuration
The shape of the acting area and where the audience are positioned in relation to it.

Stage furniture
Items in the production that can be moved but are not props, for example a chair, table or block. They might be included as part of the set design.

Stage manager
The person who runs and co-ordinates backstage proceedings.

Staging
The use of the stage as a design element, including type of stage configuration, positioning of entrances and exits and performer/audience relationships.

Stalls
Seating on the ground floor of a theatre, nearest to the stage.

Status symbol
A possession that is seen to show someone's wealth, social position or sense of style.

Stimulus
Something that inspires something else, such as an image or object that is used as a starting point for devising (plural is **stimuli**).

Structure
The way that something is sequenced, put together or built.

Style
Distinctive appearance, often typical of a particular person, period or place.

Stylised
Non-realistic, non-naturalistic, where style features are dominant.

Subculture
A cultural trend in society that is not the dominant one, such as goth, punk.

Swatch
A small sample of fabric that gives an idea of how an item made from it would look and feel.

Symbolic use of colour
The use of colour to communicate a certain meaning or represent a particular theme or mood.

Synchronised
Two or more sounds operating at the same time.

Synthetic
Man-made (fabric).

Tacking
A fast, long, hand-made, temporary stitch to hold seams together ready for trying on or for permanent stitching.

Tarpaulin
Large, heavy-duty, waterproof cloth/sheet, usually of woven plastic.

Texture
The surface feel of fabric, for example. Raised fabrics, such as velvet and cord, have a different texture from smooth ones, such as silk, which are flat.

Three-point lighting
A method that shines light from three different directions to give good coverage.

Thrust stage
A stage that extends into the audience area, with seats on three sides.

Transition
A change between lighting states, such as a snap or a fade.

Traverse
A stage configuration where the audience is in two parts that are seated opposite each other along two sides of the stage.

Truck
A wheeled platform on which a piece of scenery is built – to make scene changes quick and easy.

Underscore
Sound (often non-diegetic) that is played quietly while performers are speaking, to add atmosphere.

Upcycle
Taking an existing garment and changing it in some way to make something different.

Uplight
A light that shines from low down, perhaps positioned at the front of the stage.

Voicing
Creating the speaking voice for a puppet. This will usually be produced by the puppet animator.

Wardrobe
The wardrobe department is where the costumes are produced in a theatre. Alternatively, our wardrobe is the collection of clothes we own.

Weight
How heavy or light is the fabric? Does it drape or hang heavily?

White-card model
A simple 3D representation of a set design.

INDEX

allergies 95, 97, 106, 119
amplifier 42–43, 51, 62
analysing 9, 27, 30–31, 37–38, 44, 56, 61–62, 66, 77–78, 80, 104–105, 124–125, 128–129, 131, 137, 144, 154–155, 161, 168, 175, 181–182, 185–186, 191, 193, 195, 198, 202–203, 205, 210–212, 219–221, 225, 228, 230, 233, 237, 242, 246, 250, 254, 258, 262, 266, 270, 274, 278
animation 12, 108, 117, 122, 126
appliqués 94, 106
artistic intentions, agreeing on 184–185
artistic intentions, recognising 131
atmospheric 14, 23, 37–38, 41, 61–62, 209
audience appeal 116, 118, 122, 126, 181, 189, 274
automated moving lantern 17, 25, 38

backcloth 74, 76, 80
backlighting 15, 22, 38
backpack/rucksack puppet 115, 120, 126, 274
barn doors 16–17, 28, 32–33, 38
Beauty and the Beast 189
birdie 16, 38
blackout 26, 31, 35, 38, 60, 62, 195
body proportions, drawing 99
book flats 71, 80
Brecht, Bertolt 15
bruise wheel 97, 106

character and language
   costume design 82–88, 91, 94, 96–98, 100, 102, 128, 130, 181, 188, 221, 266, 268–270, 272–273
   lighting design 25, 37, 188, 195
   puppet design 109–113, 116–123, 126, 181, 236, 274–276, 278–279
   set design 68, 79–80, 188, 212, 258, 262, 263
   sound design 41, 44, 61–62, 188
collaboration 9, 83, 90, 95, 106, 180–182, 190–195, 198, 203, 206, 212, 215, 221, 224, 230, 233, 247, 255, 263, 271, 279
colour count 29, 38
colour filter 16–17, 29, 199
colour frame 29
colour palette 17, 38, 80, 83, 86, 106, 181, 218, 227, 261, 263, 270, 278
colours, selecting 73, 86–87
constant sound 40, 62

context 11, 67, 83–84, 96, 105, 137, 139–141, 144, 150–151, 154, 159, 164–165, 168, 172, 240–242, 250, 258, 266, 274
   cultural 84, 242, 250, 258, 266, 274
   economic 67, 83, 140, 164
   historical 11, 83–84, 140, 172, 242, 250, 258, 266, 274
   social 67, 83–84, 140, 150, 150, 164, 242, 250, 258, 266, 274
costume design
   adapting materials 94
   colours and fabric 86–89
   development and collaboration 224–225
      devised piece 9, 182, 221–230
      documenting 98–99, 227
   evaluating 105, 228–229
   everyday 82
   health and safety 95
   history 84–85
   how to 82–83
   in live theatre 168–171
   rehearsals 104
   research 83
   resources 90
   response to a stimulus 222–223
   in the set play 164–167
      sewing 90–93
   shape and style 85
      special effects 96–97, 106
costume designer 12, 36, 83–84, 86–88, 90, 92, 102, 104–105, 132, 164, 168, 221, 244, 252, 266, 268
costume fitting 100–103
costume, making from scratch 91
critical judgement 78, 80, 137, 145
cross-fade 26, 38, 195
cross-snap 26
cue sheet 9, 28, 30–31, 35, 38, 52, 56–58, 62, 132, 182, 195, 201, 209, 240, 248–249, 255–257
cue to cue 12, 35–36, 38, 59–60, 62
cyberbullying 188

daylight 20
decibels 56
design
   assessment 182
   in performance 182
   process 12
   role in drama 11
   working in 11, 132
   in the written exam 128–132

development and collaboration 198–199, 206–207, 215–216, 224–225, 233–234
devised design realisation 9
devised piece assessment 182
devising, process of 180–181
devising log 9, 28, 34, 45, 52–54, 78, 83, 119, 131, 181–183, 191, 193–195, 200–204, 208, 210, 212–213, 217, 219–222, 224, 226, 228–231, 233, 235, 237–238
diegetic sound 41, 44, 54, 62, 148–149, 188, 251
digital lighting desk/board 18, 38
digital mixing desk 42–43, 59
dimmer 18, 23, 26, 32, 38
directional sound 54–55, 62, 203, 209
dramatic intentions 10, 96, 181, 184, 240–241, 245, 249, 253–254, 257, 261–262, 265, 269, 273, 277–278, 280
dress rehearsal 12, 36, 60, 77, 104, 124, 194
drone 48, 62

echo 44, 47, 50–51, 62, 209, 254
embellishments 86, 92–94, 96, 102, 106
end-on stage 69–70, 133–134, 189, 244, 252
exam preparation 131
exterior locations 65, 80, 242–243, 249–250, 259

fabric choices 83, 88–89, 106, 186, 269
fade 14, 26, 35–36, 38, 49, 56–57, 59–60, 62, 209, 256
fader 38, 43, 56–57, 62
fill light 22, 25, 29, 38
final rehearsal 36, 60, 77, 104, 124, 194
finish of fabric 89, 106
flood (lighting) 15–17, 25, 38
focus lighting 14–20, 25, 29, 32–35, 38, 68
focus of puppets 111, 126
follow spot 17
footlight 16, 134, 140
freehand 98, 106
free-standing flats 70, 80
fresnel lantern 16–17, 29, 37–38, 249
furnishings 64, 67

gels 16–18, 21–23, 27, 29, 32, 38, 142, 145, 201, 246

genre
    costume design 85, 186, 221, 266, 270
    and designers 186
    lighting design 15, 186, 195, 242, 246
    performance style 186
    puppet design 172, 274, 278
    set design 186, 212, 258, 262
    sound design 44, 150, 186, 203, 250, 254
glove puppet 112–113, 117–118, 120–121, 126
gobo 17–18, 27–29, 32–34, 38, 139, 195, 246–247, 249
group work 190–194

hair 9, 84, 95–98, 166, 182, 227–228, 266, 271
hand puppet 116, 126
hand-and-rod puppet 113, 126
health and safety 19, 34, 49, 66, 75, 95
historical costume patterns 84–85
human resources 19, 45, 58, 73, 76, 90–91, 248, 262

intensity of lighting 14, 20–21, 23, 31, 37–38, 77, 87, 104, 124, 140, 245, 249
interior locations 65, 80, 242–243, 249–250, 259
intermittent sound 40, 62
interpretation 10, 66, 80, 87–88, 96, 97, 129, 131, 137, 184, 215, 241–242, 246, 248–250, 252, 254, 256–258, 262, 265–266, 270, 273–274, 278, 280

key light 21–22, 25, 37–38

lamps 16–17, 19, 21, 25, 30, 33, 37–38, 56, 59, 140, 157, 244
lanterns 15–19, 21–35, 38, 114, 126, 133, 201, 246, 248
    types of 16–17
LED lantern/lights 17–18, 22, 24–25, 27
lighting, controlling/operating 11–12, 18–19, 31, 35–36, 38, 195, 201, 248
lighting design
    angles, colour and intensity 14, 20–23, 31, 37–38, 77, 87, 104, 124, 140, 245, 249
    development and collaboration 198–199
    devised piece 9, 28, 182, 195–203
    documenting 28–29, 201
    evaluating 37, 202
    health and safety 19, 34

    how to 15
    importance 15
    in live theatre 144–147
    plotting 30–31
    power 14
    purpose 14
    rehearsals 36
    research 27
    resources 18–19
    response to a stimulus 196–197
    rigging and focusing 11, 18–20, 28, 32–34, 38, 195, 201, 242, 247–249, 260
    in the set play 137–143
    special effects 24–25, 27–28, 30, 36–38, 139, 195, 201, 245–247
    transitions 9, 26, 30–31, 35, 38, 138, 182, 189, 201
lighting desk (console, board) 17–18, 23, 26, 29, 32, 35, 38, 62, 248
lighting fixture 16, 18, 38
lighting plot 28–29, 31, 38, 132, 195
lighting schedule 28–29
lighting state 14, 24, 26, 28, 30, 35–37, 77, 104, 124, 132, 145, 181, 187, 189, 201, 242, 245–246, 249
lighting styles 15–17
live sound 48, 61–62, 208
live theatre evaluation 137, 144–147, 154–156, 161–163, 168–171, 175–178
location, creating 65–66, 68, 79, 135, 189
location/setting 14, 24, 41, 44, 56, 65–66, 68, 76, 79–80, 85, 135–136, 140, 187, 189, 203, 212, 242, 245, 249–250, 258, 260, 266

make-up 9, 11, 82–85, 93, 95–99, 106, 166, 182, 221, 227–228, 266, 269–272
manual lighting desk/board 18–19, 35
manual mixing desk 42–43, 59
marionette 114, 117–118, 120, 126
masks 75, 95–98, 105, 128, 228, 266, 269
mass-produced clothing 84, 106
microphones 42–43, 45, 62
model box 28, 72, 80, 157, 262
monochrome 86, 106
montage 44, 62
mood 14–15, 22–24, 38, 40–41, 44–45, 47–48, 56, 61–62, 66, 87, 96, 105–106, 138–140, 150, 195, 201, 203, 208–209, 212, 218, 221, 230, 236, 242, 245–246, 250, 253–254, 258, 261–262, 266, 270, 274, 278
mood board 139, 149, 158, 193, 244, 268

natural fabric 84, 87–88, 106
natural light 20–21

naturalistic lighting 21–25, 38, 138, 140
naturalistic set/style 62, 66, 80, 106, 149, 186, 189, 244, 250, 252, 259–260, 266, 268, 276
night-time 20, 253
non-diegetic sound 41, 44, 47, 62, 148–149, 188, 250–251
non-naturalistic lighting 25, 139, 249
non-naturalistic set/style 48, 62, 66, 71, 80, 106, 186, 189, 242, 250, 253, 257–258

par can 16–17, 29, 38
periods, historical 11, 67, 84–86, 91, 94, 96–97, 102, 132, 134, 137, 140, 149–150, 186, 203, 209, 212, 221, 230, 241, 244, 246, 250–252, 254, 258, 260, 262, 266–270, 276, 278
pitch-shifting 50–51, 62
playback device 42, 58–59, 62, 256
practical design 10, 12, 18, 109, 180, 192
practical special effects 25, 36, 37, 244
production meeting 191
profile spotlight 17, 29, 38
promenade theatre 136
props 9, 12, 65–67, 73, 80, 130, 132, 134–136, 182, 218, 258, 261, 264
proscenium arch stage 54, 62, 134, 258
puppet booth 110, 126
puppet characterisation 121
puppet design
    advantages of design option 108
    animating 122–123
    creating 120–121
    development and collaboration 233–234
    devised piece 9, 182, 230–238
    documenting 236
    evaluating 125, 237–238
    introduction to 108
    in live theatre 175–178
    materials 120–121
    rehearsals 124
    research 118
    response to a stimulus 231–232
    in the set play 172–174
    type, choosing 116–117
puppets, cultural and historical importance of 109–111
puppets, operating 114, 122
puppets, types of 112–117

raked 134–135
realism 15, 121–122, 258
realistic set 66, 80; also see naturalistic

286   Index

recorded sound 52, 62
rehearsal costumes 83, 106
representative set 66, 80, 191, 260
responding to stimuli 9, 182–183, 196–197, 204–205, 213–214, 222–223
reverb 43, 50–51, 61–62, 150, 209, 254, 275
rig see lighting design, rigging and focusing
rod puppet 110, 113, 116–118, 125–126, 172–173, 274

safety bond 18, 27, 32, 34, 38, 54
scale (in drawings/plans) 69–71, 80, 218
scale (of puppet) 120, 126
scenery 64–65, 70, 73, 75–77, 80, 114, 125, 133–136, 195, 259
set design
   creating 65, 76
   development and collaboration 215–216
   devised piece 9, 67, 182, 212–220
   documenting 69–72, 218
   evaluating 64, 78–79, 219–220
      health and safety 66, 75
      how to 64
      levels, using 68
   in live theatre 161–163
   materials 74
   rehearsals 77
   research 67
   resources 73
   response to a stimulus 213–214
   in the set play 157–160
   styles 66
set designer 12, 28, 64–66, 68–69, 73, 75, 77, 86, 95, 132, 157, 161, 203, 212, 245, 252, 258–260, 265, 268, 276
set dressings 12, 66, 132, 163, 212, 218, 261
set play/text 15, 40, 67, 128–129, 131, 137–143, 148–153, 157–160, 164–167, 172–174
shadow puppet/puppetry 108, 110, 113–115, 117–118, 120, 124–126, 133, 172, 274, 280
silence 48, 209
silhouette 17, 38, 94, 100, 103, 106, 186, 259, 267
snap 26, 38, 56, 62, 189, 195

sound design
   development and collaboration 206–207
      devised piece 9, 182, 188, 203–211
   documenting 52–53, 209
   evaluating 61, 210–211
   health and safety 49
   how to 40
   in live theatre 154–156
   plotting 47, 56–57
   real world 40
   rehearsals 60
   research 44–45
   response to a stimulus 204–205
   in the set play 148–153
   sourcing, creating and mixing 46–48
   special effects 50–51, 209, 253–255
   stage 41–43
   transitions 9, 56, 62, 182, 209
sound, finding 45
sound equipment, operating 47, 55, 58–60, 62, 203
sound equipment, positioning 54–55
sound plot 52–53, 132
sound source 43, 52
source sheet 52
speakers 42–43, 52–55, 58, 62, 133, 209, 253–255
spotlight 12, 14–15, 17, 24–25, 28–29, 33, 38, 140, 181, 189, 245, 249
stage configurations 54, 62, 65–66, 69, 80, 118, 128, 132–136, 158, 242, 250, 258, 266, 274, 276–277
stage furniture 64–67, 70, 77
stage lantern see lanterns
stage management 12
stage manager 12, 132, 247, 255, 263, 271, 279
stage positioning 128, 132–133
stage space 133, 215
stalls 134
Stanislavski, Konstantin 15
Statement of Dramatic Intentions 10, 240–241, 249, 257, 265, 273, 280
status symbol 85, 106
stimulus 9, 180–184, 188, 190, 196–197, 204–205, 213–214, 222–223, 231–232

structure and form
   costume design 187, 221, 267
   and designers 187
   lighting design 187, 195, 243
   set design 187, 212, 259
   sound design 62, 187, 203, 251
style
   costume design 85, 186, 221, 266, 270
   and designers 186
   lighting design 15, 186, 195, 242, 246
   performance 186
   puppet design 172, 274, 278
   set design 186, 212, 258, 262
   sound design 44, 150, 186, 203, 250, 254
stylised 66, 80, 86, 102, 106, 244, 252, 261, 268, 276
subculture 85, 106
swatch 88, 106, 238, 270–271, 279
synchronised effects 55, 62
synthetic fabric 87–89, 106

tarpaulin 74, 80
technical rehearsal 12, 36, 60, 77, 104, 124, 194, 248, 256, 264, 272
texture of fabric 84, 86, 89, 92, 106
theatre in the round 54, 80, 118, 133, 136, 151, 158, 242, 244, 252, 274
theatre roles 132
three-point lighting 22, 38
thrust stage 54, 66, 135
traverse stage 54, 62, 135, 244

underscoring 47, 60–62, 150, 188, 193, 203, 254

visibility 14, 97, 116, 134

wardrobe 11–12, 82, 85, 90, 106
weight of fabric 89, 106
white-card meeting 252, 260, 268, 276
white-card models 71–72, 80, 259
wigs 84, 95–96, 269

Yevtushenko, Yevgeny 198, 214

Image acknowledgements

pp5 left, 22 centre, 29, 32–33, 53, 67 left, 93, 95, 157, 194 and 195 EMC design Ltd
pp6, 25 left, 34, 47 top, 101 top, 102 bottom, 137, 138 top, 180, 184, 192 bottom, 227, 265, 272 and 273 Neil Sutton at Cambridge Design Consultants
p11 top Jackie Ramirez from Pixabay
p14 right Mark Sepple
p15 Photo 12 / Alamy Stock Photo / Lucasfilm; Photo 12 / Alamy Stock Photo / Miramax Films
p16 (fresnel) Altman / B&H Foto & Electronics; (birdie) DTS Illuminazione / Presentation Design Services; (par cans) Lourens Smak / Alamy Stock Photo
p17 (profile) XuanFeng Pro Lighting Co., Limited; (gobos) EMEA Rosco; (AML) Martin Lighting
p18 left Equinox / Simply Sound & Lighting
p21 Stephen Chung / Alamy Live News
p22 left Brent Lees @ BCL Lighting Design
p22 bottom-right Expolmaging
p23 Netflix
p24 Winnipesaukee Playhouse; Yellow Dog Design / HotDogCollars.com
p25 top Matt Murphy; centre-right Prop Scenery Lights LLC
pp25 bottom, 108 top-right, 123 bottom, 130, 131 bottom, 146, 153 and 186 Geraint Lewis / Alamy Stock Photo
pp26 and 241 Manuel Harlan
p30 Sasel13 from Pixabay
pp31, 104 and 109 top aberCPC / Alamy Stock Photo
p37 Michele Domonkos / Alamy Stock Photo
p41 Peninsular Players
p44 20th Century Fox
p48 right George Coupe
p58 Helsinki City Theatre / Meyer Sound Laboratories
pp63, 73 and 220 Marmaduke St John /Alamy Stock Photo
p64 bottom Dan Norman
p65 Craig Sugden
p66 Lara Capelli; Arts at Michigan
p67 right BFA / Paramount Pictures / Alamy Stock Photo
p68 City Theatre Company; Elizabeth Aaron
pp69 and 111 right Ali McCaw
pp70, 71, 72 bottom, 189, 235 and 262 Sue Shewring
p72 top Juliet Shillingford
p76 Yvonne Arnaud Theatre
p78 Henry So / A Theatre Near U
p79 Craig Schwarz / USC School of Dramatic Arts
p83 Joel Stuthman / Alamy Stock Photo
p84 Alanna Sadler MUA; Collection Christophel / Alamy Stock Photo; Pictorial Press Ltd / Alamy Stock Photo
p86 bottom Sueddeutsche Zeitung Photo / Alamy Stock Photo
p87 top Bree Warner / Leviathan Lab
pp87 bottom, 113 top-left and 156 Brinkhoff-Moegenburg
pp92 and 268–270 Fi Carrington
p94 top-right Pendragon Costumes
pp96 bottom-right, 124 bottom, 154 and 160 WENN Rights Ltd / Alamy Stock Photo
p97 right Robert Workman
p97 bottom Kryolan / Face Paint Supplies Perth
p98 Alice Smith, Designer for Noughts and Crosses at Nottingham Playhouse – August 2016
p100 top University of Maryland Baltimore County; left mybluprint.com
p101 bottom See Kate Sew
p102 top Modern Millie Shop; left Infamous Commonwealth Theatre
p103 DoHope; Fabians Haberdashery & Trimmings; Duluth Trading Company
p105 S R Taylor Photography

pp108 top-left, 177 and 178 Xinhua / Alamy Stock Photo
p108 left David Rawcliffe / Alamy Stock Photo; bottom Warner Bros / Heyday Films
p109 centre Alexas_Fotos from Pixabay, bottom Pablo Hermoso on Unsplash
p110 right John Webb, bottom Thomas Gerlach from Pixabay
p111 top-left Gary Friedman / Photo: Nan Melville (New York), top-right Gary Friedman / Photo: Gisèle Wulfsohn; bottom-left Spitting Image Productions / ITV; bottom-right Ali McCaw
p112 right Trinity Mirror / Mirrorpix / Alamy Stock Photo; bottom-right The Jim Henson Company / Sportsphoto / Alamy Stock Photo
p113 top Han Yan /Xinhua / Alamy Live News; bottom Maggy Woodley / Red Ted Art (RedTedArt.com)
p114 centre-left Ellen Russell / Create in the Chaos (www.createinthechaos.com)
p115 bottom-left Liz Lauren / Moonbull Studio
pp115 right, 170 and 249 Johan Persson
p116 PA Images / Alamy Stock Photo
pp117 and 237 pixpoetry on Unsplash
p118 bottom-left Fremantle Media / CBBC; right Neil Spence / Alamy Stock Photo
p119 imageBROKER / Alamy Stock Photo; Štefan Štefančík on Unsplash
p121 centre Sevda Mujgan from Pixabay
p122 Theo Cote
p123 top Everett Collection Inc / Alamy Stock Photo
p124 top Joel Stuthman / Alamy Stock Photo
p125 Susan Small / Foxes Ridge
p131 top Maria Baranova
p134 bottom Masque Sound
p135 Timothy Mackabee; Simon Annand
p136 Andrew Billington; The Dukes
p139 Drew Mentzer on Unsplash, Tom Rogers on Unsplash, jschweikart from Pixabay, Ethan Wilkinson on Unsplash, Ninno JackJr on Unsplash, Maddy Baker on Unsplash
p142 LEE Filters / Dale Photographic Ltd; Dan Tsantilis
p144 Keith Mayhew / Alamy Live News
p145 Joan Marcus
p148 Michael Brosilow
p149 cocoparisienne on Pixabay, Gerd Altman on Pixabay, haalkab (Omar Gonzalez) on Pixabay, Ichigo121212 on Pixabay, Markus Spiske on Unsplash
p150 Mark Kitaoka / Village Theatre
p151 Roger Mastroianni
p152 Connor Herrington on Unsplash
p158 from Pixabay: Yvion, bvincent3, Gaby Stein, Aline Dassel, DarkWorkX
p162 Mark Douet
p164 Robert Day
p166 Drew Farrell / Royal Lyceum Theatre Company Ltd
p168 sjtheatre / Alamy Stock Photo
p172 Brigham Young University
p173 Alastair Muir / Peter McKintosh
p176 Little Angel Theatre
p187 Scott Kimmins
p199 top Xinhua/Alamy Live News
p200 Loop Images Ltd / Alamy Stock Photo
p204 Peter Barritt / Alamy Stock Photo
p208 right Jametlene Reskp on Unsplash
p212 Brian J Proball
p216 R. Eric Stone (Scenic Designer, The Complete Works of William Shakespeare (Abridged), Melissa Rain Anderson, Director)
p217 Alina Vilchenko on Pexels
p221 Bettina Strenske / Alamy Stock Photo
p222 Walter Bieri (Keystone)
p230 Alex Milledge; Puppet Kitchen
p232 Barry Lewis / Alamy Stock Photo; Meek; Lindsey Harris – Zelva was designed and built by

The Flying Buttresses: Danielle Brooke and Rupert Parry with an electronic control system by Nick Sparks
p234 Mike Deal / Winnipeg Free Press
p240 Oladimeji Ajegbile from Pexels
p248 Tristram Kenton
p256 freeimages.co.uk
p257 bottom EFE News Agency / Alamy Stock Photo
p258 Foteini Christofilopoulou
p260 Mike Hoban / Glyndebourne Productions Ltd
p264 Bernd Tschakert / Alamy Stock Photo
p275 Mike Eddowes / Toby Olié
p276 Retha Ferguson from Pexels
p277 Sarah Lewis
p278 Catherine Ashmore
p280 Andrea Piacquadio from Pexels

All other images: Shutterstock:
p5 top untitled; pp5 bottom, pp8–10 Iakov Filimonov; pp11 bottom and 12 bottom Lakeview Images / Shutterstock.com; p12 top Anna Jurkovska; p14 left John Arehart; p16 (background) Matusciac Alexandru, (floodlight) Roman Yastrebinsky, (barn doors) Iapandr, pp16 (par can lighting), 19 bottom and 247 Oleksandr Nagaiets; p17 (LEDs) Rajesh Narayanan; p18 top Pawel_Brzozowski; p20 Mopic; Wan bo; p27 right Oqbas; pp27 left and 116 left Africa Studio; p32 Trikona; p35 Tennessee Witney; p39 Pressmaster; p40 palidachan; p43 n_defender; tsaplia; p45 S B Stock; p46 GoodStudio, Dmitry Galaganov; p47 bottom Anutr Yossundara; p48 left Jacques Durocher; p49 Anrey_Popov; Javier Brosch; p50 Lebedev_S; pp50–51 agsandrew; p51 Petr Malyshev; Ching Design; p54 Kabardins photo; p55 ALPA PROD; p56 Andrew Berezovsky; p57 igor gratzer; p59 Syda Productions; Sergey Nemirovsky; p60 studiostoks; p64 top Photographee.eu; p81 MJTH; p82 OlegD / Shutterstock.com, x4wiz; p85 NeydtStock / Shutterstock.com, onajourney / Shutterstock.com, Dziurek/Shutterstock.com; p86 top Adil Celebiyev / Shutterstock.com, left WIJI; p87 left Tatyana Mi; p88 Photology1971; p89 Colin Ridgway-Cole, acidmit, Deep_Mind, Joaquin Corbalan P; p90 wavebreakmedia; Zb89V; p94 left Eddie Jordan Photos / Shutterstock.com; centre Mary Long, bottom Yuriy Golub; p96 top Dreamer Company / Shutterstock.com, bottom-left Tania Bertoni; p97 left AJP/Shutterstock.com, p107 ngoc tran; p110 top eriyalim; p112 top Viktor Fedorenko / Shutterstock.com; p114 top-left PJ_Photography / Shutterstock.com, right SvetaZi, left Thunder Waffle, bottom Pikul Norood; p115 top jesterpop; p118 top FXQuadro; p120 Miriam82, bymandesigns; p121 top John Alexopoulos, right s_oleg; pp127, 192 top and 210 Monkey Business Images; p128 Kiselev Andrey Valerevich; p134 top posztos/ Shutterstock.co.uk; p140 Kozlik; p174 Boguslaw Mazur; p183 Aleutie; p188 Antonio Guillem, Andreev105/ Shutterstock.com; p196 Kateryna Kon; p198 GN Illustrator; p199 bottom Yannick Martinez; p200 background faak; p202 Trueffelpix; p203 New Africa; pp205 and 208 left Lightspring; p207 Bborriss.67; p211 fizkes; p214 FooTToo, p215 Have a nice day Photo; p223 Degimages; p224 Andreja Donko; p225 stocksre/Shutterstock.com; p228 Lenar Nigmatullin; p229 gabriel12; p236 Mr.Whiskey; p238 mojamaya; p244 FrameStockFootages; p245 Independent; p246 mijatmijatovic; p252 panitanphoto; p253 Dragon Images; p254 metamorworks; p255 Jacob Lund; p257 top Rawpixel.com, hurricanehawk; p261 alexasokol83; p263 DGLimages; p271 Oleksii Didok.